▬ Mike Celizic ▬

THE BIGGEST GAME

OF

THEM ALL

Notre Dame, Michigan State, and the Fall of '66

SIMON & SCHUSTER

New York   London   Toronto   Sydney   Tokyo   Singapore

SIMON & SCHUSTER
SIMON & SCHUSTER BUILDING
ROCKEFELLER CENTER
1230 AVENUE OF THE AMERICAS
NEW YORK, NEW YORK 10020

DESIGNED BY LEVAVI & LEVAVI
MANUFACTURED IN THE UNITED STATES OF AMERICA

1   3   5   7   9   10   8   6   4   2

LIBRARY OF CONGRESS CATALOGING-IN-PUBLICATION DATA
CELIZIC, MIKE.
THE BIGGEST GAME OF THEM ALL : NOTRE DAME, MICHIGAN STATE, AND THE
FALL OF '66 / MIKE CELIZIC.
P.   CM.
INCLUDES INDEX.
1. FOOTBALL—UNITED STATES—HISTORY.   2. UNIVERSITY OF NOTRE
DAME—FOOTBALL—HISTORY.   3. MICHIGAN STATE UNIVERSITY—
FOOTBALL—HISTORY.   I. TITLE.
GV956.3   1966.c45   1992
796.332'63'0977—DC20   92-27790
CIP
ISBN 0-671-75817-9

PHOTO CREDITS

Notre Dame Archives, 1, 2, 3, 7, 8, 15, 16, 18; Notre Dame Athletic Department, 9, 14, 21; University Relations, Michigan State University, 4, 5, 6, 11, 12, 13; UPI/ BETTMANN, 10, 17, 19, 20.

This one's for you, Margaret.
They're all for you.

Acknowledgments

One of the hardest things about writing a book like this is figuring out how to thank everyone who made it possible. So let me start by saying that in nine years of covering sports, I have never run into a group of people who were more gracious, honest, and giving of their time and generally more delightful to deal with than the people involved in *The Biggest Game of Them All*. With rare exceptions, they returned phone calls, opened their homes and memories, and did everything in their power to make this book a reality. Anyone who cheered the fortunes of either Michigan State or Notre Dame in 1966 should be proud to know that the players they admired then for their athletic skill are just as admirable today for their decency and humanity.

That said, I'll start doling out the thank-yous with two people who had nothing to do with Notre Dame 10, Michigan State 10. They are Paulette Martis and John Heisler. Paulette answers the phones, feeds the fax machine, digs through the files, and greets with a smile everyone who comes through the doors of the Michigan State Sports Information Office. Ken Hoffman, the Spartan

Sports Information Director, is lucky to have Paulette working for him. Thanks, Paulette. I couldn't have done it without your help. John is the Sports Information Director at Notre Dame and he's one of the best. If a media guide exists that's better than the one John turns out, I haven't seen it. Thanks, John. I couldn't have done it without you, either.

Special thanks go to Bob Gladieux, who kept steering me in the right directions and fed me a steady stream of addresses and phone numbers. And to Bob's wife, Inge, who didn't throw me out when I kept her and probably half the neighborhood up until who knows what hour while reminiscing on her front porch with Bob about the good old days. Thanks also to Jim Seymour, who had the phone numbers Bob didn't have.

Ara Parseghian gave a lot of his time to this project during several interviews in South Bend and over the phone. Ara, you did the right thing and I hope this book proves that you never have to explain your strategy again. Tom Pagna dug into his attic or basement or wherever for old material from The Phantom. George Sefcik came up with his 1966 play book. Thank you all.

After dealing with present-day professional athletes, I was amazed at how many of the men from both teams invited me into their homes or offices and gave as much time as I asked and maybe more than they had. So thanks, Bubba Smith, Reggie Cavender, Rocky Bleier, Jim Seymour, Nick Eddy, Mitch Pruiett, Tom Regner, Kevin Hardy, Clinton Jones, Jim Lynch, Coley O'Brien, Dan Harshman, Don Gmitter, Joe Azzaro, and John Ray. And thanks to Bob Apisa, Charlie Thornhill, Jerry West, and George Webster for finding time during their reunion to talk to a writer. Sorry about the Central Michigan game, guys. You deserved better on your Homecoming. And a most fervent get well to George Webster, who is fighting throat cancer.

Then there's Larry Conjar, who came out of his way to help; Brian Stenger, who introduced me to the eleven-hour Cleveland lunch; and Pete Duranko, who didn't run away from Johnstown, Pennsylvania. That's a lucky city.

Thanks also to Fred Stabley, who was Sports Information Director for the Spartans in 1966; Robert Bao, the editor of the Michigan State alumni magazine; Dr. Nicholas Johns, a former Notre Dame team physician; Jethrow Kyles, the curator of the Notre Dame library's sports collection; Joe Doyle; Moose Krause; Joe Yonto; and Colonel Jack Stephens.

And thanks to Sandy Stephens, Alan Page, Dave Haley, Tim Monty, Terry Hanratty, Vince Carillot, Cal Stoll, Brian Boulac, Jerry Wampfler, Ron Jeziorski, Bob Kuechenberg, George Goeddeke, and Jimmy Raye. Also to Barbara Russell and Morrie Stevens. And to Barbara Jaeger, the Rock Queen. There is one more person to thank, but I don't know his or her name. That's the person who, in 1966, put together a scrap book of the Notre Dame season and sent it to the university. All I can figure is that the scrap book came from Pittsburgh. If anyone wants to confess to the deed, get in touch. I'll get a book to you. I hope I haven't forgotten anyone, but I probably have. If so, I apologize.

I owe a large debt of gratitude to Tom Connor, my agent, who believed in me and in the book and conveyed that belief to the people who could make it happen. To Jeff Neuman and Stuart Gottesman at Simon & Schuster, thanks for your expert editing, although that's probably not what I called it at the time. Thanks also to Jim Wright for chasing down mistakes and for keeping the porch light burning, and to Gabe Buonauro, my editor at *The Record*, for giving me the time to get this done.

Finally, to Margaret, Carl, Jimmy, Jane, and Zachary, who didn't laugh even when I was laughable.

Introduction

Nothing is better than God.
Warm beer is better than nothing.
Therefore, warm beer is better than God.
                    —Anonymous; found carved in
                    a desktop at Notre Dame, 1966

Most of us went to Notre Dame for the same reason, and it's neither deep nor complicated. Brian Stenger, a sophomore end in 1966, put it as well as anyone: "You can bet that just about every kid who attended Notre Dame was there for the same reason—to fulfill his mother's dreams."

That's what brought Nick Eddy from California to South Bend. The only son of a mother who was separated from his father, Eddy's flashing feet were worth a free ride to just about any school in the country. Some of those schools paid well for talents such as his. Notre Dame paid nothing. But that's where he went. Kevin Hardy, an enormous man with uncommon quickness and agility, was the son of a struggling widow. The last man in the history of Notre Dame to letter in football, basketball, and baseball, he could have gone anywhere as well. He went to Notre Dame because that's what his mother wanted.

It took twenty-five years for me to learn I had that much in common with men like Tom Regner and Pete Duranko, men who were beyond my reach or ken when they were seniors and I was a freshman, as green as the Jell-O in the North Dining Hall, but not nearly as cool.

When I checked into Notre Dame in September 1966, Regner and Hardy and all the rest of the men whose names would soon become familiar were already there, getting ready for one of the more extraordinary football seasons Notre Dame had ever seen. They were impossible not to notice. They were nearly as big as the fourteen-story library with the mural of Christ that over-looked the stadium on the east edge of the campus. As we got settled in our rooms, tracked down the bookstore and our first Notre Dame sweatshirts, and sat through freshmen orientation sessions, they sauntered across the campus in their shorts and T-shirts on their way to practice or meals or naps or wherever it was that football players went between practices. All things were pos-sible to them then, before the first kickoff, the first clash of pads, the first tackle, the first touchdown.

All things seemed possible to me as well. I was a child of the fifties, and that's how life was, as clean and orderly and defined as the haircuts we wore to school. We had grown up with Wally and the Beaver and "My Three Sons," a black-and-white world where Mom always had dinner ready and Dad always came home smiling at six. We had practiced standing against the walls in the corridors of our grammar schools to protect ourselves from nu-clear blasts, and we had survived the Cuban Missile Crisis. The sole blemish on our psyches was the assassination of John F. Kennedy, but the Warren Commission had assured us that his death was the work of a single mad gunman working alone. Now Lyndon Baines Johnson was preaching guns and butter, and the war that was getting nastier all the time in Vietnam still seemed a long way off.

There were signs all around that the times, they were a-chang-ing. The first issue of *The Scholastic*, the university's student magazine, that greeted us when we arrived in South Bend with our pathetic little piles of belongings—cheap metal bookshelves from Sears, portable typewriters, desk lamps, alarm clocks that had to be wound—contained a compelling story by Robert Sam Anson about that summer's ghetto riots in Chicago. Anson was a senior and on his way to a career as one of the nation's leading journalists. He saw beyond the distant horizon and tried to tell us about it. But most of us ignored him. The reaction to his probing stories was angry letters demanding to know what his problem was.

Folk music and hootenannies had given in to Motown and hard rock, and bubble gum sentiment was fighting the music with a biting social message on the Top 40 charts. The year had begun with songs like "It's My Life" and "Get Off of My Cloud," sentiments that the progenitors of us Baby Boomers couldn't quite figure. "Paint It Black" topped the charts in the spring and "Wild Thing" in the summer. A long-haired freaky guy with one name —Donovan—broke into the big time with "Sunshine Superman," but the biggest hit of the year was Staff Sgt. Barry Sadler's anthem of old-time American ass-kicking, "The Ballad of the Green Berets."

The newspapers were full of stories about people trying to come to grips with emerging life-styles. One of the more popular subjects was a presumed nut out on the West Coast named Dr. Timothy Leary. Leary was preaching a gospel of drop out, turn on, tune in, and was advocating the use of something called LSD. Hippies, in fact, had been discovered and named in San Francisco, but Haight-Ashbury, communal living, and free love were still ideas shunned by the mainstream college student. *The Scholastic* did, however, run stories about birth control and, not coincidentally, the radical concept of allowing women to visit men in their dorm rooms—topics that were unheard of a decade earlier. The most popular guest lecturers on campus that year were Masters and Johnson, the sex therapists, who embarrassed and amused the student body by using such words as penis and vagina in mixed company.

The drug of choice on campus was still beer, and the more popular hair styles for both college men and women were short. Neither of these trends would last. On Long Island two high school boys had already been segregated from their classmates for committing the crime of letting their hair grow outrageously long, which is to say it just brushed the tops of their ears on the sides and flirted with their collars in the back. African Americans —who in November 1966 saw Edward Brooke of Massachusetts become the first black U.S. senator since Reconstruction—were called Negroes in the papers. At Notre Dame blacks were as rare as they are in the National Hockey League today, perhaps sixty in a student population of six thousand. The media called women girls, housewives, little women, better halves, chicks, dames, and broads, and females were still considered unsuited for jobs as doctors and lawyers.

It was three years after the assassination of President Kennedy and three years before Woodstock. It was two years before the Reverend Martin Luther King, Jr., was shot and Chicago exploded in the Days of Rage demonstrations. In the summer of 1966 the Supreme Court ruled on a case called *Miranda v. Arizona* that suspects under arrest had to be read their rights before they could be questioned. We had the right to remain silent. Silence became our duty, too, when the court also ruled that reciting the Lord's Prayer in public schools was a violation of the constitutional separation of Church and State.

So 1966 was an embarkation point between "Father Knows Best" and the Me Generation. Seniors belonged to the old generation, to the Beach Boys and the Four Seasons; freshmen to the new, to the Rolling Stones and Jimi Hendrix. Seniors accepted authority without question. Freshmen learned to trust no one over thirty. "We used to tell the kids to do something and they did it," said Tom Pagna, Ara Parseghian's backfield coach. "Within a couple of years we'd tell them to do something, and they'd want to know why."

Religion was changing. On November 18, the American Catholic Bishops announced that from the start of the next liturgical year on December 2, Catholics no longer had to abstain from eating meat on Friday. Catholics with a sense of humor wondered what that meant for all the people who had gone to hell for eating meat on Friday. That same fall, the first dual liturgy wedding was concelebrated by a Catholic priest and a Protestant minister with the blessing of the Roman Catholic Church. Nuns, attired for centuries in habits that covered every inch of skin except their faces, were allowed to wear street clothes. Cloistered nuns kept their habits, but some were allowed to speak during meals. Masses were celebrated in English instead of Latin, and with guitar music and whole wheat communion hosts.

Technology was moving at a full sprint. In June the United States guided a space probe to a soft landing on the moon. Scientists breathed a sigh of relief when the spaceship didn't sink in the lunar surface. In the week leading up to the Notre Dame–Michigan State game, a spacecraft sent back pictures of an area of the moon where NASA planned to land men in 1969. That same week a two-man Gemini crew demonstrated for the first time that men could perform useful work outside a space capsule in the vacuum of space. That fall a new television series about men in space debuted, "Star Trek." It didn't catch on right away. Too futuristic. Westerns still ruled the airwaves; "Bonanza" was the top-rated show. NBC commissioned the first made-for-television movie that year, but the big trend in broadcasting was airing Hollywood movies in prime time. The programming prompted a number of lawsuits as producers and directors went to court to prevent their works from being cut apart by commercial breaks. A judge in Los Angeles dismissed one such suit, saying that television audiences were "thick-skinned about commercials." CBS purchased Alfred Hitchcock's *Psycho* for prime-time airing, but network executives finally decided against broadcasting the film because they thought it was too violent for the gentle tastes of the time.

Another new development in telecommunications had a more direct effect on the way the nation watched sports. It was a new-fangled communications satellite that could broadcast live television across the ocean. It would be used November 19 to broadcast the Notre Dame–Michigan State game, allowing American servicemen in Vietnam to watch the game as well as college football fans in Hawaii, who were used to seeing games a week late. Color television itself was still something special. Only that fall Canada joined the United States and Japan as the only countries in the world with color broadcasts. Television listings still noted which shows were in color and which were not.

Over the next few years of school the underclassmen would see society turn upside down. For the upperclassmen, school was as it always had been.

Rocky Bleier, who grew up over his father's bar in Appleton, Wisconsin, remembers it well: "Our only concern was playing that football game, winning the National Championship, and then having a good spring; trying to get laid and having a couple of beers."

As a junior he could think about trying to get laid. As a freshman I had a better chance of having an elephant jump on me from one of the vaselike elm trees that lined the main quad, which was probably another reason that it pleased my mother I was at Notre Dame. Most of our energy as underclassmen was spent trying to get beer. Cold or warm, it didn't matter. By the time I was a senior, there were visiting hours for women in the dorms, and it was legal to drink there as well. It wasn't legal to smoke grass, but that didn't stop people from doing it.

But if the old order was cracking and heaving at the seams, Notre Dame wasn't rushing into anything. In 1966 the university was just starting to join the rest of the world. It was the last year that students, who lived in cut-off jeans and torn-off sweatshirts, had to wear coats and ties to dinner, a requirement that some fulfilled by attaching a clip-on tie to a torn T-shirt and throwing on a sport coat. It was the first year that there were no curfews or mandatory lights out for sophomores, juniors, and seniors. Only freshmen still had to be in their rooms by 10 P.M. on weeknights, midnight on weekends. In the spring semester even the freshmen were given their freedom—except, of course, the freshmen in Cavanaugh Hall, where Father Matthew Micelli, a.k.a. the Black Matt, refused to go along with the new liberalism. Everyone else on campus might roam South Bend and nearby Niles, Michigan, but his kids, of whom I was one, wouldn't.

That's how Cavanaugh Hall came to miss the big spring social event of the 1966–67 school year—the panty raid on St. Mary's College, a mile across the Dixie Highway from Notre Dame. We couldn't get out of the dorm.

Panty raids were still high fun in 1966, but considering the cast-iron underwear women wore in those days, it's hard to tell why—at least in retrospect. The administration didn't encourage such shenanigans, but a food fight in the North Dining Hall that same year brought harsher discipline than the panty raid. The St. Mary's girls (adult females hadn't yet become women) didn't object either. For many on both campuses, the ritual shower of underwear was as close to a relationship as most Notre Dame and St. Mary's students ever got.

That was the reality at Notre Dame. The school was all male. It wasn't until the year before, in 1965, that Notre Dame finally gave tenure to its first two female faculty members. It was also the first year the Notre Dame Club let women attend the communion breakfast; it was on the thirty-fifth anniversary of Knute Rockne's death. When the freshmen arrived on campus, the authorities hammered home two points. The first was stated explicitly: We don't take dummies. The second was demonstrated: We don't have women, but there's always football.

First, they herded the fifteen hundred incoming freshmen together to lecture us about how common our uncommon accomplishments were. You were a high school valedictorian? Big deal, kid. We got a couple hundred of those. High college board scores? Well, look around. Odds are the kid next to you had higher scores. There were high school sports captains by the gross and student body presidents by the score. For every student in the auditorium, five others had been turned away.

Thus sobered, the freshman class was sent to St. Mary's for what was optimistically called a "mixer." There were about four Notre Dame men for each St. Mary's woman, but at the mixer it seemed more like twenty to one. Surrounded by this wealth of young men, most of whom had gone through at least four straight years of schooling without having a girl in their classes and thus had the social graces of water buffalo, the girls of St. Mary's found themselves having to turn down offer after offer of dates. Thus discouraged, we wrote off St. Mary's women forever. The only common theme at the two schools on either side of the Dixie Highway was the continual complaint about how hard it was to get a date.

Having shown us the depressing level of competition in class and the hopelessness of ever going out on a date, the good Fathers showed us what we could look forward to. Herding everyone again into an auditorium, they dimmed the lights and rolled the sacred celluloid of Notre Dame: *Knute Rockne, All American.*

There it was, in scratchy black and white: Pat O'Brien as Rockne exhorting his troops to fight, fight, fight and win, win, win. The Four Horsemen and the Notre Dame backfield shift. Ronald Reagan doing such a terrific job as George Gipp, dying so convincingly after telling Rockne with his last breath to go out and win one for the Gipper.

Yes, football would save us. It would be our comfort and our light. In the days to come we learned about Touchdown Jesus— the library mural of Christ that was built on the holy ground where Gipp used to practice. Christ, with his arms raised, looked over the north goalposts of the stadium. Outside the library was a heroic bronze statue of Moses with his index finger raised to the heavens: We're Number One. In the heart of the campus stood the statue of Father William Corby, whose arm was raised as he administered penance to the Union troops at Gettysburg. That was the story, but we knew he was calling for a fair catch.

Without women, football was our social life. Fridays before home games ended with the world's greatest pep rallies in the musty innards of the old 1899 field house. Saturdays turned into campus-wide celebrations after morning classes—a fact of academic life that underclassmen were not allowed to avoid. When the team was on the road, we retreated to the back rooms of South Bend bars and clubs, where, for a couple bucks, we could watch the games on closed-circuit television, a technology Notre Dame was pioneering, and drink as much lukewarm Schlitz beer from quart bottles as we could hold. Sometimes more. It seemed like a bit of heaven. Sundays, a substantial portion of the student body knocked heads in Notre Dame's intramural tackle football league. The university supplied the equipment from the stores of gear abandoned by the varsity. Apparently they never threw anything away because a lot of us wound up playing in leather helmets and leather shoulder pads. Some of the stuff looked like the same gear Gipp got killed in.

The university had been running the intramural program for decades, and the football was on a high level. Cavanaugh Hall's quarterback in 1966 had been an All-Stater in Montana or Wyoming or one of the Dakotas. The school was loaded with high school stars who weren't good enough to play for Notre Dame and didn't want to play anywhere else. In the days before sophisticated scouting, the program occasionally provided a varsity player. Now it just helped us let off steam.

The hormone-venting propertics of football were the stuff of campus myth and legend. Stories that had been floating around campus from the beginning of time held that the good Fathers kept statistics of attendance at the sacraments. It was said that those taking communion on Saturday mornings rose in proportion to the importance of the game being played that afternoon. It was also said that the number of sins of self-abuse admitted to in confession rose precipitously after a tough loss.

We weren't sure how self-abuse—or impure actions with oneself, as it was known in the confessional—could increase in that place.

As freshmen it didn't take us long to learn everything about the football team that was now ours. We already knew about Ara Parseghian, the Armenian coach who had taken Notre Dame to the brink of a National Championship in 1964. His stature on campus rivaled that of the golden dome. We had heard and read about the veterans on his team: Alan Page, Pete Duranko, Kevin Hardy, Jim Lynch, Nick Eddy, Larry Conjar, Tom Rhoads, John Horney, George Goeddeke, Paul Seiler, Tom Regner. But there were others we had never heard of: Terry Hanratty, Jim Seymour, Bob Kuechenberg, Bob Gladieux, Coley O'Brien. The newspapers told us the team would be good. *Sports Illustrated* said it would be the fourth best in the country behind Alabama, Arkansas, and Nebraska. The Associated Press poll guessed it was eighth best, and the United Press International twelfth, with Michigan State on top of both polls. *Look* magazine picked us second, behind Michigan State.

We guessed it would be fun, but we never imagined that it would become a season and a team for the ages. We never imagined that that season would end an era of relative innocence that had begun fifty-three years earlier and that it would usher in the modern era of big-time, big-money, high-fivin', jukin'-and-jivin' football from one end of the cable box to the other.

All we knew was that the football season was here and Notre Dame was primed to shake down some serious thunder. We didn't care what Michigan State thought; we knew with religious certainty that we were once again the center of the college football universe. We'd start proving that against Purdue, and we'd keep proving it against Oklahoma, Southern Cal, and, yes, against Michigan State, too. And if it didn't work out, well, there was always warm beer.

1

*To travel hopefully is a better thing than to arrive, and
the true success is to labor.*

—Robert Louis Stevenson

November 18, 1966, was the last time the sons of Notre Dame
boarded a railroad train to go to a football game.

It was something of an anachronism to take the train, even in
those days when trains still provided passenger service between
such places as South Bend, Indiana, and East Lansing, Michigan.
Since the early fifties the Irish had been flying to distant away
games. Closer venues were reached by bus. But for this game the
team took the Grand Trunk Railroad out of South Bend's Union
Station. No one knew it then, but it would be the last time Notre
Dame would go to battle by rail.

Few people, least of all the football players, noticed that the
world was changing profoundly in 1966, a year smack in the
middle of an era of social upheaval.

In the midst of so much change, the train was a nice touch, a
link to the way life had been when Notre Dame first changed the
game of college football. Also wonderfully old-fashioned was the
boisterous crowd that sent off the sixty-three players, coaches,
and student managers who made the trip. The fans, bundled up

against the chilly, dank day, brought homemade signs and banners. They wore buttons on their heavy, winter clothes. The banners and buttons bore such messages as IRISH ARA FORCE, ARA'S LYNCH MOB, HATE STATE, and GO IRISH. BEAT THE SPARTANS. The mayor of South Bend was there, and although the elections had passed, he made a speech. The crowd craned to touch their heroes. They screamed. They sang the "Notre Dame Victory March."

There wasn't a sports fan in the nation who couldn't name a half-dozen or more of the young men who boarded that train. One of them was an eighteen-year-old from Butler, Pennsylvania, with a narrow, hawklike face and a right arm made of solid gold. Three months earlier he had been just another anonymous sophomore, hoping to win a starting job on the football team. Now he was as recognizable as a movie star. His face had been on the covers of *Time* and *Sports Illustrated.* His name, Terry Hanratty, was already written in the Notre Dame record book alongside George Gipp, Johnny Lujack, Paul Hornung, John Huarte, and Angelo Bertelli. His favorite receiver, Jim Seymour, a tall, well-built kid from just outside Detroit, was nearly as famous. On the train with them were Jim Lynch, Alan Page, Nick Eddy, Kevin Hardy, Pete Duranko, and Larry Conjar. Leading them was Ara Parseghian, who in his third year as coach of Notre Dame was already being compared to Knute Rockne and Frank Leahy. Like Rockne, Parseghian wasn't Catholic; as with Rockne, no one at Notre Dame minded. In fact, at that moment, ecumenism seemed like the best idea the Church had ever had.

Notre Dame's football history is probably the richest in all of college football. At one time Notre Dame always seemed to be playing for the National Championship, but those days were so long ago they seem more legend than memory. Not since 1949, when Frank Leahy won his fourth national title in seven years, had Notre Dame won a championship. In 1963 they had staggered to a 2-7 season, the second worst in their history. Players who were on that team said the only break they caught was when President Kennedy was assassinated in Dallas, which led to the cancellation of that Saturday's game against Iowa and saved the team from going 2-8. Nobody doubted that they'd rather have taken the loss.

Then Parseghian, a darkly intense Armenian of the Presbyterian persuasion, went to South Bend and moved into the head coach's office in the corner of the university's athletic building, the Rockne Memorial. He got the job by having beaten the Irish for four straight years when he was coaching Northwestern. Parseghian arrived without a recruiting class of his own, but he took what his predecessors, Joe Kuharich and Hugh Devore, had left him, moved some players around, installed a kid named John Huarte at quarterback, and came within ninety seconds of a perfect season. And Huarte, who had been used by Devore and Kuharich as a holder for extra points and field goals, won the Heisman trophy a full month before he received his first varsity letter. That was in 1964. In 1965, without the benefit of a competent quarterback, the team fell to 7-2-1, outstanding by most standards but mediocre by Parseghian's.

Now, a year later, the Notre Dame faithful filled the station platform, cheering and singing. But even after the train chugged out of South Bend, the players weren't free of well-wishers. All the way to Lansing people left their homes to wave at the train and shout to players who couldn't hear them. People lined the platforms in the towns along the way. Nuns in their heavy habits, fingering big, olive-stone rosaries, brought their pupils—scrubbed and smiling children dressed in Catholic school uniforms—to see the train pass by. They lined them up in neat rows on the platforms and waved. In backyards along the route people stood and waved. Some held signs. As the train pushed deeper into Michigan, the signs changed from blue and gold to green and white, and the messages changed from GO IRISH to GO SPARTANS. But always, no matter how many Michigan State fans were about, there was someone pleading for the Irish to win.

Dave Anderson, a young reporter for the *New York Times*, was assigned to ride the train with the team. He looked with wonder at the passing scene. "It's like something out of Rockne," he thought. Even then he knew it was something that hadn't been seen in a long time and maybe wouldn't be seen again.

And it *was* like something out of Rockne and out of Frank Leahy, when the Irish rode the rails to every corner of the country, spreading their gospel of Notre Dame football and building the legends that would be handed down like heirloom christening gowns from one generation to the next. Crowds used to come out to watch those old Notre Dame teams pass through town. They were working people who saw in the Notre Dame players their own sons, who saw in Notre Dame a place that celebrated ethnicity and the religion that the immigrants brought with them.

Football made Notre Dame, and Notre Dame made football. Notre Dame didn't invent the game; the Ivy League schools get credit for that, taking the game of rugby and making it American. Princeton and Rutgers played the first intercollegiate match in 1869 in New Brunswick, New Jersey. Notre Dame was only twenty-seven years old then, and didn't take up football until 1887. By then the game was established in the East. If someone said he played football for Harvard or Yale or the Army, people knew it meant he was the best.

But Notre Dame students took to football from the first game, held in a public park in South Bend. The game was against the University of Michigan, which even then crowed about being "Champions of the West." It wasn't so much a contest as a scrimmage, held to allow the visitors to instruct the Notre Damers on how to play the new game. "The occasion has started an enthusiastic football boom," declared *The Scholastic,* the school magazine, "and it is hoped that coming years will witness a series of these contests."

The goodwill between Notre Dame and Michigan lasted exactly one year. The following year Michigan arrived for two games, played on successive days in the spring. Michigan won the first game handily but narrowly escaped with a win the next day when a Wolverine player picked up the ball during what Notre Dame thought was a time-out and ran with it for the winning goal. The referee, who was from Michigan, sided with the Wolverines, and the ensuing quarrel was so fierce it took eleven years until the two sides had cooled off sufficiently to play again. It wasn't the last time Notre Dame and Michigan feuded. After only ten years of playing the game, in fact, Notre Dame was feuding with nearly everyone that counted. The school was shunned and scorned by the powers of the day in their own Midwest. They were interlopers, the bad guys. The established powers were the members of the Western Conference, which had acquired a nickname: the Big Ten. By 1896, Notre Dame felt it was sufficiently advanced to apply for membership in the conference. It was rejected with a sneer as being too small and substandard academically. The Big Ten members also suggested that

Notre Dame's players weren't eligible under their rules. The Irish didn't like that, but they brought their rules into conformity with those of the Big Ten and waited for another chance. It came in 1905 when the University of Michigan pulled out of the conference in a dispute. Notre Dame again applied for admission and was again refused. In 1909, to drive the point home, members of the Western Conference froze Notre Dame out of their schedules.

That was the Big Ten's last chance. From that day on, Notre Dame vowed to forge its own way. Its one last big sectional game had been against Michigan. That ended, too, in an incident which had begun in 1909 when Notre Dame upset the Wolverines in South Bend; the following fall Michigan decided out of spite to cancel the return match. Michigan waited until Notre Dame was en route to Ann Arbor to make that decision. When the Irish arrived, they were told that two of their players were academically ineligible and there would be no game. Michigan subsequently rejoined the Big Ten, leaving Notre Dame with a serious problem. For the next three years it filled its weekends with games against the likes of St. Viator, Morris Harvey, Wabash, Rose Poly, and Olivet, a list that read more like a bus schedule than a football schedule.

As far as the rest of the country knew, Notre Dame belonged with those kinds of schools. It was a tiny, denominational school with a vainglorious, gold-plated administration building. It was populated by the sons of immigrants and workingmen. Academically it couldn't compete with a Michigan. Why should it athletically? In fact, Notre Dame's president, Father John W. Cavanaugh, felt his school shouldn't try to compete. He didn't think that much of football, and as far as he was concerned, Wabash and Morris Harvey were just fine.

And that's how it might have stood but for the intervention of Jesse Harper, who was hired as athletic director and football coach in 1913. Harper, like the feisty kids who played for him, had aspirations. Few people in the East knew about Knute Kenneth Rockne, Gus Dorais, and Ray Eichenlaub. Harper was going to introduce them.

In the summer of 1913, Harper wrote to a number of schools asking for football games. He didn't care where the games were, he just wanted to play top-flight opponents. He signed up South Dakota for a home game and scheduled Penn State and Texas away. He also scheduled a game against Army at West Point. Three trips of such length were virtually unheard of in those days. The Texas trip, some fifteen hundred miles, was the greatest distance Notre Dame had ever traveled for a football game. Harper was delighted.

Among those opponents, Army was the elite. As the reigning power of the East, Army excelled at a brand of smash-mouth football that was long on blood and short on beauty. The team was big, which is to say it had players as large as 200 pounds. It didn't go for finesse. That was for the ballet.

Harper, who had played for Amos Alonzo Stagg, had other ideas. In 1906 college football had reached a pinnacle of brutality. The flying wedge, in which players locked arms and trampled anyone with enough temerity to challenge it, was widely used. The game had gotten so dangerous, in fact, that President Theodore Roosevelt urged that it be banned. In reaction to Roosevelt, the keepers of the game tried to make it safer. They outlawed the locked-arm wedge and legalized the forward pass in the hope of opening up the game.

Others had fiddled with the pass. Rockne himself credited Eddie Cochems, the coach at St. Louis University—a regular Notre Dame opponent—with being the first coach to effectively employ the pass. That was in 1907. Pop Warner of Carlisle and Amos Alonzo Stagg of Chicago experimented with it but thought that it overly complicated the game. They preferred to win with old-fashioned strength. Army, too, knew about the forward pass and in fact was the best passing team in the East. But the maneuver was a last-resort play, and no one tried to shovel the ball more than a few yards forward. The ball itself, fatter and rounder than it is today, didn't seem to be suited for much else.

Dorais and Rockne were the first players to see the real potential of the forward pass. In the summer of 1913 the two seniors-to-be got jobs at Cedar Point, an amusement park in Sandusky, Ohio, where many Notre Dame students retreated for the summer. Every day they worked on throwing the ball, and Dorais perfected a spiral delivery that could send the ball 30 and 40 yards at a time downfield—phenomenal distances for the day.

When football practice began that year, Dorais unveiled his new skill. Harper wasn't impressed. No one could throw the ball like that, he said. In wet weather it would be too slick to hold. To demonstrate his point, he soaked a football in a bucket of water and dared Dorais to throw it. Dorais did. Perfectly. Harper was sold.

That was the weapon Notre Dame would use on Army, and Harper protected it as if it were the Stealth bomber. That wasn't hard to do because word didn't travel far or fast in those days. Not when it concerned Notre Dame, at any rate. Against Ohio Northern and South Dakota, the Irish threw their passes in virtual anonymity. Then, against Alma, with an Army scout in attendance, Harper shelved the weapon, relying on Eichenlaub's line smashes to roll to a 62–0 victory. The next Saturday, November 1, 1913, was Army.

Notre Dame wasn't utterly unknown to Army. The Irish baseball team had visited West Point on an East Coast trip that spring, and in losing 3–0 had shown itself to be an able but not dangerous opponent. Army knew that Notre Dame had lost only one football game in the preceding four years, but who had they played? The conservative style of play they had employed in the Alma game supported the notion that Notre Dame would be a good opponent but would present no unanticipated problems. Notre Dame would be a perfect team for Army to use as a tune-up for its tough games in the East.

If Army was blasé about the upcoming battle, Notre Dame was in a perfect frenzy. Army may have looked at the little upstart school as a tune-up, but Notre Dame looked at the game as a shot at legitimacy. It was their way of declaring, "We are here." In his autobiography Rockne recalled that "while the game was not all-important to Army, it was the supreme test of our playing careers. We went to play them like crusaders, believing that we represented not only our school but the whole aspiring Middle West."

The Notre Dame student press wrote about the game and the season that enfolded it with a modern enthusiasm. "Taken altogether, the schedule is by far the hardest arranged for our gridiron warriors since the organization of the Western Conference, if indeed it is not the hardest in the history of local football," declared *The Scholastic*. The significance of the travel schedule was also noted: "Heretofore, Pittsburgh marked the limit of Gold and Blue football excursions, but this year Coach Harper will send his men into the East for two invasions, to Army and Penn

State. In these games Notre Dame will meet the best of the East. It is needless to remark on the strength of West Point."

It's about six hundred miles from South Bend to West Point, an overnight trip on the New York Central. If Army had seen Notre Dame get on the train, it might have laughed. The entire team consisted of nineteen players, Harper, who also acted as trainer, and one assistant coach. For those nineteen players Notre Dame had fourteen pairs of shoes. The $1,000 Harper received from Army for expenses didn't cover meals, so Notre Dame brown-bagged it. The captain of the team, Knute Rockne, weighed barely 145 pounds, and he was nursing a separated rib cartilage suffered in the first game of the season, an 87–0 romp over Ohio Northern. The quarterback, Gus Dorais, wasn't much bigger. Notre Dame had one genuine monster, Ray Eichenlaub, who weighed 195 pounds. Army, it was reported, outweighed the Irish across the line by 15 pounds a man.

Intercollegiate relations were cordial back then. Army housed the visitors in its own officer's club and fed them with the cadets in the mess hall. The same informality reigned on game day when the fans were not charged admission and watched the game from whatever vantage point was most convenient. The audience, variously reported as between twenty-five hundred and five thousand, wasn't large for a game that would become the stuff of legend. Nor were the eastern media impressed with the match. The *New York Times* and the other New York papers sent their second-string football writers, who would find their full descriptive powers put to the test before the day was over.

The game started according to the Army script. Notre Dame received the opening kickoff, and Dorais promptly fumbled the ball to Army deep in his own territory. After holding Army, Notre Dame took over again. "Let's open up," Dorais suggested, and the assault began.

With Army charging hard to stop the run, Dorais stepped back and began flinging graceful spirals to his ends and backs. After missing on his first 2 throws, he hit either 13 or 14—the newspapers couldn't get together on the stats in those days before play-by-play sheets and instant replay—of his next 15 passes for 243 yards. Any quarterback in any day would gladly have those numbers, but in 1913 it was as if aliens had landed in Times Square.

"The Westerners flashed the most sensational football that has been seen in the East this year, baffling the Cadets with a style of open play and a perfectly developed forward pass, which carried the victors down the field 30 yards at a clip," the second-string writer for the *New York Times* gushed. Dorais, he wrote, was "a frail youth of 145 pounds, as agile as a cat and as restless as a jumping jack." The Army players, he reported, "were hopelessly confused and chagrined."

One of the pass plays was a 40-yard completion to Rockne, the longest pass ever completed in college football. The way the play came about told everything everyone would ever need to know about the little Norwegian. Rockne later wrote:

> After one fierce scrimmage I emerged limping as if hurt. On the next three plays Dorais threw three successful passes in a row to [Joe] Pliska, our right halfback, for short gains. On each of these three plays I limped down the field, acting as if the thing farthest from my mind was to receive a forward pass. After the third play the Army halfback covering me figured I wasn't worth watching. Even as a decoy he figured I was harmless.
>
> Finally, Dorais called my number. . . . I started limping down the field, and the Army halfback covering me almost yawned in my face, he was so bored. Suddenly I put on full speed and left him standing there flat-footed. I raced across the Army goal line as Dorais whipped the ball and the grandstands roared at the completion of a 40-yard pass. Everybody seemed astonished. There had been no hurdling, no tackling, no plunging, no crushing of fiber or sinew, just a long-distance touchdown by rapid transit. At the moment that I touched the ball, life for me was complete.

The writers were enthralled. "It is superior for ground-gaining purposes; it is less dangerous to the players," wrote one, "and it makes a prettier game to view from the sidelines."

There it was: Modern football with all that meant for attracting spectators—and money. Cash receipts didn't mean that much to Army and the Ivy League, but to Notre Dame the financial lode that football represented would later be mined by Rockne for all it was worth. The school, whose endowment back then couldn't have bought a loaf of bread, quite simply needed the money to transform a distant prairie college into the ranking academic institution that Father Edward Sorin, the school's founder, had envisioned. Notre Dame 35, Army 13 started the process which made that possible, for after that game Harper didn't have to write to schools for games. They came to him, eager to try themselves against such a team.

Back in South Bend, "the whole town turned out. Brass bands, red fire engines, speeches, as if we had repulsed and conquered an attack upon the West by the East," Rockne wrote.

Six days after Army, Notre Dame was in State College, Pennsylvania, playing and beating Penn State. Two weeks after that they were in St. Louis beating Christian Brothers, and a week after that they were fifteen hundred miles from home in Texas, wrapping up a perfect 7-0 season with a 30–7 win over Texas.

National Championship polls didn't exist back then, but they soon would. For Michigan it had been enough to be Champions of the West, but Notre Dame wanted to be champions of the world. From 1913 on they became the team to beat.

The next forty years were filled with glory and big games for Notre Dame. And then it ended.

The end came gradually. In 1953, Leahy had gone 9-0-1, his best season since his last championship in 1949. But the stress of coaching Notre Dame had destroyed his health, and, at the urging of university officials Leahy retired after the season. Terry Brennan replaced him and went 9-1 in 1954. In two years that changed to 2-8, and after two more Brennan was replaced by Joe Kuharich. Kuharich was worse than Brennan. In his four seasons he wallowed to a 17-23-0 record and left with the distinction of being the only coach in Notre Dame history with a losing record.

By the time Parseghian arrived, matters had deteriorated so that the team's home games weren't even sellouts, and a significant minority of students on campus were questioning the value of big-time football. Athletes, they maintained, were animals. Notre Dame had evolved to the point where it didn't need them.

Parseghian's first season, the 9-1 campaign of 1964, turned that around. By 1966 football again was king, and a student who admitted to being a communist had a better chance of being socially accepted than one who admitted to not attending football games.

The way Notre Dame approached football hadn't changed that much since 1913. The profits still went to the university and not to the athletic department. Although there were a few professors who taught courses in which showing up was enough work to get a passing grade, athletes received no particular favors. There were no courses in basket-weaving or bead-stringing. There was no physical education major. There were no athletic dorms or special dining facilities for the athletes. The school's weight room was a cramped facility next to the campus cobbler's shop. There were now enough shoes for each player, but the school did not splurge on equipment.

By 1966, Notre Dame no longer had to take students and athletes wherever it could find them. Now the athletes sought out the school, and not all of them found that talent alone was enough to get in. There was still a blue-collar flavor to the school, but now there was also a feeling of superiority that the university encouraged. It wasn't called that, it was called mystique, but the effect was the same.

Football was a prime source of revenue, but it was more than that. It was a symbol of Notre Dame's philosophy. The Ivy League, which had once dominated football, slowly dropped out of the hunt for National Championships and Heisman trophy winners. Big-time football at schools like Yale, Harvard, and Princeton was considered antithetical to a quality education. But Notre Dame felt that if it was going to do something, it was going to do it right and be the best at it. Football was the metaphor for that determination.

The university's president, Father Theodore Hesburgh, agreed with that feeling, but he also felt there was a lot more to life than the successful application of the two-minute drill. After Edward Sorin, Hesburgh was the most influential and visionary president the university ever had. Sorin's dream had been a Catholic university. Hesburgh made it come true, and he put football in its place as part of Notre Dame, not as all that Notre Dame was.

In 1966, Notre Dame's twelve-hundred-acre campus contained sixty buildings, half of which had been built since Hesburgh took over in 1952. It had completed its first major fund-raising drive. It had the academic vigor it had lacked before he came. Hesburgh described the university he inherited, in a 1953 grant application to the Ford Foundation:

> Our student body had doubled, our facilities were inadequate, our faculty quite ordinary for the most part, our deans and de-

partment heads complacent, our graduates loyal and true in heart but often lacking in intellectual curiosity, our academic programs largely encrusted with the accretions of decades, our graduate school an infant, our administration much in need of reorganization, our fund-raising organization nonexistent, and our football team national champions.

Hesburgh got the Ford grant and many more. He became one of the leading activists of the era, serving on so many national and international commissions that he spent half his days on the road. A standing campus joke about Hesburgh went like this: "What's the difference between God and Father Hesburgh?" Answer: "God is everywhere. Father Hesburgh is everywhere but Notre Dame."

If Hesburgh received credit for taking Notre Dame to the forefront of education, he also received the blame for the distressing state of incompetence of the football team under Brennan and Kuharich. The story was that he had deemphasized football; in truth, he had only reemphasized academics. If the football team struggled, it was because of the coaching. Since Hesburgh wouldn't fire a coach—a trait that would drive alumni crazy again when Gerry Faust succeeded Dan Devine in 1981—the team suffered. But if Hesburgh hired Brennan and Kuharich, he also hired Parseghian. Once again the words of the "Notre Dame Victory March" rang true: "Old Notre Dame will win over all."

The seniors on that 1966 team who rode the train to Lansing were well aware of what the song said. But still, as the players looked out the windows of the train at the faithful who lined the tracks to Lansing, they marvelled at the excitement they had caused.

"We had never seen anything like that," said Tom Pagna, the offensive coordinator. "It was like the old days."

And none of them knew it would never be like the old days again.

2

I've coached a lot of places, but to me, Michigan State was the epitome of what a college campus ought to be.
—Cal Stoll

Notre Dame was thirteen years old when the institution that would become Michigan State University put down roots in the middle of nearly eight square miles of central Michigan, on the outskirts of Lansing, the state capital. Like Notre Dame, it was born of a vision, but it was a vision much more prosaic than that of the priests of du Lac. Whereas Notre Dame aspired from the first to grow into a great Catholic university, Michigan Agricultural aspired to the higher practical education of the masses, primarily in the science of agriculture.

The birth of the state school was a ground-breaking event in more ways than one, for the East Lansing institution was the first agricultural school in the nation. By 1862 the concept of the college was ratified by the passage of the Morrill Act, which established the mechanisms that led to the national system of sixty-eight land-grant colleges and universities. If the University of Michigan was to be the state's selective school, dedicated to such pursuits as medicine and law, the new college was to be the gateway for the sons of Michigan's commoners to more practical careers. Unlike the University of Michigan, Michigan Agricultural would not choose its students. It would educate all who came. And since the new college's mission was to educate and not to play, it wasn't until 1896, nine years after Notre Dame, that Michigan Agricultural got around to trying its callused hands at football. Unlike Notre Dame, which started by going straight to the best in the West, the University of Michigan, Michigan Agricultural began with more modest opposition. Its first game was against Lansing High School, and the Aggies, as they were first known, came away with a 10–0 victory. In three other games, however, they lost two to Kalamazoo and tied Alma.

The following year, the college opened again against Lansing High and ended its season for the first time against Notre Dame. The Irish won, 34–0, in South Bend. By its third season, 1898, Michigan Agricultural felt ready to take on its downstate neighbor, the University of Michigan, which looked at these hicks with unconcealed contempt. On the football field it was the gentlemen from Ann Arbor in a 39–0 laugher over the farmers from East Lansing.

And so it went into the twentieth century. In 1902, Michigan Agricultural tried the University of Michigan again, and this time lost by a score of 119–0, which would remain forever the worst loss in its history. Three years later, under coach John F. Macklin, Michigan Agricultural finally got back at the Ann Arbor gang, winning 12–7 on the road and going on to its first undefeated, untied season.

The heady sense of triumph was short-lived, though. The plain reality was that Michigan Agricultural College's prime mission was to provide advanced education to anyone who could meet the entrance requirements and come up with the minimal tuition and fees. That was the whole idea behind land-grant colleges—to educate the masses. And the masses, at least in those days, were not where the athletes traditionally came from. They came from the upper classes, which had the leisure time to pursue fun and games. They were also the people who went to the more exclusive schools. Michigan Agricultural wasn't meant to be exclusive. It didn't choose its student body. It educated farmers.

After 1913, the Aggies sank back into the athletic middle class, losing regularly to both Michigan and Notre Dame, gleaning its victories from the likes of Albion, DePauw, Olivet, and even the Chicago YMCA.

If the football program was stagnant, the college was not. By 1925, Michigan Agricultural had grown and diversified to the point where it was more than an agricultural school. Accordingly, it changed its name to Michigan State College. At the same time it dropped its Aggie nickname. A contest was held to come up with a new nickname, and the winner, chosen by people of negative imagination, was the "Michigan Staters." Local newspapers were appalled at the choice, not so much because it was so prosaic but because it didn't fit in a short headline. Two local newspapermen, George S. Alderton and Dale Stafford, took it upon themselves to rectify the situation. They decided that another name submitted during the contest but rejected was shorter and therefore better. The name, suggested by Perry J. Fremont, a former Michigan Agricultural athlete, was the "Spartans." The journalists started by slipping the nickname into stories, then trying it out in small, inconspicuous headlines. When nobody complained, they used it all the time. And so the Spartans of Michigan State were born.

No matter what the institution called itself, it was still "Moo U" to the Wolverines of the University of Michigan, whose students and admirers never missed a chance to remind Michigan State that it was, at best, a poor sister. It showed on the football field. In fourteen games from 1919 through 1931, Michigan State not only failed to beat the Wolverines but also failed to score a single point in all but one of them. The single tally in all those games was a field goal in a 55–3 loss in 1926.

The rule was years of mediocrity interrupted by an occasional flash of success, such as an 8-1 regular season in 1938, before a trip to the Orange Bowl for a season-ending loss to Auburn. But things didn't get consistently better until the arrival in 1947 of Biggie Munn.

Clarence L. "Biggie" Munn, a native of Minnesota, had been an All-American lineman for the University of Minnesota in 1931. He went straight into coaching after college and worked his way up the ranks as an assistant at Syracuse and at the University of Michigan before becoming head coach of Syracuse in 1946. After that single season, Michigan State athletic director Ralph Young hired Munn to coach the Spartans. One of the coaches Munn brought with him was Hugh Duffy Daugherty, who had played the line for Biggie at Syracuse and returned after World War II to become an assistant coach.

Young knew that if his athletic program was going to grow, he needed to get into a major conference, and he set his sights on the Big Ten. But first he had to show success against an upgraded schedule. He also knew that the most prestigious team he could play was Notre Dame.

The Irish and the Spartans hadn't met since 1921 when Michigan State lost for the thirteenth time in fifteen tries against Notre Dame. But now Young called up Notre Dame for help. He asked Edward W. "Moose" Krause for a series of games against the Irish and offered to play every game in South Bend. Instead of splitting the gate, "Just give us our expenses," he said. Krause and Young were old friends—indeed, Krause was old friends with almost everyone in college athletics—and Krause refused the terms. "We'll alternate sites and split the gate," said Krause. They agreed to play five games, from 1948 to 1952.

Meanwhile, Munn immediately turned the Spartan program around. After opening the 1947 season with a depressing 55–0 loss to Michigan in Ann Arbor, Munn won seven of the remaining eight games on the schedule, losing only a 7–6 heartbreaker to Kentucky.

By 1950, Munn was ready to break through. He had a great junior tackle, Don E. Coleman, a tough sophomore guard named Frank Kush, and an All-American fullback with the headline stretching name of Everett Grandelius. In the second game of the season he served notice that the old order had changed as he finally beat Michigan, 14–7, in front of 97,239 onlookers in Ann Arbor. Munn also beat the Irish for the first time, 36–33, in South Bend, after having suffered defeats in the first two games of the renewed series. The Spartans went on to an 8-1 season. Munn beat the Irish again in 1951 and this time went undefeated. In 1952 he repeated the feat and won Michigan State's first National Championship.

By now the Big Ten was convinced that Michigan State would be a worthy member of the nation's premier football conference. All that was needed was for one conference member to drop out, and when the University of Chicago obliged after the 1952 season, Michigan State was in the Big Ten, effective in 1953. To mark the historic occasion, Michigan Governor G. Mennen Williams came up with the Paul Bunyan trophy that would be held each year by the winner of that season's game. The trophy is a four-foot-high carved and painted wooden statue of Paul Bunyan standing astride an ax that is buried in the statue's base. On the left side of the base flies a flag with the letter S, on the right a similar flag labelled M. The Paul Bunyan trophy was not exactly the Little Brown Jug, but it was a tangible sign that Michigan State, which had started life so humbly, was now the equal of Michigan—in the eyes of the governor, at least. In the eyes of the University of Michigan students, however, the school to the northwest, although a full-fledged university now, was still Moo U. Whenever the Spartans went to Ann Arbor, the Wolverine student body reminded them of that by making thunderous mooing noises when the Spartans took the field. When Michigan traveled to Lansing, Wolverine students habitually sneaked onto the campus before the game and painted blue the big statue of the Michigan State Spartan that had been erected in front of the athletic complex in 1945. In return, the Spartan students went to Ann Arbor before the games and painted green a big boulder on Washtenaw Avenue in the fraternity and sorority neighborhood. Sometimes they'd paint the bronze lions outside the art museum green and spray-paint GO MSU on construction barricades. Once they came down and horrified Ann Arbor by painting their slogans on granite buildings. But that was the level of animosity between the two schools. Year in and year out the football season in East Lansing began with a single goal: Beat the Wolverines. And when the Spartans finally reached the top, the football team actually came to enjoy the mooing in Ann Arbor. It just added to the pleasure of milking the Wolverines for ten victories in thirteen years leading to the 1966 season.

Getting in the Big Ten was a symbol of big-time status, but winning the conference title was the only way the Spartans would prove their right to be there. Munn did just that in his very first season. In 1953 the Spartans won eight times, losing only to Purdue, and celebrated New Year's Day, 1954, at the Rose Bowl by beating UCLA, 28–20.

With that triumph Munn retired from coaching and took over from Ralph Young as athletic director. He named his assistant, Duffy Daugherty, to succeed him as coach.

Daugherty had impeccable football credentials, which is to say he was the son of a Pennsylvania coal miner. Born September 8, 1915, in Emeigh, a pinpoint of a town in Cambria County, he grew up in Barnesboro, a mining town of about three thousand desperate souls just south of Emeigh on the west branch of the Susquehanna River.

Daugherty wasn't big—his nickname at Syracuse was "Stubby"—but he was tough enough to play guard at Syracuse. A picture of him from that time shows a wiry little Irishman with a determined face under a lush crop of curly brown hair. He instilled that determination in his troops when he coached the line for Munn at Michigan State, where his players were nick-named Duffy's Toughies.

He was tough and he was funny. Where others collected stamps or coins, Daugherty collected one-liners. "It's bad luck to be behind at the end of a game" was his comment on Dame Fortune. Speaking on capitalism, he said, "If I had a little money, I'd be one myself." Instead of pep talks after practices and before games, he told his squad jokes—shaggy dog stories. The bigger and more tense the game, the longer and more painful the joke he told. After a while his older players had heard them all, and they'd end up laughing not at the joke but at the underclassmen who hadn't heard them yet and thought they were funny. It didn't matter. The idea was to cut the tension, not add to it. And it worked.

His first team, the 1954 squad, had a hard time of it, going 3-6, but he rebounded in 1955 to go 9-1, the last win being a 17–14 defeat of UCLA in the Rose Bowl. The tremendous turn-around earned Daugherty national Coach of the Year honors. After two more good seasons, however, the team went into a decline. In 1961, when he went 7-2, and 1963, when he was 6-2-1, he seemed to be turning things around, but then the program bottomed out again in 1964, winning four and losing five.

In 1964, when things were going so poorly, some Spartan fans began to lament the fact that Daugherty didn't land the Notre Dame coaching job in 1957. Duffy had made it clear that he wanted it. He was an Irishman. Notre Dame was where he wanted to be, but the school hired Joe Kuharich instead.

No one ever gave a reason why Daugherty was bypassed. He certainly had the coaching credentials, and despite regularly beating Notre Dame, Fighting Irish fans liked him better than any other opposing coach. But he also had a reputation for being a bit looser with the rules than Notre Dame liked, and his life-style, which included stops at blue-collar saloons, was not quite on the plane to which Notre Dame aspired.

"Notre Dame wants its coaches to be like its priests," Jim Lynch, the captain of the 1966 Irish, once said. "They have to be able to enjoy a drink without getting drunk and enjoy the company of women without fooling around." Apparently, the powers at Notre Dame didn't feel that Duffy filled that prescription.

Going into the 1965 season, nine years removed from the memory of the past Rose Bowl, Spartan fans were getting restless, and the little Irishman was being hung in effigy on the campus. Little did they know that Duffy Daugherty's best was yet to come.

3

"C" students rule the world.

—Terry Hanratty

Normally, the Notre Dame football team ate the same breakfast as the rest of the student body—gloppy scrambled eggs that sometimes had a green tinge and bacon that wasn't anything to write home about, although it was sometimes so charred that you could write home with it. The only consideration they received was at dinner after practice when they ate after the rest of the students had finished. They also had twice as much as the regular students did of the foodlike substances served in the North Dining Hall. There was a lively debate as to whether this was a privilege or a punishment.

But game days were different. Then the players took their morning meal as a team and separate from the rest of the student body. In addition to the eggs, bacon, cereal, juice, sausage, and potatoes, they had steak. In keeping with the sports nutrition theories of the day, everyone figured there was nothing like a big hunk of red meat—or gray meat, as it usually became once the dining hall staff was done with it—to power the human machine in the big game. If someone had suggested that steak was bad and carbohydrates—spaghetti and macaroni—were better, they would have been laughed off the campus. Real men ate steaks.

The only problem was that many of the players were so nervous before games they couldn't keep their spit down, much less a steak. So the ritual game day breakfast became a bonanza for the second- and third-stringers. Not having to worry about starting or even playing until the game was decided, they fattened up on the steaks the starters couldn't get down.

September 24 was a good day for nonstarters because the varsity had more than ordinary first-game jitters. It was opening day of the 1966 Notre Dame football season, and no pushover opening day opponent was on the menu. Purdue was in town, the team led by Bob Griese, one of the best college quarterbacks of the day. The previous year Notre Dame had gone to Lafayette, Indiana, the second week of the season, and Griese had taken them apart, 25–21, with a magnificent performance. He had completed 19 of 22 passes and picked over their defense like a Thanksgiving turkey carcass. The Irish had high hopes for this season, but first they had to get past Griese and Purdue. Whether they would or not depended almost entirely on whether a sophomore quarterback who had never played a varsity game before—who had, in fact, never played any sort of college game—could overcome the pressure of starting for Notre Dame on national television against the mighty Boilermakers of Purdue.

No one had told Terry Hanratty this in so many words. They hadn't said it out loud even to themselves. You don't want to go into a football season relying on one person. But that was the fact. In 1965, Notre Dame had failed because it lacked a quarterback. If Hanratty didn't come through, they might fail again. If, on the other hand, he did throw the ball as he had shown he could in practice, then Notre Dame could start to think about winning its first National Championship in seventeen years.

As the coaches and upperclassmen considered all of this, Hanratty made his way through the cafeteria line, pushing his plastic tray along the stainless-steel rails that fronted the steam counters. He was watched carefully but not obviously; everyone wondered how he would react to the pressure. Hanratty was unaware of them. His mind was overloaded with his own thoughts, and they had nothing to do with pass patterns, cadence counts, or reading defenses. No, Terrence Hanratty had more important things on his mind.

Steak! That's what occupied Hanratty. *Eggs. Potatoes. Sausage. Bacon. More steak.* He had never seen a breakfast like it. In fact, until he got to college, he had never seen a dinner like it, either. As a kid growing up in Butler, Pennsylvania, Hanratty had heard of steak, but he'd never actually seen one. He knew all about macaroni and cheese and spaghetti, as did everyone else who grew up in the hardscrabble coal country of the Monongahela Valley. Only once had he even come within sniffing distance of a steak, and that was in a sandwich. He had been invited to Pittsburgh to meet Ara Parseghian, the Notre Dame coach. Parseghian was in town for business and thought he'd talk to the quarterback whom he knew only as number 11 on the game films that his defensive coach and Pennsylvania recruiter, John Ray, had brought back to South Bend.

"Who's that number eleven?" Parseghian had exclaimed as he watched the films. "We gotta get him."

Unlike other coaches, Parseghian didn't go to the homes of recruits to sweet-talk them into signing with the Irish. Ordinarily, he never left his office in the Knute Rockne Memorial. Woody Hayes of Ohio State, Joe Paterno who had just taken over the head job at Penn State, Duffy Daugherty of Michigan State, and Bump Elliott of Michigan would roam the Midwest, camping out in recruits' living rooms, charming their mothers, making promises to their fathers. Parseghian wouldn't do that. Only twice did he visit recruits at home, and the results only confirmed his antipathy toward the fine art of groveling: One of the kids went to Notre Dame but never played, and the other went somewhere else.

If a recruit wanted to see him, he had to go to South Bend. Parseghian didn't do this for any reason other than that he disliked groveling in the living rooms of high school kids. But it was also a powerful psychological weapon that told the recruit, *We're Notre Dame. We don't have to beg you to come. You have to beg us to let you play for us.*

But Parseghian made a rare exception for Hanratty, although he still wasn't going to go to this kid's home. He had to give a speech in Pittsburgh, and since number 11 was the best quarterback he had seen in a long time and he really needed a quarterback, he could meet with him while he was in town.

Hanratty wasn't the nervous sort, but when Parseghian called, anxiety took over. He dressed up in his best clothes and drove to the Hilton Hotel in Pittsburgh, where a lunch meeting had been arranged. After the introductions had been made and everyone got settled, Parseghian invited Hanratty to order lunch—anything he wanted.

As Hanratty scanned the menu, his eyes fell on the steak sandwich. It was tempting. He had always wanted a steak, even if it was just a sandwich. The price, which was something around $2.95, seemed steep to him, and he didn't want to appear greedy, which would have drawn laughter at a lot of other schools where players didn't have to choose between steak and tuna but between Fords and Pontiacs. Hanratty didn't know about those things. He just knew he wanted to make the right impression, so he passed on the steak and went for the club sandwich, which was about a dollar cheaper.

Hanratty learned soon enough that he could have all the steak he wanted. Recruiters from other colleges offered to furnish his mother's house and carpet it. Word was a Notre Dame booster offered a new furnace. There were offers of cars and cash. He could have anything he wanted.

Hanratty had decided at a young age that his athletic ability was going to carry him through life. He didn't know if it would be baseball or football; he was equally outstanding at both. He made his decision subconsciously during the summer before his senior year of high school. For the first time in his life his batting average in baseball dropped, and he was missing easy ground balls in the infield. When he stopped to think about it, he realized that he was spending all his time practicing football and that baseball had taken a backseat. So it would be football.

He did only enough in school to get by with C's. "C students rule the world," he said. "A students don't have the whatever. They're not imaginative. C students are a little crazy."

He had started school at the age of five, so he was only sixteen in his senior year of high school and didn't turn seventeen until January. But he ran the pro-style offense at Butler High and in nine games led his team to almost three hundred points. One of the games was a 41–21 drubbing of Beaver Falls, Joe Namath's old high school, and Hanratty scored one of the touchdowns in that game on an 82-yard quarterback sneak. People in the Monongahela Valley compared him to Namath, who had gone on to

Alabama where, in 1964, he was a senior. Hanratty didn't particularly like the comparison. He preferred to emulate another Pennsylvania kid who he felt had a bit more class—Johnny Unitas.

The youngest of four children, Hanratty didn't have it easy growing up, and athletics was his escape. His parents split up, and the kids stayed with their mother. There wasn't a lot of money. He seldom watched sports on television because he would rather be outside playing them. His mother, who was quite athletic herself, would literally drag him in the house and make him watch Joe DiMaggio. Baseball was her sport, and football scared her. In fact, the Purdue–Notre Dame game in 1966 was the first time she ever watched him play—at home on television.

Hanratty hadn't grown up immersed in the Notre Dame legend as had some of his teammates at Notre Dame. But when it came time to pick a college, the decision was between Michigan State and Notre Dame. His older brother, Pete, was already at Notre Dame on a track scholarship, but that wasn't the determining factor.

"It was just meeting Ara," Hanratty said. "He was as honest as any man could be."

Hanratty liked Duffy Daugherty, Michigan State's puckish coach, too. And odds were good he could have made a better living at Michigan State than at Notre Dame. But when it came time to decide, he decided he liked Parseghian more. He called Daugherty as a courtesy to let him know he wouldn't be going to East Lansing, and Daugherty spent the next half hour telling Hanratty what a great guy Parseghian was and what a great decision Hanratty had made.

So he went to South Bend and on vacations he went home and listened to his former high school teammates, some of whom wouldn't get beyond third-string in college, talk about the envelopes of money they found in the mailboxes every week. Hanratty, meanwhile, was scraping together money by running a barbershop in his dorm room, charging $1 a head and providing an old *Playboy* magazine for the guy waiting his turn in the chair.

But if Hanratty didn't have a car and a bank account, at least he had steak. Even freshmen got that every Thursday night. The steaks weren't the highest grade of meat, and they were done to order only if you preferred something that could be switched with a flagstone without anyone's noticing. But they were steaks.

As a freshman Hanratty hadn't eaten pregame meals with the team. Freshmen football players weren't eligible to play with the varsity, so they weren't eligible at Notre Dame for special treatment. This was his first encounter with what it meant to be on the varsity. It meant steak for breakfast.

Delighted with how good football had been to him, Hanratty piled his tray high with enough grease and cholesterol to put a small city into cardiac arrest. He found a table, sat down, spread the bounty out in front of him, and started shoveling it in.

He was so intent on his meal, he didn't even notice that the entire varsity was watching him, staring in openmouthed wonder and whispering to one another. "He's going to throw up," they muttered. "He's going to be slow," they worried. "What does he think he's doing?" they wondered.

When he was done, he looked up and everyone looked nonchalant, as if they hadn't been watching him at all. He looked remarkably calm for one who would shortly be the center of attention of millions of fans. What they didn't know was that Hanratty had no real idea of what national television meant. He didn't know which network was broadcasting the game and didn't realize how many people would be watching. He hadn't watched it as a kid, and he wasn't thinking about it now. As far as he was concerned, he was just going to play another football game.

It was fine for him to think that, but this team was heavy with seniors who knew this was their last chance to win a National Championship. If they were going to do that, the rookie quarterback was going to have to come up big. The least he could do was have the courtesy to be nervous.

Hanratty wasn't the only question mark on the Irish team. Four of the six interior linemen employed by the Notre Dame offense were new, and a fifth, Tom Regner, had only alternated at guard the year before. None of the three junior defensive backs in John Ray's 4-4-3 defense had ever started a varsity game. The safety, Tom Schoen, had been converted from quarterback and had never played defense. Still, the defensive backs were talented athletes. The offensive linemen were big, and most had some experience. Regner, who was listed in the program at 240 but bent the scales at 270, was a certified monster blocker, and George Goeddeke, the center, was as tough as old work boots. Notre Dame would also have a running attack of the highest order with seniors Nick Eddy and Larry Conjar teaming with junior Rocky Bleier. The big question was quarterback. Their quarterback in 1965 had been Bill Zloch, a fierce competitor and a terrific guy beloved by his teammates, but not a passer by the most generous definition of the term. Forced to gain yardage on the ground, Notre Dame ran into defenses that sometimes staked all eleven men on the line of scrimmage. Purdue had contained them, and Michigan State had held them to negative yardage, the only time in the history of Notre Dame football that that had happened.

After the 1965 season Parseghian vowed that he would have a passing attack in 1966. He had brought in two freshmen the year before, Hanratty and Coley O'Brien, a hotshot out of McLean, Virginia, and went through the 1965 season wishing that freshmen were allowed to play varsity football. Parseghian had also brought in people to catch the ball, notably two mirror-image ends named Jim Seymour and Curt Heneghan.

Heneghan, out of Redmond, Washington, was 6 feet 3, 190 pounds. Seymour, from Berkeley, Michigan, was 6 feet 4, 205. Both could run and catch, and both had been highly recruited. Parseghian had been so impressed with their work in spring practice that he spent the summer planning to install an offense that employed two wide receivers and only two running backs. Now a common set in college football, it was still somewhat innovative at the time. Most teams ran their big receiver at split end and used one of their two halfbacks as a flanker. Unfortunately, Heneghan hurt his knee while working out during the summer, and when fall practice began, Seymour was the single wide-out.

Like Hanratty, Jim Seymour was a highly recruited high school star. Unlike Hanratty and many of his teammates, he grew up with the advantages of a middle-class life-style including a backyard swimming pool. The fact the family had a pool was considered proof that the Seymours were wealthy, although comfortable was nearer the truth.

Seymour had grown up wanting to be a basketball player. He went out for the football team as a freshman at Shrine of the Little Flower High School, a small Catholic school in Royal Oak, but hated the game. He said as much to his coach, Al Fracassa, a former quarterback at Michigan State. Fracassa told him not to worry. "By the time I get done with you, you're going to love the game," Fracassa said.

The coach was right. Seymour went through high school starring in football, basketball, and track. He was undefeated in the high and low hurdles for more than two years. In his senior year of football he played halfback, tight end, defensive back, and punter. He caught 31 passes for 560 yards and punted for a 44.2-yard average. He was so good that Fracassa and the school retired his number, and the college offers—sixty in all from every corner of the country—started coming in.

Seymour was from a thoroughly Catholic family that was soaked in the lore of Notre Dame. As a young man in 1935, his father had gone to Columbus, Ohio, where he was among the 81,000 who watched Notre Dame go into the fourth period trailing Ohio State 13–0, and then come back to win 18–13 in the closing seconds. Seymour also had an aunt who was a cloistered nun in the Sacred Heart order. The nuns bent their rules on contact with the outside world enough to pull in the Notre Dame games, and every time Seymour's Aunt Marguerite saw him on television, she wrote him a letter to let him know how he could improve his play. His father went to the practice every Friday before home games and added his own advice.

Despite that heritage, or maybe because of it, Seymour hadn't intended to go to Notre Dame. He was a Michigander, and when you live an hour away from Ann Arbor, you dream of going to Michigan. Indeed, Bump Elliott, Michigan's coach, practically lived with Seymour from his sophomore year of high school. Today, recruiting visits are strictly limited and contact with boosters is verboten, but back then there were no limits on contacts with potential recruits. For three years Seymour was continually contacted by phone and in person. He had seats at University of Michigan basketball games. He liked the idea of going to school so close to home, and he would be able to see his girlfriend on weekends. So he decided to go to the University of Michigan and told Elliott as much.

Notre Dame entered the picture when Paul Shoults, Parseghian's defensive backfield coach who recruited in the Detroit area, showed up at Shrine High one day and asked to meet Seymour after school. Notre Dame was late but not unprepared. Shoults knew everything about Seymour and told him how much Notre Dame wanted him. They planned to use him at defensive back and as a punter, Shoults said. He invited Seymour to Notre Dame to meet Parseghian.

As luck would have it, Seymour had some friends whose father had been transferred to South Bend. Seymour had driven to South Bend before to see them, and since he hadn't seen them in a while, he figured he may as well accept Shoults's invitation. At least he'd get to see his friends.

The first order of business on a recruiting trip to Notre Dame, and most schools, for that matter, is a tour of the campus conducted by current members of the football team. Tom O'Leary, then a freshman, was assigned to take Seymour around. Two other freshmen, Tom Schoen and Jim Smithberger, joined in. Then they found out that Seymour had a car, and suddenly the campus was less interesting and the whole party departed for Elkhart, where a good, if somewhat illegal, time was had by all. Along the way the three freshmen told Seymour what a terrific place Notre Dame was and how great the coaches were. "If you don't make it at one position, they'll find a place for you," one of them told Seymour, not knowing how prophetic that statement was. Within two years both Smithberger and Schoen had been repositioned and were starting with O'Leary in the defensive backfield.

The next stop was Parseghian's office. Seymour sat down, figuring he would listen to what the man had to say, express his thanks, and then return to Michigan and Bump Elliott. Then Ara started talking, his anthracite eyes gleaming beneath a dark set of brows. Seymour soon realized he had a problem. "I'm going to play for this man," he thought. "He's just like Coach Fracassa." The next thing he knew, words were coming out of his mouth. Later, he figured it was all the nuns back at school praying for him to go to Notre Dame that kicked in. It was as good an explanation as any.

"Coach, you have a deal," Seymour heard himself say. They shook hands and Seymour stood up to go, but before he left he said, "Will you do me a favor? Before we make it official, I have to tell someone else first."

"You want to tell Bump, don't you?" Ara said.

Seymour met Ara on a Saturday. When he got home the next day, he tried to call Elliott but couldn't get him. He figured he would try Elliott again after basketball practice Monday. But when he got home Monday evening, the phone was already ringing. Seymour picked it up. It was a Michigan booster.

"You son of a bitch" were the first words Seymour heard.

"Pardon me?"

"We just heard a nasty rumor that you're going to Notre Dame," the man said.

"Yeah, I am," Seymour replied.

With that, the Wolverine patriot buried Seymour in a mountain of vituperation. If Seymour had had any second thoughts about his decision, the man removed them. Seymour hung up the phone.

Moments later the phone rang again. This time it was Elliott.

"I've been trying to get ahold of you, Jim," Elliott said.

"I've been trying to get ahold of you, Coach."

"Do you know who I'm with?" Elliott asked. When Seymour said he didn't, Elliott answered: "Ara Parseghian."

"Uh, Coach," Seymour stumbled, "that's what I wanted to talk to you about."

Elliott wasn't angry at all. Seymour had read him to be a class guy, and now he proved it. "You made a good choice, Jim," he said. "You couldn't play for a better man than Ara Parseghian."

Ten years later Seymour ran into Elliott at a social affair in Ann Arbor. Seeing Seymour, the coach, now retired, excused himself from a group of his former players and approached Seymour. "Did I tell you right?" he asked. "Isn't Ara a hell of a guy?"

"You're right," Seymour agreed. "He is."

Recruiting in college football has never been easy, but in many ways it was even more difficult in 1966 than it is today. Today, once a school gets a recruit to sign a national letter of intent, the athlete is locked into that school. In 1966 getting players like Seymour and Hanratty to commit to Notre Dame was just the beginning of the battle. That's because in 1966 the national letter of intent still didn't exist.

The letter is in essence a binding contract between the school and the athlete. Once he signs, he's yours to keep. But in 1966, once he committed, he still could go elsewhere. This happened to Notre Dame in 1963, the year before Parseghian arrived. Notre Dame had gone after Floyd Little, a spectacular high school running back. Little's grades needed to improve to get into Notre Dame, so the school stashed him for a year at Bordentown Prep, a New Jersey academy that Notre Dame used to raise the grades of athletes who had been marginal high school students. That fall he went to New York to catch his train to South Bend. His luggage was loaded on the train and he was still on the platform when Ernie Davis, the great Syracuse running back, intercepted him. Syracuse had also recruited Little but had apparently lost to Notre Dame. But until he got there, he was still fair game, and Davis turned his head at the last moment. When the train from New York pulled into South Bend, Little's baggage got off, but he was in Syracuse.

Coaches couldn't rest until the athlete actually arrived on campus. Several conferences, including the Big Ten, instituted a conference letter of intent that was binding in the conference, but didn't protect anyone from out-of-conference predators. Parseghian drew up his own Notre Dame letter of intent; it had no legal force but it increased the sense of commitment on the part of the athlete who signed it. Still, getting an athlete to commit was no guarantee he would arrive, and coaches spent their summers calling their incoming freshmen to make sure they still intended to come. They also called selected athletes who committed elsewhere, trying to change their minds.

So Parseghian breathed a sigh of relief when his freshman class of 1965 reported, including Hanratty, Seymour, Heneghan, and O'Brien. Having taken over the coaching job in December 1964, this was the first class he had totally recruited himself. He had gone through a thousand films to come up with seventy candidates. From those he settled on thirty-five who were both interested in Notre Dame and had the grades to be admitted. Of those, thirty-one made it to the varsity as sophomores.

Since freshmen weren't eligible to play, they didn't attend summer practice with the varsity; instead they arrived with the rest of their class. Once they unpacked, however, they were immediately thrown in as fresh meat for the varsity, who had arrived early for two-a-days. Filling in on the scout team that mimicked that week's opponent against the first team offensive and defensive units, they quickly learned that there was a big difference between high school and college.

One of the first lessons for Hanratty and Seymour's class came one day when Chuck Landolfi, a fellow freshman running back, suffered a compound fracture in a drill. His leg badly mangled, he was on the ground screaming. In high school such an incident would have stopped practice. At Notre Dame, Parseghian just told everyone to get to the other end of the field and get on with the drill while the doctors took care of Landolfi.

It was against this defense that Terry Hanratty and Jim Seymour got their first taste of what it would take to perform on the college level. But while Hanratty had his turns, Coley O'Brien, another freshmen recruit, got most of the work at quarterback that fall and seemed to have the inside track on the signal caller's job. O'Brien fit the mold of Notre Dame better than Hanratty. He was the product of a Catholic academy and was a better student than Hanratty. He was also blonder and, with a surname like O'Brien, more Irish.

But during the winter of 1965–66, Hanratty outworked O'Brien. Every day Hanratty went to the old field house and worked on his passing, usually with Seymour, but with anyone who would come. Besides having a stronger arm, he was also taller, heavier, and faster than O'Brien. And, a big factor in Parseghian's eventual decision to start Hanratty, he could throw the deep out pattern better than O'Brien. By the middle of spring practice Hanratty—in Parseghian's mind, at least—had a small edge. Publicly, Parseghian said both quarterbacks were even.

In the media's mind, however, O'Brien was still the leader, even though Hanratty did more work in the major spring scrimmages, including the concluding Blue-Gold game in which the first-team varsity took on a team of alumni that was bolstered by Parseghian's best substitutes. In a 33–0 victory Hanratty passed for two touchdowns and ran for two more. Seymour caught 10 passes for 166 yards, including a 50-yarder on the fourth play of the game.

During the summer of 1966, members of the football team received two letters. Both were written by Ara Parseghian, but the first was signed by team captain James R. Lynch, better known to his teammates as Jim. Lynch would have written the letter himself, but he was busy on a Peace Corps–like project in Peru. That letter went out August 2 and consisted of five paragraphs. It was direct:

> On Saturday afternoon, September 25, 1965, a capacity crowd witnessed Bob Griese and the Purdue Boilermakers topple the Irish from their No. 1 national rating. NEED ANY MORE BE SAID? The '65 game is history. There is nothing we can do about

the past, but there is a great deal we can do about our opener
with Purdue on September 24.

Our preparation for that game and the entire '66 season must
start right now. We must condition ourselves to be both mentally
and physically tough, and constantly remind ourselves of the
dream that can be ours.

Many people close to the game of football expect great things
from our team. The challenge is waiting for us. If we are willing
to work and behave like winners, one of Notre Dame's greatest
seasons awaits us. . . .

The letter also urged the players to start getting into condition.
"You owe yourself and your team a well-conditioned body," Parseghian said through Lynch before signing off.

Two days later Parseghian sent out his own letter, a detailed
epistle that ran five pages on generic University of Notre Dame
Department of Athletics stationery. He was head coach of the
nation's best-known college football team, but he didn't even
have personalized stationery. The letter opened with a prosaic
recital of reporting dates and the details of training camp.

On the top of the letter's third page, Parseghian stated the
team's objective in unequivocal terms:

Our principal goal is the National Championship. We are not
members of any conference, and basically we are known as a
major independent. The schedule we play gives us a great shot
nationally because sportswriters and fans can draw a direct comparison between our strength and the teams in their area.

The team needed little priming. Returning for fall practice, the
Notre Dame players felt that this was going to be the year they
would put it all together. Along with the feeling was the certain
knowledge that this had to be the year. The backbone of the team
was its seniors, most of whom had been in the recruiting class of
1963, a class put together by Kuharich and Hugh Devore, the
interim coach who ran the team in 1963 after Kuharich left to
coach the Philadelphia Eagles and before Parseghian was hired.
As freshmen in 1963 they had watched the team stumble to one
of the worst records in school history, but they hadn't been part
of it and hadn't learned how to lose. As sophomores they experienced the magic of Ara's first year when they went 9-0 before

blowing a 17–0 lead and losing in the last ninety seconds to Southern Cal in the season's last game.

When they had had their first meeting as freshmen, they were so big that they scared one another. Guard Tom Regner, 270 pounds of prime beef, walked into that first meeting, saw speci- mens like Kevin Hardy, who was taller and heavier than he was, and Alan Page, who went around 250, and said, "What am I doing here?"

Now they were seniors, and the one ingredient that they had missed—a passing combination—was in place. Even in fall prac- tice no one on the team knew whether Hanratty or O'Brien would start. They didn't particularly care; either one was a universe better than what they had had in 1965.

The coaches, taught by life's unpleasant vicissitudes that noth- ing is a sure shot, weren't convinced that they had a team des- tined for greatness. The offensive line was the first question mark. Goeddeke was a given at center. Regner, who had split time with Dick Arrington, was an All-American candidate as one guard, and Dick Swatland would play the other guard. Paul Seiler, who had bloomed that spring under Jerry Wampfler, the offensive line coach hired to replace Doc Urich, would play as one tackle. The other initially was Rudy Konieczny, but a big sophomore named Bob Kuechenberg from Hobart, Indiana, was pushing him and would eventually take over. Tight end was between Don Gmitter, a 220-pounder from Pittsburgh who could block, and George Kunz, who was as big as a barn and would eventually be at tackle when Gmitter got the starting job. Seymour was a lock at split end, but Brian Stenger, a 210-pound sophomore out of Euclid, Ohio, backed him up and also was a third tight end.

The running backs were also set with returning starters Larry Conjar, a classic fullback who ran with a minimum of finesse and a maximum of power and could block the biggest defensive ends around, and Nick Eddy, whose first name in most newspaper stories wasn't Nick but "All-American candidate." Rocky Bleier, whose all-world determination made up for what he lacked in size and speed, was the other halfback.

Practice began September 1, and there would be twenty-nine sessions before the first game three weeks later against Purdue. On September 10, Parseghian held a Blue-White scrimmage, pitting the starters against the second team. It was a flawless

Indian Summer day, brilliantly sunny and 83 degrees, and the performance of the Blues, led by Hanratty, was the equal of the weather. The Whites, quarterbacked by O'Brien, had the ball first, but on the second play the Blues intercepted and took over on the White 24-yard line. Two runs by Eddy and a pass from Hanratty to Eddy produced a touchdown. The Whites went 3 plays and punted, and on the next series the Blues scored in 2 plays, with Eddy going 47 yards for the score. The Whites tried again and got off 1 play, a pass intercepted by Smithberger. On the next play Eddy scored yet again.

In two hours the Blues had 27 first downs, 361 yards rushing, 235 yards passing, and 77 points on the scoreboard. The Whites had zero.

Parseghian might have been pleased. Instead he said, "We're making progress, but we could use more depth."

Despite Hanratty's performance in the scrimmage, Parseghian still didn't name a quarterback. He wanted to give both O'Brien and Hanratty a full shot, but more than that, he didn't want to put any pressure on Hanratty until he absolutely had to. He needn't have worried. Hanratty was pressure proof.

Finally, on Tuesday, September 20, the first day of preparations for Purdue, Parseghian tapped Hanratty on the shoulder and said, "You're it." But he told the press that although Hanratty was starting, he would use O'Brien at quarterback as well. Now all he had to do was keep Hanratty and the other sophomore, Seymour, calm.

Parseghian worked on Hanratty, and Gmitter, a senior, was assigned to play Dad to Seymour. Gmitter took the job seriously. "Now, Jimmy, don't be nervous," he lectured. "I know it's your first starting job. It's national television. It's Purdue. You just have to play your game," and on and on and on.

Seymour listened, then said, "Why should I be nervous?"

Gmitter looked at him and thought, "The kid's wacko."

One reason Seymour and Hanratty seemed to lack even the rudimentary nervous system of an acorn squash was that they had already played against Notre Dame's defense. Anything else, they figured, would have to be a vacation. Also, they had seen Purdue once before. Every year the freshmen went along with the varsity on a road trip just to get a feel for the travel. In 1965 they had gone to Purdue and watched Griese lead the Boilermakers to the 25–21 victory. As they watched Bill Zloch and the Notre Dame offense struggle to move the ball, they kept thinking, "If we were in there, we'd beat these guys silly." After the game, while the varsity was showering and dressing, they and the other freshmen sat on the team bus and talked about how different it would be the following year.

Parseghian had been thinking the same thing. It didn't help his highly strung nervous system to know that he had O'Brien, Hanratty, and Seymour but couldn't play them because the rules didn't allow it. As if to remind himself of what he was missing, he had worked them out in the fall of 1965 against his varsity defense and watched them move the ball down the field in ways his starting offense couldn't.

Parseghian wasn't known for his locker room rhetoric. He never pulled the sort of tricks that Rockne was known for; he would never give a "Win one for the Gipper" speech.

He left the motivating to an anonymous character called "The Phantom." No one on the team knew who The Phantom was. Twenty-five years after they graduated, many of the players still didn't know. All they knew was that every game week officially began on Monday when they went into the locker room and found The Phantom's notes in their lockers and his general comments pinned to a bulletin board that was called the Clobber Board.

On Monday, September 19, Bob Griese's picture was at the top of the Clobber Board. "Best quarterback in the Big Ten," read the caption under the picture. "Recently stated, 'Notre Dame couldn't stop me if I were handcuffed.' "

Griese hadn't said that, but that was beside the point. Tom Pagna, who did The Phantom's work in the dark of night, had a histrionic streak and believed in the benefits of taunting his troops to greater effort. His messages were, by his own admission, so corny that after a few years, when the new generation of cooler, more sophisticated players started arriving, he gave it up, only to learn that the players missed his written pep talks.

Pagna called his mysterious agitator The Phantom after another anonymous character from his college days at Miami of Ohio, where he had played for Parseghian when Ara was just starting his coaching career. It seems that there was a mentally deficient student in his dormitory who would sneak into the communal bathroom in the dead of night and deposit a steaming pile of his own excrement in the middle of the floor. To let everyone know who had done it, he would stick a coat hanger in the mess with a piece of paper attached announcing it as the work of The Phantom. Since The Phantom's initials, T.P., were the same as his own, Pagna took on the persona.

The Phantom's general message before Purdue was: "Purdue will tax us. They have pride. Because of that, we cannot play flat. We can never let up on anybody. . . . We owe Purdue something for last year. To ourselves and the nation that follows us, we owe much more."

After practice, when the team huddled together for one last message before going in to shower, Pagna led chants by the offense and defense against one another. The verses weren't much: "Roses are red/Violets are blue/Ara thinks you're great/but that's not true." But the players bought into it. Pagna even had them competing in making up verses about the opponent that week. The players would give their efforts, and Ara would judge them. The athletes' efforts were marginally better than Pagna's:

> *His name is Griese.*
> *He leads the Boilers.*
> *He throws the football all over the field.*
> *We're going to stop him.*
> *We're going to drop him.*
> *And we're never going to yield.*

The rest of the motivation took care of itself, first in the *South Bend Tribune* and *The Voice*, the student newspaper, and then from the student body.

Early in the week the campus started blooming with signs, and painted bedsheets hung from dormitory windows. For Purdue the signs mostly had to do with plays on Griese's name. "Wild Irish Rose Beats Griese Kid Stuff" played on a popular advertising campaign for Vitalis, a hair tonic that was supposed to be grease-free.

At practice George Kunz was moved to tackle to replace Konieczny, who was injured. Halfway through the week Parseghian worked out his number-one kick coverage unit against a group of prep squadders. The varsity kicked, the preppers took it straight back up the middle and broke it for a touchdown. Parseghian, who ruled over practices from a tower built of scaffolding that was mounted on the back of an old truck, was livid and ordered them to run it again. They did, and the prep squadders came within an eyelash of breaking it again.

Parseghian asked Pagna, who ran the kick return unit, what was going on. Pagna told him he was trying a new blocking scheme, the five-man wedge, that led the return cross-blocking at the point of attack. Ara told him to teach it to the varsity.

As the week went on, practices tapered off and campus excitement increased exponentially, cresting for the first time in the Friday night pep rally. The first pep rally was always one of the best, it being the freshman class's first opportunity to show what they were made of. It started early in the evening when the band, dressed in sweats, marched around the campus beating on their drums and wearing out the victory march. As the band moved on, the dorms emptied. Most of the students went straight to the field house, but usually a thousand would surround the band and escort it around campus, flinging every roll of toilet paper on campus into the trees. To protect the band from the students, a group of upperclassmen organized themselves into an extremely low class security outfit called the Meat Squad. To get into the Meat Squad you had to know somebody already on it. It also helped if you could drink a six-pack of warm Strohs in twenty minutes or less. While the band warmed up inside spooky old Washington Hall at the center of the campus, the Meat Squad warmed up outside with belly-bouncing contests on top of a garbage dumpster.

The parade led into the old field house, where almost the entire student body of six thousand crushed together on the dirt floor in a howling, sweating, chanting, pyramid-building, paint-smeared mob. Parents and alumni in for the game huddled safely out of harm's way in the back of the building. Parents tried to decide whether they should cheer for the team or pray that the kid who climbed to the fourth level of the pyramid and tried to hang from one of the steel tie-rods that held the walls together twenty feet off the floor wasn't their son. Finally, after another dozen choruses of the victory march, the team would file into a balcony at the west end of the building. No matter who spoke, Ara would eventually get to the microphone, and when he stood up and moved forward, the ocean of screaming, sweating students roared like a hurricane and chanted his name: "Ar-a! Ar-a!" Parseghian stood there with his arms raised and took it in, and as he did, he could never help thinking: "This is how Hitler got started."

After the rally the students got on with the party that would carry through Sunday night, and the team marched across campus to Moreau Seminary, where they ate dinner, had an evening meeting, and watched a movie together. Favored viewing material was anything with John Wayne and a lot of dead bodies in it. The coaches figured it got the players into the right frame of mind for the game. After the movie the players grabbed a hunk of fruit and went to bed.

On Saturday morning the entire team went to mass at the Moreau Chapel, then broke for their breakfast of steak and eggs. As Hanratty wolfed down his meal and his teammates stared in disbelief, Ara, who ate before the others, paced outside the room, circling like a starving wolf, his eyes burning beneath a furrowed brow. All week long he had written down his thoughts about the game as they had occurred to him. When the players finished their meal, he stalked into the room and always began the same way: "Let me have your attention, men."

The place went dead quiet, and for the next twenty or thirty minutes Parseghian broke the game down into its constituent parts. He told each unit of the team what to look for. He told them what he thought the rhythm of the game would be. He talked about the incentive the other team had and the incentive his own team had. No opponent was ever easy in his eyes. There was always some horrible loss to avenge, even if it happened twenty years ago. For Purdue there was the revenge factor, not only for the previous year but also for 1950 when Purdue beat the Irish and broke Frank Leahy's undefeated string at thirty-nine games, and for 1954 when Len Dawson led the Boilermakers to a 27–14 victory and broke Notre Dame's thirteen-game undefeated streak. But mostly it was revenge for 1965.

The fact that the game was on national television was worthy of headlines. One story written that week noted that ABC would be using eight cameras to cover the game, an impressive number. Teams were allowed on television only three times every two years. Only one of those appearances could be on national television, and for Notre Dame the Purdue game was it. The Novemher 19 game with Michigan State was scheduled to be a regional broadcast. Under the NCAA's new contract with ABC, each team on a national broadcast collected $112,000. In addition, Purdue would get $140,000 from Notre Dame—fifty percent of the net gate from a sellout crowd of 59,075. Tickets sold for $6 each, and 1966 was the first year in Notre Dame's history that every game was sold out before the season started. Except for the 1973 Air Force game, which was played at home during Thanksgiving break when students weren't on campus, every game since has been a sellout.

In those days the schools still dictated to television. Notre Dame, in addition to not allowing any commercial announcements over the stadium public address system, did not allow more than two TV time-outs per half and no more than two minutes of commercials before the game, two minutes at halftime, and two minutes after the game. In addition, ABC had to run promotional materials for Notre Dame prepared by the school. Commercials for beer, wine, liquor, laxatives, patent medicines, or politicians and their ideas were strictly prohibited. The commercials that were to run had to be submitted to the university for approval no later than Wednesday, along with an outline of when they would be run. The broadcasters could not mention any upcoming professional football broadcasts nor interview anyone affiliated with professional sports. Also, the network had to agree to run two announcements of no more than fifty words each about academic programs at Notre Dame. The school's publicity department would provide the copy. Other than that, ABC's broadcast team of Chris Schenkel, Bill Fleming, and Bud Wilkinson could do what it wanted. Even then the writers complained that the networks were given too much leeway. "The video barons are accustomed to getting what they want, and they are not timid in inflicting their demands," wrote one outraged commentator after sitting through a couple of commercials. "It might help matters if the college chieftains displayed stronger reluctance to surrender their sovereignty, despite the TV pot o' gold."

While the players made their way to the stadium, the Notre Dame campus was in full party mode. With no fraternities, social life revolved around the residence halls. About half of the nineteen halls had formed rock bands, which set up on the porches of the buildings—or in the case of Sorin Hall, the elite dormitory

that had once been home to Knute Rockne, on the porch roof—
and they engaged in a lively competition all morning, trying to
blast each other off campus. Since you couldn't walk 50 yards
without running into another band, the effect was chaotic but, to
the students at least, invigorating. In front of the halls and along
the sidewalks that lined the huge main quad, other groups of
enterprising students fired up barbecue grills made out of fifty-
five-gallon oil drums cut in half. Savvy fans stayed away from the
burgers and stuck with the favorite pregame fodder—hot dogs
boiled in beer.

Meanwhile, the players were pulling on their game uniforms
for the first time. Ara and Pagna had brought in the current Notre
Dame uniforms in 1964. When Parseghian came in, the Irish had
been painting shamrocks on the helmets, and Parseghian
thought they looked awful. Besides, Notre Dame's colors were
not green and gold but blue and gold. So he scrapped everything
green and told Pagna to find uniforms. Pagna settled on gold
pants with a satin finish in the front that gave them a gleaming
shine. Pagna wasn't looking for sparkle; a satin finish would be
harder for a tackler to hang on to. He added navy blue kneesocks
with no striping. Then he found that he could get each player
either one home jersey and one away jersey with sewn-on numbers in a tough, heavy fabric or, for the same price, five blue home
jerseys and five white away jerseys in a light, mesh fabric with
rubberized numbers. He went with the lighter jerseys, figuring
the team would look sharper if it had brand-new jerseys for every
game. And the players would get to keep their old jerseys or give
them to family and friends. The finishing touch was the helmet,
which would be unadorned and gold. The only problem was that
Pagna didn't like any of the shades of gold plastic the helmet
companies offered, so he hit on the idea of spray-painting them
with gold paint to match the dome. The paint contained actual
gold powder, and the look was perfect except that long days of
practice chipped and gouged the paint. So Pagna had the student
managers give each helmet a fresh coat of spray paint the night
before the game.

Game time was 1:15, and by noon people started to wander
down to the stadium at the southeast corner of the campus. An
innovation that year was the creation of a seating section for the
St. Mary's student body, who were given the northwest corner of

the north end zone. Student seating was along the west side of the stadium behind the Notre Dame bench from the end zone to almost midfield, with the seating getting closer to midfield with each year's attendance. Freshmen had the worst field position but were compensated by being close enough to the St. Mary's section to hurl insults, rolls of toilet paper, and, weather permitting, snowballs at the girls from across the Dixie Highway. On the Notre Dame students' scale of social events, it ranked just below a panty raid.

The administration was making noises about inviting some of the St. Mary's girls to try out for the Notre Dame cheerleading squad. The idea was met with near unanimous outrage by the men of Notre Dame. They figured that if they couldn't have women on campus, why pretend they were by having them on the cheering squad? Despite the opposition, within two years Notre Dame had its first female cheerleaders.

By the time the teams had finished their warmups and returned to the locker rooms underneath the north stands, the stadium was nearly full. The day was clear and bright, the temperature perfect at 66 degrees, and the wind a rambunctious fifteen miles per hour out of the northwest. In the locker room the players got their tape adjusted, maybe grabbed an orange, and huddled one last time with their coaches. With little more than a minute to go before they were to take the field, Parseghian stepped before them and gave them their final marching orders. There was a team prayer, and then they filed out of the locker room and through a tunnel under the stands, where they massed on the edge of the field. On a signal from Ara, they followed him in a charge to their bench through the ocean of noise their appearance unleashed.

To protect Hanratty, Parseghian had instructed Jim Lynch, his captain, to choose to kick off and begin the game on defense if he won the coin toss. Figuring Purdue would take the ball if it won, one way or the other Notre Dame would begin the game by daring Purdue to move the ball.

Lynch won the toss and chose to defend the north goal, which meant that Notre Dame would start with Touchdown Jesus at their backs. With the crowd screaming in anticipation, Jim Ryan kicked the ball from his 40 down to the Purdue 5, and after a return of 14 yards, Griese took the field with a first down at his own 19. A senior, Griese was a genuine triple threat who not only led the offense with his passing and running but also punted and kicked field goals and extra points. After dismantling the Irish in 1965, he had remarked on how easy it had been: "We could do anything we wanted to against them. It was mechanical," Griese was quoted in *Sports Illustrated.* The Notre Dame defense had paid twice for that remark. They paid physically the Monday after the game when John Ray, the defensive coordinator, ran them into the ground, and they paid emotionally when the humiliating quote appeared in the magazine.

Any ideas Purdue and Griese may have had that it would be another day of mechanical precision ended on the second play when Griese was flushed from the pocket and clobbered by Alan Page. Griese lost 1 yard and most of his consciousness on the play.

Griese, his head still not entirely clear, punted 35 yards to the Notre Dame 37, and Hanratty and Seymour took the field for the first time for Notre Dame. Parseghian had promised that the Irish would run a more wide-open offense, but he didn't show it on his first series. Technically, coaches weren't allowed to call plays from the sidelines. But Ara had played pro ball for Paul Brown of the Cleveland Browns, the originator of messenger guards and plays called by the coach. Ara didn't shuttle messengers in and out but instead used a signaling system developed by Pagna that was both simple and nearly impossible to detect. Pagna sent the signals by the way he stood and the way he held the game plan, which was written on a four-by-six notecard. Pagna could signal any of a hundred bits of information that way, including formations and cadences.

Parseghian, wanting Hanratty to ease into the game, called all running plays on his first series, and like Purdue, the Irish ran three plays and then let Bleier kick back to the Boilermakers. Taking over on his own 13, Griese, too, stayed on the ground and moved the Boilermakers to two first downs before he had to punt again, this time to Notre Dame's 30, where Schoen gathered it in and brought it back to his own 41. Now Parseghian was ready to unveil Hanratty and Seymour to the home crowd and the national television audience.

Jack Mollenkopf, Purdue's coach, wasn't under any misconceptions about Parseghian's offense. He had scouted the Blue-Gold scrimmage the previous spring and knew that Parseghian's two young quarterbacks could throw the ball. What he wasn't ready for was Seymour's ability to run precise patterns and go up and get the ball.

On the first play of Notre Dame's second drive, Parseghian told Hanratty to go deep to Seymour. Taking the snap at his own 41, Hanratty retreated 7 yards, eluded a blitz by safety Leroy Keyes, and let fly for Seymour.

Parseghian had said the kid could throw. The papers had written that he could throw. The fans had heard about the low, tight spirals with the velocity of bullets that Hanratty routinely launched all over the practice field. Now, with an opportunity to display that awesome arm, Hanratty sent up a knuckleball, a high, wobbling thing that even Bill Zloch would have disowned.

It did, however, travel 40 yards in the air and landed without incident in the arms of Seymour, who was so open it was practically obscene. As the stadium exploded in noise, Seymour turned at the Purdue 25 and ran to the 20. Seeing his path cut off, he spun to the inside only to find three more defenders closing in, so he turned back outside and got 5 more to the 15 before four white shirts dragged him down.

Notre Dame fans had seen this sort of performance two years before with John Huarte tossing to Jack Snow. They had longed for it the previous season, and now it was back. They had hardly settled back in their seats when Hanratty handed to Conjar over the middle on the first down from the Purdue 15. Conjar was stopped for 1, and the roar turned to a murmur. But then Hanratty dropped back again and threw underneath for 6 more yards to the tall number 85 again.

Now it was third and 3 at the Purdue 8, and the crowd was up, anticipating the kill. Parseghian called a pitchout to Bleier. Hanratty took the snap and started moving down the line to the left, sucking defensive end Bob Holmes in toward him. With Holmes committed, Hanratty shoveled the ball to Bleier, who was running parallel to the line of scrimmage at the 17-yard line. But the pitch was high and slightly behind Bleier. He reached for it, but it bounced off his right shoulder, skittered across his back, and hit the ground to his left. Bleier reached for the bouncing ball, but it hit his knee and then his arms. Then Purdue's Bob Corby slammed into him at the 7 and popped the ball free. The ball flew up and straight forward to Keyes, who got his hands on it on the

5, bobbled it to the 6, then latched on and set sail for the goal line, 94 yards away. No one touched him. Keyes's run was the longest fumble return ever against Notre Dame, and it was on national television. Bleier blamed himself for it. Later he would claim he gave Keyes his big break on national television. If he hadn't fumbled, no one would have known who Keyes was.

The coaches were livid. One thing that wasn't on the game plan was giving Griese a lead to work with. But with more than 5:30 left in the first quarter, there was no panic. They'd get it back somehow.

The Notre Dame kick return unit went out with instructions to run the center wedge return they had worked on in practice. As they waited for the referee to signal the start of play, Eddy stood inside the 5-yard line, kicking at the dirt like a stallion. He was definitely thinking about taking it back all the way, but then Eddy thought about taking it all the way every time he touched the ball. The keys to the return were the two deep backs, Bleier and Bob Gladieux, who flanked Eddy, and the three men ahead of them, Conjar, Seymour, and Gmitter. Purdue's Jim Klutcharch helped by providing a perfect kickoff that went nearly straight down the field to the 3-yard line. As Eddy gathered it in, Bleier and Gladieux sprinted ahead of him, shoulder to shoulder and heading toward the onrushing Boilermakers.

By the time the three-man convoy reached the 20, there was no one left standing. The hole at the 20 looked like someone had thrown a grenade into the middle of the Purdue line. They weren't just blocked, every white shirt was on the ground. As Eddy cruised through untouched, Gladieux spotted one guy still standing on his right, so he took him down. Conjar wiped out someone trailing the play who was presumptuous enough to think he had a chance to catch Eddy. And Bleier, who was supposed to find somebody to block, ran down the field with Eddy all the way to the end zone, arriving there just before Eddy did, a fact he still brags about. Neither one of them had been touched in 97 yards and fourteen seconds during Notre Dame's first kick-off return for a touchdown since 1957. Eddy said he had never seen a better executed kick return. No one on the Purdue sideline argued with him.

Eddy let the ball drop in the end zone and started back to the bench, only to be mobbed by his teammates. He was fighting an infected ear that was so painful he couldn't take his helmet off, but now here were all these guys banging on his helmet until the ear was throbbing like a bass guitar, and he didn't have the heart to tell them to cut it out.

Finally, he trotted to the sidelines where Ara greeted him. "Thanks," the coach said to his star halfback. "We needed that one."

Whatever momentum Purdue thought it had built with Keyes's fumble return evaporated. Notre Dame had served notice that it could score from anywhere on the field. It drove that point home after Purdue's next drive stalled just short of midfield.

After the punt Hanratty moved the Irish right back down the field, completing a 41-yard pass to Seymour to put the ball on the Purdue 6. But Jim Ryan missed a chip-shot field goal, and Purdue took over at the 20. Griese retaliated by moving Purdue straight down the field to the Notre Dame 9, but then he, too, missed a chip-shot field goal.

In the sixties college football had few kicking specialists, and kickers still approached the ball from straight-on. Kicking with their toes, field goals—and extra points, for that matter—were by no means automatic, no matter how close in. Far fewer field goals were attempted, and of those that were, a 60 percent success rate was outstanding.

On Notre Dame's next possession, Hanratty brought the stadium to its feet with a 52-yard pass that caught Seymour in full stride on his way to an 84-yard touchdown play. It was the second-longest touchdown pass in Notre Dame history, exceeded only by a 91-yard Huarte-to-Eddy play against Pittsburgh in 1964. But that play had been mostly Eddy's running. Seymour's had been a legitimate bomb, a word that was so recently applied to football that some newspapers still put quotes around it.

By the time the teams broke for halftime, the crowd was delirious. Hanratty had thrown the ball 10 times, had connected 6 times, and had racked up 202 yards. Griese had thrown 12 times, completed 6, but gained only 80 yards. Purdue had outrushed Notre Dame, 91–41, but some of those yards were the result of Griese's being forced to run for his life. Anyway, Notre Dame's defensive strategy had been to take away a team's strength, and the Irish had done that by shutting down Griese's passing and making Purdue run.

Like everything else Parseghian did, halftime was a precise drill. While the bands strutted and trumpeted outside, the players took care of any bumps and bruises, hit the johns, and sucked oranges and Cokes. Meanwhile, the coaches huddled together, going over the first half and discussing the changes they would make in the second. The assistant coaches then went to their units and passed down Parseghian's orders. Just before it was time to go back out, Ara gathered everyone together and gave another brief talk, outlining in a minute or so exactly what their mission was.

Then, as the Notre Dame band was wrapping up its halftime show, hundreds of students poured over the low brick wall that surrounds the cozy stadium and ran out onto the grass to form a double line for the team to run through on its way to the bench. The student "tunnel" had become something of an institution, and the administration put up with it because the players liked it. It was like an orderly riot, with the students clapping the players on the back as they ran out, shouting their names, whooping and hollering. But they kept the aisle between the lines clear, and when the team had passed, they leaped back into the stands without prompting. It simply didn't occur to them to stay out on the field to run around and wave and maybe catch the attention of the television cameras.

The second half was a lot like the first: Hanratty and Seymour, a bit of Conjar, Eddy, and Bleier, and that big defensive front eight making Griese's life miserable.

Midway through the third quarter Notre Dame started on its own 13 and blasted to the Purdue 12 in 10 plays—8 of them runs. But on fourth and a yard, Purdue stopped Conjar for no gain and took over on downs. Notre Dame was dominating, but as the fourth quarter began, its lead was still only seven. But then Hanratty hit Seymour for another touchdown—a 39-yarder— and after Ryan missed the point after, the score was 20–7.

With fourteen minutes to go, Griese finally caught fire. He went the length of the field in seven plays and three minutes. He completed three passes for 52 yards, but the big moment in the drive came on the second play when Tom O'Leary chased Griese out of bounds, then plastered him after the play. He earned a 15-yard personal foul that put Purdue in Notre Dame territory. Perry Williams ran the final yard of the drive, and Griese kicked the extra point to make it 20–14.

Parseghian believed in breaking points. He preached to his team about them. Every team, he told them, had a breaking point, the only exception being themselves. They didn't have one, he told them. To make sure they remembered, he put it on a sign in the locker room. WE HAVE NO BREAKING POINT! screamed at them every day from the locker room wall. Only the other guy had a breaking point. Now was the time to put that theory to a test.

Parseghian believed his rookie quarterback and split end wouldn't break. He didn't think his offensive line would break either. The team needed to gain yards and eat up the clock, and for the next six minutes they did just that, biting off rushing yardage in neat chunks, nothing more than 6 yards, nothing less than 2. Seymour, having stretched the Purdue defense, now ran patterns underneath to pick up critical first downs. The drive ground on for 12 plays to the Purdue 28 before Hanratty got greedy and looked for Seymour one more time in the end zone. Seymour was there, but so was Purdue safety John Charles, who beat him to the ball and brought it out to the 14.

Now it was up to the defense, which Joe Doyle of the *South Bend Tribune* had accused in print the week before the game of being soft and lacking intensity, just the sort of quote John Ray and The Phantom loved to use to rally the troops. The defense proved Doyle wrong. On a third-and-8 play, Page again hammered Griese in the backfield, and this time Griese fumbled and the Irish recovered.

Hanratty and Seymour settled it with a final 7-yard touchdown pass, with Seymour leaping high for the catch as Purdue defender Bob Mangene flailed helplessly at a ball he couldn't come within a foot of reaching. Hanratty and Seymour failed to connect on a try for a two-point conversion, but it didn't matter. Notre Dame led 26–14. Less than three minutes were left, and Purdue had been brought to its breaking point. It was time for Indiana State Police Sgt. Tim McCarthy to break in on the public address system for one of the going-home messages he started delivering in 1960 and has continued ever since: "Remember," McCarthy told the crowd, "those who have one for the road may have a trooper for a chaser." McCarthy had a few more like that, and they never failed to raise a cheer from the crowd, many of whom were in the process of having that one for the road. Sometimes he'd say, "The road may be rocky if you drive while you're stoned." Whatever he said, it was the signal for the final celebration to begin and for the traffic-beaters to head for the exits. Purdue was still on the field, but it was all over but the shouting.

The shouting went on for a good long time. Mollenkopf initially shouted at his pass defense, but then he went home and watched the game films. By Monday he confessed that their task had been impossible, especially since Mollenkopf refused to double-team Seymour, an oversight he would correct the next time they met. But on that day, one-on-one, Seymour was supreme. "We just had no idea Seymour had that much speed," Mollenkopf confessed. "It was just impossible for us to stop him no matter what we tried. It was not a case of trying to adjust. He was just too much for us to handle. I don't think any pro defense could have stopped him either."

When the statisticians were finished adding up Seymour's day against Purdue, the figures came to 13 catches for 276 yards and three touchdowns. In one afternoon he had outdone Nick Eddy's entire 1965 season. The 13 catches and the yards were both Notre Dame single-game records. The yardage was the second highest ever run up by a receiver in NCAA history. Only Chuck Hughes of Texas Western, who gained 349 yards receiving in one game the previous year, surpassed Seymour's total in the history of the college game. Hanratty's 304 total yards passing were only 28 off George Izo's team record. Notre Dame added 152 yards on the ground and outgained Purdue 453–293.

"They did something that had never been accomplished before at Notre Dame and might well never be accomplished again," Parseghian said after the game. "We caught Purdue by surprise, and now the element of surprise is gone. It's too early to call on the basis of one game. Remember, two years ago Huarte and Snow helped us to win nine straight games before we lost the final one to Southern Cal."

That was Ara, first praising, then putting the brakes on before the euphoria got to his rookies. And always, always reminding his team of what had happened before and what they must avoid.

Still, it was a huge victory psychologically. The team had performed beyond anyone's expectations. The defense had gotten stingy when it had to. Notre Dame had felt it was pretty good going into the game, but the team's veterans simply didn't know how the rookies would react to game pressure.

"It was supposed to happen, but when it did, there was a sense of awe," said Gmitter.

"You know they have some talent, but it's unproven," Conjar said. "But watching them perform, even for the other players, it was like, WOW, these guys have got it."

And if Hanratty and Seymour had it, so did Notre Dame.

As Pagna put it, "When we beat Purdue, we knew we beat a good football team."

Hanratty and Seymour, and with them Notre Dame, dominated the sports pages that weekend and into the next week. Seymour was named lineman of the week by both the Associated Press and *Sports Illustrated*, and the Midwest lineman of the week by United Press International. Hanratty was the UPI Midwest back of the week and was honorable mention Associated Press national back of the week. "I never dreamed it would all turn out like this," the rookie said with appropriate wide-eyed wonder when informed of the award. Parseghian was UPI's coach of the week.

The win also swept the Irish from twelfth place in the UPI coaches poll to third behind UCLA and Michigan State, both of which had played and won two games each. In the AP poll, voted by the writers, they went from eighth to fourth, behind Michigan State, UCLA, and Alabama, which was coping quite nicely after the Joe Namath era behind a left-handed quarterback named Kenny "The Snake" Stabler.

Quarterbacks were on the minds of Notre Dame fans as well. Monday after the Purdue game, Parseghian went to Indianapolis to address a meeting of that city's quarterback club. There, he was asked several questions about Coley O'Brien's role on the team.

"We've played only one game," Parseghian said. "I'm sure Coley will get his chance. Fans don't realize that every team must have a backup quarterback. We'd have been in real trouble in 1964 if something had happened to John Huarte. But this year I have every bit of confidence in Coley. He'll play, and he'll play well. Just you wait and see."

Parseghian had no real idea when O'Brien would play in a starting role. Certainly, if Hanratty continued to play as he had against Purdue, it wouldn't be soon. Ara wasn't going to say that to the O'Brien fans, or to anyone for that matter. But he knew that in football, nothing is certain.

4

If you take the challenge out of living, then you're not living.

—Charles "Mad Dog" Thornhill

Notre Dame had taken Purdue and the nation by surprise and moved in one week from eighth to fourth in the AP poll and to third in the UPI poll. But the team on top of both polls was not a surprise to anyone. Michigan State had come back into competition from an undefeated regular season in 1965 with the backbone of one of the mightiest defenses in college football history intact. Bubba Smith, George Webster, and Charlie Thornhill, a trio of primal forces, were not only back, they were seniors at the peak of their collegiate powers. Notre Dame's subway alumni could celebrate all they wanted over one win against Purdue. Michigan State's tractor alumni knew that if the Spartans performed to their abilities, neither the Irish nor anyone else had a chance at number one. They knew it because as great as the Spartans' 1965 season had been, they still had something to prove.

Michigan State had roared through 1965, literally annihilating a tough Big Ten schedule, allowing fewer than 50 yards rushing per game. They had wiped out Notre Dame and Penn State, had beaten UCLA, and had gone to the Rose Bowl. But at the Rose Bowl they had lost to UCLA in their second meeting of that season. The loss cost them number one in the AP poll, which held up its final vote until the top contenders for the National Championship—Michigan State and Alabama—played their bowl games. They captured UPI's top ranking, taken after the end of the regular season, but the loss to UCLA, a team they had already beaten, left a bitter aftertaste to a spectacular season.

Most of the stars of 1965 were back. Webster, Thornhill, and Smith headed the defense, and halfback Clinton Jones, fullback Bob Apisa, and end Gene Washington had returned on offense. These were franchise players, and there was enough behind them to form a team that could claim to be one of the best ever. They knew it, and their goal was to fulfill that claim. To do that they would have to win every game, and going into the season, Notre Dame, the last game on their schedule, was not a major worry. They were far more concerned with Big Ten foes Ohio State and Michigan, but they didn't really see how anyone could beat them.

You could call them arrogant, and they were that, but it was the arrogance of great athletes who know their own ability. Underlying that arrogance was a rare sense of team unity. Like Notre Dame, the Spartans had great coaching and great personnel, but other teams had had as much without reaching the same heights. It was the sense of family, of being in it not as individuals but as a team, that pushed them to another level. That and the sting of the lone defeat of 1965.

Michigan State could not return to the Rose Bowl in 1966. Big Ten rules prohibited a team from going two years in a row. To replace that incentive, Daugherty promised his team that if they won the National Championship, the school would buy each one of them a championship ring with a real diamond in it. Professional champions got such rings, and the prospect of winning them would be another rallying point for the team. "Don't blow the diamond," they'd tell each other when things got tight.

But Michigan State's unique standing in college football that year went beyond diamonds or a family sense of unity. What set the team apart as much as its talent was its makeup. Notre Dame had always laid claim to a national recruiting program, but Duffy Daugherty had made the Irish look positively parochial. He had scoured the country from top to bottom and shore to shore and beyond to assemble his team. When he was done, he had three Hawaiians, including a barefoot kicker, Dick Kenney. He had a black quarterback. He had eight blacks—most of them from the South, which was still practically a foreign country—starting on defense.

Blacks had been playing college football for a long time, but seldom in such numbers and seldom in such key positions. Both of Daugherty's captains, Webster on defense and Jones on offense, were black. A lot of people thought white players couldn't or wouldn't perform under black leadership. The same people thought you couldn't win with a black majority. Surely blacks and whites couldn't get along, couldn't find common ground, even on the field of play. But Michigan State took all of that as added incentive. They'd prove those ideas wrong.

As with Notre Dame, the Michigan State team was born in 1963, a pivotal season in college football. It was the last year in which unlimited substitutions were still banned. And it was the year that both Michigan State and Notre Dame harvested two of the best recruiting crops college football had ever seen. The two occurrences were related.

Football from the beginning had been a sport in which eleven men from each side went out on the field and stayed there, playing offense and defense. Substitutions were strictly limited, so the best teams were the ones that had the best all-around athletes. This was true both in college and in the pros.

In 1950 the National Football League began allowing free substitutions, and two-platoon football began. The NCAA, however, accepted the system only grudgingly and only over a long period of time. First, the NCAA allowed quarterbacks to be replaced when their teams went on defense. Gradually, the substitution rules were liberalized. By 1963 it was possible to substitute entire units, but the changes had to be made piecemeal, a limited number of men at a time. After that season and one year after Chuck Bednarik, the last two-way player in professional football, had retired from the Philadelphia Eagles, college substitution restrictions finally were dropped entirely. The era of specialization had begun in earnest.

When Ara Parseghian went to Notre Dame in 1964, part of his stunning success could be traced directly to his ability to take advantage of the new rules. Parseghian looked at the squad he had inherited and saw men of great ability who were not all playing in their best positions. He put his best all-around athletes on defense and his best skill players—quarterback, receiver, and running backs on offense. Big, fast players went to the defensive line. Big, slower players to the offensive line. His talent was in being able to identify a player's best position. The result was a 9-1 season and instant celebrity status for Parseghian.

Duffy Daugherty didn't catch on quite as quickly. Enamored with offensive football, he didn't give his defense the players it needed to succeed. He also didn't fully use all his players. George Webster, for instance, alternated between offensive and defensive end in 1964, his first varsity season. But because he alternated with Bubba Smith at defensive end, both were seldom in the game at the same time. Meanwhile, Charlie Thornhill, who would become a demon at linebacker, was playing in the offensive backfield, the same position safety Jess Phillips first played when he arrived on campus in 1964.

When Daugherty brought in his 1963 freshman class and introduced them to one another, many of them wondered, "What am I doing here?" Even Bubba was in awe as the coaches introduced the players to one another. It seemed that every person in the room was a high school All American, or All State at the least. Smith, who had played anonymously in a black conference, wasn't all anything. One of his high school coaches had told him that when he got to college there would be other big men to compete with. "You might not make it," the coach said.

"I don't care what you or anybody else says, I'm going to make it," Bubba told him.

But now, in this room surrounded by prime beef, Bubba Smith, the human mountain range, had doubts. Maybe the coach had been right. He turned to George Webster, who was sitting near him, and said, "Goddamn, George, all these guys are All Americans." And George Webster replied, "Screw it."

"Yeah," Bubba said, the bravado swelling in him, "screw it."

They received their equipment and started practicing, and soon Bubba and the rest of them knew they could compete. After letting the freshmen work out for a few days, Daugherty liked to bring the best of them over to the varsity practice and feed them to the first team to see what they had. The first batch he called up included Clinton Jones, Gene Washington, and George Webster. Later he added Bubba. From the start the newcomers beat up on the varsity and got in fights with the upperclassmen. They didn't take anything from anyone. Right then they started to think they were something special.

If they were, it didn't show right away. When they became sophomores in 1964 and eligible to play, they looked good on paper but not on the field as they stumbled through a 4-5 season. Before the season ended stuffed Duffy dummies were being strung up on campus, so eager was the student body to get rid of Daugherty and bring in a new coach who would restore the days of glory that were fast fading from memory. One of the few positive things that happened in that forgettable year was the emergence of Charlie Thornhill as a linebacker.

Duffy found Thornhill, better known as "Bad Dog," "Mad Dog," or just plain "Dog" in Virginia. From Roanoke's Addison High, Thornhill was one of the greatest high school running backs Virginia had ever seen. He led his team to three straight league titles and scored 219 points in his high school career. He was so good that even though he went to an all-black high school, the local white citizenry flocked to his games to watch him perform against other black schools, and he became the first black ever named the outstanding high school back by the Roanoke Touchdown Club. In his final high school game Thornhill remembers going into a thronged stadium. "There were eight thousand whites on one side of the field and eight thousand blacks on the other side."

Thornhill was good enough to attract the attention of Notre Dame, which didn't do much recruiting in the South but did get to Virginia. He visited the campus, a place he had only dreamed about as a kid growing up listening to the Notre Dame games on the radio. He wasn't impressed with the 10 P.M. lights-out rule or the fact that there weren't any women at the school, but he was on the verge of going there anyway when Paul "Bear" Bryant intervened.

Bryant, the coach of Alabama, was as big a name as there was in college football. He couldn't recruit blacks because the University of Alabama was still busy fighting the Civil War, but he could scout them and tell his friends about them. One of his good friends was Duffy Daugherty.

As luck would have it, several years earlier Daugherty had been slavering over a hot young quarterback out of Beaver Falls, Pennsylvania, by the name of Joe Namath. Daugherty recruited him heavily and dearly wanted him to run the Spartan offense, but try as Duffy might—and he tried mightily—he couldn't get Namath's high school transcript past the Michigan State admissions office. Unable to take Namath himself, he told Bryant about him. Alabama's lofty admissions requirements, which had no place for blacks, proved no obstacle for Namath, who helped the Crimson Tide to a National Championship in 1964, his senior season.

When Bryant saw Thornhill, he thought of Daugherty and the favor he owed him. At a Virginia awards banquet, Bryant sought out Thornhill and told him that before he committed to Notre Dame he would do well to listen to Duffy Daugherty at Michigan State. Thornhill visited the campus and liked it. He especially appreciated the fact that Michigan State allowed women to enroll and didn't make its students turn the lights out at ten.

Thornhill arrived in Lansing by bus at around five in the morning. When he got off, he had no idea where to go next, so he called the person he knew best—Vince Carillot, the coach who had recruited him. Carillot told him to stay put and drove down to pick him up. When he got to the bus station, Thornhill was sitting on the curb with his baggage, which consisted of one tiny satchel. Carillot took him back to his own house and got him some breakfast, an act of kindness that today is a violation of NCAA rules. Then he took Thornhill to the dorm.

Besides his little bag Thornhill arrived at Michigan State with an attitude. Number one, "I didn't like white people." This was a problem in East Lansing because most of the students were white. As luck would have it, one of them was assigned to be his roommate in Wonders Hall, the dorm where many of the athletes lived.

Although most of the athletes lived in the same dorm, they were assigned nonathlete roommates. Color had no bearing on the process. Since football players got to school before the regular students, Thornhill was in his room when his white roommate arrived with his parents. Thornhill never had a chance to learn his roommate's name or where he was from because the kid's parents took one look at Thornhill and left with their son to find the housing authorities and get another room that did not come with a black man. That was just fine with Thornhill. The main reason he didn't like white people was that he had never really known any when he was growing up in the segregated South. His knowledge of the race was based on television. "I thought all white people were like Ozzie and Harriet," he said. "I thought they never fought." Quite frankly, a world of Ozzies and Harriets scared Thornhill. Then he finally met some whites and found out that "they fought more than black people did." That made him feel a little better.

Still, Thornhill's way of dealing with the predominantly white society of the university was to retreat into false pride. Nobody messed with him. Nobody.

Attitude or no, Thornhill still had tremendous skills. He stood only 5 feet 10 but weighed 205 pounds and had biceps that made him look as if he were smuggling softballs in his shirt. Fooling around in the dorm, the players used to have pushup contests, and Thornhill retired the title by doing thirty with defensive guard Harold Lucas, who weighed better than 300 pounds, sitting on his back. Thornhill did the pushups on his fingertips. Thornhill came by his strength and physique naturally, from his mother's side of the family, he said. Even when he was a grown man in his forties and his mother was in her seventies, he wouldn't cross her because he still suspected she could clean his clock.

When the team started spring practice in 1964, Thornhill was moved onto the first team as a fullback. Then one day, walking down a hallway, he met Dan Boisture, his offensive backfield coach, coming the other way. Boisture playfully popped him in the chest and said, "How you doin', big boy?"

Thornhill hit Boisture back, a lot harder than the coach had hit him. "Don't you call me no boy!" he exploded, unable to distinguish a harmless comment from an intentional slur.

That did it for Thornhill. The next day he found himself on the second team. A few days later he was on the third team, then the fourth team, and finally off the depth chart altogether. And the further he dropped, the meaner and more sullen he became.

Returning for fall practice, Thornhill was still buried. Finally, the week before the season opener, Daugherty called Thornhill into his office and told him point-blank: "With your attitude you may as well go home because you're never going to play for Michigan State."

"Yes I will," Thornhill told him.

"No you won't," Daugherty replied, and from there the conversation degenerated, with Thornhill saying "Will!" and Daugherty sputtering "Will not!" Thornhill had the last word, though. He had a scholarship, and he wasn't going anywhere. Duffy was stuck with him.

So Daugherty let Thornhill come to practice, but that was it. When the team went to North Carolina for the first game of the 1964 season, Thornhill was left behind. The Spartans lost, 21–15, but worse, from Thornhill's point of view, was the fact that many of his friends and relatives went to North Carolina to see him play, only to discover that he hadn't made the trip. After the game he had to field a lot of calls asking what was wrong. Some had even heard through other players that Thornhill practiced with the Spartans but wasn't on the team.

Two home games followed, and Daugherty underscored his point by not even allowing Thornhill to dress in a Spartan uniform with the rest of the scrubs to stand on the sidelines. Instead, the coach gave him two tickets and told him to sit in the stands.

By the fifth week of the season, when the team beat Northwestern, 24–6, at home with Thornhill watching from the stands again, he was desperate. Thornhill had hit rock bottom, and he said to himself, "Everybody's against me. I need a miracle."

That Sunday, Thornhill opened his Bible, got down on his knees in his dorm room, and prayed for his miracle. He went to bed and slept soundly. When he woke up on Monday morning, he felt different. He felt good for the first time since Carillot had found him sitting on the curb more than a year earlier. He went to class and took his books with him. He found himself actually listening to the lectures and taking notes. That afternoon he went to practice feeling so good that he was singing.

Bubba Smith looked at him with undisguised amazement. Here was a man who hadn't said ten words to anyone in who knew how long suddenly breaking out in song. "Why are you so happy?" he demanded to know. "You ain't even on the team."

"Don't worry about it," Thornhill said. "I feel good."

Monday was a soft day for the varsity. The main activity of the afternoon was the scrimmage between freshmen and the scrubs who hadn't played Saturday. The players had various names for the scrimmage, most of them variations of the Toilet Bowl. But

Thornhill wasn't even fit for that game, and the scrimmage began without him, as it usually did.

He wasn't concerned. He found someone else who wasn't playing and started playing catch on the sideline while the scrubs went at it. "Don't worry," he told himself. "Something's going to happen."

Just then a linebacker went down, and one of the coaches was yelling to the sideline: "We need a linebacker over here!"

An inner voice told Thornhill, "Get in there." He tossed the ball back to his partner and ran onto the field.

"You're not a linebacker!" Carillot hollered when he saw Thornhill coming out. But before he could tell him to get off the field, he had an idea. "This might be good for you," he said. "Get in there." In the huddle Thornhill received some quick instructions on the basics of the position. "If he goes there, you go here. If they come at you, just block them." That kind of stuff.

The scrimmage resumed, and the first play the offense ran, Thornhill made the tackle. He made the tackle on the second, third, fourth, and fifth plays, too, until Daugherty finally pulled off his cap and asked the team, "Can't anybody out here stop that guy?"

"No, you can't," Thornhill said back. "Today, I get *you.*"

Daugherty wasn't one to be shown up. He gathered the offense around him in the huddle and called the next play: "All of you get Thornhill. Knock him over the soccer field. I don't care about the play. Just get him."

One of Thornhill's fellow defenders told him what was coming, but Thornhill had already figured it out. As the team broke the huddle and lined up, he cast a quick glance heavenward and said, "One more time, Lord. One more time."

The snap count was two, and Thornhill lined up in the middle and watched the center's hand on the football. The quarterback barked, *"Hut one."* He barked, *"Hut . . ."* and the tendons on the center's wrist tightened as he anticipated the count. That was all Thornhill needed to see. *"Two"* was just coming out of the quarterback's mouth when Mad Dog went airborne. He leaped over the center and hit the quarterback square in the chest just as he was pulling the ball up. The quarterback's helmet went one way, the ball went another. Duffy, watching from behind the backfield, pulled his cap off again and slammed it to the ground.

"Thornhill!" he barked. "Get over here!" Thornhill trotted over as Duffy called over Hank Bullough, his defensive coordinator, as well. "Hank," he told Bullough. "I'm taking Thornhill to Wisconsin and I'm starting him."

Thornhill was made for defense. He had tremendous speed, and with his low center of gravity he was nearly impossible to knock down. And if he did get knocked down, he was back on his feet and pursuing so quickly, you wondered if he had ever actually hit the ground. He was like the Tazmanian Devil, a whirling human buzz saw, destroying everything in his path. "Dog wasn't subtle" was the way Bubba Smith put it. Even as a running back, he loved hitting people, carrying the ball in one arm and swinging the other like a club at anyone who tried to stop him. "I tried to annihilate folks when I hit them," he admitted. And on defense he could hit to his heart's content. That weekend in Wisconsin he made a pile of tackles. Daugherty never suggested he stay home again.

After the 4-5 1964 season, Duffy and his assistant coaches sat down for a serious talk. The team was talented, they knew that, but they had to make it work. Hank Bullough, his defensive line coach, and Vince Carillot, the defensive backfield coach, argued long and strenuously that they needed some of Duffy's best players on defense if they were going to turn things around. Two players they particularly wanted were Webster and Thornhill. Both players were also wanted by the offense. Finally, the defense prevailed.

The coaches settled their depth chart right there, determined that they would go into spring practice with a set lineup in which everyone knew his place. After the meeting Daugherty called a team meeting. It was two weeks after the season's last game.

Daugherty didn't pussyfoot around. "Mickey," he said, looking at George Webster. "You will be our rover back." He shifted his gaze to Smith: "Bubba, you will be at defensive end." Then, turning to Bob Viney, "You will be at the other end."

So it went through the entire lineup. Every player was given his assignment. There would be no more waffling on positions. And as he spoke, the players felt their confidence growing; they felt they were on the verge of something wonderful.

"Every time he called a name, I was getting more excited," Bubba Smith remembers. "We figured we could be good if he played all of us, and that's what he was doing. I knew we would win."

Bubba was right. In 1965 it all came together in a way that exceeded everyone's expectations except maybe the players themselves. Daugherty thought he had the makings of a great team, and he even refused to take any speaking engagements that fall to put his full energies into the football team. But even he wasn't thinking undefeated—at least not out loud. Before the season began Hank Bullough, the architect of the defense, predicted that no Big Ten team would get through the conference schedule undefeated, including the Spartans. Most observers thought Michigan State would be lucky to get through their first four conference games—Illinois, Michigan, Ohio State, and Purdue—with only one loss. But before they could even think about teams in their conference, they had to face UCLA and Penn State.

The Spartans cleared the first hurdle cleanly. UCLA ran into Spartan Stadium on the afternoon of September 18 and ran out two and a half hours later on the short end of a 13–3 score.

It was a good start but not spectacular. The players felt all along that they were special, but lots of people felt special and never demonstrated that they deserved the feeling. "Life's littered with those," said Bubba, the noted Spartan philosopher. "And most of them are alcoholics." The coaches, raised to never expect the best, crossed their fingers and got down to the business of convincing their team that the following week's game against Penn State in State College, Pennsylvania, would be a true test of their mettle.

Getting to State College was no easy matter. The closest airport to the campus was a long and winding bus ride through the Nittany Mountains. As the starters rode on their bus and thought about the game, someone in the back started humming the school's fight song. Others picked up the tune until the whole bus was humming and then singing the fight song.

The coaches, who were sitting in the front, were amazed, and when they stopped to think about it, so were the players. The "Michigan State Fight Song" isn't exactly the "University of Michigan Fight Song" or the "Notre Dame Victory March." The Spartan fight song, though lively enough, is Muzak by comparison. And then there are the words—no thunder from the skies or conquering heroes, no winning over all, just doggerel rhymes:

On the banks of the Red Cedar
Is a school that's known to all;
Its specialty is winning,
And those Spartans play good ball.
Spartan teams are never beaten,
All through the games they fight;
Fight for the only colors,
Green and White.
Go right thru for MSU,
Watch the points keep growing.
Spartan teams are bound to win,
They're fighting with a vim.
RAH! RAH! RAH!
See their team is weakening,
We're going to win this game.
Fight! Fight! Rah! Team, fight!
Victory for MSU!

So the fact that these large and worldly young men were actually singing these lyrics and singing them again and again was truly a sign that they had been suffused by the spirit, that they had become true believers. This was key. These men, for all their bluster and bravado, were not cynics. They hadn't gone to school in the expectation of putting in their four years and going off to make a million dollars in the pros. Nobody made that kind of money in pro football, at least not when they entered college, and whatever fringe benefits they enjoyed at Michigan State, it wasn't any more than they could have gotten at dozens of other institutions of higher learning. They had gone to Michigan State because they wanted to, and once there, they had accepted it as their home. Being a Spartan meant something to them.

"One thing we never wanted to do when we ran out on the field in Spartan Stadium was embarrass the university," said Smith. "We would do anything rather than lose in front of our classmates." And, it turned out, they would also do anything rather than lose in front of anyone.

One of Penn State's strengths was supposed to be speed. They had one running back, Mike Irwin, who was said to be one of the fastest kids around. Sure enough, Irwin wound up turning the corner and heading upfield with no one in front of him for what looked like a sure touchdown. Carillot and Boisture, the two coaches who sat in the press box and called down the defensive and offensive signals, saw the play develop and groaned in unison.

"He's gone," said Boisture.

Carillot was about to agree when he saw Bubba Smith, who was on the other side of the field, set sail along the long leg of a right triangle to cut off the runner. Carillot looked at Irwin and at Bubba, made one of those calculations that a physics major with a slide rule could do in a couple minutes and that the mind can do in a nanosecond, and said, "No, he's not. Look at Bubba."

Bubba caught Irwin around midfield and didn't even bother to tackle him. He just herded him out of bounds, and had enough breath left as he did it to ask, "Hey, man. Where you goin'?"

Nowhere, as it turned out. Penn State lost 23–0, and now the Spartans knew they were good, maybe as good as they thought. They showered, dressed, and climbed back on the buses for the trip to the airport. On the long way back they sang the fight song.

Friday nights before home games the Spartans stayed in the Kellogg Center, the university's hotel and conference center that is located within easy walking distance of the stadium. After breakfast and team meetings on Saturday morning, the team would walk to the stadium to dress. Their path started along the banks of the Red Cedar River. After the Penn State game, the players began humming the fight song on the way to the stadium. From then on it became their pregame mantra.

Later, when the Spartans met Michigan in Ann Arbor, the Michigan faithful brought signs to the stadium with arrows printed on them. When Michigan State's defense took the field, the fans held up the signs so that Bubba would know which way to run. Michigan fans thought that was pretty funny, and it was, especially when compared to the game. On defense, Bubba, Webster, Thornhill, Harold Lucas, Bob Viney, Jess Phillips, and company held the Wolverines to −51 yards rushing, forcing Michigan to pass 42 times, which yielded yardage—305 passing —but also led to three interceptions and only one score. It was Moo U 24, Michigan 7.

Woody Hayes and Ohio State were next. If there was one thing Hayes believed in, it was running the football. Three yards and a cloud of dust was his watchword. Passes were for sissies and communists. The Spartans stuffed Hayes's vaunted ground attack for −22 yards and forced Hayes to put the ball in the air 29 times. Final score: MSU 32, OSU 7, and lucky to get that much. It was a beating that Woody did not forget.

Only one team stood between the Spartans and a perfect regular season—Notre Dame. In 1964 the Irish behind John Huarte and Jack Snow had rolled over Michigan State 34–7. This time, as the Spartans rode the Grand Trunk to South Bend, they were bent on revenge.

The Spartans arrived Friday, dressed in sweats, and held their light workout at Notre Dame. By sheer coincidence, Notre Dame insisted, the Irish marching band was practicing on a field next to the Spartan walk-through. From the moment they ran out onto the field until the end of practice, Michigan State players swear that the Notre Dame band practiced nothing but the "Notre Dame Victory March." After practice the Spartans changed, left the stadium locker room, and walked outside and into the band. It was still playing the fight song, which by now even Bubba was tired of hearing. Words were exchanged, and news soon got out around campus that the Spartans had slurred the Fighting Irish band.

The next afternoon, after the Spartans had finished their warm-ups and had returned to their locker room, they received word that the Notre Dame students had retaliated against the MSU band in the stadium tunnel. Someone said something about one of the band members being stuffed inside his tuba.

That was enough for the football team. When they came out for the game, Mad Dog Thornhill was foaming at the mouth and his fellow members of the defense were looking for someone to kill. Their game plan called for them to do just that. They would put the whole team on the line of scrimmage and dare Bill Zloch to throw the ball if he could, which they already knew he couldn't. If he wanted to hand off to his vaunted backfield of Nick Eddy, Bill Wolski, and Larry Conjar, let him. They would eat them alive.

Notre Dame collected a grand total of −12 yards rushing, 24 yards passing, three first downs, and 12 total yards. It was the worst offensive performance in the history of the school. And what made it worse was the jeering of Mad Dog and Bubba. Today, players talk to one another constantly on the field. It's called woofing or talking trash. But in 1966 most teams were still taught to do their job and keep quiet. Showing up the opposition was considered poor taste. Mad Dog and Bubba had heard that theory but rejected it. They talked every chance they got, and not just to the players. When they drove somebody out of bounds in front of the Notre Dame bench, they looked for Ara and told him what they thought of him as well.

"There was a lot of spitting, a lot of bad-mouthing," Eddy remembers. "You don't mind getting beat by someone who is a good sport about it, but when somebody rubs it in your face, it stays with you."

And when they beat you up physically, it stays even longer. "They beat the hell out of us," Irish guard Tom Regner said.

"Yeah," Mad Dog agreed. "We beat the dog doo out of them."

Losing 3–0 at the half, the Spartans scored in the third quarter on a run by Clinton Jones and again in the fourth on a pass from Steve Juday to Dwight Lee and won 12–3 to close out a 10-0 regular season and a trip to the Rose Bowl, where UCLA, a team they had already beaten, would be waiting for them.

In 1964, Los Angeles had derailed the Irish, and on January 1, 1966, it would do the same to the Spartans.

Among all his excellent qualities, Duffy Daugherty had one that was not so excellent. He was paranoid.

Many coaches will tell you that a little paranoia is a good thing. You can't trust the writers. You can't trust the opposition. You can't always trust your own players. Otherwise, why would you have curfews?

All of this was true to some extent, but Duffy tended to go overboard. Fearful that the writers would divide his team, he let the players talk to the press after their games but not during the week. That way, questions would be confined mostly to the game and not the personalities. As for the opposition, he had every coach's fear that someone was spying on his practices. But when it came to curfews, he was at his best.

With the Rose Bowl coming up, which meant a week in sunny California, Duffy felt he needed to get his team away from everything a few days before the game. At the beginning of the week he let the team have a good time, but he wanted them to get away from the good life the night before the game. Searching for a place to hole up, somebody told him about a monastery.

Duffy told his coaches about the place. "It will be quiet. Nobody will bother them," Duffy argued, genuinely excited by the idea. His coaches tried to talk him out of it, but he wouldn't listen. A monastery it would be.

Duffy had been born an Orangeman—an Irish Protestant. But he had converted to Catholicism, and a monastery probably seemed cozy and comforting to him. But to southern Baptists, it was as foreign and disturbing as mini-skirts in Iran. The players didn't even have roommates. It was one man to a room, and the room was furnished in true Spartan style: a narrow, rock-hard bed, a crucifix on the wall, and a bible on the nightstand. And while some players found it restful, others got the willies just being there. Another problem was that they had already beaten UCLA, and Daugherty and his assistants had a hard time convincing the team that they were facing a dangerous opponent. Finally, Duffy felt that since the Rose Bowl was the last game for his seniors, he should give as many of them as possible a chance to shine in this showcase game.

One of the seniors Daugherty hoped to reward was defensive back Don Japinga, the team's co-captain. Duffy appointed him to return punts. Japinga was a fine defensive back and one of the fastest men on the team. In previous years he had handled punt returns, but he was replaced that year by defensive backs Jess Phillips, Mitch Pruiett, and Drake Garrett. Sure enough, in the second quarter, Japinga was driven back inside his own 5-yard line by a UCLA punt, and instead of letting it fall and roll into the end zone as punt returners are taught, he tried to field it and ended up fumbling. UCLA recovered and quickly scored one of its two second-quarter touchdowns for a 14–0 halftime lead.

Steve Juday, the senior quarterback and co-captain, had a rough first half, and Daugherty talked to his backup quarterback, sophomore Jimmy Raye, at halftime, telling him that he was thinking of putting Raye in to start the third quarter. When the team came out for the second half, Raye warmed up on the sideline, thinking he would go in on the team's first series. But Daugherty had a change of heart and told Raye he was going to give Juday one more chance. "Steve's a senior, and this is his last game," Duffy said. "You'll be in the same position someday."

So Juday went in for one series and then another and another. The Spartan offense went nowhere as the third quarter turned into the fourth. Finally, with about half the fourth quarter gone,

Daugherty sent Raye in. The sophomore responded immediately, driving the Spartans to a touchdown to make the score 14–6. The score came on an option play, just the sort of play that the quick Raye excelled at. Raye started around the end, the UCLA defense closed in on him, and he pitched the ball to fullback Bob Apisa, who rambled 38 yards for the score. Instead of kicking the extra point, Daugherty went for a 2-point conversion, but it failed.

The defense stopped the Bruins and Raye went to work again, teaming up with Gene Washington for a couple of big gains and getting the ball to the UCLA 1-yard line. Then Duffy put Juday in again, and the senior ran a sneak for the touchdown to pull the Spartans to within 2 points, 14–12.

State needed a 2-point conversion to tie, and Duffy switched quarterbacks again, putting Raye back in to run the same option play with Apisa that had resulted in the first touchdown. Raye and Apisa executed it perfectly, but Bobby Stiles, a UCLA defensive back who was outweighed by some 50 pounds by Apisa, made the tackle of his life and preserved the victory.

It was a bitter defeat. The defense had held UCLA to 212 total yards and recovered 2 fumbles, but the offense, despite outgaining UCLA by 102 yards, turned the ball over 3 times on interceptions and twice on fumbles. Many players still feel that Daugherty shouldn't have stuck so long with Juday, who had set a dozen team passing records that year but was only 6-for-18 passing for 80 yards against the Bruins. Raye, in his short stint, was 2-for-4 for 30 yards.

While the players blamed the coaches for not playing the sophomores and juniors more, the coaches blamed themselves. "We, as coaches, did a poor job," says Carillot. "We didn't get the players ready."

The Spartans didn't come away from the game totally empty. If nothing else, like Notre Dame they now had a special incentive going into 1966. The Irish had that loss to USC in 1964, and the Spartans had the Rose Bowl.

But while Notre Dame went into the 1966 season thinking about November 19 and Michigan State, the Spartans were thinking about the Big Ten and their diamond rings. Notre Dame wasn't a particular worry to them. They were more concerned with getting through the Big Ten season and trying to repeat as conference champions. It was the only goal that Daugherty ever stated, and it was a daunting task. No other team in the Big Ten had repeated as champions since 1955 when Ohio State had done it.

The key for the Spartans in 1966, as it had been in 1965 and as it was for every great team, was the defense. Except for the Rose Bowl, the offense had come up big when it had to in 1965, but the defense had created the opportunities and held the opposition in check. Going into the 1966 season, the Spartans had reason to be concerned about losses to graduation, most of them on the defensive front. Harold Lucas, the middle guard, was the biggest departure, both literally and figuratively. Lucas weighed 300 pounds and was quick. His replacement, Pat Gallinagh, was 5 feet 10, barely 220 pounds, and was not quick. Starting tackles Buddy Owens and Don Bierowicz were replaced by Charles Bailey and Nick Jordan, who went 205 and 215 pounds respectively. Phil Hoag at right defensive end was also new, replacing Bob Viney. Ron Goovert, the middle linebacker who had been sharing time with Thornhill, was also lost to graduation.

Overall, the 1966 defense was slower, smaller, and less free-wheeling than the 1965 edition. "We had to stay at home more," Bubba said. Unlike in 1965, they couldn't be confident that someone would be able to cover for them. It was an impressive unit, but everyone associated with both units felt that the 1965 unit was the best ever at Michigan State and one of the best ever anywhere.

Still, any defense that had George Webster on it was not a pleasant thought for anyone who had to face it. At 6 feet 4 and 218 pounds, Webster was described in many articles as "a giant." Physically, he was big enough for the times, but when he played, he seemed to expand until he occupied the entire field. You could hit him, but it was virtually impossible to block him. He simply ran through you or stepped away from you and got on with the business of putting a world of hurt on the ballcarrier. Those who played against him insist he was the best college linebacker ever —better than Dick Butkus, better than Tommy Nobis, better than all of them.

Yet he wasn't technically a linebacker. He wasn't technically anything in normal defensive terminology. He played a hybrid position created by Duffy Daugherty in 1959. It combined the skills of every man on the defensive field. He was, in Duffy's scheme, a rover back, and he was the one piece Daugherty's defense could not do without.

Daugherty's defense defied easy definition. In its basic alignment it looked like a 6-1 front, with six linemen and a middle linebacker. Webster turned up just about anywhere between them and the three defensive backs. Teams that had to block it treated it as they would a 4-3, that is, a four-man front with three linebackers.

But even then Webster made it different. Sometimes he'd show up on the line of scrimmage playing over a tackle or end from an upright stance. Sometimes he'd line up as a linebacker, either in the middle or outside. Sometimes he'd join the deep backs. It took an extraordinarily talented individual to do all this, someone who combined strength and speed with intelligence and desire. Webster was all of that and more. What Lawrence Taylor did for the outside linebacker's position in the pros in the eighties, Webster did for his position in the sixties. The difference was that Taylor worked primarily from the line forward into the offensive backfield while Webster worked primarily from the line backward into the defensive backfield. In either case, because of the ground he covered and because he showed up in so many different positions, he made the field smaller for the offense.

Daugherty found George Webster in Anderson, South Carolina, just seventeen miles from Clemson. Webster grew up wanting to play basketball. As a kid he nailed a hoop to a pecan tree in his backyard and played every day. As he got older he decided he wanted to take up football, but his mother, fearing he'd get hurt, wouldn't sign the permission form he needed to play. He begged and begged until she finally gave in. He was good from the start, but he almost gave up the game his freshman year in high school when he dropped off the team and just hung around with his friends. His principal, B. M. Wakefield, talked to him after that freshman year and told him he could do big things in sports if only he stuck with it. Wakefield was persuasive, and Webster went out for the team again as a sophomore.

In high school he played defensive tackle, offensive tackle, linebacker, and end, and helped Westside High to two state championships, the second in 1962. After football season he averaged eighteen points his senior year in basketball and won a state basketball championship in the spring of 1963. Then he moved on to track and won the state shotput championship.

Webster would have loved to go to Clemson, and he came to know Frank Howard, the Clemson coach, well. But like other southern schools, Clemson didn't admit blacks. Howard, another of Daugherty's buddies, told Webster to look at Michigan State, and when George went up there, he fell in love with the campus and almost equally in love with Duffy.

Duffy would fall in love with Webster as well. Years later Daugherty still called the kid they called Mickey "the best football player I've ever coached." A consensus All American in 1965, he would repeat that feat in 1966, becoming the first Spartan so honored. He was only the second Spartan player ever to have his uniform number—90—retired.

Although Webster was the unchallenged superstar of the defense, Charles "Bubba" Smith easily outdistanced him in yardage of newspaper columns. That was no knock on Webster, it was just an acknowledgment of the fact that Smith was *sui generis*, one of a kind.

Daugherty found Bubba in Beaumont, Texas. Again, one of his vast network of coaching friends helped him land the big man. In this case the friend was Willie Ray Smith, a legendary Texas high school coach and Bubba's father. If Bubba wasn't the best player Daugherty ever signed, he was certainly the most spectacular. He stood 6 feet 7, weighed 285 pounds, wore size 52 extra-long suits, and could run sprints with the backs. He was so fast that Fran Dittrich, the Michigan State track coach, claimed, "I'd like to have Bubba on the track team, but he's too big to run in one lane."

As Bubba had shown at Penn State and on numerous other occasions, he was capable of prodigious feats on the football field. Fortunately for those who played against him, however, he was as happy-go-lucky as he was big and delighted more in finessing an opponent than in overpowering him.

Like Thornhill, Smith went to Michigan State never having experienced white society. And like Thornhill, he was waiting in his room in Wonders Hall when his new roommate came in freshman year. The roommate, from the lily-white Upper Peninsula of Michigan, walked into the room with his parents. Bubba, who had been relaxing, unfolded himself from the bed and stood to his full height. The roommate and his parents nearly fainted, but they didn't leave. Unlike Thornhill, Bubba didn't have an attitude about anything. He took life as it came and enjoyed new experiences, and having a white roommate came under that classification. In time he and his roommate were good friends. And as Bubba moved on in school, he even joined a Jewish fraternity.

He was a free spirit who tested the limits of authority at every turn. He drove around campus his senior year in a brand-new white Oldsmobile with his name in gold letters on the door. At Michigan, Wolverine fans claimed that it was in order for him to find his car in the parking lot. In addition to the car, he always seemed to have plenty of money, presumably given to him by philanthropical alumni. Whatever he did, the student body loved it, whether it was parking in university president John Hannah's parking place or cruising Grand River Avenue, East Lansing's main drag, on the night before a game. He even received the award given to the school's most popular student.

Despite his popularity, Bubba caused so much trouble that after the 1965 season, Duffy went to George Webster and Clinton Jones, the new co-captains for the coming season, and asked them to straighten Bubba out. "We threw him out of school for a quarter," Webster said. But if Webster and Jones were stern, they weren't crazy. The quarter he was thrown out didn't include the football season.

Although Smith at times moved to middle guard, his primary position was left defensive end, and other teams avoided him as if he were radioactive. That put enormous pressure on the other defensive end, Phil Hoag. Although newspaper stories continually pointed out that his name was pronounced *Hoyg*, to everyone and for evermore he was Hoge.

Hoag had gone to Michigan State from Toledo, where he was an All-State linebacker and fullback at Toledo Central Catholic. He wasn't big by any standards, just 5 feet 11 and 208 pounds. He wasn't particularly fast, either, but he was tough and strong, and he was intense. "The quarterback comes out of the huddle and looks one way at Bubba," Hoag recalled. "Then he looks the other way at little old me. 'This is the way we go, boys,' he shouts."

At left tackle was Charles Bailey, another Ohio product, from Dayton's Dunbar High. At 6 feet even and 204 pounds, he was, like Hoag, undersized for his position. Unlike Hoag, however, he had exceptional speed for an interior lineman. Playing against bigger men never bothered Bailey or any of the Spartans, who were generally outsized everywhere they went. "Size has never really handicapped me," he once told a reporter. "You can't convince me two or three inches more in height makes that much of a difference."

Men like Bailey were typical of the 1966 team. Several years earlier Daugherty had recruited big athletes and had not won with them, so he turned to smaller, quicker athletes in the belief that small and quick would beat big and slow. And because so many of the players were small, they lifted weights as much or more than any other team in an effort to gain bulk. At Notre Dame, where the athletes were both big and fast, virtually no one lifted. At Michigan State, at least half the team did.

At the opposite tackle was Nick Jordan, who at 6 feet and 233 pounds was one of the few linemen other than Bubba who did not have a size problem.

The defensive guards were Pat Gallinagh and Jeff Richardson. Gallinagh, a senior from Detroit, stood only 5 feet 10 but weighed in at 220 pounds. Still, considering that he was replacing the 300-pound Lucas and was slow afoot as well, he had his work cut out for him. With the guard position open in spring practice of 1966, "I told myself it was my last chance and I had to go out there and bust," Gallinagh said. He won a starting job that spring and held it through the year. At the same time he carried a 3.13 average as a history major and earned academic All-American honors; he also won several Michigan State awards for scholar-athletes.

Richardson, the right defensive guard, had the size coaches liked to see in the middle—6 feet 2 and 250 pounds—but until 1966 he seemed to lack the desire. Richardson played only thirty minutes as a sophomore and then moved to the wrestling team where he won the Big Ten heavyweight championship. But as a junior he played fewer than ten minutes with the football team and lost his wrestling championship as well. He didn't impress the coaches in spring practice of 1966 and went into the fall still listed as second team on the depth chart. But by the time the season started, he had become a starter. "He came to play football this year," Bullough said of him. And he played well enough to earn several All-American mentions.

In addition to the starters, George Chatlos, a junior from Youngwood, Pennsylvania, would also play a key role in the defense, going in at left end when Bubba was moved over center in certain defenses and spelling Hoag at right end. Only 6 feet and 215 pounds, Chatlos was nearly as reckless as "Mad Dog" Thornhill. "It's hard to keep someone like him on the bench," coach Cal Stoll told a newspaper, and indeed, by season's end, Chatlos would work his way into the starting lineup at defensive tackle.

Thornhill was the middle linebacker, and no one expected any problems there. With Webster playing rover, all the front line had to do was pick off the blockers, and either he or Thornhill would clean up.

The Spartans were deepest in the defensive backfield, where Jim Summers, Drake Garrett, Sterling Armstrong, Jess Phillips, and Jerry Jones could rotate among the cornerback and safety positions and where Daugherty and Bullough could bring in defenses with multiple defensive backs in passing situations.

They were a hard-hitting group, but the one person you really didn't want to meet in that defensive backfield if you were a receiver was Phillips. His teammates insist that no one was better at laying a lick on a receiver than Phillips. A junior, Phillips was 6 feet, 195 pounds, and one of the fastest men on the team. Like Bubba, Phillips arrived courtesy of Willie Ray Smith at Charlton Pollard High in Beaumont, Texas. East Lansing was also home to Bubba's little brother, Tody, who was on the freshman team, and sophomore reserve defensive backs William Ware and Clinton Harris. Daugherty wasn't the only beneficiary of Willie Ray's program, though. Twenty of the twenty-two seniors in Phillips's high school class also received college football scholarships.

Phillips was quiet and polite and by all accounts a fine person. He didn't drink or have any apparent vices other than a taste for gambling and fine clothes. He would wear tailored suits around campus topped off by a fedora, and he liked to carry a cane. On the field he went in for artistic taping and never took the field without the tape being just so on his wrists and shoes, which he decorated so that it looked as if he were wearing spats, a style popularized by Lenny Moore of the Baltimore Colts.

The defensive corners going into the season were Jim Summers on the left side and Drake Garrett on the right, although Sterling Armstrong would eventually take over from Garrett. Overall, the defensive backfield was where the team was deepest.

If this defense was not as great on paper as the 1965 team, it still looked impressive. It started to show how impressive it would be under game pressure on September 17 when the Spartans opened their 1966 campaign at home against North Carolina State. As with many Spartan openers, the game was played before a decidedly less-than-capacity crowd of 55,418. The crowd didn't reflect a lack of interest but rather the fact that Michigan State's academic year was organized into quarters instead of semesters, and the fall quarter hadn't begun yet.

Before the game Duffy Daugherty adopted the standard line of coaches before their first game of a new year; he told his players that North Carolina State was going to test them as they had never been tested before. His own team, he told the writers, "could be anything from excellent to mediocre." Everything, he said, depended on how his team adjusted to the revamped offensive and defensive lines and to his new quarterback, Jimmy Raye, a North Carolina product and a junior. Daugherty also didn't know how junior fullback Bob Apisa, who had had a spectacular sophomore season, would respond after undergoing off-season knee surgery.

If Daugherty was properly cautious about the prospects of the coming season, others—who had already circled November 19 on their calendars and were planning on unbeaten Notre Dame meeting unbeaten Michigan State—were not. Three days before the game was played, the Spartans were reminded of what their season would come down to. As they were practicing, a small plane flew over their practice field. Behind it trailed a banner that read: GO IRISH BEAT STATE.

"I can see overlooking one opponent," Duffy quipped when asked about the banner, "but eight?"

On a perfect 70-degree afternoon, Duffy soon learned that, like the 1965 squad, this team had the annoying habit of starting slowly and giving up an early lead. In the first quarter the Spartans looked as if they might strike first when Jimmy Raye broke free for 33 yards to the Wolfpack 9-yard line, but a clipping penalty pushed the Spartans back to their own 48 and stopped the drive. North Carolina State fared no better, though, as the new defensive line held the Wolfpack without a first down for the first fifteen minutes.

But in the second quarter the Wolfpack intercepted a Raye pass at their own 26 and then drove down to the Spartan 32 in a series in which they collected three straight first downs. From there Harold Deters kicked a 49-yard field goal, the longest of his college career, to give the Wolfpack the lead, 3–0.

That woke up the Spartan offense. Starting from their own 40 after the kickoff, the Spartans ran into a fourth-and-1 just short of midfield, went for the yardage, and made it. Two plays later Clinton Jones, Daugherty's All-American halfback, took a pitch and rambled 39 yards for the go-ahead touchdown.

That was all the scoring either team would do in the first half, but the Spartans had established control. The Wolfpack had already put together its longest drive of the day with its three-first-downs effort that led to the field goal. And the Spartans had more to show.

They waited a bit to show it. Early in the third quarter, after another drive had stalled, Dick Kenney came in to punt for the Spartans and had the snap from center sail over his head. A less athletic punter may have gotten nailed, but Kenney averted disaster by running the ball down deep in his own territory and across the field to avoid the rush, and getting off a kick while on the run. The kick made it only to the Spartan 39—a 3-yard loss—but it was enough. The defense stuffed the Wolfpack right there, and after a punt, the offense got down to business.

Raye, who would have preferred to be playing for his home state Wolfpack but couldn't because his skin was the wrong color, engineered an 80-yard drive on the next series. He picked up the first 30 yards himself on a fake pass and a run to midfield. Three more plays netted 13 yards, and then Apisa answered questions about his knee by taking a pitchout around left end for the final 37 yards and the touchdown that put the Spartans up 14–3.

Any worries about the defense now disappeared as the unit, finally in synch, pushed the Wolfpack back 9 yards in three plays to their own 7-yard line. Jess Phillips took the short punt that followed at the Wolfpack 36 and returned it to the 22. From there it took six crunching runs to get it into the end zone again, with Raye sneaking the final yard to up the score to 21–3.

The Spartans added another touchdown in the fourth quarter on a 15-play drive that covered 74 yards. Sophomore fullback Frank Waters, whose father, Muddy Waters, had also played fullback for the Spartans and was now a college coach, went the final yard for the score.

North Carolina State got a late touchdown against the second team defense—the kind of touchdown that coaches hate—on a 43-yard pass. But the end result, a 28–10 victory, was enough to keep the Spartans on top of the wire service polls.

The game showed that the Spartan ground attack was going to be potent again in 1966. Jones had gained 129 yards in 19 carries, Apisa 90 yards in 12 carries, and Raye 84 yards in 10 tries, which didn't include the long first-quarter run he lost because of the clipping penalty. Raye's figures were especially reassuring to Spartan fans. The new quarterback had been advertised as a good runner, and he had come through. But while he had completed 6 of 10 passes, they had gained only 33 yards, and the jury remained out on how well he could pass.

As for the defense, it had held North Carolina State to 8 first downs, only 2 of which came on the ground. The Wolfpack had attempted 31 running plays and had netted only 27 yards on them. Passing, the Wolfpack was 11-for-16 for 127 yards, a big chunk of that coming on their fourth-quarter touchdown. Overall, Michigan State outgained the Wolfpack 396 yards to 154.

Michigan State had unveiled a few new wrinkles on both sides of the line during the game. On offense, they had come out in a balanced line with their star end, Gene Washington, lined up tight against a tackle instead of split wide. And on defense, Bubba Smith had moved to nose tackle several times to get pressure up the middle on the passer and to give Hank Bullough a chance to get George Chatlos into the game at end.

"North Carolina State was a tough opponent for an opening game," Duffy said, repeating what every coach says about every overmatched first-game opponent. "We had some glaring first-game mistakes and will have to correct them quickly if we want to be a good team. We had several offsides, and missed assignments on offense and defense—like that touchdown pass they had with only ten seconds to go. If we make that type of mistake in the first game, we can make it again when it could really hurt."

Washington hadn't caught a single pass all day, but Daugherty wasn't concerned about that. The Wolfpack had double-teamed him all day, as other teams would soon be doing to Notre Dame's Jim Seymour. And Al Brenner, a sophomore end on the other side of the line, had caught one pass, which Daugherty liked.

But the big question that no one could answer yet was, What was Raye's ability as a passer? Six completions in ten tries for 33 yards showed nothing. Maybe next week against Penn State the Spartan fans would learn more. As Joe Hart, sports editor of the *Saginaw News,* put it: "If Michigan State is going to defend its Big Ten title and protect its rating as the No. 1 collegiate football team, Raye is going to have to bloom as a passer to keep enemy defenses honest."

Under rookie head coach Joe Paterno, Penn State had opened the season with a 15–7 victory over Maryland. Going to East Lansing on September 24, the Nittany Lions were installed as nineteen-point underdogs to the Spartans.

On the same day that Hanratty and Seymour were lighting up Purdue, the Spartans tore Paterno's team into little pieces. For a change the Spartans didn't give up an early touchdown. In fact, with Bubba Smith coming up as big as his program weight, they didn't give up anything until the game was out of reach.

But the Spartans did have their usual trouble getting untracked. Finally, late in the first quarter, Clinton Jones got the offense rolling when he took a pitchout to the right, found his way barred by tacklers, and reversed his field around the left side for 31 yards to the Penn State 8. From there Jones carried twice more to give the Spartans a 7–0 lead. Penn State, meanwhile, could barely make it back to the line of scrimmage. Three times during the game Paterno's troops were pinned so deep that the coach called third-down quick-kick punts. Penn State punted seven times in all, had one punt blocked, and lost the ball three times on fumbles. But the biggest insult to Penn State pride came when Bubba Smith caught up with quarterback Jack White and hit him so hard he had to leave the game with a bruised hip and kidney.

In the second quarter Michigan State put fourteen more points on the board on two touchdowns, the first on a short run by Apisa set up by long runs by halfback Dwight Lee and Jimmy Raye. The second brought the stadium to its feet when Raye, who had misfired on four straight long-distance heaves to his wide receivers, Washington and Brenner, finally hit Washington with a 36-yard strike for the touchdown.

The Spartans didn't let up in the second half. In the middle of the third quarter Raye hit Washington again with a second touchdown bomb, this one covering 50 yards. Then Jerry Jones came through with a blocked punt to get the ball on the Penn State 12, from where Apisa scored again.

Rip his head off! Rip it off!

—John Ray

One of Bob Gladieux's earliest college football memories is the unforgettable sound of John Ray's cigarette-wracked foghorn of a voice cutting through the noise of a scrimmage. It was 1965 and Gladieux was a freshman running back from Louisville, Ohio, getting his first taste of action as cannon fodder for the Notre Dame varsity defense. Gladieux knew something about that defense, and for a running back, none of it was comforting. As a senior in high school he had gone to the Notre Dame–Iowa game in late November of the previous year. Gladieux remembered two things about the game: It was snowing, and Notre Dame's defense looked like its offense. "They kept pushing Iowa backwards and backwards and backwards."

Now, just a few days after he had arrived in South Bend for his freshman year, he was a "white rock." That was what they called the scrubs who ran against the first team. No one knows where the phrase came from. Maybe it meant the white jerseys they wore. Maybe it was because they got pounded like rocks in a Hollywood prison yard. There were arguments for both. Anyway,

Leading 36–0, Daugherty put in his reserves for a garbage-time fourth quarter, and Charles Wedemeyer, his backup quarterback, directed yet another touchdown drive with sophomore fullback Regis Cavender going the last yard. Joe Hart watched that touchdown and wrote, "Who ever heard of Regis Cavender?"

Had Daugherty and Bullough left the first team defense in for the entire game, Penn State, which collected only 163 yards on the day, probably would have ended up with negative rushing yardage. But the coaches let the reserves play, and Penn State gained most of its yardage and its only touchdown against that unit. The first-team defenders had begged Duffy to let them back in to preserve the shutout, and Daugherty let them throw back one fourth-quarter threat. He finally relented, and Penn State slunk out of town with a 42–8 thrashing pinned to its record.

It was a little harder for Daugherty to find things to complain about after this game. Even he had to admit the defense was "full of fire and enthusiasm. That's the way we like them." He also couldn't complain about the 236 rushing yards and 145 passing yards—143 of them accounted for on four completions to Washington—rolled up by his offense, even if Jones had gained only 49 yards and Raye only 31 on the ground.

Instead, Daugherty sang the same song that Ara Parseghian was singing in South Bend about the lack of depth, especially on the defensive front. "We're in trouble when we use our second-stringers," Daugherty told the writers. Some answered, When you have Bubba Smith, George Webster, Dog Thornhill, and Jess Phillips, who needs reserves?

even for a white rock, Gladieux didn't look like much. He had weighed 170 his senior year in high school, but he had contracted mononucleosis that summer; when he arrived on campus, he was down to 155 and wasn't near full strength.

But there he was in the backfield, running pass plays against the first team defense, which included many of the players who had pushed Iowa around so easily. The coach held up a card diagraming the next play, which called for him to run a pass pattern across the middle of the defense, where the linebackers —Jim Lynch, John Horney, Dave Martin, and Mike McGill— roamed. Gladieux studied the play, took his position when the huddle broke, and took off on the snap, across the line, and then curled into the short zone in the middle of the field and the heart of the defense. That's when he heard it.

"Rip his head off! Rip it off!" some maniac was screaming. "Make him never want to come across the center again!"

Gladieux, who was known as "Harpo" because he had a head of curly blond hair and because he was something of a cutup, wasn't the most industrious student on the planet, but he wasn't dumb. "He's talking about me!" he thought just before the defense did its best to follow orders.

Harpo Gladieux laughs at that story. So does everyone else who has ever heard that voice. But the man behind the voice laughs the loudest. "Yeah," John Ray rasped. "That's me."

If you played for Ray, you loved him and you hated him. "He's a dear, dear man—a great guy," said Jim Lynch, the captain and soul of the 1966 defense. "But he was a tough son of a bitch."

"He was," said Gladieux, searching for the right word, "I don't know . . . ruthless?"

Yeah, that's about right. Ruthless. A regular Vlad the Impaler of the gridiron. A grinning sadist who wasn't happy with a win, wasn't happy with a shutout, was hardly happy over holding a team to no first downs. A mad genius who lived for the game in which he held an opponent to zero points, zero first downs, zero yards passing, and minus yards rushing. A man whose defenses inspired a spontaneous cheer that would rise from the student section when the rout was on and the foe was in miserable retreat: "Blood! Blood! Blood makes the grass grow!"

"If a team personifies the personality of the coach, then Notre Dame's defense did that," said Gladieux. "The reckless abandon, attacking, voracious, ferocious defense—that's the way John Ray's personality was."

Ray went to Notre Dame in 1964 with Parseghian. He was a Notre Dame product, sort of. A native of South Bend, he had started at center on the 1944 Notre Dame team. After that season he enlisted in the Army and didn't return until the spring semester of 1947. Then he transferred to Olivet College in Michigan where he finished his playing career and started his coaching career as a student assistant. From there he went into the high school ranks, working his way up to head coach at Three Rivers High, also in Michigan. He took that team to its first undefeated season ever, but when he talks about it, the thing that stands out in his mind is not that his team scored almost 250 points but that they gave up two touchdowns.

By 1959, Ray had worked his way up to the head coaching job at John Carroll University in Cleveland. In those days there were two divisions in college football: major colleges and small colleges. John Carroll was a small college, but it had some football tradition. Don Shula, the longtime Miami Dolphin coach, had played his college ball there. Ray made it as big as a small college could get.

In five years Ray went 29-6, with all six losses coming in two seasons. In 1962 his aptly nicknamed Wolfpack set six national small college defensive records and accomplished one of his life ambitions by allowing his opponents an average total offense of −1 yard per game.

By the end of his 1963 campaign Ray was a hot property nationally, as was his defense that was wreaking so much havoc. Some people called the defense a split-six, but Ray called it a 4-4 because it featured four down linemen and four linebackers behind them. It was designed to stop the run, and by presenting what essentially was an eight-man front, it did that admirably. Because of that, it was no surprise to Ray when his phone rang one day and Ara Parseghian was at the other end asking him to speak to six thousand coaches about defense at that winter's national coaches' convention. He had first met Parseghian a few years earlier when Ara, who had played for the Cleveland Browns, was coaching at Northwestern and was named major college coach of the year by the Cleveland Touchdown Club. Ray attended as small college coach of the year.

As the convention drew nearer, Parseghian began calling Ray more frequently. "How are you coming along on the presentation?" he'd ask. "This is the big-time now, you know."

"I know, Ara," Ray told him. "I'm ready. Don't worry about it."

In December, Parseghian got the job at Notre Dame, and in January he left to coach in one of the postseason all-star games. When he returned, he called Ray again. "I want to meet you," he said.

By now Ray was getting a bit exasperated. "I'm on top of it," he insisted. "I've done this before."

"I still want to meet you," Ara insisted. Finally, Ray agreed to go to Notre Dame to meet him, if that would make him happy. Meanwhile, he had something else on his mind that loomed larger than the presentation at the convention. Wake Forest had fired its coach after the 1963 season and had contacted Ray about taking over. It was what Ray wanted: the top job at a major university. The deal was all but done. All Ray wanted to do before he made a commitment was visit the campus and meet with the school's president. In his mind it was just a formality.

In the meantime, he had to make Parseghian happy. When he got to South Bend, he sat down with Ara and said, "So what do you want to know about my talk?"

"It's not about the talk, John," Ara replied. "I want you to come to Notre Dame."

Ray tried to protest. He was all but signed at Wake Forest, he said. He didn't know if he could be an assistant coach after running the whole show. He didn't this, he couldn't that.

Parseghian was ready for every protest. "You'll run the defense," he said. "You'll be like an assistant head coach." Then Ara played his trump: "Anyway, you being a Catholic and going to Wake Forest is worse than me being a Presbyterian coming to Notre Dame."

Ray still wasn't sure, so Parseghian picked up the phone, made a couple of calls, tracked down the recently fired Wake Forest coach, and handed the phone to Ray. The coach, who had no reason to be nice to Wake Forest, swore to Ray that it was a can't-win job and the Baptist South was no place for a Yankee Catholic, and so on and so forth until he had talked Ray out of Wake Forest and into Notre Dame.

That spring of 1964, Ray gathered his new defense around him and told them how it was going to work. He explained the idea of a perfect game and told them he didn't want the other team to make a single first down. He particularly didn't want to give up a rushing first down. In the fourth game of that first season, against UCLA, with the Irish leading 24–0, the Bruins, through some combination of luck and execution, finally ran for a first down. Just one. But even after correcting the situation by getting the ball back, Jim Carroll, an All-American linebacker, came off the field with tears in his eyes. "I'm sorry, Coach," he said. "I tried. I really tried."

Ray's defense was so fanatical that even when a game was well in hand and the second team defense had taken over, the first team would get up and reenter the game whenever the opposition threatened to score. They wanted the shutout. Ray loved that kind of spirit, but it drove Parseghian to distraction. It didn't look good, Parseghian said. Intellectually, Ray understood that, but viscerally, he couldn't stand the sight of any number other than zero on the opponent's side of the scoreboard.

Ray spelled out his defensive philosophy in the playbook that each player received at the beginning of the season:

> The major objective of defensive football is to keep your opponent from scoring. Every member of the defensive team should have this fact uppermost in his mind at all times. To repeat, the first and only mission of the defense is to prevent a score. Strong as it may seem, defensive players often lose sight of this vital fact.

He then listed "ten basic musts":

1. Do not allow the *long pass* for an easy TD.
2. Do not allow the *long run* for an easy TD.
3. Do not allow the offense *to score* inside our 5-yard line by running.
4. Do not allow a *kickoff return* for a TD.
5. Cut down on *kickoff returns* so as to allow no more than 5 yards per kick.
6. The defense must intercept *3* out of every *14* passes attempted.
7. The defense must average *20 yards per interception*.
8. During a season we must return *3 interceptions for TD's*.

9. The defense must make our opponents fumble at least *3 times a game*.

10. We must *recover* at least *2 fumbles* of our opponents every game.

These points were not negotiable. They were, Ray insisted, reasonable expectations. Then again, it was a stretch to call Ray a reasonable man in matters of defense.

Since the strength of most teams was running, the first thing to do in the quest for victory was to take away the run. And the first place Ray attacked was the middle of the line, where he bunched two tackles and two linebackers over two offensive guards and one center. The offensive tackles were left uncovered, but two more linebackers covered the tight ends. The ends lined up two and a half feet outside the end man on the line.

With good athletes, the defense was deadly, and Ray had the best. His guards were Pete Duranko, a 240-pound converted fullback, and Kevin Hardy, who was listed at 6 feet 5 and 270 pounds but went closer to 295. Of the pair, Hardy was considered the finesse player, which gives an idea of what Duranko was like. Both were All Americans. The two inside backers were Jim Lynch, the team captain and a dogged defender, and Mike McGill, 6 feet 2, 220. When McGill got hurt, John Horney, 5 feet 11 and 205 and a determined hitter, took over. At 6 feet 1 and 225 pounds, Lynch was big for a linebacker, bigger than most of the ballcarriers he had to tackle. He was an All American and an academic All American. He would later play eleven years for the Kansas City Chiefs.

At right end next to Hardy was Alan Page, who at 6 feet 5 and 240 pounds was quick and strong and terrifying. Another All American, Page later became the first defensive player ever to be named the National Football League's most valuable player. His fifteen years of excellence in the pros eventually earned him a bronze bust in the Pro Football Hall of Fame in his hometown, Canton, Ohio. At left end was Tom Rhoads, 6 feet 2 and 220 pounds, another guy who was too small for the pros but more than big enough in college.

The outside linebackers were John Pergine, 6 feet and 210 pounds, out of Norristown, Pennsylvania, and Dave Martin, who was the same size and hailed from Roeland Park, Kansas.

Ray had pages of instructions about what these men were to

do, but the basic idea was for the eight men to establish a new line of scrimmage at the snap of the ball a yard behind the offensive line. "How you get there is your problem, but you get there" is how Joe Yonto, who coached the defensive line, put it.

The way Duranko did it was fairly basic. "My job was to go in there and kick the hell out of the guard," he explained. "Pinch in on him, knock the hell out of him, and knock him into the center. Keep him off the linebackers. Just hit the hell out of the guard in the face. Move him away, and then do whatever you have to do."

By all accounts Duranko was the toughest man on that defensive front and the strongest man on the team. He was also one of the funniest. He came by his grit and determination honestly, growing up as the fifth of ten children of a working-class family in Johnstown, Pennsylvania, a gritty town where coal meets iron ore and the combination spreads a patina of sooty rust on everything. It's a town of rock-ribbed values, where a church—most of them Catholic—seems to sprout from every other street corner. Any corner not taken by a church is occupied by a shot-and-beer bar where the shots are Seagram's or Carstair's and the beers are Iron City.

As a kid in grammar school, Duranko was given his report card by one of the priests at his church. On one such occasion the priest looked at the boy who was growing so big and strong and, before handing him his grades, asked, "What school are you going to go to?"

"I don't know," Duranko answered, for he hadn't really thought about any school beyond the one he was in. Kids from Johnstown didn't think about college. They thought about the mills and the mines. They dreamed about getting out of high school and going somewhere big and glamorous, someplace like Pittsburgh.

The priest had an answer for him. "You're going to Notre Dame," he said. The priest didn't say this to every kid in the school, but he said it to Duranko because even then he knew the kid was special.

Hardy, the other tackle, was as laid-back as Duranko was intense. The second of four children of a widowed mother, he grew up in Oakland without any of the advantages of middle-class America. If he didn't have money, he did have one thing—incredible athletic talent. That would be his ticket out. The only thing was, he never figured he'd wind up playing football. He was a basketball player and a baseball player for a high school team that almost never lost a game in either sport. It wasn't until his senior year in high school that he even thought of going out for football, and he did that only because he figured that someone as big as he was ought to give that game a go. But he hurt his knee, said the hell with it, and never played a game.

Colleges didn't care that he never played football. Coaches looked at his size and his athletic ability and figured they'd make a believer out of the big kid. Bill Walsh, who was then coaching at Cal, recruited him there. Then, late in the year, his high school principal contacted a Notre Dame alumnus he knew from Tulsa and asked him if he could interest Notre Dame in his prize student-athlete. Hardy never learned the man's name, but suddenly Notre Dame was inviting him out for a recruiting visit and offering him a scholarship.

John Ray liked Hardy—he professes to have liked all his players—but he didn't understand him. Hardy was simply too gentle, too sensitive, too laid-back. It said right there in the playbook on the bottom of the page about defensive tackles: "TACKLES MUST BE DEDICATED, MEAN AND VICIOUS, OUTSTANDING TEAM MEMBERS." Ray had written it in capital letters and even highlighted it in red ink, so it should have been clear enough what he was looking for.

Hardy judged himself by his performance, not his attitude. He didn't see any point in destroying an opponent if he got the job done. And with his size and quickness, he didn't have to be vicious. "There wasn't anybody going to get by me," he said.

But Ray wanted fire. It wasn't just him; a lot of coaches demanded the same thing and used similar methods. Hank Bullough, his counterpart at the University of Michigan, played the same sorts of head games with his defense that Ray did at Notre Dame. And his players had the same sort of love-hate relationship with him.

One of Ray's remedies for timidity in practice was to make a man he thought wasn't hitting hard enough take a 10-yard run at some hapless white rock and knock him into the next area code.

Hardy couldn't accept that. Ripping off the head of someone

who was wearing an enemy jersey and was a stranger was one thing. If the game required it, you did it. But taking a run at a teammate seemed senseless, especially for someone as large and powerful and capable of inflicting damage as he was.

Never having played football, Hardy didn't understand the games the coaches played. He was used to basketball and baseball coaches, who were more relaxed in their techniques. They might make you run laps, but they didn't want you to practice beating on people.

Hardy's partner on the right side of the defensive line was Alan Page, who had weighed nearly 300 pounds in high school, 240 in college, and ended his Hall of Fame pro career around 220. At any weight Page was the sort of physical specimen who made other players think about getting into another sport.

In 1964, Page had been one of three blacks on the team. By 1966, with the graduation of Jim Snowden and guard Dick Arrington, he was the only black on the team and one of about sixty in the entire six-thousand-member student body. But Page had plenty in common with his teammates. Like the other players, Page came from a solid, working-class background and was the product of a Catholic education. He chose Notre Dame over Michigan State and Purdue—the other schools he was seriously interested in—because Notre Dame didn't offer him anything other than a good education.

Parseghian felt lucky to have Page. "The school was lily white," he said. "Other coaches would talk to a black player we were interested in and tell him, 'There aren't any girls there. You'll have no social life. They turn the lights out at ten at night.' Trying to find a black athlete who was academically qualified and was willing to accept Catholicism as it was in those days, at an all-male school, was a problem." It wasn't until 1974, when Parseghian was getting ready to retire, that the social situation changed with the addition of women and a minority recruitment program.

The word on Page going into his senior year was that he, like Hardy, wasn't vicious enough for Ray's tastes, and Page admitted with a chuckle that "I was too nice for him." But he had enormous talent. He could run, he had great quickness, and he had the athletic ability to leap over a blocker and the strength to run through one. His arms seemed extraordinarily long, and he had hands that looked big enough to palm a medicine ball. Ray looked at all of that and went to work. He made such a career out of hammering on Page that Alan took to calling him "the meanest white man I know." He said it with some affection, and Ray took it as a compliment.

Page came to that conclusion in the second game of the 1964 season, against Purdue. It happened on a play in which Hardy blocked a Purdue punt. Page, rushing outside of Hardy, was supposed to keep containment on the punter, which meant that he was supposed to stay outside the punter's shoulders so that he couldn't pull the ball in and take off around the end. But Page had a special knack for being in the right spot to take advantage of a turnover, and when Hardy nailed the punt, Page was in front of the punter to pick up the loose ball and ran it 57 yards into the end zone for a touchdown.

Scoring a touchdown is a big deal for a defensive player. Some never get the chance to hear the cheers that such heroics inspire. And Page, in only his second varsity game, had done it. So when he dropped the ball in the end zone and trotted off the field, he was smiling broadly.

Then he ran into Ray. "You son of a bitch!" Ray screamed at him. "You weren't supposed to be there. You had contain. I'm going to run your ass off Monday."

Ray was right. Page wasn't supposed to be in front of the punter being a hero. He was supposed to be outside the guy's shoulder, playing his position. Things had worked out well enough and Page had turned the game around, and still Ray was screaming at him. That's when he decided that Ray was unequaled in meanness.

The fourth member of the front four was Tom Rhoads from St. Xavier High in Cincinnati. Rhoads wasn't as big, as strong, or as quick as his more famous teammates, and he had such skinny wheels his teammates called him "Bird Legs." "A nice, easygoing kid," said Ray. He would end up at end after being tried at linebacker and coming up a step slow. "He wasn't big enough to be a defensive end," Ray said. "But if you talk about courage, Tom had it. He was like what Mike Ditka calls the A.C.E.—great Attitude, great Character, and great Enthusiasm. You win with aces."

Ray worked with the linemen a lot, but Joe Yonto was the

actual line coach. Ray's guys were the linebackers, the tough guys of the defense who moved into the holes created by the line and cleaned up. In the era of dominant middle linebackers, no one was more important to the Irish defense than Jim Lynch.

Lynch was everything a Notre Dame captain was supposed to be, to both the alumni and the coaches. He was Irish Catholic for starters. For the alumni, that was enough right there. He was smart, an academic All American, in fact, and the winner of an NCAA postgraduate fellowship. He was also as clean-living and upstanding a man as you could find on a college campus, and had lodgings that befitted his stature—one of the corner turret rooms in venerable old Sorin Hall. He was not only a man of good reputation but of good deeds. He was a member of a student-founded social-action group called CILA, the Council for the International Lay Apostolate. The organization operated on the same principles as the Peace Corps but predated it.

Lynch started six straight games as a sophomore, then hurt his knee against Navy and missed the rest of the season. He started at outside linebacker in 1965 and by the spring of 1966 his leadership role was acknowledged by his teammates, who elected him team captain and presented him with the shillelagh that had been handed down from captain to captain for no one knew how long.

"It was the most meaningful honor that I've ever received in sports," Lynch said. "Bigger than the Maxwell trophy, bigger than All American. It was part of the tradition of Notre Dame and the essence of what Notre Dame athletics is all about. You have to have people like me who absolutely buy into the program, who aren't going to win in the wrong way and aren't going to lose because you quit."

Ray used the captaincy to squeeze every last drop of blood out of Lynch he could. To get Page's attention at practice, Ray would grab his face mask and shake him. Horney got clubbed on the helmet. Duranko and Hardy he might move a notch down on the depth chart for a day or two until they were smoldering. He got to John Pergine by challenging his manhood, calling him yellow and making him go stand on the sidelines until he found some guts. He could bring Pergine practically to tears that way, but when Ray let him back in the scrimmage, he'd hit the white rocks so hard they turned into pea gravel. Then Ray would say something like, "That's a little better, John. You have a long way to come, but that's a little better."

He couldn't do any of that to Lynch. His pride wouldn't bear it. Instead, Ray would simply stroll past Lynch and mutter in a voice that only Lynch could hear: "You're the captain? What a disgrace. We ought to have a new election. You're a disgrace to the uniform."

Lynch would listen to that and then go rip someone's head off.

Ray's front eight were thoroughbreds. They were men to whom the challenge of yielding no points and negative yards was not just a coaching ploy, it was the great challenge that great talent can rise to. The real but unspoken message Ray gave them was: "You guys are too good to be satisfied with stopping them for no gain. You want to stop them back there, behind the line of scrimmage."

The three deep men were Jim Smithberger and Tom O'Leary at the corners, and Tom Schoen at safety. All were juniors. All had started their first game against Purdue. But only Smithberger and O'Leary had experience playing defense.

Smithberger was from Welch, West Virginia. He was a defensive halfback with the size—6 feet 1, 190 pounds—of an offensive back. He was described in at least one scouting report as "not outstandingly fast but smart." Like everyone on that defense, he could hit, and in the defensive secondary he had the reputation of hitting the hardest. At the other corner was O'Leary, a former All-State performer at St. Charles Prep in Columbus, Ohio, who had played sixty-six minutes in 1965. At 5 feet 10 and 185 pounds, he was the fastest of the defensive backs and usually drew the job of covering the opposition's best receiver. Smithberger and O'Leary were steady performers, but the spectacular member of the trio was Schoen, a 5 feet 11, 178-pound reformed quarterback out of St. Joseph's High School in the Cleveland suburb of Euclid, Ohio. Schoen's father, Norman, had been a standout college athlete at Baldwin-Wallace College in Ohio and dreamed of his son quarterbacking the Fighting Irish.

As a sophomore, Schoen backed up Bill Zloch, the quarterback who couldn't throw straight. He saw just enough action to win a letter and was 13-for-24 passing with 1 touchdown. But, like Zloch, he was more of a runner than a passer. As a sophomore he ran 35 times for 81 yards.

When Zloch graduated, Schoen had hopes of becoming the starting quarterback. But Parseghian knew that with Hanratty and O'Brien joining the varsity, it wasn't likely. Determined to get Schoen's athletic talents into his lineup, in the spring of 1966, Parseghian decided to move him to safety to replace All-American Nick Rassas, who had led the 1965 secondary with six interceptions and had scored three touchdowns returning punts and another one with an interception.

Ara told Ray to break the news to Schoen. It wasn't well received. "He was madder than hell," Ray says. And as mad as he was, Norm Schoen was even madder.

That night Norm called Ray. "I'm transferring my kid," Norm said.

"That's your prerogative," Ray replied.

"You said he'd play quarterback," Norm complained.

"I never said that," Ray shot back. "I said we'd give him every opportunity to win the job, and we did. We never guarantee anyone any position."

Then Ray got started with his sales pitch. "I don't know whether you want Tom sitting on the bench as a third-string quarterback or being the number-one defensive back and probably being an All American. It's your choice."

"You're just saying that," Norm said, wary of coaches and their promises.

"I'm not just saying it," Ray insisted. "Look, if you want to transfer Tom, transfer him. But you're doing him an injustice. He'll love playing safety. He'll be great at it."

Norm didn't buy it. He and Ray jawed at each other over the telephone for a long time, two proud and unyielding men fighting over the future of a kid they both had high hopes for. Ray finally tired of it and told Norm Schoen to come to South Bend and take his kid home if that's what he wanted. After talking it over with his son, he decided to go along with the program. The decision turned out to be critical to Notre Dame, which gained a safety who was a deadly punt returner and a ball hawk in the secondary. He picked off 7 passes that year, the second highest total in school history, and ran them back for 118 yards and 2 touchdowns. He added another touchdown on a punt return. And true to Ray's promise, he, too, became an All American.

From a fan's perspective, the defense came through with honors against Purdue, but from Ray's vantage point, much work remained. They had won and they had held Griese in check, but they had surrendered fourteen points, seven of them the result of a sustained fourth-quarter touchdown drive. John Ray's men were supposed to be made of sterner stuff. One touchdown was unacceptable, and the Monday after the game, Ray made them pay for their generosity. After the workouts he put them through, they'd think twice about letting their next opponent, Northwestern, cross the Notre Dame goal line.

6

*Duffy made a statement to the sports world when he
brought in all those blacks.*

—George Webster

Before the 1960s, men like George Webster, Bubba Smith, Charlie Thornhill, and Jimmy Raye probably wouldn't have played at Michigan State or at any other major university. Neither would have many of their teammates. It didn't have anything to do with skill. Bubba and his teammates had as much of that as almost any team that ever played the game. It had to do instead with the color of their skin. They were black. And they were from the South.

Perhaps Duffy Daugherty's greatest gift as a coach was that he was color-blind when it came to winning. Blacks had played college football for a long time (Jackie Robinson was a star football player at UCLA long before he broke baseball's color barrier, and Paul Robeson played for Rutgers during World War I), but predominantly white universities still did not recruit and play blacks in large numbers. And for the most part, coaches from around the country did not recruit in the South.

Southern universities were still as white as a loaf of Wonder Bread and would remain so into the late sixties; a black athlete would not take the field for Alabama until the early seventies. Southern schools, the Supreme Court and Little Rock notwithstanding, were segregated. In many states black high schools weren't even allowed to play white high schools, which only added to the anonymity under which players like Bubba Smith labored. If they wanted to go to college, their best hope was to play for black colleges, such as Grambling, Howard, or Southern. But many potentially great athletes didn't go to college at all. They had been taught that college was not for them, that their lot in life was to finish high school and get on with a life of working with their hands.

Daugherty had recruited blacks before, as had other Big Ten coaches. He didn't discover that blacks could be good students as well as good athletes. He wasn't even the first to realize that a black could play quarterback in a big-time program. Murray Warmath, the head coach at Minnesota, had gone to the Rose Bowl in 1961 and 1962 (when the Big Ten allowed a team to go to the bowl two straight years) behind quarterback Sandy Stephens. A product of the same western Pennsylvania mining country that produced Terry Hanratty, Joe Namath, Joe Montana, Dan Marino, Jim Kelly, and so many other great quarterbacks, Stephens became the first black quarterback to be named first-team All American after the 1961 season. He was also the first black quarterback to lead a team to a National Championship.

Stephens was the real ground-breaker. He played both offense and defense and led the Big Ten in interceptions, punt returns, and kickoff returns. He was a great running quarterback and ran the option with consistent success. When Stephens arrived at Minnesota as a freshman, he was the only black in the football program, but by the time he graduated, Warmath had added four other black starters: linebacker Bobby Bell, defensive lineman Carl Eller, center Greg Larsen, and running back Bill Muncie.

Ironically, Stephens wanted to go to Michigan State, but Duffy Daugherty was one of only two Big Ten coaches who didn't try to recruit him (Bump Elliott at Michigan was the other). He also almost joined Ara Parseghian's Northwestern squad but was turned off by the size of Northwestern's small stadium.

When Daugherty saw what Stephens, Bell, Eller, and company had done at Minnesota, he went them one better. Instead of a limited number of blacks, he started recruiting totally regardless of color. And he harvested the talent-laden South as no one had before. Gregarious by nature, Daugherty formed close friendships and working relationships with southern coaches on all levels.

In addition to Bubba Smith and his high school teammates, Daugherty snared a tall, swift receiver named Gene Washington who came highly recommended by Willie Ray Smith. Washington, the son of simple, hardworking parents, was from LaPorte, Texas, and played ball at Baytown High School. He was 6 feet 3, close to 220 pounds, and could run like the wind. At Michigan State he became the perennial Big Ten high hurdles champion and also won an NCAA high hurdles title.

From the start Duffy realized that Washington was the swift receiver who could stretch opposing defenses, a man who could score at any time from any place on the field. He was something of a raw talent when he arrived in East Lansing. His one major flaw was that he had a hard time catching the football. But Duffy turned him over to Cal Stoll, his ends coach, and Stoll worked him to exhaustion to improve his concentration to the point where, when the ball was in the air, he thought of nothing but catching it and hanging on. Stoll knew he had succeeded when Washington went several rows deep into the marching band on the sideline during a game to catch—and hang on to—a pass.

Washington's other shortcoming wasn't as glaring. Because of his large size, he had trouble cutting patterns short and breaking them to the sideline. The coaches could live with that, though, as long as he could go deep. He did that so well that by the end of his junior year, he was Michigan State's all-time single season and career pass receiver. In 1965 alone he had caught 40 passes for 683 yards and 4 touchdowns, and was all Big Ten. His two-year totals were 75 catches for 1,180 yards. On top of all that he could block like a lineman, and in Duffy's balanced line he often found himself taking on and defeating defensive ends and tackles.

Washington was also one of the finest men you'd meet anywhere. He was active in East Lansing as a Big Brother and was named president of the school's Letterman Club. As a senior he and Clinton Jones were elected to the university's Excalibur Club, an exclusive honorary fraternity that, until they came along, had never gotten around to admitting black students.

Clinton Jones, Washington's fellow Excalibur member, hadn't gone to college with Washington's credentials. In fact, Jones had hardly played football at all at Cleveland's Cathedral Latin High School. He was on the team, but he just didn't play much until his senior year. A convert to Catholicism who came from a broken home in an east-side working-class neighborhood, Jones had dreamed of going to either Notre Dame or Villanova—the alma mater of one of his heroes, Frank Budd—where he wanted to run track. Although he played varsity football his senior year, Jones suffered an injury early in the season and played only three and a half games, so his football achievements didn't merit the attention of any big-time programs. But when he set a national prep record in the hurdles at the Ohio high school championships in the spring of his senior year, Ohio State coach Woody Hayes took notice.

Hayes, who considered it a personal affront whenever any star Ohio high schooler left the state to play football, regularly went to the state track meet on the off chance of finding someone who might be converted to football. When he saw Jones, who was 6 feet and weighed nearly 200 pounds, he was in love.

It was already May of Jones's senior year, and he had hardly been recruited as a football player. The one offer he had received that spring came from Bob Devaney, the coach at Nebraska. Jones, who struggled with a learning disability, already knew that his S.A.T. scores weren't good enough to get him into Notre Dame or Villanova and had signed a conference letter of intent to go to Nebraska. But after Hayes saw Jones at the track meet, he declared the letter Jones had signed void, and told him he would be going to Ohio State to play football.

Jones was a shy young man, raised by his hardworking mother to be respectful and polite, so he listened to Hayes and said nothing. He didn't have the heart to come right out and tell Woody that his most fervent desire in life was to travel around the world, and the first step toward that end was to get the heck out of Ohio. Luckily, news of his track prowess spread quickly, and Hank Bullough soon invited him to visit Michigan State to talk to Duffy. He had graduated from high school by then, and at a time when most athletes were preparing for fall practice, he still didn't have a school to go to. One of the last things holding Jones back was that he wanted to go to a Catholic university. He even thought about going to the University of Detroit, which was Catholic, where athletic officials told him that the university would start a track team in his honor. Jones thought about all the offers and finally chose Michigan State. Although he was a great track star, he wanted to play football.

"I wanted to play football because football had eluded me," said Jones, who had grown up watching Jim Brown do wonderful things for the Cleveland Browns. "I had to prove something."

He had gone out for football as a freshman at Cathedral Latin but then gave up the sport as a sophomore and ran track. He returned as a junior and scored one touchdown as a reserve. In his abbreviated senior season, he scored two more touchdowns, hardly the stuff of legend.

Jones himself doesn't know why he became obsessed with making it as a football player, but he was. He went at his job with a religious, almost mystical, fervor. "I determined I would make it in football or die trying," he said. "It came to be a very spiritual thing, a challenge for my life that I became obsessed with. I think a high school coach called me a coward one time, and that might have been the reason."

His freshman coach at Michigan State was Wayne Fontes. "He gave me that spiritual aspect I needed. He had compassion for a sensitive kid like I was. When I have that sort of connection to a person, I don't want to disappoint him. I would do anything for him."

Football was never easy, never natural for Clinton Jones. He continually fought his own low self-image and the doubts that gnawed at him. And so he began to see the game as a test of faith. As his religion tested his spiritual faith, football tested his physical faith and let him come face-to-face with his limitations. In high school he would stand on the sideline during games reciting the rosary to tap into that strength. Sometimes he did the same thing in college. And when he could break through his own self-doubt and the war he fought within himself, he did marvelous things. "Once I got real angry," he said, "all the doubt would leave, and there was total commitment that I would die to make it."

He made it. Big. As a junior on the 1965 squad he had rushed 165 times for 787 yards and a 4.8-yards-per-carry average. His longest run, an 80-yarder against Ohio State, was the longest in the Big Ten that season, and his 11 touchdowns—4, a Big Ten record, against Iowa—and 68 points led the Big Ten. He also caught 26 passes for 308 yards and was elected co-captain with George Webster of the 1966 squad.

In addition to all that, he found time to convert Gene Washington to Catholicism and stood up for his teammate as his godfather when Washington was baptized at the university's Newman Center.

Unlike Ara Parseghian, Duffy Daugherty couldn't sit in his office and wait for recruits to come to him. Instead, he divided the country into recruiting territories for his assistants. He also took a territory for himself. "As things worked out," he liked to say, "I ended up with California and Hawaii." So while his assistants spent the winter scouring New England and the Midwest along with the South, Duffy, who never took a recruiting trip without his golf clubs, was sweating it out in the American paradise.

Few people seriously recruited Hawaii in those days, particularly coaches from the Big Ten. After all, why would a kid from Honolulu want to spend four years fighting frostbite? Daugherty gave them reasons, most of them having to do with winning football games in the big time. In 1963, Duffy went to the islands and came away with Dick Kenney, one of the new breed of kicking specialists. Growing up in Hawaii, Kenney had learned to kick barefoot. In the snow and cold of the Midwest, he continued to kick that way.

Bob Apisa, a baby bull of a fullback, went to Michigan State in 1964. Born in American Samoa, Apisa moved to Honolulu when he was young. There, he grew up big and thick and remarkably fast, and as a sophomore in 1965 he teamed with Clinton Jones for a powerful running attack. He was third in the Big Ten in rushing that year, with 666 yards in 122 carries for a 5.5-yard average and 9 touchdowns. The performance brought him an All-American mention and raised hopes for a long and brilliant career. At the end of his sophomore year, however, he went down with torn knee cartilage, and off-season surgery revealed a torn ligament in the same knee that he had suffered in high school. The doctors repaired both injuries, and all Duffy could do was hope over the summer that he would come back in 1966 at something near his 1965 form.

The third Spartan running back was Dwight Lee, whose first

name, as far as the sportswriters were concerned, was "Unheralded," as in "The unheralded Dwight Lee did thus and so Saturday against Whozits State." But that's the way it was working in the same backfield as Apisa and Jones, who got most of the carries and the ink that went with them while Lee blocked for them.

Lee, one of ten children whose father made neon signs, had been an All-State halfback for New Haven (Michigan) High School, where he had scored 20 touchdowns his senior year. At 6 feet 2, 195 pounds, he had been a great all-around scholastic athlete, collecting sixteen varsity letters in four high school years in football, baseball, basketball, and track. Unlike Jones, who liked to make tacklers miss, Lee was a straight-ahead runner, and when he joined the Spartan-varsity as a sophomore in 1965, the coaches decided his talents could best be used as a blocking back for Jones and Apisa.

He would rather have carried the ball, but he took to his role with such gusto that Dan Boisture, the backfield coach, nicknamed him the "Human Machete" for the way he cut down would-be tacklers. On the occasions when he was called on to carry the ball, he performed admirably. But when the season started he was in his old blocking back role again, collecting newspaper clippings about how unheralded he was.

Pete Waldmeir of the *Detroit News* wrote, "Lee's time . . . has been taken up mostly with falling on the barbed wire and otherwise gentling the path for MSU All-American halfback Clinton Jones."

Another *Detroit News* reporter, Larry Middlemas, wrote, "Hearing about Michigan State football games, you'd think the Spartans played with a three-man backfield. The unknown fourth man is Dwight Lee. He blocks."

Lee didn't know it at the time, but he was enjoying the best years of his life. He was a member of a fraternity and roomed with his quarterback, Jimmy Raye. Thinking that football was going to be his life forever, he skated through school taking anything to stay eligible and nothing that would get him a degree. It took many painful years after college and after the dream of playing pro ball ended in the World Football League—some of those years spent in jail—for him to realize his mistake.

But that was still far away in 1966. Then, he was well liked, he was on top of the world, he was playing football for Michigan State.

Lee's fraternity roommate, Jimmy Raye, was the only real change in the Spartan backfield for the 1966 season. Raye, a junior, was a skinny kid from Fayetteville, North Carolina, who hadn't even weighed 150 pounds as a freshman. He had shown up that year in baggy jeans and a baseball cap, and introduced himself to his freshman roommate, Mitch Pruiett, who had come to State as a running back. Pruiett took one look at him and thought, "This is a quarterback?" He was to discover that this, indeed, was not only a quarterback but a prototype of the modern college option quarterback, a wiry, quick kid who was a superior runner and an adequate passer. What made him remarkable back then but wouldn't raise an eyebrow today was that he was black. Despite the accomplishments of Sandy Stephens, everyone knew you didn't win with a black quarterback. In the pros there was a joke that wasn't really funny that went like this: With nine blacks on offense you can win the division. With ten blacks you can win the conference. With eleven blacks you can't beat Pittsburgh (a perennial loser in the sixties). No one had to explain that the eleventh black would be the quarterback. Fortunately for the Spartans, Daugherty didn't believe any of that and let Raye run his team. In fact, one of the reasons Raye went to Michigan State was that Daugherty didn't tell him, as other black quarterbacks were still being told twenty years later, that he would have to switch to wide receiver or defensive back. All Duffy said was that if he could win the job, it was his. It was the same speech Warmath had given Stephens at Minnesota.

One of five children, Raye had been known as a passer in high school, where he led Smith High to a 21-3-3 record in his three varsity seasons. But at Michigan State he was primarily a runner. As a sophomore he had thrown only 2 passes in his backup role to Steve Juday. He completed one to his team and one to the opposition. However, he had gained 192 yards on only 28 carries —a 6.8-yard average—and had a 45-yard touchdown run against Northwestern to his credit. He was so marked as a running quarterback that even the team's media guide noted that "his throwing was good in the spring, with a surprising number of completions."

Still, he had completed two of four in the Rose Bowl loss and had led the team nearly to victory. If nothing else, that performance had marked Raye as a winner, and that quality put him at the helm for the 1966 season.

Raye and the rest of the backfield would be operating behind an undersized offensive line, the result of downsizing that Daugherty began in 1963. A small man himself, Duffy had initially populated his line with the biggest people he could find. At first it worked, but in recent years his behemoths were getting beaten by smaller and quicker men. So Daugherty went with small and quick himself. The personification of that philosophy was tackle Jerry West, whom Daugherty found just thirty-five miles from East Lansing in Durand, Michigan. West weighed only 200 pounds as a high school star, but he was good enough to attract offers from a number of other Big Ten schools as well as Bob Devaney at Nebraska. West's preference was to join Bump Elliott's Wolverines at the University of Michigan, but he went to State to be with his high school sweetheart, whom he married as a junior.

Starting the season at right guard next to West was David Techlin, another smallish lineman at 5 feet 11 and almost 215 pounds. A junior from Essexville, Michigan, Techlin had been the number-one backup tackle on the 1965 team, but in the spring Duffy toyed with his line and moved him to guard, where he won the starting job.

At center was another junior, Larry Smith, who went to Michigan State from Chicago's St. Rita High School and whose job it was to replace the formidable Boris Dimitroff, who had been lost to graduation. Smith was one of the taller linemen, at 6 feet 1, but at 200 pounds he too was small.

The left side of the offensive line was somewhat beefier than the right. Tony Conti, another junior, was 5 feet 10 and 225 pounds, and was moved in spring practice to the offensive line from defense, where he had worked as an understudy the previous year.

At left tackle Duffy had another junior, Joe Przybycki, but unlike Smith, Conti, and Techlin, Przybycki was a veteran starter from the 1965 team. He was also Duffy's biggest lineman, topping out at 6 feet 1 and 240 pounds.

The last member of the line was sophomore Al Brenner, a 6 feet 2, 192-pound end from Niles, Michigan. Brenner was a con-

verted high school halfback, and Stoll said he was a better receiver out of high school than Gene Washington had been. He
didn't have Washington's near-world-class speed, but he was
more than fast enough, and what impressed Stoll were his exceptional hands. And he could block. Like West, Brenner was mar
ried and, though only eighteen, was also a father, student, and
athlete.

If Daugherty's defense was made up mostly of black players,
the interior offensive line was all white. It probably wasn't intentional, but Notre Dame's Jim Lynch remembers that that pattern
wasn't uncommon even when he got to the pros. The racist views
of the day held that blacks, especially linemen, belonged on defense, where their instinctive skills and high aggression levels
could best be exploited. And because offensive blocking schemes
were often complicated, coaches, whether consciously or not,
tended to put white linemen there just as they tended to put black
backs at halfback instead of quarterback.

Still, Duffy sent his team out on the field with twelve of his
twenty-two starters black. It was one of the first teams to field a
totally integrated lineup. Other coaches, who held the majority
view that you couldn't win with large numbers of blacks, made
jokes about Duffy's team even after it had crushed ten straight
opponents in 1965. One alleged joke that made the rounds went
like this:

"Did you hear about the plane crash in Africa?"

"No. Was anyone hurt?"

"Just Duffy and his coaching staff."

Har. Har. Har.

Then there was the line that showed up in a Chicago newspaper. Duffy would never have trouble recruiting, it held, as long
as he didn't run out of bananas.

Yes, newspapers wrote lines like that in those politically incor-
rect days, and no one got fired over them. It was one reason
Daugherty didn't like his players to read the newspapers.

But those sorts of slurs only made the Spartans closer. "We
heard those comments," Mitch Pruiett said. "And it shows how
much guts it took for Duffy to do what he did. He was very
progressive. A good human being." His teammates shared that
opinion. Most of them, whites and blacks alike, were from similar
backgrounds—blue-collar, working families who hadn't had any-

thing handed to them. When Duffy gave them an opportunity, they didn't look for ulterior motives or for reasons why they should be unhappy. They jumped at it.

"It was a melting pot team," said George Webster. "It went back to the family unit, which was so much different then. We were brought up differently than kids today—not just black guys but white guys, too."

Most of them came from homes of traditional families, a phrase that still held meaning back then. The blacks may not have had as much money as some of the whites, but that didn't mean the whites came from rich backgrounds. What they had in common were old-fashioned values and a common belief in the American Dream, a belief that if they could get their foot in the door and work hard, good things would come to them.

"Segregation existed in the South when we grew up," said Webster. "The fact was instilled in us growing up, so we had more to prove when we went to Michigan State. Just going there was a frightening experience in itself, but we had this chance, and we were going to go for it."

Thornhill, who was frightened of whites, was not typical of the team. Most of the blacks who went to East Lansing were curious about whites and wanted to learn about these people they had grown up next to but not with. When they found that their values and family experiences were similar, they discovered they liked the new order. They became more than friends, hanging out together, living together, studying together. It didn't hurt that they were winning together as well.

The fact that the team was the object of jokes and snide comments simply because it was so thoroughly integrated was just another reason for the players to support one another: No one else was going to support them. They turned the enmity they generated into strength. "It was us against the world," said Webster. They knew they had to hang together or, as Benjamin Franklin once put it, most assuredly they would all hang separately.

"It was amazing that prejudice didn't exist with us, even though it was prevalent everywhere else," Webster said. "Duffy made a statement to the sports world when he brought in all those blacks. It wasn't a fluke. He knew what he was doing."

The Michigan State players may have been happy in East Lan-

sing, but the rest of the nation was starting to simmer and perco-
late and finally boil over in riots and hate. Watts had gone up in
flames in the summer of 1965, and the summer of 1966 saw riots
and racially motivated shootings seemingly all over Michigan.
"The glue that held us together was the football team," said
Clinton Jones.

They used to talk about racial issues. They couldn't help but
talk about them. One of the biggest issues was their social lives.
It had been an unwritten rule, but a rule just the same, that black
players didn't date white women. Not only couldn't they date
white women, they couldn't even be seen walking and talking
with white women. Herb Adderley, who had played for Duffy
from 1958 to 1960 and was co-captain of the 1960 team, had
gotten in trouble for being seen with white women. Usually, the
sanction for a black who dated a white woman was to be demoted
to second string.

Of course, the blacks did date white women, both out of curiosity and out of necessity—there weren't that many black women
on campus—and in their senior year Webster and Jones went to
Duffy and talked to him about the no-dating rule and convinced
him that it should be dropped. Duffy himself didn't seem to care,
but as with the makeup of his team, he had to walk a tightrope
between what he knew to be right and what the alumni thought
was proper. And as long as the team won, the alumni were a lot
easier to deal with.

But Duffy wasn't one to just give lip service to civil rights. He
demanded that his players not divide along racial lines. Once,
when he came into the players' training table and found the black
players and white players sitting apart from each other, he gave
the team a lecture about how they were one team and he didn't
want to see blacks at one table and whites at another. The players
hadn't really noticed that they had segregated themselves, but
they didn't do it again.

Another time, during the 1966 season, Michigan had gone on
the road to play Indiana, and in the Friday walk-through practice,
Bubba Smith gave Pat Gallinagh a hard time. This was nothing
new; Bubba gave everyone a hard time. It was his way of staying
loose and also a way of goading his teammates to higher levels of
performance. This particular time, Gallinagh had taken about all
he could from Bubba, and when they got in the locker room, he

went after the big end. The players thought it was one of the funniest things they had ever seen. Bubba was so big, he just put a hand on Gallinagh's head and held him away while Gallinagh swung wildly and futilely at Bubba. When he had swung himself out, the incident ended.

Later that night at dinner, Duffy, who had heard there had been a fight between two of his starters, walked into the dining room and launched into a lecture about how they couldn't have any racially motivated fights. Although Bubba was black and Gallinagh was white, race hadn't had anything to do with it, but Duffy wanted to make sure. So he made both players get up in front of the team and apologize before anyone was allowed to eat. Gallinagh was so guilt-stricken that he apologized for about twenty minutes while his teammates yelled at him to sit down so they could eat.

The fact that there were so many blacks on the team lent a sense of pride and solidarity to the black players. "We knew it was the first time so many blacks had been on one team," Bubba Smith said. And in an era when black athletes didn't have as many choices, that meant something, for Michigan State wanted them there. It helps explain the extraordinary affection they had for the school.

But while Daugherty was building one of the great teams, he was also sowing the seeds of his and the Big Ten's downfall. As he had taken the lead from Murray Warmath, others, seeing his success, started blanketing the South and stopped worrying about what the alumni would think. Eventually, the southern schools got around to keeping their athletes at home. And when that happened, the great flow of talent into the Big Ten from the South slowed to a trickle.

7

Ratings are a good stimulus for college football and create interest.

—Ara Parseghian

If God had been a football coach, he wouldn't have rested on the seventh day. He would have watched films and worked on his next game plan.

Players, at least, got Saturday night off and most of Sunday, but by Sunday morning, college football coaches were busy planning. By Sunday afternoon, they had the team out for a run, just to get the kinks out, and after that back to the meeting rooms to look at the films of the previous day's action. And there's not a coach worth the title who ever notices much good about what he sees. You can win 100–0 and average 20 yards on every play, but when the film rolls the coach will find the play on which you gained only 16 yards and point out so many flaws that by the time he gets done, you'll swear you lost the game.

Terry Hanratty discovered this quirk of coaches the day after his day of days against Purdue. Along with the rest of the team, he sauntered to the film session, feeling, by his own admission, "pretty damn good." Oh, he had taken a generous amount of ribbing from his teammates, especially after they were finished reading all the wondrous adjectives that the sportswriters had sacrificed in his honor in the Sunday papers. But he expected that. What he didn't expect was the way Tom Pagna, the offensive backfield coach, would dissect his performance.

The projector was barely warm before Hanratty started hearing it. His footwork was wrong. He sidearmed this ball, threw off his back foot on that ball, threw into coverage here, missed a receiver there. The touchdowns to Seymour were okay throws, but the rest of it, well, there might be some hope, but you could never tell. By the time Pagna was done clicking the film back and forth, replaying every perceived flaw, Hanratty was convinced he had just played the worst game in the history of football.

That wasn't true, but when coaches talk to their teams, truth means less than it does to a presidential candidate explaining his views on taxes. To Pagna's credit, he did such a good job that Sunday and on subsequent Sundays that Hanratty was out of college before he realized all the coach was doing was making sure that the rookie didn't have a chance to get so cocky he'd soon be useless. Instead, he came out convinced of how far he had to go and how hard he had to work before he'd be good enough to be called mediocre.

Pagna was only following Parseghian's lead. From the day Ara first addressed a Notre Dame team in the winter of 1963, he had drilled into them that football under Ara Parseghian was serious business, and when he told them something, they had better listen. The meeting had taken place in a lecture room in O'Shaughnessy Hall, the university's liberal arts building. Early in his speech he told the players there would be no smoking or drinking, and that it was a twelve-month rule. Violators, he said, would be tossed off the team and out of school. The upperclassmen had heard it all before from Kuharich and Devore, and they took Ara about as seriously as Goliath took his coach's advice to watch out for the kid's slingshot. They took it in and tried their best not to laugh. Even when Parseghian said, "If you don't believe me, try me," they didn't take it seriously.

Now Ara wasn't about to patrol every gin mill in South Bend, but he did expect his players not to be obvious about flouting the rules. But when Dave Pivec, an end who was considered a lock to be an All American in his senior year, got caught drinking, Parseghian booted him off the team and out of school. From then on he had everyone's attention, and while players still sneaked a few beers or a cigarette or cigar, they were discreet about it.

The players' attention extended to Parseghian's game preparations. If Ara told them they couldn't take an opponent lightly, then, by golly, they didn't. It didn't matter if they were playing the Little Sisters of the Poor and the papers had installed them as an eighty-point favorite. If Ara said those Little Sisters had a cunning aerial game and were lying in wait for the Irish—and remember, boys, back in 1908 they upset our tennis team and we have to get even—the team bought into it.

"He never let up. He always had that intensity," said Joe Doyle, the former *South Bend Tribune* sports editor who covered every one of Parseghian's games. "All good coaches have the fear that everything is going to go wrong. Every pass is going to be intercepted. There'll be a fumble on every play. Every call will go against them."

For Northwestern, there were two messages. One was that despite having beaten Northwestern the year before, the Irish still had to atone for the four straight defeats Notre Dame had absorbed at the Wildcats' hands from 1959 to 1962. It didn't matter that Parseghian himself had been the architect of those defeats and he would, in effect, be getting revenge on himself. The other was that Northwestern may have lost its first two games of the season and Notre Dame was favored by three touchdowns, but the Wildcats had a capable passing game and were dangerous and ready to spring an upset before a home crowd at Dyche Stadium.

On campus that week students were struggling to understand a radical, new philosophy at Notre Dame. The concept, utterly foreign to the school since its very founding, was called personal freedom. Curfews had been abolished for all but freshmen, and instead of a rector ruling each dorm with an iron hand, students were being organized into dormitory sections and were being asked to decide on their own communal rules. A number of halls sprang into action immediately, voting to abolish curfews and establishing their own parietal hours. No one knew what parietal actually meant, but they knew the sense of it was that students could receive women in their rooms at approved times. If you happened to know a woman, it was the best thing to hit campus since Father Brennan's philosophy class, where the requirements for an A were to show up most of the time and not snore too loudly. If you didn't know any women, it was still nice to dream about. The administration, in establishing hall autonomy, hadn't prohibited parietal hours, but as soon as halls started voting to allow them, the administration discovered that it had meant to do that but had neglected to say so in the new rules. Within a week, the dean of students informed the student body that, with the exception of the exceptionally mature and squarish maids who came in every day to make the beds, dust, and sweep up, women in the dorms were still a very large no-no. So much for freedom.

Still, what was left of hall autonomy struck at the very core of campus life. Until then you changed dorms every year, and the rules you lived under were imposed on you. Now students could stay in one dorm for the entire four years. The dorms became communities instead of warehouses. Because Notre Dame was primarily a residential campus and because the school did not allow fraternities, even without visiting hours for women, the changes were far-reaching. And not all students approved, particularly the upperclassmen who had grown used to the old order. *The Scholastic* mocked such sentiments and speculated that "the possible loss of all rules and restrictions threatens the very way of life for the Notre Dame student: with the rules will go the sacred right of all students to complain."

Alumni and Catholic traditionalists didn't approve either. That was apparent that summer when the parents of Notre Dame students received mailings decrying changes at Notre Dame. A Chicago group called Advocates of Our Lady sent out one of the letters, charging that Notre Dame was guilty of promoting "liturgical aberration." The Advocates specifically objected to the radical move toward allowing students at the university freedom of speech. That could only lead to the erosion of Catholicism, the Advocates of Our Lady declared.

The religious reactionaries weren't the only ones wary of change under the Dome. *The Scholastic* reported that Dr. Robert Hassenger, a sociology professor, had surveyed alumni during that summer's class reunions and found that, with the exception of the classes of 1961 and 1916, alumni wanted rules tightened, not loosened. Dan Murray, writing for the student magazine, looked at the other survey results, extrapolated them for current students, and came to these conclusions: "[We] can count on being rich, Republican, and racist. We will find birth control, natural or otherwise, the only answer and therefore will have only one and one-half children. And we will sport a streak of cruelty: We will likely clamor as ND alumni for a tightening of the rules."

The two youngest classes, 1956 and 1961, both opposed open housing by substantial majorities and also felt no moral obligation to actively work to desegregate schools, the magazine reported.

The fact that Murray was writing about these issues reflected the reality that Notre Dame students were at least thinking about them, and not without rising guilt.

The next week's issue of *The Scholastic* was dedicated to civil rights issues. Notre Dame's civil rights commissioner, Tom Figel, introduced the block of articles by explaining why students had been apathetic toward the subject: "It is simply something that doesn't concern him."

Figel hit it squarely on the head. Notre Dame students were from the homogeneous world of Catholic suburbia. They had read about the riots and were reading that fall about shootings in Benton Harbor, which wasn't far away in Michigan. But it hadn't touched them personally. Their biggest priority was the same as it was at most campuses—studying. When they weren't studying, they gathered in the rooms of the lucky few of their peers who had a record player. The state-of-the-art in stereos—as far as anyone knew in the dorms—was a box that looked like a cardboard overnight case. The lid of it swung up and broke into two detachable pieces that contained speakers capable of reproducing any sound, as long as the sound was that of a cat being strangled. The turntables could accommodate stacks of LPs or 45s, and the accepted method of balancing the tone arm was to tape a couple of nickels to the top of it to make sure the needle dug through the vinyl grooves like a John Deere single-bottom plow.

In 1966 twenty-seven different singles hit number one on the charts, more than any other year before or since. That week, The Association had checked in at the top with a treacly ballad called "Cherish," which immediately became "our song" to millions of teenage lovers. Those who weren't in love could console themselves with "You Can't Hurry Love" by the Supremes, and those who had already been bludgeoned to despair by differential calculus or the infamous *Norton Anthology of English Literature* could turn to Napoleon XIV and his unforgettable ditty, "They're Coming to Take Me Away Ha-Haaa!" which was being made famous by a new disc jockey who called himself Dr. Demento. The Beatles, Los Bravos, Simon and Garfunkel, Junior Walker, The Critters, Herb Alpert, the Four Seasons, the Four Tops, and ? (Question Mark) and the Mysterians all had songs on the charts that week, and radio stations were playing a just-released tune called "Last Train to Clarksville" by a brand-new made-for-television outfit called The Monkees.

The Monkees were described as "mop-topped" in the papers, the adjective of choice for anyone affecting a hair style based on those introduced by the Beatles. Their television show, said Jack Gould of the *New York Times*, was "suggestive of the Marx Brothers in adolescence." The first episode of the series, which had aired Monday, September 12, had David Jones, Peter Tork, Mickey Dolenz, and Mike Nesmith saving "the princess of the Duchy of Harmonica from the homicidal intentions of Archduke Otto."

The Monkees were the second hit show to tap into the changing pop culture. In 1965 the campy "Batman" series had checked in with considerable success. The fascination with space and science fiction that had spawned "Star Trek" also gave birth to "Voyage to the Bottom of the Sea" and "The Time Tunnel."

An early manifestation of what would become the women's movement was reflected in "That Girl" starring Marlo Thomas as an independent career girl.

The big hit at the theaters that fall was a science-fiction film called *Fantastic Voyage*, about a submarine that gets shrunk to molecular size and goes for a cruise through a human body. The men of Notre Dame flocked to the film, not for the special effects, however, but to ogle the film's female lead, a hitherto unknown actress named Raquel Welch. She created such a sensation that Robert Neville, an entertainment writer for the crusty *New York Times*, was assigned to dredge up a couple of thousand breathless words to tell the world about her. In the feature, headlined "OK, OK, but Can She Act?" Neville, after conducting assiduous research, reported:

> Her known attributes are mainly physical. She is certainly an uncommonly striking example of feminine excitement. Her height is five feet six inches, she weighs 118 pounds and mea-

sures out at 37–22½–35½. She has long thick brown tresses, a smooth, tanned skin, a mouth which smiles a perfect set of teeth, and big deep brown eyes.

As for her work in *Fantastic Voyage*, Neville resorted to the *Times*'s own movie review, which had called her "the most pneumatic looking thing in a skin-diving suit that has yet appeared."

The great majority of students, after three or four critical viewings of the film, had to agree that Neville had it just about right.

At other colleges, weightier issues prevailed. At Kentucky State College in Frankfort, students were outraged when they were forbidden to sit on any part of the campus that faced the main highway. The previously all-white school was afraid that the local white citizenry might not like seeing students of contrasting skin tones sitting on the grass together. Meanwhile, students at the University of Georgia were pushing for an extension of the Fourth and Fifth Amendment prohibitions against such things as illegal search and seizure and the right to legal representation in campus disciplinary proceedings.

The future had arrived, but it was hard to recognize because it came disguised as feature stories and seemingly isolated events. *Life* magazine, still a weekly, trumpeted a story in which the reader "can watch the room take off and watch your blood beat. And turn yourself inside out. Happily, without going near LSD. This week, *Life* presents a symphony in mind expansion. In dizzying color. Psychedelic art. Or what it's like when you're turned on. You've never seen anything like it. Certainly not in a magazine."

The American death toll in Vietnam hit five thousand in mid-September, and if anyone had said it would reach ten times that number before it was over, few would have believed it.

Violent death wasn't confined to overseas. There had been the riots in the Chicago ghettos that summer and shootings of blacks in Atlanta and a half-dozen other cities that fall. But the most shocking slaughter came at the hands of madmen who suddenly started popping out of America's wood veneer paneling with guns blazing and knives slashing. In mid-July, Richard Speck, a twenty-four-year-old drifter and ex-con, entered the apartment of nine student nurses in Chicago. He didn't leave until after he had strangled or stabbed eight of them. The ninth, Corazon Amurao, escaped by rolling under a bed and hiding. The country hadn't recovered from that outburst of mayhem when, two weeks later, Charles J. Whitman, a student at the University of Texas at Austin and the unwitting host of a brain tumor, climbed the university's clock tower with three rifles, a shotgun, and three pistols and started picking off everyone in sight. He killed twelve and wounded thirty-one before police killed him. Then, in September, Valerie Percy, the twenty-one-year-old daughter of U.S. Senate candidate Charles H. Percy, was stabbed eleven times and beaten over the head with a blunt object in his Kenilworth home.

This was the world, but it seemed far away for most students. It was something to talk about, but it didn't seem real, not among the ivy-covered Neo-Gothic buildings and the towering elm trees. Raised to respect authority, most students, whether they admitted it or not, still believed in the motto, "God, Country, Notre Dame."

For the freshmen, the team's first road game was another rite of passage. For a few dollars, which was all most of them had, they could buy into a "smoker" in the back room of a gin mill, where they could watch the game on television, suck on cheap Dover Rum Crook cigars, and drink beer until they were looking at life from the underside of a Formica-topped table. No one had any doubts the Irish would crush Northwestern like bugs. The only questions were the final score, how many passes Hanratty would complete, and how many of those Seymour would catch.

Through the bottom of a beer bottle the game looked terrific. Notre Dame took the opening kickoff, failed to move, and punted to the Wildcats, who couldn't move either, and punted back. Notre Dame took over on their own 44-yard line, and on the first play Hanratty pitched right to Eddy, who cut sharply behind blocks by Conjar and Bleier, outran the pursuit, and arrived seven or eight seconds later untouched in the Northwestern end zone.

It was a good start, but Alex Agase, the Northwestern coach, wasn't going to be ambushed by Seymour and Hanratty as Purdue had been. Having had a week to look at the films, he figured out soon enough that it would behoove him to take away Seymour's deep routes and not try to cover him with a single defensive back. Of course, Parseghian hadn't just fallen off the turnip truck, either; he figured Agase would do that. So he sent Seymour into the middle of the defense on curl patterns, threw Rocky Bleier into the receiving mix, and went for shorter gains.

With six minutes to go in the first quarter, Notre Dame banged down to the Northwestern 21 and was poised for another score when they unreeled a succession of plays that had Parseghian literally hopping mad on the sideline. First, Eddy came up shy of a first down on a fourth-down plunge. But Northwestern was flagged for jumping the snap count, so they tried it again from the 16. This time Notre Dame was flagged for holding, and the refs marched the Irish back to the 31, where it was still fourth down. No problem. Seymour went deep, Hanratty dropped back to the 40 and threw, and Seymour beat two defenders to the ball in the back of the end zone. But another flag was down. Seymour had left too soon, and the play was brought back again. This time Bleier punted and the offense went off to regroup.

The next time they got the ball, Eddy fumbled it away at the Northwestern 29. Again the defense held and again the offense took over, this time at their own 36. Joining the offense for the first time that year was tackle Rudy Konieczny, a junior from Fairview, Massachusetts. He got burned almost immediately when Hanratty called a pass and Konieczny missed his block on defensive end Bob Tubbs. Tubbs blew in and blindsided Hanratty, who fumbled the ball away at his own 18.

It was gut-check time for Ray's defense, and after surrendering a first down at their own 7, they showed their mettle. Three runs got the ball to the 2, fourth down and goal to go. Eschewing the field goal, Agase sent in a pass play, but Denny Boothe could find no one open and threw it high and incomplete through the end zone.

In the second quarter, with the wind at his back, Hanratty completed passes of 12 yards to Seymour and 13 to Bleier before the team was moved back again on a holding penalty by Paul Seiler. Unruffled, Hanratty gained 29 more on 2 consecutive passes to Seymour to get it to the 14, from where Bleier and Conjar took over, with Conjar bashing the final yard for the score. Jim Ryan missed the kick, and it was 13–0.

Notre Dame left the field with the game in control, but it had hardly been Parseghian's idea of what Notre Dame football should be. Penalties, fumbles, and interceptions were things the other guys did, and he wasn't amused to see it happening to his team.

The third quarter was more of the same—episodes of offensive might sandwiched between costly errors. With 6:16 left in the quarter, the Irish drove 39 yards for another touchdown, the final yards coming on a 12-yard Bleier run. Hanratty ran a quarterback draw for a two-point conversion to run it to 21–0.

The defense by now had asserted total control and soon forced another Northwestern punt. It was Schoen's turn to discover the joys of playing safety. Fielding Cas Banaszek's punt at his own 35, Schoen ran left, showed a flash of leg to two Northwestern defenders, took it back as they skidded past, and turned the play upfield for a 65-yard touchdown dash. His elation was short-lived, though. An Irish blocker had been caught clipping, and Notre Dame had its second touchdown of the afternoon called back on a penalty.

And the sloppiness still wasn't over, not that anyone at the smokers back in South Bend was noticing anymore. Given the ball again early in the fourth quarter, Hanratty threw yet another interception, and Parseghian decided he and the first unit had had enough for the day. Hanratty had completed 14 of 23 passes for 202 yards. Nine of them went to Seymour, who finished with 141 yards but no touchdowns. Seymour had now caught 22 passes in his first two games.

As Northwestern kept practicing their three-and-out routine, Coley O'Brien and the second unit got their first taste of combat. After stalling on his first drive, O'Brien engineered a 45-yard touchdown drive in 7 plays that included a 16-yard pass to Brian Stenger. Frank Criniti, a sophomore halfback from West Virginia, carried the final 2 yards. At 5 feet 8, 173 pounds, Criniti was the smallest man on the team and also the one man no one wanted to be hit by.

After Criniti's score, Joe Azzaro came in to kick the extra point, making it 28–0 with 4:34 remaining.

Schoen, who had tasted the end zone once, only to have it taken away, wasn't done. Bill Melzer, in to replace Boothe at quarterback, was determined to get Northwestern on the board. On his second play he threw a pass that was tipped and picked off by Schoen at the 36. This time the blocks were made cleanly, and Schoen had his first defensive touchdown. Azzaro kicked again to run the score to 35–0 with 3:50 remaining.

Then in the closing minutes, with Notre Dame's second defensive unit on the field, Melzer completed 4 straight passes, the final one for 32 yards to Roger Murphy in the end zone. With only thirty seconds on the clock, the shutout was lost.

"I don't like to be hoggish about it," Ray snarled after the game, "but I don't like to see the reserves make mistakes to allow a score."

Parseghian had to be pleased with the way Hanratty and Seymour had adjusted to new coverages and the fact that the 425 total yards his offense rang up was divided nearly equally between rushing and passing. But he saw more things to give him concern. The 85 yards in penalties assessed against his team was the highest total in his twenty-two-game Notre Dame career. Five turnovers—two interceptions and three fumbles—were galling, too. He knew that mistakes were a part of football, but this was going too far.

Going into the game Ara had also been concerned about the team's kicking game. Jim Ryan, who had started the season at place kicker, had missed one of three extra points and a short field goal against Purdue and had followed that up by missing one of two extra point tries against Northwestern.

The kicking game took care of itself, or, more accurately, Joe Azzaro took care of it for the Irish. Azzaro was an uncommon player for his day because he did nothing but placekick. Azzaro grew up in Pittsburgh, where his father raised him listening to Notre Dame games on the radio. From an early age Azzaro dreamed of playing for the Irish, but his hopes were nearly shattered when he broke both his ankles in an automobile accident just before he entered Pittsburgh's Central Catholic High School. The ankles were a long time healing, and part of Azzaro's home-made therapy consisted of placekicking footballs through the uprights of a grape arbor that stood on a hill behind the family's house. He became good enough at it so that in his senior year of high school he went out for the football team and got the place-kicking job.

Azzaro's father was determined that his son would go to Notre Dame. Parseghian didn't offer him a scholarship, but he told him he was welcome to try out for the team as a walk-on. That was good enough for Azzaro. He made the team, and in the middle of his sophomore season in 1964, he became the number-one kicker for several games, kicking seven extra points and the field goal that gave Notre Dame a 17–15 victory over Pittsburgh. But he tore some muscles in his thigh and missed the end of the season.

Still, Parseghian was impressed enough to give Azzaro a scholarship, but while working out during the summer of 1965, Azzaro tore his thigh again. The tear was so bad that he underwent surgery to repair it. The repairs involved removing about half of his quadricep, and he was out for the season. The doctors warned him that he might be out for life.

When the 1966 season started, Ryan was the number-one kicker and Azzaro was a spectator. When the forty-four-man traveling squad to go to Northwestern was announced, he wasn't on it. Parseghian had wanted to bring him, but he had a strict limit on the number of players he could take to the game at university expense. Since Evanston, Illinois, wasn't that far away, Ara gave Azzaro the keys to his new Oldsmobile and told him to drive up Saturday morning and to bring his equipment with him. That's what he did, and when he showed up, Ara got him into the game. When Azzaro nailed two extra points and delivered two deep and booming kickoffs, Parseghian started thinking about changing kickers.

It wasn't hard for the kickers to tell when they were on the ascent. During practice when they were working on extra points and field goals, Parseghian would pick out one of them and start yelling at him and throwing his clipboard in front of the ball as he was about to kick. When he started doing that to Azzaro the week after Northwestern, Joe knew he was probably the new starting kicker.

Azzaro was one good thing to come out of Northwestern. Another was the news that arrived the following Monday: Notre Dame had slipped past Alabama in the Associated Press poll to take over the number-three ranking behind second-place UCLA and top-ranked Michigan State. The Irish remained in third place in the UPI poll but edged closer to UCLA and further ahead of Alabama. After three weeks of the season, the entire national Top Ten was still undefeated.

To casual followers of college football, the brief stories accompanying the weekly rankings made it look as if Michigan State had had an easy time in the 26–10 win over Illinois that kept the Spartans on top of the polls. Nothing could be further from the truth. The fact was that the Spartans felt lucky to come out of Champaign, Illinois, with their lives.

In five previous trips to face the Fighting Illini, Duffy Daugherty had never returned with a win. Were it not for his defense, he might not have done it this time either. Illinois, which had a veteran team, clearly had an upset on its mind. Pete Elliott, the Illinois coach, went into the game with the same strategy that so many others would apply against the Spartans: Stop the run and force them to pass. On the other side of the ball, Elliott wanted his own quarterbacks to throw the ball against Michigan State's run-crushing defense. One of those quarterbacks was sophomore Bob Naponic, who had been a teammate of Michigan State's George Chatlos at Hempfield High in western Pennsylvania. Coming out of high school, Naponic had been rated ahead of another western Pennsylvania star, Terry Hanratty, and had started ahead of Hanratty in the Big 33 high school all-star game that Pennsylvania played annually against Texas. Elliott's strategy may have worked if his offense had been able to hold on to the ball. But three lost fumbles and two interceptions ultimately did him in.

The game had started like too many games for the Spartans—with a scoreless first period. Worse, Elliott's plan to stop Clinton Jones and Bob Apisa was working, and the Spartans found themselves relying on Jimmy Raye's scrambles and runs by Dwight Lee for their yardage.

Illinois got the first break of the game in the second quarter when Lee fumbled on his own 38 and defensive end Ken Kmiec recovered for Illinois. The Spartan defense stopped the next 2 plays for 3 yards, but on third-and-7, Bob Naponic hit Bob Robertson for 19 yards on a tackle eligible pass to put the ball on the 16. The Illini went back to the run and picked up 6 more yards on 2 plays to bring up a third-and-4 at the 10. Naponic went back to pass and had halfback Ron Bess open at the 4, but missed connections, and Elliott sent in Jim Stotz to kick a 27-yard field goal for a 3–0 lead.

As it did so often, the Michigan State offense responded immediately. In their longest drive of the day, Michigan State covered 71 yards in only 4 plays, the biggest of which was a 50-yard bomb from Raye to Washington that took them to the Illini 10. Raye got the rest of the yardage himself on the next play when he ducked inside of right end for the score that gave the Spartans a 6–3 lead. Dick Kenney, who had missed a first-quarter field goal attempt, hit the extra point to make it 7–3.

Illinois took the kickoff and moved downfield to the Michigan State 46. Naponic missed 1 pass from there to bring up second down and one of the biggest plays of the Spartan season. The play started innocently enough, with Naponic dropping back to attempt another pass. But before he could throw, Chatlos, his former high school teammate, crashed into him from the blind side. For the fourth time that season the ball popped free after a Chatlos hit. While it was still in the air, Phil Hoag, who was also rushing on the play, grabbed it and started to run, but an Illinois player grabbed his arm and started to spin him around and to the ground. As Hoag was spinning, he caught sight of Pat Gallinagh, who was rushing into the fray with his hands against his chest to block someone. "Here!" Hoag yelled, and he tossed the ball to Gallinagh, who later confessed that if it hadn't hit him directly in the chest, there was no way he could have held on to it. But hold on he did, and he was still holding on when he collapsed panting and wheezing under a pile of his happy teammates in the Illinois end zone at the end of an unlikely 54-yard touchdown play.

"Gallinagh is the second slowest football player in the world," one of his teammates told the press after the game. "The Illinois guy chasing him was the slowest."

The touchdown gave the Spartans a 13–3 lead (Kenney missed the point after), and both teams retired to the locker rooms for halftime.

Whatever Elliott told his players at the break, it seemed to work. Early in the second half, Naponic went back from his own 38 and threw the ball as far as he could for his end, John Wright. The pass was a little short and Wright had to hold up for it, giving Jerry Jones a chance to close in on him. Both players went up for the ball. Wright won the battle, shook off Jones's attempt to tackle him, and sprinted into the end zone to cut the Spartan lead to 13–10.

Again, Raye brought the Spartans back downfield, gaining big yardage along the way on his own around both ends. He got his team down to the Illinois 19, but on a first down from there, he tried to hit Al Brenner at the 3 and hit the Illinis' Bruce Sullivan instead. The interception brought the crowd of 57,747 to its feet.

Illinois couldn't move the ball and punted. Again Raye brought his team down the field, moving to a first down at the Illinois 6. From there, Jones, Lee, and Apisa each took a crack at the end zone, but the 3 plays netted only a yard each. On fourth-and-goal at the 3, Daugherty decided to go for it instead of trying a field goal, and he told Raye to take it in himself. Raye tried but could come up with only 2 of the 3 yards before being run out of bounds at the 1.

Then Illinois's luck ran out. After rushing twice for no gain, Naponic sent halfback Bill Huston on a sweep around right end. The Spartans stormed through the Illinois line and greeted Huston in the end zone, where he was crushed by the left side of the defensive line. By the time Huston hit the ground, he had neither his consciousness nor the ball, which squirted out of his hands and out to the 3-yard line, where Phil Hoag, who recovered all three Illinois fumbles that day, fell on it. Huston was taken off the field on a stretcher.

This time the Spartan offense didn't fail. On the first play, Raye went the 3 yards for the touchdown. A pass for a two-point conversion fell incomplete, and Michigan State had a 19–10 lead with a quarter to play.

From then on it was all defense on both sides. The only score of the fourth quarter came when Al Brenner took a 53-yard punt by Tom Smith on his own 5, caught a couple of blocks, and cruised 95 yards untouched for the longest punt return for a touchdown in the history of the Big Ten.

Brenner's return was a nice cap on the victory, but even that didn't bring a lot of jubilation to the Michigan State locker room. The players and coaches knew they had been lucky to win. The stat sheets bore out the difficulties they had had. Illinois had matched them in first downs at 13 each and had nearly matched them in total yardage, 243 for the Spartans to 221. Illinois had gained most of its yards in the air and had only 16 on the ground, but even that was misleading since 90 yards in advances had been offset by 74 yards lost rushing, and 45 of those were lost attempting to pass. George Webster had accounted for 22 of those yards personally, with 4 tackles for losses.

So the Spartans dressed quickly and got out of town. On the way out they didn't even sing the fight song. It didn't seem like a time to celebrate.

The following Saturday, October 8, brought another big test. Bump Elliott and the Michigan Wolverines were going to East Lansing for the annual battle of Michigan. The Wolverines had opened their season with consecutive wins over Oregon State and California, and had moved up to eighth place in the AP poll. But then they lost 21–7 to North Carolina and dropped out of the rankings altogether. That didn't mean they weren't dangerous, especially against the Spartans.

Bump Elliott's primary weapons were quarterback Dick Vidmer, a red-shirt junior quarterback who had been another teammate of Chatlos at Hempfield High, end Jack Clancy, and a deep backfield led by Jim Detwiler and fullback Dave Fisher. It became apparent early in the game that Elliott, who had watched his team lose yardage rushing the year before, was going to use Vidmer and Clancy until they were worn out. Defensively, he wanted to cut off Michigan State's sweeps and force them to run up the middle or pass.

The game attracted a record Spartan Stadium crowd of 78,833, almost 3,000 over the stadium's listed capacity. The game was worth the price of admission. Jimmy Raye later called it the hardest hitting game he had ever played in, and both Daugherty and Elliott agreed it was certainly up there with the roughest they had ever seen. "It was a rip-snorter all the way," wrote Bob Hoerner, sports editor of *The State Journal* of Lansing. "Maybe not all of the tackles were heard on Grand River Avenue, but a couple of times when Spartan and Wolverine met head-on, the windows in Ag Hall must have rattled."

Michigan State again couldn't score in the first quarter, but it did manage to score first. Before the tally, however, it had to survive an early scare on Michigan's first possession. The drive initially stalled and Michigan punted. The short punt hit Michigan State's Mitch Pruiett, and an alert Wolverine fell on the ball at the Spartan 43. They couldn't move, though, and the punting battle continued through the quarter. Finally, Al Brenner fielded a Michigan punt at the Wolverine 47 and brought the crowd to its feet when he blazed all the way back for an apparent touchdown. But the cheering was short-lived. A Michigan State blocker had been flagged for clipping—one of seven 15-yard penalties called on the Spartans that day—and the play was brought back.

Raye was unfazed and simply began again the drive that would give the Spartans the lead. The big play was a simple inside handoff to Bob Apisa, who had a terrific day with 140 yards gained on 18 carries. The play gained 15 yards and an additional

15 yards on a Wolverine penalty, one of their five major fouls. From the Wolverine 18 Apisa ran for another 11, and Raye finally got it across from the 5 on the seventh play of the drive. When Dick Kenney kicked the extra point, the Spartans had a 7–0 lead early in the second quarter.

It would be nearly thirty minutes before anyone scored again, although it took some defensive heroics to keep the Wolverines off the board. Just before halftime the Spartans were forced to punt from deep in their own territory. Kicking into the wind, Kenney got off a feeble effort that carried only to his own 28. Vidmer came out and immediately hit Clancy for 19 yards to the Michigan State 7. With the crowd begging Bubba Smith to "kill, Bubba, kill," Vidmer went back to pass twice more without success. On the second attempt the Wolverines were flagged for being offsides and the ball was moved back to the 12, where it remained second down. Again Vidmer passed, this time for Detwiler, but Jerry Jones broke it up. On third down, Jones did it again, barely tipping away a ball in the end zone that was heading straight to Clancy and what had looked like a certain touchdown. On fourth down, Rick Sygar tried a field goal but hit the right upright.

Early in the fourth period, with the score still 7–0 and the tension as thick as the federal tax code, Michigan jarred the ball free from Raye and recovered on the Michigan State 43. Again, the Spartan defense refused to budge, yielding just 4 yards before the Wolverines punted into the State end zone.

Taking over on the 20, Raye finally put everything together for the team's one long drive of the day and the touchdown that would allow the huge crowd a chance to exhale an ocean of noise. Apisa again got the big yards, ripping off a 49-yard run on a quick-hitting trap play over Jerry West at right tackle and taking the ball to the Wolverine 16. Three plays later, Apisa rode the same play into the end zone from 6 yards out.

Desperate now, Michigan tried to come back, but almost immediately coughed the ball up when halfback Ernie Sharpe was nailed by Pat Gallinagh and fumbled. Jimmy Raye wasted no time taking advantage of the turnover, throwing 25 yards to Gene Washington for a 20–0 lead and putting the game out of reach.

If there was any doubt, it was erased on the next series when Dog Thornhill clobbered Sharpe and again forced a fumble. This time Jess Phillips fell on the ball, and the defense trotted off the field to turn it over to the reserves as the East Lansing crowd started their night-long celebration. Charlie Wedemeyer came in at quarterback in place of Raye to try to get yet another score, but after throwing one incompletion, he threw an interception, the Spartans' first of the game.

Now Vidmer drove his team the length of the field in 10 plays, with the big yardage being ripped off by fullback Dave Fisher who carried twice for gains of 40 and 26 yards in the 77-yard drive. Detwiler got the last 10 yards and the touchdown on a pass from Vidmer.

The touchdown made it 20–7 and aggravated the defense, which had wanted a shutout. But the annoyance didn't last. They had won another tough game, and while they didn't hold the Wolverines to negative rushing yards as they had in 1965, they did limit Michigan to 47 yards on the ground and 168 in the air while gaining 245 rushing themselves and 45 more passing.

It was a particularly satisfying day for George Chatlos. Before the game the writers noted that he had sacked one high school teammate, Naponic, the week before and wondered what he would do to Vidmer. "I don't want to play favorites," he said. "I'll just have to make sure I get Vidmer, too." Late in the game he got him, an event both could joke about later but only Chatlos could enjoy that day.

Vidmer was more impressed by the pressure Bubba had put on him all afternoon. "You can't see him, but you can sort of feel him creeping up on you," the quarterback said. "He comes at you so hard, you find yourself throwing off balance, hurrying your plays." His passing stats bore that out.

Another Michigan player, defensive lineman Dave Porter, who had grown up in Lansing, had looked forward to playing in the Michigan–Michigan State game since he was a kid. Now a junior, he had finally gotten his chance. "I see now why they build this game up," he said afterward, a bit ruefully. "This is the hardest I've ever been hit."

The Spartans could sing again, but they couldn't celebrate long. The following week Ohio State was waiting for them in Columbus, and the week after that they'd have to see how well their pass defense held up against Bob Griese. In the Big Ten there weren't many weeks off.

While the Spartans had been preparing for and then defeating Michigan, Notre Dame was facing Army in its third game of the season. Despite the fact that the Cadets had given up only six points in their first three games and were 3-0, they were going into South Bend as twenty-eight-point underdogs. Parseghian, of course, disagreed with the odds makers and tried to convince his team that Army, which was led by star linebacker Townsend Clarke, would test them severely.

In truth, Army was entering a long period of decline and was light-years away from its glory days of the mid-1940s. The lure of pro ball kept many players away from West Point, and the service academy's strict limitations on physical size also hurt them as athletes continued to get bigger.

Another factor was that Army, like many other schools, waited until the mid-sixties before suiting up its first black football player. That pioneer was named Gary Steele, and in 1966 he was a sophomore, playing his first season of college football.

Parseghian concentrated during practice that week on improving his running attack, pointing out that if you took away Nick Eddy's 56-yard run against Northwestern, the team averaged only 3 yards a play on the ground. "We are not supermen," Ara had told reporters during the week. Some may even have believed him.

Meanwhile Ray complained loudly that his second unit defense, despite the humiliation of having given up a meaningless touchdown (although Ray would never agree that such a thing existed), still wasn't displaying the proper predatory attitude in practice.

The excitement level at the pep rally was rather ordinary, which is to say there were no reports of anyone's being hospitalized because of it. But this was Army, and the student body expected the rout the papers were predicting.

While the team and the campus slept before the game, three Notre Dame students were sneaking into the South Bend Armory, where Army had billeted its mule mascots for the night. They didn't steal the mules. That would have created too many other problems since no one was sure if the cancellation of parietal hours in the dorms meant mules, too. Instead, they painted large green shamrocks on their hindquarters. The next morning the Cadets who were supposed to be guarding the mules spent a memorable hour with soap and scrub brushes erasing the damage.

Game day, October 8, 1966, dawned clear and sunny, and by the time the team took the field, it was 72 degrees with a southwest wind blowing at sixteen miles per hour. The pregame party on campus had been enlivened when a student stole the campus police captain's Cushman vehicle and drove it wildly around the quad, chasing down St. Mary's girls. The spirit of the chase carried over to the stadium, where the Notre Dame section and the St. Mary's section spent a good part of the afternoon hurling insults at each other.

That's the kind of day it was. From the moment Notre Dame's leprechaun led the team out onto the field, the game was essentially over. The leprechaun himself, now a fixture at all Notre Dame games, had been created only that year by a sophomore with access to some Hollywood costuming people. He had dropped $250 of his own money—enough to carry the average student through the entire winter—on his brown custom-tailored outfit. The makeup department at Warner Brothers donated a $40 beard to complete the effect. When he presented himself to the appropriate officials, the leprechaun became the official mascot.

Army's biggest moment of the game came before it even started when the Cadets won the coin flip and elected to receive. Azzaro kicked it into the end zone, Army returned to the 23, and 3 plays and 7 yards later, the Cadets were lining up to punt. Army's punter, Nick Kuriko, had been suspended for missing curfew, and his replacement, Ron Wasilewski, advanced the ball only 16 yards, to the Notre Dame 46.

On the first play Hanratty went back and missed Seymour. No matter. On the next play Hanratty went to Seymour again, 19 yards downfield, and the big end went high in the air to pull the ball in. As he came down, one Army defender hit him in the back and dropped him to the ground. Once there, two more Army defenders piled on, helmets first. They stayed on Seymour a little longer than necessary, telling him what they thought of him, which turned out to be not much. The writers kept calling Army scrappy, but the teams that played against them considered them just plain dirty.

"They were gnats," said Duranko. "They'd throw dirt in your eyes."

"They were the dirtiest team we played all year," added Gmitter. "They had this Cadet hustle and gang tackling, and a lot of it was after the whistle. So we started crunching some people, and they got the idea. After about three minutes they weren't talking anymore."

It took just a little longer than that for Notre Dame to find the end zone. After the pass to Seymour, Notre Dame ran seven straight times, with Bleier going the last 2 yards for a touchdown. Azzaro kicked the point, and it was 7–0.

Army returned the kick to the 23 again, but this time they didn't keep it long enough to punt. On the Cadets' third play, Carl Woessner took a handoff and ran directly into Kevin Hardy. The impact knocked the ball loose at the Army 33, where Duranko jumped on it. The offense, which had been on the sidelines less than two minutes, trotted back out and didn't waste any time getting back to the bench. Hanratty faked a handoff to Bleier into the line, dropped back 7 yards to the 40, and heaved it to the back of the end zone, where Seymour hauled it in behind two Army defenders. Azzaro swung his leg again and it was 14–0, and the first quarter was barely half over.

Those scrappy Cadets came back out to try again. This time they marched down to the Notre Dame 39 before stalling and punting 15 yards to the Notre Dame 24. Helped by two 15-yard personal foul penalties against the Cadets for late hits, the offense needed only 6 plays to score their third touchdown.

By halftime Notre Dame had scored twice more for a 35–0 halftime lead. As they trotted happily to the locker room, Parseghian faced a dilemma: What do you tell a team that's up by 5 touchdowns and has outgained the opposition 323 yards to 97 yards? He thought about it until it was time for him to address the squad. The team went silent as it always did when Ara stood before them. They waited to hear their instructions for the second half. Ara looked at them and said, "Hi, fellas." Then he sent them out.

Parseghian could have avenged Notre Dame's 59–0 wartime loss to Army, but he didn't. He sent in his second team offensive unit to start the second half and eventually used forty-eight players, including Bob Belden, his third-team quarterback, and eight different running backs. They didn't score, but Army didn't either, and the second half ended as it had begun, 35–0.

As the teams ran off the field after the game, the students ran onto it. Three of them brought a sign that left a sour taste in everyone's mouth. Unfurling it on the field and in front of the eight hundred Cadets who had made the trip from West Point for the game, they paraded around with the message, a bad word-play on the acronym for the campus Reserve Officers Training Corps, or ROTC. The banner said: ARMY ROTS-SEE?

The banner was a sign of the antimilitary sentiment that would spread to Notre Dame and nearly every other campus during the next four years. In 1966, however, most students thought it was in exceptionally poor taste. The real sentiment of the student body toward the military would become apparent later in the year when the students voted on the university's Patriot of the Year award and chose Gen. William Westmoreland, the commander of American troops in Vietnam.

After the game Parseghian had to dig a little deeper to find something to worry about. He found it, though, in the inability of the second unit to score in the second half. "We're just not as deep as some people have been saying we are," he told the writers. "Those kids on the second string made plenty of mistakes out there—penalties, ragged handling of the ball, mechanical errors."

Army coach Tom Cahill didn't see it that way. "The thing about this team that beats you is their balance," he said. "You try to stop them one way, and they'll beat you the other. I thought we were well enough prepared, but we just couldn't stop them. They're much better than last year."

Cahill was saying what Parseghian was thinking. Ara had built the team so that it had no weaknesses, and he had succeeded. They had shown in the first two games that they could score with the big play. Against Army they had also shown that they could grind it out on the ground if they wanted. Purdue had taken away the run but got killed with the long pass. Northwestern had taken away the long pass and had gotten killed with the short pass. Army just got killed every which way.

The key to the first-half ground attack against Army was Parseghian's fullback, Larry Conjar, who took seven handoffs and ripped off 44 punishing yards. This was on top of Conjar's customary devastating blocking, a pastime he positively loved because it gave him a chance to hit defensive ends and linebackers just as hard as they hit him when he had the ball.

Conjar was 6 feet even and went around 215. An ideal fullback might have been a little bigger, but nobody played bigger. For the fans, that's what Conjar was and always had been. But the coaches, his teammates, and Conjar himself knew that wasn't even close to the truth, and they liked him more because of it.

Conjar grew up in Steelton, Pennsylvania, a mill town just outside of Harrisburg, the son of a steelworker and part of an extended family that included fifty-five first cousins. He was a handsome kid with glistening black hair and dark sparkling eyes. He was also painfully shy.

As a boy he used to lie on the floor at home with his father on Saturday afternoons and listen to Notre Dame football games on the radio. That was where he listened to the call as the Notre Dame team of Dick Lynch and Nick Pietrosante broke Oklahoma's forty-seven-game winning streak in 1957. It was there he decided that he, too, wanted to study under the Dome and play football for the Fighting Irish. He visited Notre Dame in November of his senior year in high school, and he still remembers turning down Notre Dame Avenue on a gray, chilly day and feeling the goosebumps break out all over his body when he saw the Golden Dome shining against the overcast sky.

He went in with the great freshman class of 1963, but he wasn't an immediate hit. Like Charlie Thornhill at Michigan State, he couldn't get with the program. He didn't have Thornhill's racial problems, but he had problems just the same. Most of them concerned his high school sweetheart, who had stayed back home and whom he missed to distraction. To the coaching staff he was a major disappointment.

Conjar knew it, too. Three weeks before the end of the 1964 season, when he was doing nothing and going nowhere, his father had come out to watch a game. Afterward he told Larry that all the guys in the steel mill were razzing him because his kid had gone to Notre Dame, where he wasn't playing, when he could have gone to a teacher's college nearer home and been a big deal.

The comments hurt, and Conjar thought about them and where he was going the next day, Sunday, when he was running the stadium steps with the rest of the team. He got to the top of the stadium and looked out across the campus he had dreamed of coming to. "Tomorrow night," he told himself. "Tomorrow night is going to be *my* night."

Monday was the Toilet Bowl, when the scrubs played the freshmen, and there was no question that Conjar was a scrub. Conjar had told himself before that he was going to perform, but he had only gone through the motions. This time he was committed.

Whatever came over him had been spotted that same Sunday by John Murphy, the freshman coach. He even told Tom Pagna and Ara to keep an eye on Conjar in the next day's scrimmage because there was something going on.

The first play of the scrimmage was an off-tackle run. Conjar's assignment was to kick out the defensive end ahead of the ball-carrier, who would cut inside. At the snap Conjar exploded into the hapless freshman who had the misfortune to be playing defensive end. Conjar didn't even know who the kid was. He just put his helmet in the kid's chest and ran him over.

Parseghian was waiting when the squad huddled for the next play. "Not bad," Ara said. "Let's run that play again."

He called the same play four straight times, and Conjar ran the end over all four times. After the fourth play he came back to the huddle, and Pagna looked him square in the eye. "It's about time," Pagna said.

While the team spent the weekend after Army going over films and starting to get ready for the next victim, North Carolina, the campus waited for Monday afternoon when the wire service polls came out. They weren't disappointed. In both the AP and UPI polls the Irish had moved up to second place, behind Michigan State, which had beaten Michigan, 20–7, and ahead of Alabama and UCLA. The writers were already starting to circle. *Sports Illustrated* and *Time* were both working on stories about Notre Dame and the sophomore pitching and catching combination, and Roger Valdiserri in the sports information office was locked in daily and mortal debate with writers over an appropriate nickname for Hanratty and Seymour. One of the Chicago papers dubbed them the "Kiddie Korps." Valdiserri settled on the "Baby Bombers," although as they grew up in future seasons, he took to calling them "Mr. Fling and Mr. Cling."

8

I've always thought the object of the game was to win. Apparently they expect more of us.

—Duffy Daugherty

The 1966 World Series ended on Sunday, October 9, when Dave McNally pitched the Baltimore Orioles' third consecutive complete-game shutout against the Los Angeles Dodgers. The Dodgers, who were led by pitchers Sandy Koufax and Don Drysdale, never led in any of the four games and were blanked for the final thirty-three innings. The postmortems continued for a few days, but by the end of that week college football was again king of the sports pages.

The coming weekend was critical for Michigan State. Woody Hayes had been looking forward to October 15 ever since the day, a year earlier, when Michigan State had humiliated his Ohio State Buckeyes 32–7 in East Lansing. Losing was bad enough, but the Spartans had held Woody's men to negative rushing yardage. That had never happened to a Woody Hayes team before, and he would be damned if it would happen again. As if he needed more incentive, Ohio State had lost its two previous games, to Washington and Illinois, and both losses were at home. Hayes had never in his fifteen years at Ohio State lost three games in a row. He told his players it wasn't going to happen now. An avid student of military history who had more than a touch of General Patton in him, Hayes had also been plotting his revenge against Daugherty and the Spartans for almost a year. He had started his psychological warfare in spring practice when he dressed some of his scout team players in green-and-white jerseys—Michigan State colors. He had them run Spartan plays, and he had his varsity learn every move they could expect from Duffy Daugherty.

This time the Buckeyes would greet the Spartans in Ohio Stadium in front of 84,282 screaming partisans who had the endearing habit of showering enemy teams with buckeyes—walnut-sized nuts—as they stood on the sidelines. The Spartans knew it wasn't going to be easy. And although they said they never looked at the wire service polls or worried about rankings, they all knew that Notre Dame was breathing down their necks and that any slip on their part combined with another big Notre Dame win could make them number two.

Thursday was the last full practice day of the week, and Daugherty liked to close out the practice with a little fun. Sometimes he'd match his players in foot races. Often he would work on some gimmick play he had concocted. Duffy was big on trick plays. He was an extremely bright man and equally creative, and if it weren't for his assistants, who dreaded his departures from football orthodoxy and did their best to keep him in check, there's no telling what sort of craziness he would have sprung on the field.

But this Thursday, Duffy was in no mood for tricks. He didn't know that Woody Hayes had had his troops beating up on green shirts since spring, but he knew Hayes wanted this game in the worst way. So practice was straightforward right up to the end when it was time to practice extra points against a live defense. Duffy's holder and kicker, Charlie Wedemeyer and Dick Kenney, were both Hawaiians. A sophomore backup quarterback, Wedemeyer was just 5 feet 7 and 170 pounds, but he had thrown for 348 yards in the final freshman scrimmage the year before and was the best pure passer on the team. Kenney, at an even 6 feet and 214 pounds, was more than just a kicker who didn't wear a shoe or sock on his right foot. A senior, he had led the Spartan baseball team the previous spring with a 5-1 record and a 2.31

earned run average. As a kicker he was accurate for his time and straight-on style, and he was also long. He had hit kicks in practice from as far away as 60 yards.

Wedemeyer and Kenney liked to fool around together, and one day they came up with a fake extra point or field goal play in which Kenney took the snap directly from center while Wedemeyer got up from his kneeling position and sprinted into the end zone, where Kenney hit him with a pass. They hadn't shown the play to anyone until the Thursday before Ohio State. Then they pulled it in the practice, unannounced.

Duffy wasn't amused. He wanted to see a well-oiled extra point unit, not a trick. He told them to do it right.

The team flew down to Ohio State, arriving Friday in time to get in one walk-through practice before dinner. From the start, nothing went right. The weather was atrocious, pouring cold rain and high winds. The plane hit the runway and slid sideways to a stop.

At their walk-through practice, the team was sky-high. The excitement carried into the locker room where someone started yelling and the rest of the team picked it up until the entire room was one sustained scream that didn't stop until they had finished showering and dressing. Reggie Cavender, Bob Apisa's backup at fullback, remembers thinking in the midst of all the noise that maybe the team had peaked a day early.

The weather didn't let up that night or the next day, and somewhere, Woody Hayes was raising his eyes to the heavens in thanksgiving. He had prepared his team to stop the Spartans' fast and powerful runners, and now the weather was going to help him, too. Clinton Jones and Jimmy Raye both relied on speed and quickness, and the Spartan offensive line, having been built not on size but on speed, relied on it even more. On a muddy field much of their advantage was gone. So Woody thanked the football gods for the rain and ordered his grounds crew not to cover the football field with a tarp, as they would normally have done to keep it as dry and firm as possible until the game.

By game time the uncovered field was more swamp than gridiron, and still more water was falling on it. The rain, which came in waves, was so hard at times that fans in the stands could barely see from one side of the field to the other. Players taking their stances put their hands on the ground and watched them disappear to the wrist. Running was not going to be easy, and passing was going to be next to impossible.

And it nearly was, especially for the Spartans. They fumbled seven times that day and had two snaps sail over Dick Kenney's head on punts. Though they lost only one fumble, the slick ball kept them from getting anything going. Ohio State, on the other hand, somehow didn't have nearly as much trouble holding on to the ball. They couldn't move it for much of the game, but at least they didn't give it up.

Hayes and the Buckeyes got their first break on the Spartans' second possession of the game. Trying to work into a thirty-six-mile-an-hour gale, the Spartans went nowhere, and on third down Raye fumbled the ball and fell on it on his own 31 to bring on the fourth down and the punting team. The Spartans had a new long snapper for punts and field goals, Ron Ranieri, who was making the first road trip of his career. It rapidly became a trip from hell. Trying to center the slick football, he sent it sailing over Kenney's head and into the end zone. Two Buckeyes chased the ball down and tried to fall on it for a touchdown, but they couldn't handle it; it slithered out of the end zone for a safety and a 2–0 Ohio State lead. Not a good way to start.

Kenney put the ball into play on a free kick that sailed down to Bo Rein at the Ohio State 24. But Rein couldn't handle the ball, one of the few Buckeye mistakes of the day, and George Chatlos leaped on it for the Spartans. Any hope of scoring off the recovery was short-lived. Two plays gained nothing, and a third resulted in a 9-yard loss when Clinton Jones couldn't handle a pitchout. With the ball on the 33, Kenney tried a 50-yard field goal into the teeth of the storm but couldn't come close with it.

The rest of the first half was scoreless and brutal. On one play even the indestructible George Webster was laid out by a vicious block that caught him in the ribs. As he lay on the field gasping for breath, an Ohio State player, on his way back to the huddle, looked down at Webster and said in his best schoolboy accent, "Aaawww, big George Webster got hurt." Bubba Smith, standing nearby, heard the line and couldn't help himself. He broke up laughing, and when Webster looked up and saw Bubba, he couldn't help but laugh too. Then he got up and rejoined the fray.

Michigan State had one scoring chance in that first half. Starting on their own 21, they got all the way to the Ohio State 21, the biggest gain coming on a 29-yard screen pass from Raye to Brenner. The pass carried to the Buckeye 33, but when Raye tried it again from the 21, Jim Nein stepped in front of Brenner, picked it off, and headed downfield for what Nein figured would be a touchdown. But Raye, who had made one big mistake, would not make another one. He chased Nein down and dragged him to the slop at the Michigan State 49. It was the only time Ohio State crossed midfield the entire half.

The second half wasn't much prettier than the first. Early in the third quarter Hayes ordered a punt on third down from his own 26, but the strategy backfired when the kick carried only to his own 46. From there Raye moved his team to a first down at the Ohio State 11. Two running plays got the ball to the 5, bringing up third-and-4. The Spartans had earlier lost Dwight Lee, who was tossed out of the game for trying to register his displeasure by going after the Ohio State defense. Now on third down, Raye pitched around the right side to Lee's replacement, Dick Berlinski, but Berlinski lost 4 yards and Daugherty sent Kenney in to try a field goal. Kenney made it from 27 yards out, and for the first time the Spartans had a lead, 3–2. It was a score more appropriate to a baseball game, but it was still a lead.

The defense held again and forced another punt, and Mike Current hit a beauty that put the Spartans in business at their own 12. Raye couldn't move the team, and on fourth down with the ball on the 18, Kenney came in to punt. The game nearly ended right there as Ranieri again snapped the ball over Kenney's head. But this time Kenney didn't let the Buckeyes take advantage. He quickly picked up the ball at the goal line and somehow managed to get off a kick that carried all the way to the Spartan 47.

The kick was the last play of the third quarter. After the teams changed ends, Michigan State came out of its defensive huddle with all eleven defenders massed at the line of scrimmage, anticipating an Ohio State run. Normally, that was a good call. Woody Hayes viewed passing as if it were a communist conspiracy, but he shocked the Spartans and everyone in the stadium by faking a run and throwing a pass to split end Billy Anders coming across the field. "Woody never did that before or since," said Vince Carrilot. "It fooled us so bad we had to try to catch the kid from behind." Jerry Jones tried to catch him, but by the time Anders caught the ball at the 15, Jones was so far behind him, Anders could have walked into the end zone. As the big crowd filled the air with soggy cheers, the scoreboard put six more points on the Buckeye side. But everything would not go Woody Hayes's way that day. Gary Cairns, who had kicked a 55-yard field goal earlier in the year, hit the crossbar with his point-after attempt, and instead of a 9–3 lead, Ohio State led only 8–3.

If the Spartans were going to do anything, time was starting to run out. The opportunity had come for Jimmy Raye to show what he was made of. Robert Markus of the *Chicago Tribune* spun a prize-winning story about it that began:

> Jimmy Raye did today what they said he could not do, and he saved Michigan State from a football disaster. Jimmy Raye cannot pass, his critics said, but today the whole state of Ohio knows that this is not so.
>
> Thru a driving rain and against a wind that was howling like all the hounds of hell, Raye threw and threw again and he moved the unbeaten Spartans 84 yards to a fourth-quarter touchdown that brought an 11 to 8 victory over Ohio State.
>
> With a desperation born of despair, Raye put the soggy, slippery football in the air seven times on this advance and he connected four times. The other three passes were on target, too, but his receivers simply could not hold on to the treacherous ball.

Up until that drive, Bubba Smith had been having conniptions on the sidelines watching the Spartan offense struggle. The defense had been stopping Ohio State all day, but the offense wasn't capitalizing. There had been tension between the offense and defense all year. Duffy liked to play the two units against each other as a way to inspire each one. But the defense felt that it was the heart of the team and that the offense didn't always do as much as it should have. "They didn't have anybody on offense like Dog that had that kind of fire to get them going," Bubba said of Thornhill. And now, as the offense continued to have problems in the Ohio Stadium swamp, Bubba was stalking the sidelines yelling, "Let me play offense. I'll play tackle. At least I'll give them a hole."

That was Bubba Smith, the born dramatist, always ready with the heroic gesture or the grand overstatement. The coaches had been listening to him for three years, and they ignored him.

Finally, after the Buckeye touchdown, the offense slogged out to try again. After the kickoff, the ball was at their own 16-yard line. They had to have a touchdown, and they had to have it soon. As they huddled and Jimmy Raye came off the sidelines, they knew it was now or never.

A year earlier, with Steve Juday at the controls, there would have been some yelling and maybe an edge of panic in the huddle. Now there was icy calm and firm resolve. They didn't know how they'd pull it out, but they knew they would. "It was suck it up, guys, we got to get one," remembers Jerry West, the right tackle. "We knew we were going to score."

Raye didn't say much. He told them to watch the penalties and to concentrate. That was about it. And the confidence he showed rubbed off on his troops.

The drive was one of those dream sequences in which things are happening and nobody remembers exactly what they were. They just knew they were gaining yards, the chains were moving, and the Ohio State goal line was getting closer. "Jimmy ran, he passed, he rolled out, he did it all," said Mitch Pruiett, who had started his first game at offensive right guard and had stepped right into the drive of his life.

What made the drive amazing was that the bulk of it was accomplished through the air in impossible conditions. Raye kept running bootlegs and hitting Gene Washington and Al Brenner for 69 of the 84 yards in the drive. The first of his four completions was to Washington for 28 yards to the Spartan 44. Then he hit Washington again at the Ohio State 42. Brenner was next, and he pulled one in at the 25. From there they banged out 12 yards in the mud and a first down at the 13. Again Raye went back to pass, and again he found Washington alone at the 5, but this time the big end couldn't hang on to the slick ball. It fell harmlessly as 84,000 roared for the Buckeyes to stop the drive. But Raye went back and found Washington again, this time at the 2. Here's how Markus described the final series of the drive:

> [I]t took Michigan State all four downs and all the muscle and sweat it possessed to score from there. Raye himself dived three times into the swarming scarlet Buckeye line. The first time he budged it a yard. Then he got a foot and then another foot. On fourth down with 12 inches still showing between the ball and

the Ohio State goal, fullback Bob Apisa lunged over left guard and barely into the end zone.

The scoring play was called 4 Veer Trap, and Apisa remembers taking the handoff and leaping into the crest of two waves that had crashed together and were foaming at each other, with what was left of the white chalk marking the goal beneath them. Apisa looked down, saw the line, and holding the ball with both hands, shoved it forward. All he had to do was get the ball across the line for an instant. After that, it didn't matter. As the Ohio State defense drove forward and pushed him and the ball backwards 4 or 5 yards, Apisa only hoped he had gotten it in.

The crowd saw Apisa being thrown backwards and roared with delight. But the officials—who had to be brave and honest men to do such a thing in front of 84,000 partisans—had seen the ball break the plane of the goal line and threw their hands straight up. Touchdown, Michigan State.

The crowd didn't buy it. They screamed in protest. They threw buckeyes, pennies, soda pop bottles. It didn't matter. Michigan State had the lead, 9–8, and now Duffy had a decision to make. A full seven minutes remained in the game, and it was likely that Ohio State would be able to mount one last effort to wrest the lead back. If Duffy kicked an extra point, his lead would be only two points, and he could still lose by a field goal. If he could get a two-point conversion, Hayes would need a touchdown to win. Knowing Woody Hayes, Duffy felt certain if he had the choice, Hayes would rather lose than tie the game with a field goal.

Now Duffy remembered the fake extra point that Wedemeyer and Kenney had worked on in practice. He told them to go in and run it. If they failed, there was no difference in being ahead one point or two, so it was a safe play. Wedemeyer and Kenney went in, Ranieri snapped the ball to Kenney, Wedemeyer dashed into the end zone uncovered, and Kenney hit him to make the lead 11–8.

Chet Sullwold wrote in *The Toledo Blade*, "Richard Kenney, barefoot boy with shirt of green, today shattered Ohio State's upset dream."

Ohio State battled back, and they nearly pulled it off. They got to the Michigan State 35 with 3:37 to play and seemed to have broken Rein clear for a pass, but Jim Summers leaped in front of him and picked it off. The Buckeyes forced the Spartans to punt, and Michigan State obliged the cause by committing a personal foul to bring the ball to their own 25. This time Drake Garrett made the game-saving interception at his own 10-yard line.

Finally it ended, and when it did, a funny thing happened that Raye remembers as if it were yesterday: "The minute the game ended, the sun came out full throttle."

In Hawaii the next day one of the papers that kept close track of its native sons ran a banner headline about the game in which the Hawaiian kicker, fullback, and backup quarterback had accounted for all of Michigan State's points. It read: HAWAIIANS 11, OHIO STATE 8.

Another place closer to home than Hawaii was pretty excited about the game because of the success of a native son. That was Benton Harbor, Michigan, hometown of Mitch Pruiett.

When Pruiett left Benton Harbor for East Lansing, you could have made a lot of money betting people that Pruiett would wind up starting at offensive guard. There was no way it was going to happen. Pruiett was a great athlete in Benton Harbor, a four-sport letterman as a senior in high school. But he wasn't a guard, and at 5 feet 9 and 188 pounds, he didn't look like the sort to become one.

The son of a foundry worker, Pruiett was the oldest of three boys who shared a single bedroom in a small house on the edge of Benton Harbor's housing project. He was one of the few kids on the Michigan State team, white or black, who had grown up in a racially mixed environment.

By his junior year in high school he had attracted the attention of college coaches all over the Midwest. Every Big Ten school contacted him. The phone was ringing constantly. Pruiett visited Michigan, Michigan State, Central Michigan, Western Michigan, Wisconsin, and Indiana. What finally swayed him was the fact that Michigan State was within an easy drive of Benton Harbor, which would make it easy for his mother—his number-one fan—to see his games.

Going to East Lansing was an awakening, especially when he saw that his competition for his three varsity years would be Bob Apisa, who outweighed him by 30 pounds. During his sophomore year he played a little at running back, but mostly he played defense where he backed up George Webster, the best rover back in college football. Fortunately, the Spartans won a lot of games by a wide margin, and he played enough to get a letter. Still, it was clear if he hoped to have a future, it would have to be someplace else.

In the spring of his junior year the team was short on guards, and the coaches, remembering how well he blocked when he was in the backfield, suggested he give the offensive line a try. He did and was good at it, although he was still grossly undersized. That summer Pruiett hit the weights and got himself up to 212. He started the year backing up Tony Conti on the left side of the line, but Daugherty liked the way he played a lot bigger than he was. When Dave Techlin faltered at right guard halfway through the season, the coaches moved Pruiett over there next to West and started him in the Ohio State game. From then on, although he and Techlin were sometimes used alternately to run in plays, he was the starting right guard.

After the Ohio State game the Spartans showered quickly, got on the bus, and headed back to East Lansing, happy to have escaped with a victory. But they had seen the scoreboard during the game and knew that Notre Dame was beating up big time on North Carolina. And though they said they didn't look at the national rankings, they knew their reign as number one was in danger.

They weren't the only ones who lost ground that week. Alabama, *Sports Illustrated*'s preseason number one, faced Tennessee that week and was lucky to survive. Trailing 11–10, Tennessee had driven to Alabama's 2-yard line with sixteen seconds remaining, but didn't have enough time-outs left to try to run the ball in. So the Volunteers tried a field goal from 19 yards away and missed. 'Bama kept their undefeated season going, but that narrow escape effectively cut them out of consideration for the national title as long as either Notre Dame or Michigan State remained unbeaten.

Notre Dame's day was considerably easier than either Michigan State's or Alabama's. For starters, it wasn't raining. For another, the Notre Dame running game had finally hit full stride, and now that it had, Parseghian finally revealed that Conjar had started the season with bone spurs on his heels. The injuries were the result of a summer spent running on pavement in thin-soled track shoes that provided no cushioning. Conjar, a fanatic when it came to conditioning, had worn them because he thought they'd make him faster. But as he had shown the previous week, he was healthy again.

Parseghian's main worry that week was the status of his offensive line, where Rudy Konieczny had reinjured his knee and was out indefinitely. To replace him, Ara and his line coach, Jerry Wampfler, turned to sophomore Bob Kuechenberg, another precocious eighteen-year-old.

"Kooch," as he was called, hadn't gone to Notre Dame by the usual route. Although he had been an All-State end in Hobart, Indiana, and stood 6 feet 2, he weighed only 195 pounds as a high school senior. And because he wasn't really fast enough to play end, most big-time recruiters weren't beating down his door. In fact, they weren't calling at all. But Kuechenberg had one asset: his brother Rudy, who had been a three-year, two-way starter for the University of Indiana. Rudy's last season at Indiana was 1964, Bob's senior year in high school. After the football season Rudy, who would go on to play five years in the NFL as a linebacker, was chosen to play in the North-South college all-star game, which was being coached by Ara Parseghian.

After the all-star game, in which Rudy distinguished himself by detaching Roger Staubach from his senses, Rudy cornered Ara in an elevator on the way out of the stadium. "I don't know if you have any scholarships left," Rudy told the coach, "but if you do, I have a kid brother who really deserves one. He's not very big, but he's got a lot of heart." Ara listened, thanked him for the tip, and left it at that. Two days later Bob Kuechenberg received a phone call at home from Ara. Did he want a scholarship to Notre Dame?

Kooch didn't have to think long before answering. Ara told him he would be tried at linebacker because of his size, or lack of it. Bob was willing to try anything. As a freshman he was still undersized and spent his days being hamburger for the varsity. He went home for the summer and threw himself into the accepted body-building program of the day, eating a lot. By his sophomore year he was up to 235 pounds and had moved up to second on the depth chart at left tackle behind Paul Seiler. When George Kunz got hurt, he moved to the right side and stepped in when Rudy Konieczny's knee acted up. He started for the rest of the season.

It was the only full year he played offense in college, a fact that would later amaze Don Shula, his coach in the pros. In his junior year injuries on the defensive line forced the coaches to move him to the other side of the ball. Meanwhile, Kunz, who was Kuechenberg's roommate, came back and became an All-American tackle and the second player taken in the 1969 NFL draft. Kooch went in the fourth round, which didn't carry nearly the signing bonus that Kunz got. After the draft Kooch told "Barn," as Kunz was known because that's what he was as big as, "You know, you got my signing bonus." Kuechenberg made Kunz buy him dinner and made him pick up the checks ever after, determined to get his signing bonus back.

In addition to the changes on the offensive line, the Irish would be playing without Tom "Dusty" Rhoads who was down with a shoulder injury. He was replaced by Allen Sack, a standout high school quarterback who, like John Pergine and Tom Schoen, had been converted to defense. Sack, from Boothwyn, Pennsylvania, had captained both his high school football and basketball teams and threw the discus in track. But as a defensive end at Notre Dame he was pushed as far as his 6 feet 3 and 205 pounds could take him. He played well for Notre Dame, but he didn't enjoy it.

"It's hard to have a good time when your major concern is survival," he once wrote after he had finished school and gone on to a career as a sociology professor in Connecticut. The humiliation the players put up with during the weekly film sessions and the brutality of the practice sessions struck him as particularly inhuman. He left school without a high regard for big-time amateur athletics.

None of that was a concern to John Ray and Joe Yonto. As long as he hit and contained and tackled, he could think what he wanted. And Sack always did his job.

Finally, on Friday, Hanratty came up with a pulled muscle in his throwing arm. The doctors checked him out, stuck a syringe of cortisone in his arm, and pronounced him fit enough to play, although he couldn't throw with a normal, overhand motion and had to sidearm the ball instead. Now more than ever the running game had to come through.

North Carolina had had two weeks to prepare for Notre Dame. They came into the game undefeated and counted Michigan among their victims. Offensively, they were led by quarterback

1

Ara Parseghian, Notre Dame's fiery head coach, helped bring back the days of football greatness, but will be forever linked to his final decision in the big game.

2

3

The stunning performances of sophomore quarterback Terry Hanratty *(left)* and sophomore end Jim Seymour *(right)* against Purdue made Notre Dame an instant contender for the National Championship.

4

Michigan State recruited players from across the country and across racial barriers to assemble the best team possible. *Left to Right:* Bob Apisa from Hawaii, Clinton Jones from Ohio, Bubba Smith and Gene Washington from Texas, and George Webster from South Carolina.

5

6

Charlie "Dog" Thornhill found a home at linebacker, and galvanized the Spartan defense with his ferocity.

Safety Jess Phillips may have been the hardest hitter on a team of hard hitters.

Notre Dame's Friday night pep rallies in the old field house left students literally hanging from the rafters.

The Irish backfield was led by Bob "Rocky" Bleier, Larry Conjar, and All-American Nick Eddy.

Opposite: Quarterbacks Terry Hanratty *(left)* and Coley O'Brien *(right)* battled against each other before the season began, but were both needed before it was over.

Quarterback Jimmy Raye *(right)* decided to go to Michigan State because Duffy Daugherty *(left)*, unlike many other coaches, said he could lead the team if he won the job.

11

12

13

The Spartans were led by senior cocaptains
Clinton Jones *(top left)* and George
Webster *(top right)*, but Bubba Smith
(bottom) was the team's unofficial
spokesman.

14 Notre Dame's huge defensive line included *(left to right):* Alan Page, Kevin Hardy, Pete Duranko, and Tom Rhoads.

15

The Irish defense was led by team captain and senior All-American middle linebacker Jim Lynch.

Defensive mastermind John Ray was so ruthless in motivating his players that Alan Page called him, affectionately, "the meanest white man I know."

16

Terry Hanratty, protecting the ball here from Michigan State's Sterling Armstrong after being brought down by George Webster and Jess Phillips, injured his shoulder in the first quarter and was forced to leave the game.

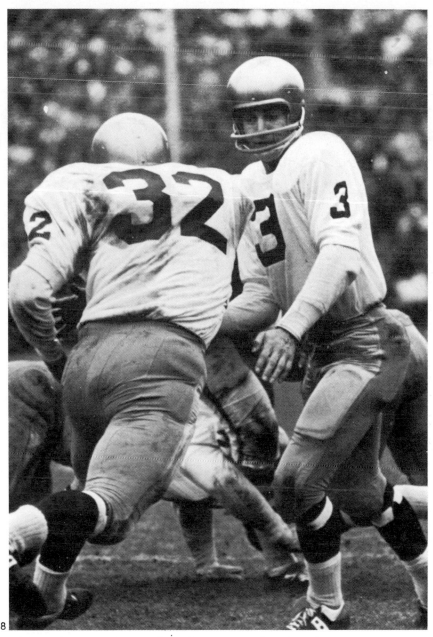

18

Coley O'Brien, who replaced Hanratty, hands off to Larry Conjar, the fullback known as "the crushing Croatian."

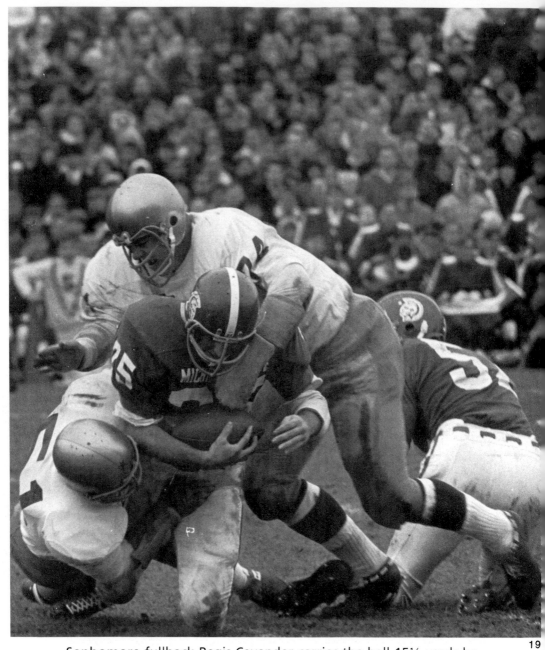

Sophomore fullback Regis Cavender carries the ball 15½ yards before being brought down by John Horney and Kevin Hardy to set up a crucial fourth-down play in the fourth quarter.

Joe Azzaro's 28-yard field goal past the outstretched arms of George Chatlos in the fourth quarter tied the score at 10–10.

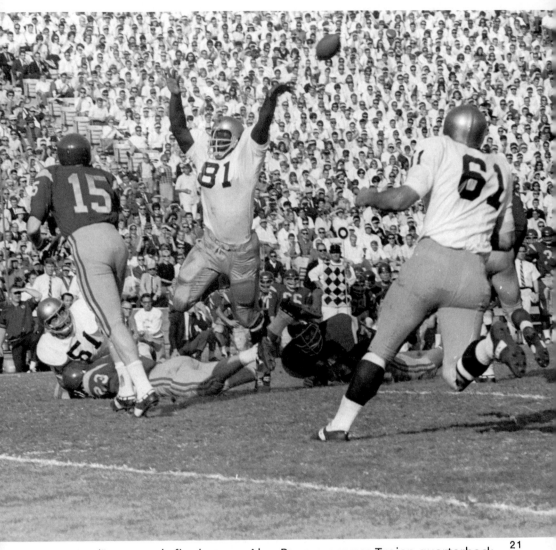

In the season's final game, Alan Page pressures Trojan quarterback Troy Winslow, helping the Irish to destroy Southern Cal 51–0 and convince the UPI voters that Notre Dame should be named National Champions.

Danny Talbott, another triple threat who accounted for much of the team's yardage with his running and passing.

Talbott lasted less than a quarter before he was sent to the sidelines with a sprained right ankle. Jeff Beaver replaced him and immediately completed a 14-yard pass. Then his day ended with a separated shoulder, and the Tar Heels were down to Tim Karrs, a reserve fullback who had never played college quarterback before.

Defensively, North Carolina, which didn't know Hanratty had a sore arm, was determined to stop Jim Seymour. They double- and triple-teamed him everywhere he went. The strategy worked, too. For all of the first quarter and half of the second, Seymour, who had caught 30 passes in his first three games, didn't catch a single pass. They also didn't allow Notre Dame to move the ball in its first two series.

Then on Notre Dame's third possession the Irish started moving. Conjar ripped for gains of 8, 14, and 11 yards. Eddy slashed for 16. Once, on third-and-8, Hanratty had to throw, but instead of going to Seymour, he went to tight end Don Gmitter, who made one of the two catches he had all year. Conjar went the final 3 yards, Azzaro kicked the point, and it was 7–0 with 1:54 left in the quarter.

Talbott went down on the ensuing series while being sacked by Lynch. Beaver followed him a play later, and Karrs came in and finished his first series by being sacked for 15 yards. Now Hanratty fired to Eddy for 12, handed to Conjar up the middle, first for 20 and then for 11 more before it was Eddy's turn to carry for 8 more to the North Carolina 4. Three plays later, Conjar scored again. When Azzaro missed the point, it was 13–0 with 10:27 to go in the half.

North Carolina tried again and managed to get two first downs before halfback Dick Wesolowski fumbled a handoff. Kevin Hardy jumped on it, and the Irish had the ball again. By now the Tar Heels were tired of watching Conjar bust through gaping holes while one-fourth of the defense was chasing Seymour around the field. With Notre Dame at its own 44, North Carolina switched back into its normal defense, a run-stuffing 5-4. Hanratty brought the team to the line and recognized the situation immediately. With nine defenders crowding the line of scrimmage, North Carolina had only two defensive backs, and only one of them could cover Seymour. Hanratty's arm was hurting, but he couldn't pass this up. He discarded the play he had called in the huddle and called Seymour's number at the line. Hanratty faked a handoff to Bleier to freeze the defense, dropped back to his 35, and let fly. Fifty-three yards later, the ball's trajectory intersected with Seymour, who took it in full stride at the 13, stepped away from a diving tackler, and strolled into the end zone.

It was the only play all day on which the Tar Heels left Seymour with single coverage, and it was the only pass Seymour caught.

In the third quarter Notre Dame went back to the ground, and for the third time in four games Nick Eddy put down one for the highlight films. With four minutes to go in the period, John Pergine had intercepted a Karrs pass and returned it to the Notre Dame 48. On the first play Hanratty handed to Eddy who cut off left tackle, faked a move inside, cut to the left sideline, cut back to the inside, and with nearly everyone on the team cutting down defenders left and right, took it into the end zone untouched. The blocking on the run was so thorough that even Seymour, who disliked blocking more than a cat hates mud baths, cut somebody down.

With the score 26–0, Parseghian sent in the reserves. He had spent a lot of time during the past two weeks complaining about the performance of his second unit and even more time working them over on the practice field. Now Coley O'Brien and the rest of the backups showed that they were learning their craft. O'Brien completed 4 of 5 passes, including 2 to Harpo Gladieux for 50 yards, and the second team pushed a final touchdown across for the 32–0 final and Notre Dame's second consecutive shutout.

Hanratty had completed only 5 of 11 passes, and Notre Dame's passing attack netted a modest 183 yards. But they had rung up 432 yards of total offense to bring their average for four games to 429.5 yards, the second highest total in the country behind UCLA's 431.2 yards per game. Their 238.5 yards per game passing total was good for fourth in the nation behind a trio of pass-happy lightweights—Tulsa, Texas Western, and Louisville. Michigan State wasn't among the Top Ten in any offensive category.

The voters in the polls considered all of this, and when the new rankings came out on Monday, Notre Dame was number one.

Ara took the news tactfully. "I see no reason why we should be ahead of three or four teams, and on the other hand, why they should be ahead of us," he said, covering all the bases.

Duffy was less diplomatic, and with reason. Normally, once a team got to the top of the polls, it stayed there until it lost. That's the way it worked in boxing. If you wanted to be champ, you had to beat the champ, and no one had beaten Michigan State. The Spartans had won but apparently not impressively enough, at least not for the voters who didn't know and didn't want to know about three inches of mud and an Ohio State team that had been practicing for one mighty effort for six months. All they saw was Michigan State 11, Ohio State 8, and Notre Dame 32, North Carolina 0. They also saw a Michigan State team that had had to come from behind more than once, that had had trouble scoring in the first quarter, that had shown an inconsistent passing game. Then they looked at Notre Dame and saw a juggernaut.

The Michigan State players knew how the media—and thus the voters—worked. It was a fact of life that Notre Dame was the darling of the media in New York, the media capital of the nation, and was also almost the home team in Chicago, the Midwest media center. Neither of these two great cities had a major football power to call its own. Chicago adopted Notre Dame because of geographic proximity. New York had come to embrace the team over the decades since the Irish arrived at West Point in 1913 and introduced the nation to the modern passing attack. Over the years Notre Dame had returned regularly for its series of great games against Army in Yankee Stadium; New York's great population of Catholic immigrants took the team as its own and came to be known as the subway alumni. Rockne had charmed the writers in his day, who repaid his attentions by making him a legend. And when Army surrendered its place atop the Eastern football world, Notre Dame replaced it. Given a choice between Notre Dame and any other team, the New York writers, many of whom were of Catholic immigrant stock, were going with the Irish. It didn't matter if the southern block was as anti–Notre Dame as the Eastern block was pro–Notre Dame. There were more writers with more influence in New York than there were in the rest of the country combined.

The Spartans didn't like it, but they couldn't do a thing about it. They hadn't lost a game and had lost the top ranking. Such things happen when championships are decided by popularity contests, especially when one of the contestants looks a little bit shaky and the other contender is Notre Dame.

"It was us against the world anyway," one Spartan said, and he was right. They were considered the outlaws, and Notre Dame could do no wrong. The Spartans didn't like it, though. They felt that Notre Dame had been intentionally running up scores just to get the top ranking. That wasn't true, but that's what they thought. It's what they still think.

"I've always thought the object of the game was to win," Duffy protested. "Apparently, they expect more of us."

The complaints did no good. And Michigan State knew it. What's more, they decided they didn't care. They would get their chance to straighten out the pollsters in their final game. In the meantime, they had to worry about Purdue.

9

Those weren't jiggles. Those were ripples.

—Jim Riley

Notre Dame went into the week of October 16 as one of nine undefeated teams in the nation. In order of ranking they were Notre Dame, Michigan State, UCLA, Alabama, Southern Cal, Georgia Tech, Nebraska, Florida, and Oklahoma. Purdue, ranked ninth, was the only team in the Top Ten with a loss. Alabama, alone among the undefeateds, did not have any of the other eight teams on its schedule. Notre Dame still had to face three of them: Oklahoma, Michigan State, and USC Oklahoma was scheduled for that Saturday, October 22, the fourth undefeated opponent in five games for the Irish.

The rest of the nation was starting to think seriously that the season could come down to the November 19 showdown with Michigan State, but Parseghian and his staff had no trouble concentrating on Oklahoma. No team they had played yet, including Purdue, concerned them as much as the Sooners. Some of that concern was generated by the unknown. Notre Dame hadn't played Oklahoma since 1962, before Parseghian took over. They hadn't been highly rated going into the season, but under first-year coach Jim MacKenzie they were one of the major surprises of the year. MacKenzie, who had been a first assistant at Arkansas, had a theory that small, fast, superbly conditioned athletes were superior to bigger but slower players. One of the first things he did when he went in was put his team on a diet until they were all as lean and sinewy as college wrestlers. Jim Riley, a defensive tackle who played at 270 pounds in the pros, dropped below 230 for MacKenzie. Oklahoma's middle guard on defense, a marvelously quick and agile star with the equally marvelous name of Granville Liggins, was sent in against offensive guards and centers with barely 200 pounds on his frame.

MacKenzie wasn't the only one who had fallen in love with the theory that quick and small was better than slow and big—Duffy Daugherty shared some of the same ideas—but he had taken it to an extreme. For four games the formula had worked. Oklahoma had beaten its opponents by an average score of 25–5. Now he told his team not to be impressed by the monsters on Notre Dame's offensive and defensive lines. They were fat and they were slow, and Oklahoma was lean and quick.

None was quicker than Liggins, who didn't bother running through blockers. He simply leaped over their heads or spun around them. His nickname was the "Chocolate Cheetah," and when the offensive line watched the films of Oklahoma at the beginning of the week, Liggins would have looked like the fastest man alive except for the fact that everyone else on the Sooner team looked just as fast. The defense, watching films of Sooner quarterback Bobby Warmack, receivers Ben Hart and Eddie Hinton, and halfback Ron Shotts, had the same impression.

While the Notre Dame players gasped at the team speed they saw on the films, their coaches enjoyed a silent chuckle because they knew the films were running at a higher speed than usual.

That was the first volley in the psychological war the coaches were going to wage with their own players that week. The second volley came on Monday when Parseghian gathered the team at practice to give out the weekly awards. Accolades went to offensive backs and linemen and to defensive backs and linebackers, but none went to the defensive line. Sure, they had rung up another shutout, but they had surrendered 121 net yards rushing to North Carolina, and that was unacceptable.

Those were just the preliminaries. Then the coaches got serious. Ray moved Duranko off the first team defense. Pete had been hampered by a bum ankle all year, and the coaches had laid off. But now Ray wanted him to know he had to pick it up. For good measure, Ray also booted Hardy off the first team for a day. On offense, word was sent through Joe Doyle, the *South Bend Tribune* writer, that Regner hadn't been working to his capabilities. Just in case reading that in the papers wasn't enough to get Regner cranked, Jerry Wampfler, the line coach, kicked Regner off the first team.

Regner hadn't liked Wampfler from the first day of spring practice when Jerry was introduced as the new offensive line coach, and the demotion stung deeply. Regner and the other upperclassmen on the line had learned their blocking under Doc Urich, Ara's first line coach with the Irish. Wampfler had played tackle for Ara at the University of Miami of Ohio from 1951 to 1953. After college he coached high school ball in Ohio, until 1963 when he went back to Miami and became an assistant to Bo Schembechler who had succeeded Ara. While there, Wampfler continued to develop his theories of blocking, which he finally brought to Parseghian when Urich left.

Ara made Wampfler work hard for the job, and with good reason. Jerry wanted to totally change the schemes and philosophy of the offensive line, which was a bold move considering that Urich had built one of the better lines in the country. Wampfler knew he was going to have to sell Parseghian on the changes, and he had discussed his strategy with Schembechler before going to South Bend. "You have to get in and sell it," Bo told him. "If you don't sell it and you don't believe in it, you'd better not go there."

So Wampfler sold it. For an entire day he talked about his theories, and when it was time for Parseghian to go home, he told Wampfler to stick around and come back the next day for another session. They talked and they argued and they yelled at each other. Finally, Parseghian looked at Wampfler and said, "You believe in this very strongly."

"Yes, I do," Wampfler said.

"He sat there and looked at me with those snake eyes of his for about five minutes," Wampfler said. Finally, Parseghian broke the silence. "Okay, you have the job." Then he added either a warning or a promise: "It's your baby, and if this works, I'll be the first one to pat you on the back. But if it screws us up, I will fire your ass. I don't give a damn if you played for me or not. If you screw it up, you're gone."

The sophomores on the line didn't have major problems with his philosophies, but the seniors—Regner, center George Goeddeke, and tight end Don Gmitter—went along with the program only grudgingly. They figured as long as they were getting the job done, who cared how they did it? Wampfler cared. "You could block the guy halfway to the sideline, but that didn't suffice. If you didn't knock him in the nickel seats, he didn't want you out there," Goeddeke said of Wampfler. "He was hell-bent." However much they disagreed on technique, when they got on the field, they were implacable.

Of the three, Goeddeke was the most famous, at least on campus. He was big at 6 feet 3 and 228, but probably heavier than that. But what really set him off was his hair, of which he had none. He had had Nick Eddy, who, like Hanratty, gave haircuts for a buck a head, shave his head the previous spring for St. Patrick's Day. Only not all of it was shaved. He had Eddy leave furry shamrocks on each side of his head, which Eddy's wife dyed green with food coloring. After painting the town green, Goeddeke had Eddy shave his head completely, leading to one of his nicknames: "Mr. Clean." His other nickname was "Mouse."

Goeddeke was from Detroit, where he grew up in a family of twelve children. He was the crazy kid in the family and claimed it was his duty to be wild because he had two brothers and two sisters in religious orders, and they needed someone to pray for. Given his personality, no one really thought Goeddeke was likely to pay attention to the rules. Goeddeke smoked a pack a day during the off-season and liked a beer now and then, sometimes more now than then. He'd show up on the first day of fall practice, stroll into the locker room, and exclaim: "Jesus Christ! Is it football season already?" Then he'd go out and get in his stance, and his fingers would be stained with nicotine. He knew the coaches could see it, and they made him pay by working him until his tongue was down to his knees. When asked whether he had done his summer conditioning work, he'd declare, "I ran around the block once in June, once in July, and once in August. I'm ready."

"The first couple of practices, we'd almost have to take him to the undertaker," teammate Ron Jeziorski said. But as bad as he was hurting, he remained a fountain of good cheer. And after a week or so of double sessions, he was a positive inspiration. Double sessions were a football player's hell, especially in the days before year-round conditioning programs. It was the time when the coaches flogged them into shape, and after a week or ten days, the players were hurting in places they didn't know existed. The locker room before an afternoon session looked like death row, with the condemned staring glumly at the floor, wondering why the guards didn't just shoot them now and get it over with. Suddenly they'd hear a noise like a 230-pound chicken, and George would come pushing one of the cloth-sided carts that they threw their dirty clothes in. He'd have a red coxcomb on his head and a wattle hanging from his neck. He'd be cackling and crowing and jerking his head this way and that, and they'd all crack up. Sometimes instead of being a rooster, he'd make like a baboon.

Parseghian knew Goeddeke didn't obey every rule, but unlike Dave Pivec, the unlucky player Parseghian had thrown off the team in 1964 for drinking, George didn't get caught. He'd drive a few extra miles up to Michigan to raise his hell, figuring that the coaches wouldn't roam that far afield looking for him. The truth was that Goeddeke played so hard and was so great for team morale that they let him be himself as long as he performed. In 1965, on the eve of the seventh game of the season, he showed how far he'd go. Struck with appendicitis, George went into the hospital and had the offending organ removed, a procedure that was then major surgery. He missed that game and the next game, but thirteen days later and 25 pounds lighter, he was back in the starting lineup.

Parseghian loved Goeddeke. Loved his spirit, loved his sense of fun, loved his fierce loyalty to friends and school, loved the way he played the game. He and George had a little game they'd play. Whenever George got dinged on the practice field, he'd grab his knee and start howling. It didn't matter where he was hurt, he'd always grab his knee.

"Where are you hurt, George?" Ara would ask.

"It's my arm, Coach," he'd say, hanging on to his knee.

"How's your knee?"

"My knee's fine, Coach."

And so it went. His teammates swear that when George got appendicitis, he doubled over in pain and grabbed his knee.

Goeddeke was the class clown. Regner was just the big guy. At 270 pounds, he was as big as they came on the offensive line, and the breadth of his shoulders combined with his shortness of neck prompted his teammates to call him "Peahead" and "Turtle." Tom grew up in Kenosha, Wisconsin, where he played for St. Joseph's High School, a small Catholic school. When he arrived at Notre Dame, he brought some extra baggage in the form of a backhanded challenge that came from some of the coaches in his high school conference. Regner, the word was, would never make it in college because he wasn't mean enough, and even if he was, he'd never get through college because he wasn't smart enough.

When Regner saw the size of his teammates at Notre Dame, he initially thought his critics might be right. When his teammates saw him, they had to agree. "He was funny looking," says Gmitter. "He had this massive neck, a little head, these little black glasses, a crew cut, and a baby complexion. Somebody looked at him and said, 'What a waste of a scholarship.' "

Then they went on the field, and Regner was lined up against Alan Page. Regner destroyed Page, and they brought in Kevin Hardy. Regner destroyed Hardy, too. It was about then that somebody remarked, "Some waste of a scholarship."

"Nobody hurt more, and I faced them all," Ron Jeziorski testified.

He put the big hurt on everyone he faced for three varsity years, and when he was done he was not only a first-team All American, he was an academic All American as well.

The job of blocking Granville Liggins would fall mainly to these remarkable specimens, Regner and Goeddeke. Dick Swatland, another senior who played right guard, would also be called on to help, but because Liggins liked to start over center and work to his right, he would be mostly involved on Regner's side of the line.

To give Goeddeke, Regner, and Swatland an idea of what Liggins would do, the middle of the offensive line went full contact all week with two senior reserve linebackers, Leo Collins and Ron Jeziorski, playing Liggins. The coaches tutored both reserves in all of Liggins's tricks and had them head-slapping and leap-frogging Goeddeke, and spinning like wild men. The offensive line beat Collins and Jeziorski to pulps. They hit them high, leg-whipped them, did everything but drop a piano on them, and the two prep squadders just kept on coming like a bad hangover. Regner, working with the second unit, wasted a dozen white rocks during the week until Wampfler finally decided that Regner had worked into a suitably homicidal state of mind to merit his return to the varsity.

On the defensive side of the ball, Ray was playing the same sorts of games with Hardy and Duranko. By Friday when the team left for Oklahoma, and Regner, Duranko, and Hardy were all restored to the first units, the Irish were as ready as they could be. They boarded a charter jet at South Bend Airport that was supposed to fly them directly to Will Rogers Airport in Oklahoma City. Then the real fun began.

The chartered jet hadn't been in the air a half hour when the pilot came on the intercom to inform the team that he had equipment problems with the plane and would have to divert to Chicago's O'Hare Airport for repairs. As soon as he made the announcement, Larry Conjar, who was no great fan of flying, announced to everyone that he had had a dream the night before: Their plane was going to go down in Lake Michigan, and he couldn't swim and was going to drown. They looked out the window, and sure enough, they were swinging over the lake on their approach to Chicago.

They landed safely, though, and the problem—a balky auto-pilot gyroscope—was repaired. Then they sat on the runway for the usual O'Hare ground delay and finally got into Oklahoma City, where they would stay the night before the game, two hours late. They got off the plane figuring they had licked that little problem and climbed on the two chartered buses that were waiting to take them to their hotel, varsity on one, subs on the other. They had hardly settled in their seats when a driver regretfully informed them that one of the buses had broken down and they would have to transfer to the remaining bus that would take them —standing in the aisles—to the hotel.

Ara Parseghian was not a particularly superstitious man, but he was starting to get bad vibes about the trip, fearing that the plane and the bus were trying to tell him something about the game the next day. He couldn't think about it long, though. They still had to get to their rooms, have dinner and their evening meeting, and get to bed. When they got to the rooms, they found that some of them hadn't been made up yet. When they got down to dinner, things got even worse. The Irish knew they weren't particularly welcome in Oklahoma and that this game had been trumpeted in the papers for weeks, but it was starting to get ridiculous. First, Parseghian had a minor conniption when he saw big plates of butter on every table. Parseghian, believing that too much butter was bad for a football player, allowed each player only one pat per meal. (He had given orders to that effect to the restaurant.) Then when the waitresses served the steaks, several of them were dropped—accidentally, of course—in players' laps. Ara finally cleared the room of hired help.

They got through dinner and the meeting without further incident and finally retired to their rooms, only to discover that all the rooms faced on a courtyard where exceptionally loud music was being broadcast. Ara called the desk and asked them to turn off the music so his players could sleep. The management complied after a polite wait of about twenty minutes. Again, Ara lay down and closed his eyes, only to have them snap open when new, louder music replaced the previous music. It was the nightclub; Ara's room and those of many of his players were directly over it. Parseghian hit the phone again and demanded that they all be moved. Finally, much later than he would have liked, peace prevailed so they could all sleep.

Saturday morning, the team went to Mass, had breakfast, and listened to Ara's speech, in which he talked about all the things that had happened—how the locals were trying to jinx them and how that wasn't going to happen. In another motel in Oklahoma City, MacKenzie was telling his Sooners about how Notre Dame wasn't the Green Bay Packers as some of the writers were suggesting. Sure they were big, but they were fat and they were slow. The Sooners were small and quick, and the good quick man would beat the big slow man any day.

The Irish climbed on their buses to drive to Norman for the game. This time both buses worked, which was a good thing because it seemed that everywhere they looked they were surrounded by red-clothed Oklahoma fans who made no effort to hide their contempt for the Catholic interlopers. Some of them even brought signs to wave at the bus. Two stuck in Gmitter's mind: KILL THE CATHOLICS and PISS ON THE POPE.

The dislike was mutual. Father Edmund Joyce, Notre Dame's

vice president, had written a letter during the week to Edward W. "Moose" Krause, his athletic director, asking for help with a problem. It seems that Oklahoma's president had asked Joyce to sit with him in the press box during the game, and Joyce had declined "with the excuse that I would be on the Notre Dame side of the field." Joyce's problem was that he really did want to sit in the press box, but now he was trapped. "Are you planning to sit in the press box?" Joyce asked Krause. "If so and a seat is available, I might watch the game with you. However, don't request a special seat for me . . . as I declined to sit in the box with President Cross."

The field itself was another problem. It was built on red clay, a brand of dirt most of the Irish had never seen before. To promote drainage, it had a crown down the center that was so high, if you stood on one sideline and looked across the field, you couldn't see anybody on the other side below the knees. It was something else that Terry Hanratty would have to adjust to when passing.

The Oklahoma fans hooted at them during the warmups, and MacKenzie told his players to look at them as they worked out. "Look at the jiggles on them," MacKenzie said. "Look at their asses jiggle." The Notre Dame players didn't dare take their helmets off for fear of getting hit with the pennies that the fans were throwing at them.

By the time Notre Dame got back into the locker room after their warmups, they were steaming. Larry Conjar gave the only pregame speech of his life. "I feared them the most," Conjar explained. "We were playing in their stadium in front of those damned hillbillies, and we all knew how people can play inspired ball." Then they went out to deal with Granville Liggins and company.

Notre Dame won the toss and elected to receive. The kickoff carried to the 1, where Rocky Bleier fielded it and headed upfield. Ahead of him, Gmitter was among the players in the wedge. As luck would have it, he drew Granville Liggins to block on the kick return. Gmitter was a dogged blocker and rarely missed his man, but this time when he turned around to get Liggins, the Chocolate Cheetah disappeared. "I know I didn't blink my eyes, but I don't know where he went," Gmitter said. "I don't know if he went over me, under me, around me, through me, or what. I just couldn't believe I missed him."

But miss him he did, which is something that Liggins did not do when he encountered Bleier at the 27 and put him down. Notre Dame started out on the ground, and Conjar, Eddy, and Bleier quickly moved them to the Oklahoma 48. But on third-and-3, Hanratty slipped while going back to pass, was forced to run, and gained only a yard. Liggins made the tackle, his third in 6 plays and fourth overall.

After Bleier punted into the end zone, Oklahoma replied with a 3-play series that included 2 incomplete passes and a 2-yard run. The Sooners punted back, and again Notre Dame couldn't move, failing to gain a first down and again punting to the Sooner 22.

After two runs that netted a single yard, Warmack went back to pass again; this time he found Hart for 12 yards and a first down. Another run and pass to Hart gained 15 more yards and another first down at midfield. After an offsides penalty on the Irish and 2 more running plays that lost yardage, Warmack again hit Hart for 12 yards to the Notre Dame 36 and another first down.

The crowd was already starting to smell upset, but now the Notre Dame defense asserted itself. A run was stuffed for no gain, and another Warmack pass fell incomplete. On third-and-10, Warmack dropped back again and rolled to his right, where Alan Page had just shed a blocker and was closing in on him. Rather than take the loss, Warmack flung the ball downfield directly into the arms of Jim Lynch, who caught it on the 30 and brought it back to the 39.

When the Sooner defense came back on the field, they immediately started talking trash to the Notre Dame players. In 1966, Parseghian and most coaches taught their players not to point or talk to the other team. Drill them. Make them wish they'd never met you. Rip their heads off. But do it within the rules, and then get on with business. Their philosophy had been summed up by Paul Brown, the stone-faced coach in the 1950s who had raised the Cleveland Browns to the top of the National Football League. "When you get to the end zone," Brown told his players, "act as if you've been there before."

The Sooners didn't care about being gentlemen athletes. To them and to their fans, Notre Dame represented everything they hated, and now they told the Irish on the field what they thought of them.

The Notre Dame offense responded by opening holes that sprang Hanratty for 5, Conjar for 9, and Bleier for 2 more before Hanratty, on second-and-8 at the Oklahoma 45, dropped back to pass and found Seymour for 17 yards to the 28. After the catch, as Seymour was lying on the ground and the play had been whistled dead, a Sooner leaped in and speared him. The foul was so flagrant, even the Big Eight officials had to throw a flag, and now Notre Dame was on the Oklahoma 14 with a first down. After Conjar failed to gain, Notre Dame picked up 5 more yards without running a play when Liggins jumped the snap count and leaped offsides. Two more plays, a 2-yard run by Eddy and a 2-yard loss by Hanratty, who fell on his own fumble, brought up a fourth-and-5 at the 9-yard line.

Instead of trying a field goal, which was still an uncertain art, Ara decided to go for a touchdown. But when Hanratty's pass was deflected by defensive back Bob Stephenson and fell incomplete, the Sooners had dodged a big bullet.

As the fans celebrated the defensive stand, they had no way of knowing that they had seen everything good that was going to happen that day. Neither team managed to sustain a solid drive until early in the second quarter when the Irish offense came on the field determined to break the scoreless tie. Hanratty, starting at his own 21, threw for 12 yards to Eddy and for 15 more to Bleier. After an incompletion, he found Eddy again for 10 yards down the sideline. He also found a Sooner helmet in his ribs long after he let go of the ball. While Hanratty was being mugged in the backfield, Eddy was run out of bounds by the Oklahoma pursuit. They didn't stop there, though. They didn't stop, in fact, until they ran him over the team bench and into the brick wall that surrounded the playing field. As Eddy remembers it, they were also gouging at his eyes and calling him names. The officials flagged the hit on Hanratty for 15 yards to the Oklahoma 37.

Already reeling, on the next play the Sooners took the one hit they couldn't afford. It was a pass play, and as he had been all day, Liggins was rushing. Liggins had been everything he was advertised to be up to that point—quick and agile. Although he hadn't had a solo tackle since the first series of the game, he kept getting into the backfield and disrupting plays. And he was making George Goeddeke and Tom Regner work overtime. Now the center and guard took care of him once and for all.

As Liggins rushed, Goeddeke stood him up. Liggins started to turn to spin out of the block when Regner threw his 270 pounds into Liggins's legs from behind. "I think we got his Achilles tendon," said Regner. "George had him up, and I just blocked him down and he went down."

It's called a chop block, a technique that has since been outlawed in college football because of the injuries it can cause. In Oklahoma they called it a dirty play, but the block was perfectly legal. Regner was going for Liggins's side, Liggins turned, and Regner crashed down on his leg. "We weren't trying to hurt him. It just happened," said Regner.

But they did hurt him and sent him to the sidelines, and that was the end of Granville Liggins, the Chocolate Cheetah. After Ara Parseghian saw the films of the play Sunday, it also very nearly finished Jerry Wampfler, the offensive line coach who was in charge of teaching blocking techniques to his players. Parseghian had been leading an effort to outlaw injury-causing blocking techniques, the chop block among them. While watching the films of the game, he saw two of his players chop-blocking an opponent and putting him out of the game. Parseghian called Wampfler into his office, closed the door, and went ballistic. He told Wampfler he never wanted to see that kind of play again, that Notre Dame didn't block that way, that Notre Dame didn't intentionally try to hurt the opposition.

Wampfler defended Regner and Goeddeke and took the blame for the incident, telling Parseghian that he had instructed them to chop Liggins. Wampfler had given no such instructions; the two players had simply done what they had to do within the rules. But Wampfler felt he had to protect them, so he absorbed Ara's rage and never mentioned it to the players. He also neglected to pass on Parseghian's instructions not to let it happen again. No sense troubling them with more rules, especially when they might have to do it again someday.

After the session, Joe Doyle, who had heard what had happened, asked Wampfler if he had feared for his job during Parseghian's tirade. "I wasn't afraid of losing my job," Wampfler said. "I was afraid of losing my life."

Oklahoma was in trouble with Liggins in the lineup. As much as he could do on defense, he couldn't help the offense, whose scramble blocking techniques had been quickly solved by Duranko, Hardy, Page, and Rhoads. And without him, as Hanratty and company were about to demonstrate, the defense wasn't going to rest for the rest of the day.

On the play after Liggins left, Hanratty hit Bleier for 20 yards to the Oklahoma 21. Then it was Conjar over left tackle for 6, Bleier through the same hole for 9 to the Sooner 6, Bleier again for 4, and finally Nick Eddy scoring over left end behind a devastating lead block by Conjar, who took on an Oklahoma defender at the 2 and blew him backwards 4 yards into the end zone. Azzaro kicked the point with 8:36 left in the second quarter to make it 7–0.

Eddie Hinton did what he could for the Sooners, taking Azzaro's kick in the end zone and returning it to the 36-yard line, but from there, Wamack ran 3 plays and wound up 8 yards behind where he started. After the punt Notre Dame took over on its own 46, and now it was Bleier over left tackle again for 6, Hanratty to Seymour for 22, Bleier left again for 3, Hanratty to Bleier incomplete, Hanratty to Eddy for 8, Conjar over left guard for 5, Conjar over the middle for 3, Hanratty over left guard for 4. Now it was first and goal on the 3. Oklahoma dug in as best it could, but 3 plays later, Hanratty was in the end zone, and after Azzaro's kick, it was 14–0 with 2:36 left in the half. As the Irish players remember it, the Sooners stopped talking trash about then and played the rest of the game in respectful silence.

Azzaro kicked into the end zone, and this time the Oklahoma drive lasted 2 plays. The first, a run by Warmack, gained a yard. On the second, a delayed handoff to halfback Ron Shotts, Duranko burst into the backfield and clobbered Shotts, separating him from the ball. Dave Martin fell on it at the Oklahoma 21, and Notre Dame was in business again.

After a pass completion to Seymour for 8 yards to the 13 and a loss of a yard by Eddy, Hanratty rolled right and looked for his favorite target in the end zone. Throwing on the run, Hanratty's pass was high. Seymour went up as far as he could in a vain attempt to get it, and as he was coming down, Stephenson hit him from behind in the legs. As Seymour came down, Stephenson slid down his legs and landed on the receiver's left ankle just as Seymour's foot was planting. The impact ripped the ligaments loose in the ankle. Seymour twisted away from the searing pain as he fell, landing on his back and doing a backward roll. As he rolled, he reached with both hands for the ankle.

The joke around the team was that Seymour wasn't particularly tough, at least when it came to blocking, a chore he approached with little enthusiasm. But now he showed how tough he was. Time was running out in the half, and Notre Dame still had a chance to score. To do that they might need their remaining time-outs, and if Seymour stayed on the field writhing in agony as he felt inclined to do under the circumstances, it would cost a time-out. They had all been drilled on what to do if they were injured. Although it runs contrary to today's medical procedures, every player on every team was told the same thing: *Even if you have to crawl on your belly like a reptile, get off the field.* Unless you were unconscious, you got off the field, and the doctors did their work on the sideline while the game went on. The only time a player might stay on the ground was to buy a time-out if the clock was running out and his team was out of time-outs. Sometimes a player might do that even if he weren't injured. Frank Leahy used to have his players practice being injured, a ploy that helped him win a game or two. Once, when one of his players had twice faked injuries in the same game, stopping the clock so that Notre Dame could score—and win—he explained his actions later by saying: "If you looked up and saw Notre Dame losing and time running out, you'd feel hurt, too."

Anyway, Seymour crawled across the end zone, and the team still had its time-out. What Seymour remembers most, however, isn't the pain, which was considerable, but the sound of the Oklahoma fans laughing at him as he crawled and applauding his injury. When he got off the field, the doctors put his foot in an inflatable cast—an innovative medical item that had been developed for wounded soldiers in Vietnam—and prayed that the damage wasn't as severe as it appeared.

Parseghian, meanwhile, sent in Azzaro to try a field goal, his first attempt of the year. He nailed it, hitting it so well that it smacked the scoreboard at the back of the single level of stands and broke some of its lights. Later, someone told Azzaro it was the first time anyone had hit the scoreboard with a kick. Whether it was or not, a week or two later Oklahoma officials sent a letter to the Notre Dame athletic department complaining about the damage.

Azzaro's kick closed out the first half with Notre Dame leading 17–0. Their domination had been near total. Oklahoma's total offense for the half was 45 yards, all but 3 of that total coming on one drive. Notre Dame had answered with twelve first downs, 87 yard rushing, and 115 yards passing. The statistics show that the Sooners had good reason to stop talking, but that didn't stop their fans. Notre Dame went to the locker room under a shower of debris, both verbal and physical.

Although Stephenson's hit on Seymour had been completely clean, Notre Dame carried the memory of it and Oklahoma's spearing, gouging, and bold talk into the locker room with them. While the coaches had their halftime meeting, the players thought about the first half and got even madder. They were so steamed and so impatient to get back to kicking Sooner butt that they didn't have any patience to listen to Parseghian's little speech before he sent them out for the second half.

Ara talked about staying on top of them, about there being just thirty minutes left, and he was getting to the particulars of what they were to look for when Gmitter talked back to Parseghian for the only time in his life: "Why don't you go out, Coach, because we're keyed up enough."

Notre Dame followed its 17-point second quarter with 21 more in the third. By now they knew that Oklahoma's allegedly smaller and faster players were merely smaller. The Irish didn't do anything fancy. "It was like, 'Here we come, try to stop us,' " said Gmitter. "Those 4-yard plays started turning into 6 yards, then 12 yards, then 16 yards." And almost every one of them went over left guard and tackle, behind Regner and Seiler. They would come up to the line, look at the defender over them, and say, "We're comin' again." The Sooners would glare back, thinking, "They were lucky last time." And, boom, they'd drill the guy again, and the two geezers in the striped shirts holding the first-down chains would pick up their equipment and march down the field. For Oklahoma it was like the Bataan Death March in reverse. Before it was over the defenders on the right side of the line had tears in their eyes from the effort and the frustration of trying to stop men who outweighed them by 50 pounds or more each.

Oklahoma got one drive in that quarter, a 44-yard effort that took them to Notre Dame's 27, but a field goal effort on fourth down was wide and short. Notre Dame's third and final touchdown of the quarter was rung up by the second team under Coley O'Brien. After that the fourth quarter was garbage time. The game ended 38–0, Notre Dame's third straight shutout. The Irish had gained 430 yards, 273 of that on the ground, to 158 for Oklahoma, all but 39 of that in the air. Ara had cleared his bench, with nine players carrying the ball for him and six catching at least one pass. Three players intercepted passes, and Notre Dame had had to punt only three times to seven punts for Oklahoma.

The Oklahoma players trudged to their locker room after the game like Napoleon's army retreating from Moscow. When they got inside, they sat down and stared at the floor, broken and disconsolate. They might have stayed that way forever if Riley hadn't spoken up. "Those weren't jiggles," he finally said, harking back to MacKenzie's description of the supposedly fat Notre Damers. "Those were ripples."

The Sooners couldn't help themselves. They had been beaten every which way by a team worlds better than they. They knew it, and there was no sense in denying it. Riley's one-liner was the excuse they needed to stop pretending, so they did the only thing they could: They laughed.

What might have been a scene of unbridled celebration in the Notre Dame locker room was muffled by the injury to Seymour and a knee injury to linebacker Mike McGill. The doctors theorized that Seymour's injury was a sprain and guessed that he would miss one game, but they wouldn't know until X rays were taken in South Bend. Seymour, who was on crutches, said the ankle didn't feel that bad, a sentiment he would change when they took the inflatable cast off in South Bend and the pain that rushed into the joint soared off any scale he had known.

The team dressed quickly, went outside, and got on the buses that would take them directly to the airport. Both buses worked this time, which was a good thing because as they were pulling out they were surrounded by angry Oklahoma fans who took out their frustrations by rocking the buses and pelting them with rocks. The Irish didn't look back as the buses pulled out.

The destruction of Oklahoma ended once and for all the idea that smaller was better on the football field. Small, quick guys still had a place and would continue to give big guys fits, but you couldn't go with a whole team of them, not against a team like Notre Dame, which was big and quick.

If there can be a turning point in an undefeated season, Oklahoma was it for Notre Dame. The team had been genuinely worried about the Sooners, and the ease with which they won convinced them that they were riding something special. "We knew we had crossed the bridge," said Joe Yonto. "Now we had a chance to have a great season."

"After Oklahoma, we felt unstoppable," said Joe Azzaro, "There was so much hype about Oklahoma going into that game, and we weren't quite sure what to expect. They were supposedly the fastest team in America, and they couldn't keep up with us."

While Notre Dame was giving Oklahoma a lesson in the advantages of size and speed over mere speed, Michigan State was finally putting together the kind of dominating performance against Purdue that it expected of itself, the kind of performance that, had it come a week earlier against Ohio State, would have kept the Spartans on top of the polls.

The Spartans didn't score the first time they had the ball, but that was one of the few times the offense failed in front of another standing-room-only crowd of 78,014. It was the third-largest crowd in the university's history, and it was in a festive mood because it was also Homecoming. Adding to the excitement was the fact that Purdue was going into the game undefeated in the Big Ten. The Spartan players and fans knew that if they could knock off the Boilermakers it would virtually assure the achievement of their first goal of that season—winning the Big Ten title for the second straight year.

Purdue won the toss and elected to start the first quarter with a stiff thirty-seven-mile-an-hour wind at their backs, hoping that Bob Griese could pass the team to an early lead. For a moment it even looked as if the strategy would work when the Spartans had to punt into the wind after a brief possession and gave Griese the ball at the Spartan 40-yard line. Griese came out and immediately hit Jim Bierne for a 12-yard gain to the 28. Whatever hopes that raised on the Purdue sidelines were quickly dashed. With Daugherty and Bullough lining Bubba Smith up over center and sending him straight at Griese, the Boilermaker quarterback missed his next 3 passes and 9 of his next 10 in the half. On fourth down Griese tried a 45-yard field goal with the wind howling at his back, but the kick fell short and Michigan State took over on its 20.

Raye, who was supposed to be no match for Griese at quarterback, took over and marched the Spartans 80 yards into the wind in 9 plays. Along the way he drilled a 22-yarder to Clinton Jones and a 19-yard completion to Gene Washington. Dwight Lee picked up the final 3 yards on the ground, and Kenney, who was finally overcoming season-long inconsistencies in his kicking, nailed the extra point to make it 7–0 midway through the first quarter.

It didn't take long for the roof to cave in on Purdue. The beginning of the end came when Purdue fumbled a punt on the 6-yard line and Al Brenner fell on it. The Spartans didn't get a score immediately as Purdue stopped Apisa on fourth-and-a-foot at the goal line. But with the teams changing ends of the field for the second quarter, Griese was forced to punt the ball back from his own end zone after Purdue had picked up only 4 yards in three tries. Griese's punt was blown down by the wind after sailing only 11 yards to the 16. From there Raye rolled left, caught a great block by Brenner, and wriggled into the end zone. Another conversion by Kenney made it 14–0.

The teams traded punts again, and Michigan State won the battle for field position when Kenney's kick rolled out of bounds on the Purdue 6. Now it was George Webster's turn to shine. On a running play Webster crashed into Purdue fullback Perry Williams, who put the ball on the ground at the 16, where Sterling Armstrong pulled it in. From there Raye scrambled for 9 yards, then lobbed a short pass to Apisa at the 5. Apisa did the rest to push the score to 21–0 and set the stage for the halftime celebration.

In the first half Raye had totally turned the tables on Griese. While the Purdue All-American candidate was going 2 for 11 passing, Raye hit on 8 of 15 and began to convince people that maybe the skinny kid from North Carolina might be a decent passer after all. Maybe it was his heroic touchdown drive at Ohio State a week earlier or simply that he was becoming more familiar with the offense and receivers, but whatever the reason, Raye seemed more confident, and it showed on the scoreboard.

The second half was a festival of scoring, with both teams trading touchdowns and threatening to burn out the scoreboard. Bullough and Daugherty moved Bubba back to end in the second half, and without the huge lineman staring at him over center, Griese rediscovered his passing touch, completing 15 of his 18 second-half passes. Unfortunately for Purdue, by the time he got in gear, Michigan State had scored again early in the third quarter to stretch the lead to 28–0. The score came on Michigan State's first possession of the half and covered 61 yards in 9 plays, with the big gainers a 13-yard run by Raye and a 10-yarder by Jones to put the ball on the Purdue 2. From there Apisa bulled over for his second of 3 touchdowns of the day.

The game was out of reach, but Griese at least made the rest of it entertaining. After Michigan State kicked to the 13, Griese completed 6 passes on an 11-play drive that covered 87 yards. Griese got the touchdown himself on a 6-yard run. Purdue coach Jack Mollenkopf, trying to climb back into the game, ordered an onside kick after the touchdown, but his team couldn't get that right either. The kick traveled only 8 of the required 10 yards, and the Spartans took over on the Purdue 48. Raye fired long to Brenner, who wrestled the ball away from two defenders at the 10. From there Apisa needed only 1 carry against the disheartened Purdue defense to make it 35–7.

Now both teams were running up and down the field as if it were a scrimmage. Griese moved Purdue 77 yards in 9 plays to make it 35–13, and Raye came back with a 66-yard drive in 12 plays, with Reggie Cavender getting into the scoring party on a 2-yard smash. After that touchdown Kenney finally missed a conversion, and Michigan State, with 41 points, was finished scoring.

Griese wasn't, not that anyone really cared. He drove for a final touchdown to make the score 41–20 and a little less embarrassing. Even so, Michigan State had scored 6 touchdowns, which was 2 more than either Michigan State or Purdue had scored in any previous game in their long rivalry. Perhaps the best thing about the blowout from Daugherty's point of view was that the wealth of 376 total yards had been spread evenly among all facets of his offense. Jones had gained 67 yards rushing, Raye 40 yards, and Apisa 45 yards, and the team had rushed for 198 altogether. Then there was Raye's passing. He finished with 10 completions in 17 attempts for 159 yards. Wedemeyer added another completion, and the Spartans finished with 168 yards passing, as balanced an attack as they had yet shown.

The defensive statistics showed Purdue with 72 yards rushing —53 by Griese—and 186 passing, but most of that came in the second half when the game was out of reach.

A pleased Daugherty said after the game that Raye had followed the game plan exactly as it had been drawn. The first half, he said, in case someone had not noticed, "was our best of the season."

Mollenkopf claimed to be pleased with his team's ability to move the ball through the air in the second half, but, he said, echoing words he had used earlier in the year after playing Notre Dame, "nobody can run against State."

Michigan State had only Northwestern, Iowa, and Indiana left on its schedule, all weaker teams in the Big Ten. Now at last it was possible to look ahead to November 19 and Notre Dame. Since Purdue had played both of the top teams and had lost to both, Mollenkopf was asked who he thought was better. Mollenkopf sidestepped the question, saying only that "Michigan State seemed to be faster than Notre Dame." Pressed for a prediction, he begged off, saying, "It's going to be a heck of a game."

When the polls came out on Monday, the voters showed that they were more impressed by Notre Dame's win over Oklahoma than they were by Michigan State's blowout of Purdue, and the Irish increased their lead over Michigan State. A reporter asked Daugherty what Notre Dame's continued top ranking meant to Michigan State, and Daugherty snapped back: "I guess it means we're number two." He was asked, as both he and Ara were every day now, about the November 19 meeting of Spartans and Irish, and again he said, "We are not even thinking of Notre Dame."

He was thinking of Notre Dame, though, just as Parseghian was thinking about Michigan State. They couldn't help it. Every day the reporters asked each of them about November 19, and every day they said they weren't thinking about it. If they really weren't, they were the only two people involved with college football in the country who weren't. The two teams were now on opposite ends of a single track, steaming full speed at each other like two runaway locomotives, destined to collide in East Lansing in a storm of noise and sparks that would be heard from one end of the country to the other.

10

I couldn't understand why two snot-nosed kids should be on the cover of Time.

—Terry Hanratty

Is God dead?

Søren Kiekegaard, the Danish philosopher, had introduced the idea in the nineteenth century, and in 1966 the debate, fueled by such seminal theologians as Harvard's Harvey Cox, erupted in the popular media, which became somewhat less popular for even daring to put the question into print. But if there was a single statement that embodied the new intellectual order, this was it. If one could question the existence of God, one could question anything, from the idea that short hair for men was good to the idea that birth control pills for single women meant the end of Western civilization.

At Notre Dame the debate proceeded a bit more slowly. The final word on such subjects could usually be found carved with a Bic pen into the wood veneer top of a study carrel in the library, and on the subject of the health of the deity, the graffito had a two-line answer:

"God is dead"—Kiekegaard.
"Kiekegaard is dead"—God.

The student body's general adherence to tried-and-true values was evidenced in another, more prosaic death. During the week of the Oklahoma game, *The Voice*, the campus newspaper since the spring of 1963, folded, the victim of its own quest to be provocative. The paper had done well at the start, but it lost its credibility on campus in the spring of 1966 when it ran a story charging that the university provided jock courses for its athletes and that certain professors gave athletes better grades than nonathletes. The story was picked up by the national media, embarrassing the school, which traded heavily on its image. Notre Dame's well-oiled public relations department sprang into action and conducted a survey of the courses in question and the grading patterns in them. It found no discrepencies between the grades for athletes and nonathletes, and effectively discredited the stories.

In truth, certain courses were known around the campus as being easy grades, and many athletes sought these courses out. But by 1966, Father Hesburgh's personal mission to upgrade the university had eliminated all but a handful of such courses. The ones that remained were at the undergraduate level, and although athletes did find them easy sources of A's and B's, so did everyone else who needed points on their average.

Anyway, the student body wasn't ready for crusading journalism, especially the sort that was badly done, and *The Voice* died. Plans were announced to start a new newspaper, *The Observer*, which would be edited by Robert Sam Anson, a man who wouldn't back away from controversy, but also a man who dealt with facts. The newspaper he helped establish has existed ever since.

Anson's move to the newspaper meant *The Scholastic* would lose his considerable talents, a loss that was not mourned by the student body at large, which had little taste for his stories about social and racial injustice. The week he went to the newspaper, the magazine ran a cover story on the American military. The story suggested that conscientious objectors to the Vietnam War "have scant rights to call themselves Americans." It also declared that Americans have no right to question the justness of a war but have to accept that they "inevitably have to die in defense of worthless causes, against their wills." An officer in the U. S. Army Reserve saw the article and wrote the magazine: "The Vietniks, Beatniks, Pseudopatriots, and others among the Unwashed student body and faculty failed either to recognize its significance or to appreciate it, but we who are proud of the *God–Country–Notre Dame* tradition congratulate you. . . ."

In 1966 such sentiments could be printed and arouse only a minority of the students. Within four years such an article would have been burned on the main quad. Patriotism, like God, was not yet dead at Notre Dame. Nor were most other traditional values.

That same year a *Teen* magazine poll declared that the "in" things were granny dresses, wire-rimmed glasses, wood and plastic jewelry, long straight hair, pizza, and coffeehouses. At Notre Dame pizza was always in, but the rest of what was called "Mod" culture wasn't. *The Scholastic* ran an item it gleaned from the Northeastern University *News* that began with the admonition: "If you're thinking of growing a beard, forget it." A beard was socially unacceptable except "for a few—who have a small number of acquaintances, who are pretty much loners, and who really don't mind being stared at."

Culturally, the university's sophomore class inaugurated a free film series that would include viewings of *Mein Kampf, Lord of the Flies, The Making of the President: 1960 and 1964, We'll Bury You, October Madness,* and *Let My People Go.* At the theaters the films that dominated the Academy Awards were *A Man for All Seasons, Who's Afraid of Virginia Woolf,* and *The Fortune Cookie.* On Broadway, *Man of La Mancha, Hello, Dolly, Fiddler on the Roof, Cabaret, Mame, Annie Get Your Gun,* and *Wait Until Dark* were all drawing big crowds, while *The Fantasticks* was New York City's longest running show at seven years and counting toward eternity.

These, though, like the debate about the continued good health of the deity, were ongoing things. By far the biggest news on campus in the days after the sack of the Sooners was the cover story in *Time* magazine. There, in profile, were the Baby Bombers themselves, Terrence Hugh Hanratty and Jim Seymour. The headline that slashed across the top right corner of the magazine read: THE POWER OF TALENT & TEAMWORK. In the lower right, on Hanratty's painted shoulder, it said: NOTRE DAME'S SEYMOUR AND HANRATTY. Two years earlier Ara Parseghian had occupied the same cover. Now two of his players took his place.

Parseghian hadn't wanted it. He hadn't particularly liked being on *Time* himself, but having two players—two *sophomores*

—was something no coach wanted to see. He had done everything he could all season to keep the two kids humble, and now
they were on the cover of *Time*. How would his seniors, players
he felt had earned recognition—Eddy, Duranko, Lynch, Page,
Regner, and the rest—feel when they saw two rookies so glori-
fied? How would the kids take it? Hanratty, he was told, was the
youngest person ever to appear on *Time*'s cover.

Ara had gone as far as refusing to allow Hanratty and Seymour
to pose for a *Time* photographer for the cover shot, so the magazine used existing photographs. The pose, Hanratty in the fore-
ground with his helmet off and Seymour higher and behind him
with his helmet on, seemed to have been from a newspaper pho-
tograph taken during the Army game, and the magazine commissioned a painting from it. However, Parseghian did not deny the
magazine's reporter access to the two stars. He had always maintained an open policy toward interviews, and only later in his
career, as the media coverage increased exponentially, would he
declare Fridays before games off-limits to reporters. The *Time*
reporter went to both players' hometowns and spent a lot of time
interviewing Hanratty and less time with Seymour, who remembered being asked only about five questions.

When the story came out, Seymour didn't recognize himself.
He learned, among other things, that he could run a 100-yard
dash in 9.7, a speed he could only dream of. He learned he could
also " 'juke' his hips, dip his shoulder, toss his head, flutter his
eyelashes, and leave a safety man twisted up like a pretzel as he
cuts downfield for a pass. . . ." Don Klosterman of the Houston
Oilers told *Time*, "This boy is the best pro prospect I've ever seen
at any position. I believe he could make any professional team in
the country right now."

"It's all made up," Seymour thought, although it was likely
that Roger Valdiserri had a hand in inventing some of the numbers. Valdiserri was famous for putting a favorable spin on his
players. He was the man who several years later would greet a
skinny quarterback prospect from South River, New Jersey. The
kid, Joe Theismann, had grown up thinking his name was pronounced *Thees*-man. Valdiserri straightened him out immediately. It's *Thighs*-man, Valdiserri said. Rhymes with Heisman.
Joe Theismann never won the Heisman trophy, but it wasn't for
Valdiserri's lack of trying.

"I couldn't understand why I was on the cover of *Time* magazine," Hanratty said. "I couldn't understand why two snot-nosed kids should be on the cover of *Time*. I realize now why. We were Notre Dame. If we played anywhere else, we'd be on the inside sports pages of the newspapers. At Notre Dame, we're on the cover of *Time*."

Within two weeks they would be on the cover of *Sports Illustrated* as well. But as amazed as they were, there were good journalistic reasons for it. Hanratty hit on the biggest one—they were from Notre Dame. But what they had done at Notre Dame was what made them cover boys. In Hanratty's first four games he had thrown for more yards than George Gipp, Harry Stuhldreher of Four Horsemen fame, Heisman trophy winner Johnny Lujack, and Daryle Lamonica had in their best seasons under the Dome. With 178 alumni clubs across the country—not to mention those on foreign shores, including the Notre Dame Club of Rome, Italy —and a radio network that included 245 stations covering 90 percent of the nation, Notre Dame was the one truly national college football team, and the media had learned long ago that they couldn't go wrong writing about the Fighting Irish.

Whatever delight Hanratty and Seymour felt at their distinction was tempered the day the magazine came out by the fact that they had to go to practice and face their teammates. Neither player was sure how he would be received. "The seniors had been there four years working their butts off, and two punk kids are on the cover," Seymour thought. To their relief no one was jealous of them. Rather, the team was as proud of them as their parents were. That didn't stop guys like Goeddeke and Duranko from razzing them silly, but in a locker room, a well-turned insult is the surest sign of affection. The real resentment came from other teams, and for the rest of the season it seemed that every time someone got a chance to drill Seymour or Hanratty, he'd ask politely, "How'd you like that, *cover boy*?"

One reason for the team pride was that the *Time* article heaped lavish praise on the whole team. Army's defensive backfield coach, Ralph Hawkins, was quoted as saying, "At least twelve of those guys will be drafted by the pros." North Carolina athletic director Chuck Erickson called the 1966 Notre Dame team "the strongest Notre Dame team ever."

The article did not play well in East Lansing, where the local heroes had seen their place atop the polls taken over by Notre Dame even though the Spartans had not lost a game. And now Notre Dame was being hailed as a team whose only possible competition was the Green Bay Packers. Larry Werner, sports editor of the *Lansing State News*, shot back:

> Sure, Notre Dame is the No. 1–rated team in the country, and the famous pass-catch duo have impressive statistics, but the question is: have they been tested?
> Hardly.
> The "fabulous" aerial combination has been outstanding in a 26–14 victory over Purdue. No one-sided victory, by any means, over the team that MSU annihilated. . . .
> Northwestern, Army, and North Carolina were bothered by Notre Dame and its passing, but none of these teams are exactly national powers. When Ara Parseghian's end had to play against a rated team, Oklahoma, he left the game with a badly sprained ankle.
> They'll shine against the remaining pushover teams on the Irish schedule, like Navy, Pittsburgh, and Duke. If Seymour is even healthy for these games.
> But Bubba Smith won't let an 18-year-old quarterback give him a stiff arm and complete a pass, and guys like Jess Phillips and Jim Summers won't enjoy getting beaten by a rookie like Seymour.
> In short, Notre Dame will be playing against a good, tough football team on Nov. 19—a sensation they won't have experienced until then.

If Notre Dame had Navy, Pittsburgh, and Duke, the Spartans had their own lineup of pushovers—Northwestern, Iowa, and Indiana—to practice on between then and November 19. If you wanted to split hairs, Michigan State's pushovers were on average tougher teams than Notre Dame's. On the other hand, the *Time* cover gave added incentive to Notre Dame's opponents to knock the cover boys on their gold-plated backsides.

The Phantom jumped on that at the beginning of the last full week in October. The Phantom wrote:

> Fifty percent of your season is over. You are now number one in the country. The five remaining teams will each week repre-

sent an aroused group to steal the mark you've made. If we can keep our heads, never feeling superior, still working to be so, if we can dedicate ourselves to each week's opponent as they come, we can be number one—all the way. This week—Navy!

Navy coach Bill Elias, whose team had lost three straight to Southern Methodist, Air Force, and Syracuse, knew his team wasn't going to win any national titles, so he primed his team to make up for everything by beating Notre Dame.

Elias laid the groundwork for the game, which would be played in dilapidated, old J.F.K. Stadium in Philadelphia in front of more than 70,000 fans, by building up the Irish into the greatest team in history. "This Notre Dame team is every bit as good if not better than Frank Leahy's best teams," Elias said. It was, in fact, he told the writers, "the strongest team ever put on a football field."

Asked whether the Irish had any weaknesses, Elias quipped, "They have not yet blocked a single point after touchdown." Elias was a sportswriter's dream—a man who fed them bright quotes. How would he play Notre Dame? "We're going to play them like David played Goliath. We'll throw stones. They may blow us out of the ballpark, but if we do what other Notre Dame opponents did, we'd be blown out anyway."

Translated, Elias would install a new defense to face Notre Dame, and if Parseghian wanted to know what it was, he'd just have to show up for the game. Elias, like Parseghian, was from Ohio, and the two coaches had played against each other in high school. And like Parseghian, Elias didn't enjoy losing, and after he got done praising Notre Dame, he said as much. "I've never seen a team as high as this team since I've been here," he said of his Midshipmen. "I think we'll win it. Notre Dame is the best college football team I've ever seen as a player or a coach, and we're going to beat them."

Elias had one thing going for him that even he didn't fully appreciate. Seymour, who was as close to an irreplaceable player as Notre Dame had, wouldn't be able to play because of the injury to his ankle. Parseghian's first choice to replace Seymour was Curt Heneghan, whose knee had been well enough for him to play against Army, but he had reinjured the joint. Paul Snow, younger brother of former Notre Dame great Jack Snow, was another possibility, but he got hurt in practice that week. Finally, Kevin Rassas, younger brother of former Notre Dame All-American defensive back Nick Rassas, was moved onto the first unit and wound up sharing time with Stenger.

The offense suffered another loss that week, although this one wasn't due to an injury. During the Oklahoma trip, Hanratty noticed that his roommate, backup quarterback Coley O'Brien, kept getting up all night to go to the bathroom. He suggested that he get himself checked out. O'Brien, who was also feeling unusually fatigued, decided that Hanratty was right and told the coaches about his problem. He was sent for a checkup, and the doctors found he had diabetes. At the time very few athletes with diabetes attempted to compete; it required insulin injections and, during periods of high exertion, high doses of orange juice and candy bars to maintain blood sugar levels. The doctors told O'Brien that he could attempt to continue playing if he wanted, but not until they had stabilized his blood sugar, which would take a couple of weeks. O'Brien said he'd give it a try, but he would not make the Navy trip and third-string quarterback Bob Belden was moved up on the depth chart.

Game day, Saturday, October 29, was a perfect Indian summer day: 70 degrees, clear skies, and brisk, twenty-mile-per-hour winds. Hanratty had performed well in similar conditions all year, but without Seymour it soon became apparent that the Irish passing game wasn't going to click. In fact, against Elias's new defensive wrinkles, nothing worked for Notre Dame early on. Hanratty missed his first 5 passes, and the Irish didn't even get a first down until the first period was nearly over. They managed to score less than six minutes into the game on a 42-yard field goal by Azzaro, but only because Tom Schoen returned a punt from the Navy 42 to the 27. After 3 plays gained only 2 yards, Azzaro kicked the field goal.

Things hadn't started well for Navy either. In their first possession the Midshipmen had come up to the line, took their stances, and did what Elias had told them to do. Don't look at them, Elias had said. Don't let them intimidate you. So they dutifully stared at the hands of the men they would block instead of at their massive bodies. But when the tackle who had to block Duranko tried to concentrate on Duranko's huge hands, he saw the bottom of the pad Pete wore on his forearm. On the pad, the future officer of the Navy saw the letter *D*. His eyes were drawn up a fraction, and he saw *U*, then *R*, and *A*, but before he got the rest of the way up his arm, the ball was snapped. The letters and the forearm went into action, and he found himself contemplating how blue the sky was as he looked up at it from flat on his back. Duranko had no more trouble with him the rest of the day.

After Azzaro's field goal, Navy started to drive, and for a moment it looked as if they might make good on Elias's prediction. The Midshipmen marched to three first downs in a drive that took them from their own 21 to the Notre Dame 35. After losing yardage they got to the 28 on a face-mask penalty against Alan Page, but on fourth-and-2, the Notre Dame defense did its thing and the drive ended. Still, Navy was encouraged. If they could gain 44 yards and three first downs once, surely they could do it again.

Actually, they couldn't. Navy got only two more first downs and 20 more yards the rest of the afternoon. In one brief drive they had gained two-thirds of the yardage they would get all day. For the rest of the game the Navy offense ended their drives by turning the ball over, with their quarterback, John Cartwright, throwing four interceptions, three of which were picked off by John Pergine who was playing in front of a hometown crowd and making the best of it. His first interception, at the end of the first quarter, was deep in Navy territory, and after a Navy player speared him on the ground, the Irish took over on the Navy 12.

From there Conjar scored on a 7-yard run on the first play of the second quarter. With Azzaro kicking the extra point, it was 10–0. And that was it for the scoring in a first half that was hardly vintage for the Irish.

The second half was a different affair. As they had against Oklahoma, Parseghian and his assistants decided to abandon the pass and grind it out on the ground behind Conjar, Eddy, Bleier, and Hanratty. On their first possession of the second half, the Irish drove from the 50, where they had taken over after a punt, to a touchdown in 10 plays, not one of them a pass. Three plays later, Pergine intercepted again, and Notre Dame drove 45 yards in 11 plays for another score, again entirely on the ground. After three quarters, it was 24–0.

It looked as though it would be the fourth straight shutout for Notre Dame. It should have been. Navy could no more move the ball against the Irish defense than the Pentagon could dislodge the Vietcong half a world away. But then, early in the fourth quarter, Bob Gladieux came in to punt in place of Rocky Bleier, who along with Nick Eddy had been knocked out of the game with minor injuries. Gladieux was a competent punter, but he was left-footed, a trait that reversed the blocking schemes on the line. Unfortunately, no one told the line, and a Navy defender broke through, blocked the punt, and Navy fell on the ball in the end zone. The crowd was treated to the rarest sight of the year— one of only five touchdowns scored against the Irish.

Notre Dame would add another touchdown late in the game, but the damage was done. Parseghian was livid on the sidelines. First, Hanratty, who ended the day with a miserable total of four completions and two interceptions in fifteen attempts, had undertaken a foolhardy scramble, and then the offense had compounded it with the biggest sin of all—allowing a blocked kick. And if Parseghian was mad, John Ray was even madder. No matter who allowed the score, it broke the shutout string, which his defense had taken a lot of pride in. Now it was over. They'd pay come Monday. That much was sure.

While Ray and Parseghian were disappointed, the voters in the polls were not. Although Michigan State had beaten Northwestern, 22–0, while holding the Wildcats to only 6 yards rushing, Notre Dame increased its lead over the Spartans in both wire-service polls.

The increased lead was the result of the Spartans' performance. Michigan State had crushed Northwestern defensively. Charlie Thornhill and George Webster each had 13 tackles, and between them had 4 tackles for losses totaling 26 yards. But offensively the Spartans had been listless. After ripping off a 74-yard scoring drive in 11 plays on their first possession, the offense operated only in fits and starts the rest of the way. Five penalties for a whopping 80 yards didn't look very neat against a weak opponent either. The Spartans also scored in the second quarter on a 31-yard pass from Raye, who was 7 for 17 on the day, to Washington. Kenney kicked a 39-yard field goal in the third quarter, and in the final period Raye hit Washington for an 8-yard scoring play at the end of a 17-play, 91-yard drive.

Statistically, the game looked good. Michigan State had 24 first downs to 7 for Northwestern and piled up 254 yards on the ground and 125 in the air compared to 6 rushing and 88 passing for Northwestern. Bum knee and all, Apisa gained 73 yards on 14 carries, while Jones had 72, Lee 60, Raye 29, and Cavender 14 on 4 carries. But with that much yardage, the score should have been higher, a point that Daugherty would drive home during the next week's practice.

The object for both Notre Dame and Michigan State was to stay healthy until November 19, and until October 29, the Spartans had been doing a better job of that than the Irish. George Webster, State's great linebacker, had been hurting all year from a variety of injuries. Once the season began he didn't even practice most weeks, trying to conserve himself for the games. Most players can't perform that way. They need practice to keep their timing and conditioning, but Webster was not a normal player. Week after week he'd somehow show up on game day and make others hurt a lot worse than he did. The other chronic injury for the Spartans was more serious. Bob Apisa, their fullback, was operating on a bum knee, and in the Northwestern game he finally limped off the field, unable to go any farther.

In his place Duffy Daugherty called on a sophomore, Regis Cavender. Cavender wasn't big for a fullback—just 6 feet and 200 pounds. But Daugherty already knew he was as tough as they came. Cavender had shown that his freshman year when, on his first day of practice, they asked him and a few other freshmen to go up to the varsity practice field to run on the scout team. The Spartans were opening that season against UCLA, and they needed someone to play the role of the Bruins' flashy tailback, Mel Farr. Cavender got the job.

Cavender was so nervous he could hardly talk. Growing up in Detroit, he was well aware of the Michigan State defense, and even though the Spartans had not had a good year in 1964, the first sight of Bubba Smith and Harold Lucas, at a combined weight of more than 600 pounds, was enough to take the words away from any freshman. In the huddle the coaches told Cavender that he was just supposed to give the defense a look. As far as he knew, no one would be doing any real tackling, which made him feel somewhat better.

The first play was a pitchout to Cavender around right end. After studying the play on a card, the team went to the line, the quarterback pitched the ball to Cavender, Cavender headed for the corner, and Bubba came steaming across the line and mashed the kid into the grass. Gasping for air, Cavender picked himself up and staggered back to the huddle.

"What's going on?" he asked a coach. "Those guys are hitting full bore."

"Protect yourself," the coach advised, and then he called the same play again.

The second run started the same as the first. Cavender got the ball, looked upfield, and there was Bubba coming at him as if he were a starving wolf and Cavender was a lamb chop. "He's going to kill me," Cavender thought. With that, the instinct of a childhood spent growing up in Detroit took over. Cavender threw the ball away, went after Smith, and wrestled him to the ground, where they rolled around for a while with Cavender swinging and Bubba trying to figure out what manner of maniac he was dealing with. After the coaches pulled them apart, Cavender went back to the huddle, and the scout team, charged up by his display, ripped off 30 or 40 yards in several plays. That started Hank Bullough screaming, and before it was over, the walk-through scrimmage had turned into a free-for-all.

The coaches liked what they saw in Cavender, but Bubba wasn't completely sold, so over the next few weeks he got after the freshman whenever he could. Finally, one hot day, the team broke for Popsicles. It had seemed to Cavender during the grueling workout that the defense hadn't been doing much and the offensive backs were working their tails off, so he wasn't amused when Bubba, who was lying on the ground enjoying his Popsicle, yelled at him: "Rookie!"

When Cavender ignored him, he yelled again. "Hey, rookie, I'm talking to you." After another silence, he tried again, "Hey, punk!"

Cavender looked down at him and sneered, "You look like a beached whale. Why don't you do some work?"

Bubba didn't get up. It was too hot for that. Besides, the next day was defense day, and Cavender would have to run against him. So he just said, "Tomorrow, Cavender. In the stadium."

The next day, in the scrimmage against the defense, Cavender took his position, prepared to carry the ball at Smith. Bubba recognized the formation, realized what was coming, and called across the line: "Here, Cavender, here."

"I remember green," Cavender says, "just green"—the color of Smith's jersey. And he heard a sound coming from Bubba. It was a little snort of a laugh.

In the huddle the coaches called a play on which Cavender was supposed to block Smith. He lined up, and again Bubba called mockingly to him. This time, though, instead of trying to hit Smith high, Cavender drove into his ankles, knocking Bubba over like a sequoia. And even though Smith crashed down directly on top of him, Cavender smiled to himself. "I guess we're even," he said out loud, and from that day on, Bubba had to admit that they were.

Now, a year later, Cavender found himself thrust into a starting role, and being a sophomore and not knowing any better, he didn't realize what a big thing that was. Like Hanratty, he had no trouble with pregame steak-and-eggs breakfasts.

While Michigan State prepared for Iowa, another weak opponent in the Big Ten, Notre Dame looked forward to its own day off against the Pitt Panthers, losers of six of seven games in which they had been outscored 200–67. In 1965, Notre Dame had hung a 69–13 defeat on Pitt, and there was no reason to expect anything different, especially since they'd be playing this one at home on Homecoming Weekend. If nothing else, they'd want to blow away the intruders to impress their girlfriends. Even the 39-point spread set by the few bookies who would take the game didn't look like an unreasonable expectation.

The Phantom's message that week was directed mainly to the offense:

> We were not sharp against Navy. . . . Our offense lacked explosiveness.
> Why can't the Regners, Goeddekes, Conjars, Seilers recognize that four weeks more can immortalize their playing careers, that we have a chance that few others will ever realize in their lifetimes?

With that, Pagna, as The Phantom, laid it out in the open. Duffy Daugherty could tell his team they were going for the Big Ten title, but The Phantom would tell his own boys they were going for nothing less than immortality. He had to say something to keep their interest.

The week before Navy had been complicated by the *Time* cover story. Now, the piece was reduced to a campus joke, thanks to a spoof of the article in *The Scholastic* titled "Babes in Wonderland." Hanratty, the lampoon reported, originally wanted to go to Harvard to study Oriental philosophy, but then, one day "while meditating upon the truths of the Bhagavad Gita, he had a green vision in which one of the wee folk himself appeared, floating on a cloud of shamrocks and wearing a Notre Dame sweatshirt."

People who knew Hanratty, the dedicated "C" student preparing for a career in practical jokes, laughed at that one. But by mid-week the same people were leaping to his defense when a Pittsburgh newspaper, in writing advance stories about the coming game, decided to ask Penn State's rookie head coach, Joe Paterno, how he and his staff managed to let Hanratty, a Pennsylvania boy, get away. Paterno replied that Penn State had tried to recruit Hanratty but that his grades weren't good enough to get into Penn State.

The implication was obvious: Notre Dame had lowered its vaunted standards below even those of a state school to get the recruit it wanted, and all the pious posturing of the Notre Dame publicity mill was just that—posturing. Along with Paterno's allegations came more. There were reports that Notre Dame stocked up on talent by awarding forty and fifty scholarships a year as opposed to the thirty allowed by the Big Ten. Yeah, someone else chimed in, those Notre Damers can do everything with a football except sign it.

In fact, Notre Dame awarded thirty-three scholarships a year, three more than the Big Ten, but far fewer than many other schools. As for academic standards, Notre Dame did indeed bend the line to get Hanratty in, but it did the same for other students it wanted for talents that had nothing to do with athletics. "It's unfortunate," Parseghian said, "that when you are winning there is always someone ready to point an accusing finger at you."

He didn't go beyond that and neither did Hanratty, but both were livid at Paterno, who had begun in his first year as head coach to build his legend as a pillar of honor and integrity surrounded by a cesspool of cheating scoundrels. Hanratty knew that one part of Paterno's story was true. Penn State had contacted him and he had spoken to them. But before things got down to business, Notre Dame came through with a scholarship offer, and Hanratty told Penn State he wasn't interested. The school couldn't have rejected him because he hadn't applied.

South Bend was blanketed with an early six-inch snowfall that Thursday, and Parseghian ran Friday's final practice in the cramped space underneath the grandstands of Notre Dame Stadium. He had hoped to test the condition of Jim Seymour's ankle and had toyed with the idea of starting his split end, who had started running again. But without a dry field to test him, Parseghian decided to go one more week without him.

After spending the week building Homecoming displays and anticipating another blowout, the student body showed up Saturday afternoon in the stadium ready for fun. The temperature had improved to 40 degrees, but there was plenty of snow left in the stands to fuel a pregame snowball fight between the Notre Dame section and the St. Mary's section. Some critics of campus life saw it as a defining moment of the relationship between the two schools' student bodies.

Parseghian had talked all week about how there was no such thing as an easy opponent, about how dangerous Pitt could be. No one, including his own team, believed him.

They should have listened. Pitt came out sky high, and Notre Dame came out at sea level. The Irish took the opening kickoff and marched smartly down the field only to see Eddy fumble the drive away at the Pitt 25. From then until just under five minutes were left in the first half, Notre Dame did nothing. Pitt didn't do anything offensively either—emotion always translates more easily to defensive success than it does to offensive success, especially for a bad team. Finally, with 9:30 left in the half, Notre Dame got a drive going. It took nearly five minutes to complete, and every one of the plays was a run. At the end Hanratty ran the ball in himself from the 3, and with 4:59 to go, Notre Dame finally had a 7–0 lead.

Whatever good feelings the score generated evaporated when word came over the public address system that Michigan State was at the same time blowing out Iowa, 35–7. If the Irish didn't increase the scoring pace, they were in danger of losing their top ranking without losing a game, just as the Spartans had earlier in the season.

There was no more scoring in the first half, and in the second, Notre Dame, properly motivated, promptly restored order. On the opening kickoff Nick Eddy took a skittering kick near the right sideline at his own 15, broke for the middle, bounced off two tacklers, picked up a couple of blockers, cut outside, juked one last defender out of his shoes, and cruised into the end zone for his second touchdown on a kickoff return that year. What made the run more remarkable was that Notre Dame had received only nine kickoffs in seven games and had scored two touchdowns on them.

Eddy's return opened the floodgates. Tom Schoen chipped in a 63-yard punt return for a touchdown; Gladieux scored twice, on a pass and on a run; reserve fullback Paul May scored on another 2-yard pass; Coley O'Brien, his blood sugar stabilized, returned from his week off to direct the last touchdown drive; and when the final gun sounded, the scoreboard registered a Notre Dame–style score: 40–0, a score big enough to offset the 59–7 final Michigan State put up against Iowa.

Eddy's second kickoff return for a touchdown that year against Pitt had tied a school record. Amazingly, it had been only his fourth kickoff return of the year and gave him an average of 48.3 yards per return, a number unsurpassed by Heisman trophy winners Paul Hornung and Tim Brown and All-American wonder Rocket Ismael. What no one knew then was that Eddy would not return another kickoff for Notre Dame.

Eddy had come out of the Pitt game twice with an injured right shoulder. The injury, described as a bruise, was not expected to make him miss any work. Parseghian, like all coaches, didn't believe in resting a player with an injury that was considered minor. He could have done that with Eddy against Duke on November 12, Notre Dame's last game before the showdown with Michigan State. "If a player could play, he played," Parseghian said. It was as simple as that.

But the injury was worse than anyone knew. Diagnostic tests for most injuries were limited to X rays, which could not show the sort of soft tissue damage that is now routinely discovered by Magnetic Resonance Imaging (MRI). The doctors figured if you couldn't see the damage, it probably wasn't that bad. Certainly, Eddy was not going to admit he was really injured. Missing a game could hurt his chances for a big professional contract, and during his senior year, Eddy often thought about what professional football could do for him. It was his ticket out of a life defined more by what he didn't have than by what he had.

Today they'd write stories about Nick Eddy focusing on the difficult life he had growing up. But in 1966 writers stayed away from such stories; they were too personal. Features instead centered on what swell and well-adjusted people college football players were. In those stories someone who tore bars apart every night was "fun-loving." Someone who went through women like Kleenex was "sociable." Anyone who had ever read a book was "a good student." Even Terry Hanratty, who put only as much work into his studies as he needed to stay eligible, was invariably described as being a diligent student. Writers went out of their way to report that he even had a B in Russian, of all things.

Eddy's story was better than most, and barely a word of it ever got into print. Nick Eddy's mother married young, had her only child, and then the marriage went sour. After a difficult divorce, Eddy's mother, a Mexican American, moved to a small northern California town, Tracy, where she managed to find work. Keeping her Irish married name, she raised her son, on whom she doted, alone. The father kept in contact with his son and taught him about Notre Dame. Like so many of his teammates, he listened to Notre Dame games on the radio, but he never thought of going there. He was a homebody and was very attached to his mother. Growing up he had taken a train to visit his father's relatives in Utah, and that had seemed like a million miles away.

Even as a star running back in the Valley Oak League, he didn't think of Notre Dame, and Notre Dame didn't think of him and was not one of the more than one hundred schools that recruited him in high school. But in his junior year of high school he had been coached by Tom "Cowboy" McCormick, a halfback who had played for the Rams and the 49ers in the mid-fifties. McCormick had played his college ball at the University of the Pacific under Joe Kuharich, and when Eddy became a standout as a high school senior, McCormick, who was no longer coaching Eddy, nonetheless gave Kuharich a call and suggested that he offer the kid a scholarship. Sight unseen, Kuharich agreed. He didn't invite Eddy for a recruiting visit and didn't ask for any of his high school game films. He just took McCormick's word, such was the state of college recruiting in 1962. When Kuharich called Eddy and told him a scholarship was waiting for him, Eddy was smitten. "I'm on my way," he said.

He arrived on campus in the fall of 1962 and went through freshman football without incident. In the spring of 1963 he graduated to the ranks of those hoping to make the varsity the following year. What the university called his "family difficulties" arose during that spring practice season, and he had to leave school.

The difficulty had nothing to do with family; it had to do with a cigarette machine in Keenan Hall where he lived. The machine had a habit of taking in money and dispensing nothing, and one of Eddy's friends, who had been victimized by the machine several times, got the idea that he should get even with it. One day South Bend was hit by a freak spring snowstorm and practice was canceled, so Eddy was lying around the dorm with his friend and several others. The friend was consumed by the idea of getting even with the cigarette machine, and he outlined a plot to kidnap it and make it pay for its sins. To do that he needed a few strong bodies to physically move the machine to the dorm elevator. Notre Dame dorms were four stories each, and although each had an elevator, the students weren't allowed to use them except to move their belongings in and out in the spring and fall. Other than those times, the doors remained locked. But the leader of the great cigarette machine caper had gotten hold of a bootleg elevator key. If Eddy, who was big and strong, and another kid, who was a weightlifter, could carry the machine down the hall, he'd open the elevator and they'd take it into the basement, break it open, and no one would be the wiser.

The surprising thing about the scheme was that the co-conspirators were all sober. "It was a stupid prank," Eddy admitted, but he agreed to take part and he shared in the profits from the coin box. The triumph didn't last even one day. By dinner time the hall rector, a Father O'Neil, had learned all about the heist, and the next morning he told Eddy and his partners they had a date with the Dean of Students. O'Neil liked Eddy, as did everyone who met him. Eddy had readily confessed to his role and had voluntarily given back the money, but the university didn't tolerate larceny. Nick Eddy and his partners would have to sit out two semesters. That meant that the spring semester, for which he had already completed most of his classwork, was wiped off the books, and he would miss the fall semester and the football season.

Missing the 1963 football season turned out to be a blessing. Eddy didn't have to suffer through the misery of going 2-7 and also didn't lose the year of eligibility. If he wanted, he could play in 1966, the year after his class graduated. It didn't look like a blessing at the time. Kicked out of school, Eddy had to go home and face his mother, unsure whether she would even let him in the door after the humiliation he had brought on himself and the family. The plane ride back to California was the longest of his life, but when he got home, his mother welcomed him and told him he would take his punishment and go back and get that Notre Dame degree.

He didn't have to return to play football. John McKay, the coach of the USC football team, was one of several coaches who called Eddy and told him he was welcome to play for their schools, and he wouldn't have to miss a year. Indeed, at most schools a little matter like hijacking a cigarette machine wouldn't have gotten a football player any punishment beyond a stern lecture. Eddy told them all the same thing: "No thanks. I made a mistake and I have to go back to Notre Dame and prove to them that I can be a Notre Dame man."

Eddy got a job working for a gas pipeline company. He did some heavy manual labor and a lot of riding around the countryside in trucks looking at pipes. In the fall when Notre Dame played Stanford in Stanford Stadium, he bought a ticket and went to the game. Afterward, they let him in the locker room to see his old teammates, an experience that was more pain than joy. In January 1964, he applied for readmission to Notre Dame and was accepted.

After earning a letter on the 1964 team, Eddy went into 1965 as a certified star. But while all was well on the football field, off it Eddy was miserable. That summer he had started dating a girl with whom he had gone to high school. Jean had been a majorette then, but wasn't aware of the hotshot halfback. She didn't know he had played football for Notre Dame; what's more, she didn't care.

Jean didn't think she cared for him, either, even as they were dating and exchanging daily letters. She thought he was just a good friend; in fact, she was engaged to a local attorney who also happened to be a Notre Dame graduate. But as Nick kept calling and writing and she kept responding, her fiancé finally told her that she wasn't in love with him; she was in love with Nick. Eddy first proposed to her over the phone during preseason practice in 1965. Jean thought it was one of the funniest ideas she had ever heard. But they kept talking and exchanging letters, and Nick finally convinced her that they should get married as soon as possible. He even had a date picked out, October 16, 1965. Picking the date was easy. It was the only open week in the football schedule. Telling the coaches wasn't quite so simple.

Ara Parseghian didn't want his players dating more than once a week, and here was his star halfback standing in his office telling him he wanted to get married—*in the middle of the football season.* Parseghian and Pagna tried to talk Nick out of it, but he couldn't be swayed. Having the coaches mad at him was far preferable to being miserably in love and separated by two thousand miles from his sweetheart. So he got married. In the middle of the football season.

Jean got a job that year, and the couple lived in the university's married student housing on the north fringe of the campus. In the spring when Jean gave birth to their first child, Dr. Nicholas Johns, one of the team doctors, delivered the baby without charge. Today he couldn't do that. NCAA regulations prohibit football players from receiving free services not available to other students. But Eddy had no money, and Johns had never been one to ask a patient how he was going to pay.

After the 1965 season Eddy was drafted in the first round of the American Football League draft by Denver and in the second round of the National Football League draft by Detroit. He still had a year of eligibility, but because his class was graduating, he was eligible for the pros. It was the last year that the NFL and the upstart AFL would operate as rival leagues, which meant it was the last year that the two leagues would get into bidding wars over draft picks. Joe Namath had already shown how much money could be made with the reported $400,000 he received from the AFL New York Jets. Eddy could get a lesser amount that year, or he could play one more year in college and possibly make even more, depending on what kind of season he had. Eddy decided he would play his senior year, if for no other reason than to get his Notre Dame degree.

Eddy's only problem was finding enough money to pay the rent and buy groceries now that his wife had to stay home with their child and couldn't work. His solution was to scalp football tickets. It was illegal, which he knew. He also knew he had to support his family, so he did it. He'd buy the tickets through the athletic department, as football players were allowed to do, and then a friend of his handled the actual resale so that Eddy would not be connected with the operation. The procedure had been taught to him earlier in his college career by an upperclass teammate who did the same thing.

Because he had never had money, getting as much as he could from the pros was important to Eddy, and he was lucky enough to be in the last draft before the AFL and NFL merged in 1966. He used to talk to Pagna about how important it was for him to have an outstanding senior season.

And then, against Pittsburgh, he took a hit and felt the pain shoot through his shoulder. Well, he figured, he'd just have to play through it.

While Notre Dame was celebrating its Homecoming win over Pittsburgh, East Lansing was buzzing with what the Spartans had done to hapless Iowa before 68,711 in Spartan Stadium.

The Spartans took the field determined to make up for their lackluster offensive performance against Northwestern, and although Daugherty denied it, the idea of running up a big, Notre Dame–type score might have occurred to them. In addition, Bob Apisa's knee proved to be in worse condition than the doctors had thought, and he was definitely out of the game. That put the load squarely on Regis Cavender's young shoulders. In case he didn't know what his job was, the campus newspaper ran a picture of Cavender with a huge pair of shoes. The caption read, CAN CAVENDER FILL APISA'S SHOES?

Cavender confessed that he was thinking the same thing. "I felt I had to prove myself," he said. "I have a lot of respect for Bob."

He wasn't the only one. The entire team fell behind their injured fullback, and Clinton Jones told Apisa that he would do everything he could to make up for his absence.

Jones would more than deliver on that promise, but first the Spartans had to spot Iowa an early lead. On Iowa's first play from scrimmage, Ed Podolak pitched to fullback Silas McKinnie around left end, and nobody caught him until he had charged 43 yards to the Michigan State 47. Halfback Tony Williams went 10 yards on a counter on the next play, and then Pokolak passed to Allan Beam for 12. Another pass to Williams picked up 19 to within a yard of the goal line, and from there Williams charged through the befuddled Spartans for a 7–0 lead with only 4:41 gone in the first half.

On the sidelines the defense huddled with Hank Bullough and

determined that Iowa was running its normal plays but was doing it from new formations. "We just got together on the sideline and said to ourselves, 'Let's get together and do a job,'" said George Webster.

While the defense was collecting itself, Raye was getting the touchdown back on a 64-yard drive in 9 plays highlighted by a 15-yard pass to Brenner, a 17-yard dash by Cavender, and a 12-yard scramble by Raye. The quarterback went the final yard himself, but Kenney missed the point after and the Spartans still trailed 7–6.

The Spartans got the ball back just before the end of the first quarter when Webster intercepted a Podolak pass on the Iowa 37. Raye quickly passed for 14 yards to Washington and handed to Cavender for 14 more before Cavender scored on a 1-yard run. The Spartans tried for a 2-point conversion and failed, but they had the lead. The next time they got their hands on the ball, they scored again, this time on one play—a 53-yard pass from Raye to Washington. This time the Spartans tried their Kenney-to-Wedemeyer, 2-point conversion play, which they had used against Ohio State, but failed.

The Spartans had the ball three more times in the first half and scored on every possession, adding a field goal by Kenney from 27 yards out, a spectacular 79-yard run by Jones, and a 10-yard Raye-to-Washington pass. The second touchdown pass to Washington gave him 15 receiving touchdowns for his career, breaking Bob Carey's school record. It wasn't the only record that would fall that day.

Clinton Jones also set a few records. He had gone into the game with a double burden. The first was the knowledge that Apisa would be out, and the second was the gnawing feeling that he hadn't been doing enough for the team in the previous few games. His 3.7-yard-per-carry rushing average suggested he had a reason for that belief. "I just had to do it," he said. "I felt if I didn't perform well, I'd be letting my team down. I didn't want to end the season regretting."

After he got done with Iowa, there wasn't anything to regret. In addition to the 79-yard touchdown run, he had a 70-yarder on the third play of the second half. On the drive after that, he carried eight more times, and by the time he carried the final 2 yards for another touchdown, he had shattered not only Michigan

State's single-game rushing record but the Big Ten's as well. Jones's total for the day was 268 yards on 21 carries for an impressive 12.8 yards per carry.

With the offense scoring points at a record rate, the defense relaxed enough to allow Iowa 150 rushing yards, considerably more than the 41-yards-per-game they had been allowing, and 120 more passing. However, they did not allow Iowa to score again. Once had been enough. The offense, meanwhile, scored 8 touchdowns and a field goal, rolled up 450 yards rushing (Cavender had 110) and 157 more passing, and punted only once the entire afternoon.

The only conceivable negative about the game was the loss of Jones's backup, Frank Waters, who was knocked out while covering an Iowa kickoff return. Although he didn't sustain any major damage, he was unable to relieve Jones late in the game, and Daugherty was left with Ken Heft, a reserve fullback, who had to be taught the halfback plays on the sideline before being sent in.

With the final score 56–7, Daugherty was assaulted in the locker room by writers who wanted to know why he had run it up. He had left his starters in for the first ten minutes of the second half and for all but one of the State scores. "Who did you want me to put in?" he demanded. "Anyone who says I was trying to run it up doesn't know coaching."

He could say that if he wanted. After all, Ara Parseghian said similar things about some of the scores his team produced. But if he did say it, he relinquished his right to criticize Notre Dame's big scores. And though the Michigan State writers would continue to lay that charge on Notre Dame, they didn't have a leg to stand on either. If the polls were impressed by big scores, then both teams would have to play along, and pity the poor souls who got in their way.

And the next batch of poor souls belonged to Indiana, the last obstacle to another unbeaten Big Ten campaign and the last team standing between Michigan State and the November 19 date with Notre Dame. The game was in Bloomington, and even at home the Hoosiers could draw only 30,096 fans to see the home team get whipped.

The final score was 37–19, but it could have been a lot worse if Daugherty, looking ahead now and wanting to keep everyone healthy, had not pulled his starters early to rest them for Notre Dame. The defense was again death to running backs, holding Indiana to − 10 yards rushing, but if Notre Dame was looking for a ray of light, Indiana quarterback Frank Stavroff provided it by completing 23 of 36 passes for 316 yards. The yardage set a Big Ten record, surpassing the 310 yards Iowa's Gary Snook had piled up against Purdue two years earlier. And if Stavroff could pass for that much yardage, the experts thought that Terry Hanratty might be able to double it the following week.

Michigan State scored first on a 73-yard drive that ended with Cavender again proving his worth by taking a pitch from Raye around left end for 14 yards and a touchdown. The Spartans scored again early in the second period when Dwight Lee capped a 62-yard drive by taking an 8-yard pass from Raye into the end zone. Then Brenner, who had proved that his early season success returning punts was no fluke, started the next drive by bringing a punt back 38 yards and ended it by catching a 29-yard touchdown strike from Raye, who would throw only 9 times but would complete 7 of them for 173 yards and 3 touchdowns.

Brenner's touchdown brought the score to 20–0, and on the next drive Stavroff gave faint and momentary hope to the home crowd by throwing 24 yards over the Spartan rush to Al Gage, who took it into the end zone and cut the lead to 20–7. The touchdown revved up the Indiana defense, who charged onto the field and promptly forced Michigan State to punt. But they had hardly started celebrating when John Ginter fumbled the punt and Tony Conti recovered at the Indiana 32. From there Raye needed only 2 plays to get into the end zone, with Cavender running for the score. Then, with only twenty-four seconds to play in the half, Michigan State took over after a punt on their own 13. Instead of running out the clock, Raye went for it all with one big heave to Washington, who was 5 yards in the clear when he caught the ball 64 yards downfield, lost his balance, and fell. With time running out, Kenney made the best of the situation by booting a 27-yard field goal.

In the second half Stavroff put 2 more touchdowns on the board while the Spartans answered with one of their own, on a 29-yard pass from Raye to Washington on the first drive of the half. After that it was just a matter of surviving until the final gun and getting ready for Notre Dame.

Robert Markus, writing for the *Chicago Tribune*, sounded the properly sober note for what was to come with his game story out of Bloomington:

> Bring on the thunder, the Spartans are ready!
> Michigan State's muscular giants claimed their second successive Big Ten title today when they brushed aside Indiana's challenge with the ease of an elephant stomping on an ant. The final score was 37–19, and it could have been worse.
> So now Michigan State, having won 14 consecutive [conference] games and owning a 9-0 record this season against all opponents, goes home to meet the challenge of mighty Notre Dame.
> And if the Irish are preparing to shake down any thunder from the sky, they'd better know this: Michigan State will return aerial lightning for thunder.

Other than Apisa's knee, the Spartans would go into the game at full strength, and Cavender had already shown that he was a capable substitute. Jones, who had gained 97 yards against Indiana on 20 carries, also seemed to be in top form, and Raye was hitting passes at a rate that would make any coach happy. The only injury suffered during the Indiana game had been to tackle Joe Przybycki, and since it happened to his head, it wasn't considered the least bit serious. In fact, the Spartans, enjoying their romp through Bloomington, found it downright funny. Przybycki had had his bell rung chasing a loose ball that eventually wound up in Hoosier hands. He made it off the field all right, but he didn't feel real certain about where he was. Being a good football player, he didn't tell anyone, and when the offense went back on the field, he jogged out with them, only instead of joining his own huddle, he wandered into Indiana's defensive huddle. He was pointed to the proper huddle, but on the following plays he kept trying to rejoin the Indiana defense. The coaches finally took him out and gave him the rest of the day off, which he spent on the bench enduring bad jokes not only from the Indiana fans behind the bench but from his own teammates. With a name like Przybycki, it was about what he had come to expect.

Duke went to Notre Dame that week thinking that, despite its 4-4 record, it could beat the mighty Irish. The Blue Devils hadn't started the week that way. Years later Bob Foyle, the team's nose guard, met Rocky Bleier and told him that when coach Tom Harp told the team they could beat Notre Dame, the players didn't know whether to laugh or cry. But Harp persisted. "We've studied their films," he said. "We know when they're going to pass and when they're going to run. If we know that, we can shut them down."

Harp explained that on running plays, George Goeddeke, Notre Dame's center, would get into his stance on the balls of his feet. On a passing play he settled back on his heels. It was a subtle difference, but if Foyle, who would be playing over Goeddeke, could learn to recognize the difference in the stance, he could tell the defense what was coming.

Harp was persuasive, and that week during practice Foyle learned to crane his head around the scout team center who was imitating Goeddeke. When Goeddeke was on his toes, Foyle would yell *"Meat,"* and the defense, which included All-American and future pro linebacker Bob Matheson, would shift to stop the run. When Goeddeke settled on his heels, Foyle yelled *"Black,"* and the defense got ready for a pass. At the end of the week the Blue Devils flew to South Bend convinced that they would win.

"Only one problem," Foyle told Bleier. "They forgot to tell us about Notre Dame Stadium and all the noise the fans made. So they start the game, and I'm looking around Goeddeke and he's looking at me like I'm some kind of jerk. I'm yelling 'Meat! Meat!' and nobody can hear me."

On the first play of the game Conjar gained 4 yards up the middle. On the second play Hanratty dropped back as if to pass and handed to Eddy on a delay, and all the meat in Durham couldn't combine to get as much as a finger on him as he raced 77 yards for a touchdown that gave Notre Dame its first score a minute into the game. To make matters worse, Duke jumped offsides on the point-after attempt, and so Parseghian took the yard and ran for a 2-point conversion to make it 8–0.

Duke's offense took over on its own 32 after the kickoff, moved in 5 plays to the 48, and then another bad thing happened. Duke quarterback Larry Davis, who had completed his first 2 passes for 13 yards, threw his third pass to linebacker John Horney, who took off down the left sideline. When he ran into a traffic jam at the 30, Horney lateraled the ball to Tom O'Leary, who took it the rest of the way for a 15–0 lead with only 3:35 gone in the first quarter.

Duke took the kickoff, ran two plays, punted on third down, and eleven plays later Notre Dame was on the scoreboard with yet another touchdown. The first quarter still had 5:48 to go.

The fans loved it, and they went crazy with joy when one of the passes Hanratty completed on the touchdown drive was caught by Seymour, who had returned to action wearing high-top shoes and with his ankle so heavily taped he couldn't feel it. In the scoring frenzy that Notre Dame had begun, no one noticed that Eddy, after his touchdown run, had been in for only two more plays before going to the sideline to be replaced by Gladieux. Out of the game, he told Pagna he had reinjured his shoulder throwing a block, and Pagna, seeing that the Irish would have no trouble with the Blue Devils, told him to take the rest of the day off. Pagna wanted to save Eddy for Michigan State the next week.

By halftime Coley O'Brien and the second unit were already in the game, Notre Dame had intercepted 3 passes and gained a total of 296 yards to 81 for Duke, and the score was 43–0.

Parseghian started the second half with his second unit and kept sending in reserves until sixty-four players had played. If he had been able to play the cheerleaders and the leprechaun, he might have thrown them in, too. O'Brien threw only 2 passes the entire second half, but the Notre Dame defense picked off yet another pass, recovered two fumbles deep in Duke territory, and blocked a kick. And the reserves, working against a Duke team that had given up sometime in the second quarter, kept sticking the ball in the end zone. Notre Dame made only 17 first downs the entire game and scored 9 touchdowns, 3 on plays of 45 yards or more.

"I pulled the starters, I kept it on the ground, I used standard defenses. I just wanted to run the clock out and get out of there," Parseghian said. He even ran on fourth down in Duke territory rather than take three more points on a field goal. The Duke defense couldn't stop the play, and Notre Dame wound up with yet another touchdown.

Duke was Notre Dame's last home game before the two final games on the road against Michigan State and USC. It was also the last home game for the seniors. The senior reserves got as much playing time as possible, and Parseghian started some of them so they could say they started at least one game in their careers. As the game wore on and the carnage mounted, Don Gmitter, Tom Regner, Alan Page, and Kevin Hardy got an idea. They were all seniors (although Hardy, because he was injured one season, had one more year of eligibility), and they had been the team's original Big Four defensive line in 1964. Gmitter and Regner had played the last two years on offense, but now they decided it would be a kick if the original defensive line went in for one last play in their final home game.

The idea became an obsession, and they went to John Ray late in the fourth quarter and presented their petition. "No way," Ray said, sprinkling in a few choice expletives. "You're crazy."

"C'mon, Coach. Just one play," they begged like four kids asking their mother if they could go to the movies by themselves.

To get rid of them, Ray sent them to Dad—Ara—figuring that would be the end of it. But they badgered Parseghian until he finally caved in. "But just one play," he said. "One play, god-damn it! Do your show and get off. Just don't do anything be-cause no one had better get hurt."

While this was going on, Duke was mounting its only drive of the day and was steadily moving into Notre Dame territory. The four kids scampered over to Ray and told him that Ara said they could go in. "Okay," Ray said. "You go in there for one play. That's it."

It was third down and long near the Notre Dame 30, and the four players grabbed their helmets and were running onto the field when Ray barked one last order. He didn't give a rat's tail if they got hurt. That was their problem. But he yelled after them, "If you let them score, I'm going to have your butts."

So they ran out, and the student body, remembering past glory, stood and cheered. Duke cooperated by throwing an incomplete pass that preserved the shutout and cleared the last bit of business out of the way before the showdown in East Lansing. Michigan State was waiting with its own unblemished record to settle this number-one issue once and for all.

The whole week, all over the campus, every newspaper reporter in the world was there. Everything was just hype, hype, hype, hype.

—Tom Regner

Nothing in college football gets the juices flowing in fans and players like a late-season match between the number-one and number-two teams in the country. This is because it so rarely happens. In fact, when Notre Dame and Michigan State met in 1966, it was the latest in the season that such a match had ever happened. Even today when fans expect to see the top teams meet with some regularity in a postseason bowl game, it's rare for both to be undefeated. So any clash of undefeated teams is special. But in 1966 it was more than special. With bowl games not counting toward the National Championship and without as many bowls as there are today, such games had to take place during the regular season, which meant it was sheer luck when it happened. First, the schedules, made out from six to eight years in advance, had to bring two top teams together not at the beginning of the season but at the end. Second, the teams couldn't stumble along the way, either because of injury or from meeting a sky-high opponent on a bad day. That's why writers start the hype for potential matchups so early in a season. With so many chances for either team to do something dumb, like lose a football game, writers know they had better start beating the drum early or they might not get to it at all. The reality is that great matchups seldom materialize, which is why, when they do, they are almost invariably called the "Game of the Century."

To show how serendipitous such games are, when the 1966 schedule was first drawn up, the Irish weren't even supposed to play Michigan State. Instead, they were scheduled to meet Iowa on November 19. Then, after agreeing to the game, Iowa decided it would rather spend the weekend before Thanksgiving in Florida playing the University of Miami Hurricanes, a team that hadn't yet gotten football religion. This was in 1960. Needing a tenth game to fill the schedule, Notre Dame's athletic director, Edward W. "Moose" Krause, called his old friend Clarence L. "Biggie" Munn, who was Michigan State's athletic director. Moose said something like, "Hey, Biggie, Iowa dumped us, and we need a game November 19, 1966. You got an opening?" And Biggie, who was allowed to play ten games but had only nine scheduled, said, "Yeah. We'll play you."

So it was that two grown men called Moose and Biggie, strictly as a matter of courtesy and convenience, scheduled a game that would outlive them both. Neither man had any clue that the game would amount to anything special. At the time they came to their agreement, the Spartans and the Irish were both in a bit of a decline. Duffy Daugherty, the man who had taken over the Spartan coaching job from Munn in 1954, hadn't had a great season since 1957, when he was 8-1, and hadn't been to the Rose Bowl since 1955. Notre Dame, under Joe Kuharich, a nice guy who seemed determined to prove Leo Durocher right, was coming off a record of 5-5 in the 1959 season and was on its way to a 2-8 record in 1960.

No one knew that Ara Parseghian would bring his Era of Ara to Notre Dame, that by 1966 Notre Dame would be back on top of the heap, and that Michigan State would be there to meet them.

As big as the game was, the world didn't stop spinning on its axis as of Sunday, November 13, 1966, no matter what the sportswriters thought. An unmanned spacecraft was busy snapping pictures of the moon, where America intended to plant a flag and swat a golf ball by the end of the decade. A manned Gemini craft was orbiting the earth. Ralph Nader was filing a $26 million lawsuit against General Motors, which had admitted to hiring private investigators to inform them about the young consumer advocate who had burst onto the scene with the publication of his book, *Unsafe at Any Speed*. Because of Nader's consumer advocacy, the federal government adopted laws that would soon have seat belts, padded dashboards, collapsible steering columns, and other safety devices in every automobile, including the hot new Camaro Z-28, which GM had introduced that fall to take advantage of the market Ford had created two years earlier with its sporty little Mustang.

Stein and Day Publishers were running quarter-page ads in the *New York Times* trying to get bookstores to take a chance on carrying their shocking book, *One in Twenty*, "the first book to reveal what being a male or female homosexual is really like." Written by Bryan Magee, the book, the *Times* wrote in a review, combines "thoroughness with taste." Elsewhere on the sexual front, the city of Newark, New Jersey, closed down a burlesque house and arrested six women performers "for using lascivious language and giving the illusion of nudity." In New York City, Mayor John Lindsay succeeded in amending the city's cabaret code to outlaw topless waitresses. To dramatize the ordinance, police busted the Crystal Palace, "the city's first—and possibly last—topless-waitress night club," as the newspaper put it. Before the arrests, publicity about the bar "brought swarms of customers—mostly middle-aged men—to the club. Last night they were being charged a $6 minimum, and drinks at the bar were priced at $1.75."

Such prices were extraordinary in a day when newspapers sold for five to ten cents. Those same papers occasionally ran features on the horrors of heroin addiction which described men who had "$10-a-day" habits—a fortune. Factory wages averaged $113.44 a week. Of that, $13.11 was withheld for taxes. New York City's teachers were seeking a new contract that would pay a beginning teacher $7,500 a year and an experienced one $15,000. A secretary could make as much as $135 a week in New York and rent a furnished room in a residential hotel for $85. You could buy a serviceable used car for as little as $25 and a good-sized house for $25,000, although you had to pay an outrageous 6 percent interest on the loan, the result of the high inflation rate of 3 percent. At some public colleges tuition rose as much as 10 percent the previous year, newspapers reported, and the average tuition at state schools was $250 for in-state students and as much as $528 for out-of-staters. The $800 you could pay for a twenty-five-inch color television would buy twenty all-wool tweed suits.

Joe Namath was finishing his sophomore season with the New York Jets. Caroline Kennedy was nine years old. Ronald Reagan, a retired actor, was basking in the glory of having been elected governor of California, while Alabama was congratulating itself on its cleverness in replacing Governor George Wallace, who couldn't run for reelection, with his wife, Lurleen Wallace. UCLA basketball fans were eagerly awaiting the beginning of basketball season and the debut of the heralded sophomore Lew Alcindor, who had yet to become Kareem Abdul-Jabbar. That was just as well. Cassius Clay had already changed his name to Muhammad Ali, but newspapers and broadcasters kept calling him Clay. Ali knocked out Cleveland Williams in three rounds on Monday, November 14, before 35,460 fight fans in the Astrodome, his second title defense in three months. He introduced the Ali Shuffle in the fight. "Clay devised the Ali Shuffle to give the [closed circuit] television fans, some of whom paid as much as $10 for a seat, something to talk about on the way out," observed Robert Lipsyte in the *New York Times*.

Jack Nicklaus and Arnold Palmer split a purse of $1,000 for beating back an international field and winning the Canada Cup in Tokyo. CBS Television announced it would bring back the Smothers Brothers, who had bombed in a half-hour situation comedy in 1965, in a variety show format. In England, Prince Charles celebrated his eighteenth birthday and officially became next in line to the throne. "Except for a special tea party that the Prince gave for his school friends, the day was the usual mixture of study and athletics," the newspapers reported. Michelangelo Antonioni was preparing for the debut of his avant-garde movie, *Blow-Up* with Vanessa Redgrave and twenty-five-year-old David Hemmings. "The Poor Side of Town" by Johnny Rivers, last week's hit song, was giving way to "You Keep Me Hanging On" by the Supremes, which would be number one on the charts for two weeks before giving way to "Winchester Cathedral" by the New Vaudeville Band, which would abdicate after another week to "Good Vibrations" by the Beach Boys.

The Warren Commission report on the assassination of President Kennedy came under attack that week as *Esquire* magazine printed photos that purported to show another gunman crouched behind a station wagon parked in front of Kennedy's limousine at the instant of the shooting. Eddie Fisher sued Elizabeth Taylor for divorce that Tuesday, saying that Taylor's 1964 Mexican divorce and marriage to Richard Burton were invalid

On college campuses, birth control was an issue of hot debate. At Louisiana State University, an investigation revealed that doctors in the school infirmary were writing prescriptions for birth control pills for unmarried coeds, a practice that was called an "abuse." At Notre Dame, campus security was looking into allegations that architecture students were mass-producing fake university IDs which were used by as many as three-quarters of the school's underaged students to drink illegally. It was not seen as a major problem. Xavier University in Cincinnati adopted "Booze and Broads" regulations that set forth the rules for off-campus male students who wanted to hold parties involving both beer and females. And Georgetown University became the first Catholic university to lift its total ban on alcoholic beverages in the men's dormitories. Meanwhile, Stonehill College in Massachusetts adopted a regulation calling for a $5 fine for any male student not wearing a jacket and tie.

Finally, that Friday, as college football was moving into a weekend such as it had not seen in decades, followers of professional baseball were shocked when Sandy Koufax, fresh off a 27-9 season in which he struck out 317, allowed only 1.73 earned runs per game, and won his third Cy Young Award, suddenly announced his retirement.

Somewhere, people were concerned with all of these things. But not at Notre Dame or Michigan State. The moment Notre Dame dismembered Duke 64–0 and the Spartans trashed Indiana 37–7, with Jimmy Raye throwing for 3 touchdowns and the defense holding the Hoosiers to −10 yards rushing, the world may as well have stopped spinning. A week of classes remained, a week that at Notre Dame included midterm exams. Few cared. All that mattered was Saturday and the Game of the Year, the Game of the Decade, or the Game of the Century, depending on who was writing about it. Or simply the Poll Bowl.

The players found it nearly impossible to concentrate in class. Several Notre Dame professors—a tiny number really—later apologized for sticking to the midterm test schedule and not holding off a week. For most of the players, as for most students, though, tests came first, hoopla later. At Michigan State some professors finally dismissed classes altogether, since no one was paying attention anyway.

Each school had scheduled a pep rally for the end of the week, but on each campus the rallies started Sunday and never stopped. Groups of students, giddy at the prospect of the coming battle, paraded around both campuses, stopping outside the rooms of athletes and calling them out to speak. Pete Duranko gave a speech from the porch roof of Alumni Hall. Jim Lynch interrupted his studies to answer a knock at his Sorin Hall door and was confronted by a gang of cheering classmates outside.

Bubba Smith was sitting in his room on Monday after practice talking about the game to his roommate, John Gorman of Chicago. "I can't see them beating us," Smith was saying when he began hearing chanting outside. He had heard the chant many times before but never on a Monday. It had always been on Saturdays when the team needed a big defensive play: "Kill, Bubba, kill. Kill, Bubba, kill."

Bubba got up and opened the blinds. He saw what looked to him like ten thousand students screaming. When he opened the window, they stopped their chant and switched to, "Speech. Speech."

Bubba thought a moment and began, "Uh . . ."

The crowd went nuts. It was all the speech they needed to set them off again.

When the crowd left, Smith sat down again with Gorman. "You got a hundred dollars?" Gorman asked. (Asking Smith if he had a hundred dollars was like asking a bird if it had feathers. Bubba had long ago learned the fine art of extracting cash from people close to the Michigan State football program. His size and free-spirited personality had made him a hero of the highest order, the first black, in fact, to be voted the most popular man on campus.) Gorman extracted the hundred bucks from Bubba, and the next day went downtown and had several thousand "Kill, Bubba, Kill" buttons made up. He recruited freshmen to sell them on campus, and by week's end the firm of Smith and Gorman had a satchel for each of them stuffed with dollar bills.

Most blacks who went to mostly white schools to play football

kept a low profile, anxious not to be seen as the wrong sort of
Negro. They had good reason to be anxious. Just that week Syracuse's game at Old Miss was being threatened because officials
at Old Miss didn't know how southern fans would react to seeing
blacks on the same field with whites. Bubba was the exception;
he wasn't out to please anyone but himself. He realized that the
school hadn't brought him there because it felt sorry about the
quality of education he would have gotten if he had stayed in
Texas—if he had gone to college at all. He and his black teammates were there because they could win football games, which
sold tickets, which brought fame to the coaches and money to
everyone but the athletes.

Alan Page realized the same thing, but only after his Notre
Dame career was over. As one of only about sixty blacks in the
entire school, Page's life was more difficult than anyone knew.
He got along well with his teammates and was close friends with
Larry Conjar and Don Gmitter, among others. But after he left
school, he began to feel he had been used just as Bubba Smith
and the blacks at Michigan State had been used, just as most
football players are still used. As an assistant attorney general
and trustee of the University of Minnesota, Page now advocates
paying college football players for their services.

Page and Smith and their teams were in the process of making
college football the enormously profitable game it is today. Until
Parseghian arrived at Notre Dame, you could walk up to the
ticket window of Notre Dame Stadium on many game days, fork
over $5 or $6, and get a ticket. You couldn't do that after 1966.
At Michigan State, where the stadium had recently been ex-
panded to nearly eighty thousand seats, it was the same. Until the
middle of the 1966 season, in fact, the Notre Dame game wasn't
even sold out.

That wasn't the case the week before the game. Students had
camped out all night outside the stadium at the beginning of the
week for the opportunity to buy one of the few seats reserved for
students. The rest of the population resorted to all sorts of flum-
mery to latch on to the hottest college football ticket since the
forties when Notre Dame and Army had their annual epic battles
in Yankee Stadium.

Bill Beardsley, the Michigan State ticket manager, had the
worst week of his life. It was also the most interesting week.

Among the two hundred calls he fielded each day that week was one from someone in Chicago who said, "Name your price. I have two blank checks made out in your name. I just want two tickets." Beardsley told him he didn't have any. Richard Paisley of Cleveland wrote Beardsley a letter: "If President Johnson phoned or wrote and asked for a ticket, I'm sure you would be able to send him one. Well, President Johnson will not be there, I'm certain. So why not send me the ticket you would send him." Beardsley liked that so much he sent Paisley the president's ticket. Another fan, a man of the cloth, came from Florida to East Lansing and paraded around campus with a large, hand-lettered sign on his back: FLORIDA MINISTER NEEDS ONE TICKET. WILL EXCHANGE ONE ORANGE BOWL TICKET FOR A MICH. STATE–ND GAME. TEMPERATURE TODAY IN FLORIDA: 90 DEGREES. The sign had a palm tree painted on the bottom.

The *Wall Street Journal* ran a front-page story about the pregame madness. The *Journal* usually didn't cover sports, and if it was writing about the game and had reporters at both campuses, it meant only one thing—big money was at stake. The article only made Beardsley's life that much more hectic. After the Paisley story got out, he received calls and letters from people everywhere asking for the vice president's seat, the defense secretary's seat, the secretary of state's seat. There were no such seats. There was only the seat being reserved for Michigan's governor George Romney. The governor had originally intended to be out of the state on vacation that week, but after declaring "Spartan Victory Week," he announced, "I'm not going anywhere until I see that game."

A radio station auctioned off two tickets for charity and netted $260. Mike Schrems of Saginaw offered to sell his liquor store, which had done $65,000 worth of business in 1965, for four tickets plus $1,700 for the beer in the storeroom and $4,000 for goodwill. Schrems didn't receive any offers. Scalping was illegal, but in East Lansing a men's haberdasher tried to get around that by selling $10 Stetson fedoras for $150. In the hatband were two tickets on the 50-yard line. Face value of the tickets was $5.

At Notre Dame the situation wasn't any better. Of the five thousand tickets originally available for the visiting team before the season, Notre Dame had received student requests for only five hundred. So that's all they got, and the school ran a lottery to see which lucky students would get them. The school's cross-country team came up with a novel idea: They organized a team of runners to carry a football in relays the 158 miles to East Lansing. When they got there, they figured someone would be impressed by their determination and give them tickets. They figured wrong and watched the game in a bar. Roger Valdiserri, snowed under by ticket requests, insisted to one and all that he couldn't get tickets even for his own parents, so forget it.

Those who just wanted to watch the game on television had another problem. Notre Dame had used up its allotment of national television. The game could only be broadcasted regionally, as part of the first college football doubleheader. The second game, between USC and UCLA, would determine the PAC-8 Champion. Until that Saturday the nation had one game and one game only each week. But ABC thought showing two big games back-to-back was an idea whose time had come. Because the Notre Dame–Michigan State game could not be shown nationally, ABC announced that the South and Pacific Northwest would get a different game while the rest of the country got the Game of the Millennium, which would be beamed for the first time via the Lani Bird satellite to Hawaii, Vietnam, and the U.S. armed forces in Europe. This was too much for football fans in the blacked-out areas, and as the game drew nearer, Beano Cook, the ABC Sports publicity chief, found his life every bit as hectic as Beardsley's.

Several weeks before the game, Cook began to sense what he had to look forward to when a petition arrived asking that the game be shown nationally. It was signed by 20,000 people. He also received a letter from an inmate in a Texas prison, where the blackout applied. "If I weren't here, I would travel to see the game on television, but I won't be out by November 19," the inmate wrote. In all, 50,000 pieces of mail buried the ABC mail room. Cook estimated that that was 49,900 more letters than the network had received before any other game. Another man in the blackout area filed a lawsuit claiming he had a constitutional right to see the game on television. The suit was thrown out. Moved by that sort of fervor, Cook quipped, "This will be the greatest game since Hector fought Achilles," an allusion that most of the general public still understood. As for the amount of publicity he was distributing, Cook said, "We're putting out enough material to make *Gone with the Wind* look like a short story.''

To get around the blackout, the Michigan State and Notre Dame alumni clubs announced plans to show the game to its members on closed-circuit television. For $5 anyone could become an instant member at the door.

Faced with this unprecedented demand, ABC finally hit on a compromise that the NCAA could live with. It decided to broadcast the game on a tape-delay to those parts of the country that were blacked out.

One man who didn't want to wait was Dan Ginsberg, a Miami, Florida, attorney. Ginsberg paid $150.99 for a plane ticket, food, and lodging so he could go to New York and watch the game live rather than wait two hours for the tape delay.

While fans were willing to do anything to see the game, other coaches at smaller schools worried about what the game would do to their attendance.

John Bateman, the coach at Rutgers, said, "The Notre Dame–Michigan State game on television this week will hurt the gate at every game in our area." San Jose State decided not to fight it and simply delayed the start of its scheduled game that Saturday so that it wouldn't conflict with the end of the Notre Dame–Michigan State game. To do otherwise, the school feared, might mean not having any fans at all. Many high schools that played on Saturday afternoon also rescheduled their starting times.

Even religion took a backseat in some regions. Fathers Gerald Corrigan, James O'Connell, and John O'Mara, and a Father Franklin, who said, "Put me down as mostly Irish," told their parishioners at Our Lady of Mercy R.C. Church in Plainville, Connecticut, that confessions would be heard a half hour later that day so that they wouldn't have to miss the end of the game. To prove that Notre Dame didn't have every Catholic in the country fingering the beads for victory, six nuns from the East Lansing area sent Duffy Daugherty a tape they had made in which they sang "We Love You Spartans" to the tune of "We Love You Conrad" from the hit musical *Bye, Bye Birdie*. Duffy played it for the team one night after dinner. Four Sisters of Charity at the St. John's Student Center on the Michigan State campus went public with their love of Spartan football, which was not a revelation considering that starters Clinton Jones, Bob Apisa, Gene Washington, Dick Kenney, and Pat Gallinagh were all regulars at the center and frequently went on Sundays to watch the pro games on television with the nuns.

The game even affected wildlife. November 19 was the start of deer season in Michigan, and normally the woods were filled at the crack of dawn with hunters on the trail of fresh venison. But on this Saturday few Michiganders were setting foot in the woods until they had seen the game, and the deer had a reprieve.

Both fueling and feeding off the public frenzy were the newspapers. It had been twenty years since a regular season game this big had come around. That game was Notre Dame–Army, and it had been played in New York where a huge crowd was guaranteed and where the nation's media were centered. This game was in East Lansing, a backwater midwestern town. But times had changed since 1946. No longer was aviation a hundred stops in a DC-3 and no longer was the train the primary means of transportation. Big Boeing 707s prowled the skies, making it possible for sportswriters from all over the country to get to the game quickly and easily. Or get to each campus a week early, for that matter.

The game drew more than seven hundred reporters from every corner of the country, and it seemed that every one of them spent the entire week at one of the two campuses. Those who had come to cover the Notre Dame–Duke game simply stayed, while those who had followed Michigan State to Bloomington for the Indiana game returned with the Spartans to East Lansing. For a week they prowled the respective campuses, telling and retelling every fact and fable they could dredge up. And while most of them were chasing football legends, Jimmy Breslin of the New York *Daily News* wrote about the ground-breaking work in liberal theology being done by Notre Dame's young, activist priests and about how academics were considered by some Notre Damers as more important than football.

Parseghian and Daugherty were used to seeing writers even a couple days before the game, but to see them a week early was unheard of. And their sheer number was overwhelming. Daugherty was better prepared than Parseghian. He had decided long ago that he would protect his players during the week. They were available only after the Indiana game on Saturday and Sunday. After that they were off-limits, as were his practices, which were held on a field surrounded by a fence draped with canvas. The reporters tracked the players down anyway.

Parseghian always believed in cooperating as much as he could with the writers. He made his players available daily, and his office seemed to be filled with writers day and night, asking him questions and smoking his cigars. The days turned into nonstop press conferences for him, and the nights provided no relief. The simplicity of the time was such that he kept a listed phone number and answered every call. The death-defying prose and stories of the writers, both rookies and veterans, were on the front of every sports section for a week.

Old Notre Dame hands, those who had been around in the good old days of Rockne and Leahy, naturally said that while the media were something else, the students lacked the spirit of the old days. The players and the students couldn't imagine anything more frenzied than what was going on all week. Spirits were so high on both campuses that leaders of the respective student governments felt compelled to hold a meeting at a neutral site between both campuses to discuss ways of preventing violence between the huge Michigan State throng and the tiny band of Notre Dame students who would be at the game. Ever since some students had hung a banner at the Army game suggesting that the Irish "kick Army's ass"—meaning their mule, of course —defenders of a more peaceful world had been decrying the actions of the student body. There was the banner before the Navy game that said SINK THE SEAMEN. That and the anti-USC slogan of PUNCTURE THE TROJANS were favorites among tittering underclassmen, but it scandalized the blue noses. Then there was the giant deodorant can erected on the freshman quad before the Homecoming game against Pitt. IRISH PITT STOP read that legend, an indelicate pun in the eyes of the old-timers who also thought the practice of throwing rolls of toilet paper into the trees before pep rallies was crude. The snowball fight at the Pitt game seemed to be the last straw. Some people had been injured, it was said. Where would the violence stop? *The Observer*, making its debut, responded in a lengthy editorial under the headline ND STUDENT BODY NO. 1:

> A lot has been said of the bawdy Notre Dame man at a football game, with his pint of spirit in one hand and his lewd bedsheeted message in the other. So much has been said, in fact, that many aspiring social critics seem prepared to publish paperback exposés on the immaturity and grossness so prevalent at such a

bastion of culture and higher learning. Oh, sure, there would be truth captured within the penny plot: students have been known to get out of line with their inebriations, their occasional hostility toward musical instruments, and at times a general disdain for the rights of opposing players and fellow spectators. Yet, as journalists, we feel it significant to note that not one scathing literary attack has succeeded in curbing this underlying element of spirit-fused immaturity in those who display it. And the fact is, no such attack ever will. For as long as Notre Dame produces a great football team, for as long as Notre Dame's cherished spirit is still cherished, a certain type of student will continue to boo and hiss and drink and sweat and yell and scream and live and die for dear old alma mater. . . .

All this brings us to Saturday. The Game promises to be, at the very least, one of the hardest fought in collegiate history. It also promises to be watched by diametrically hostile forces on each side of Spartan Stadium. . . . Even a squadron of Marines would be forced to evacuate should a referee call back a winning touchdown or should Bubba Smith kick Nick Eddy in the shins. . . . After admitting the impossibility of curbing pre-game and post-contest emotion, some have suggested that perhaps the series should be cancelled, causing surely the biggest disaster since somebody stuffed a State band member into his tuba . . . [which] would hardly have been noticed had Hofstra been playing Temple at the time. . . . Cancelling the series is clearly not the answer.

The only answer is simply a good hard-fought football game. Excesses there will always be. Our stand is with the mature, the responsible, the student body as a whole. . . . Hate-Staters are we all; Hate-Baiters none.

On both sides students vied for the best prank. A gang of Notre Dame commandos stole onto the Michigan State campus one night and painted the big Spartan statue Kelly green. But some Michigan State fans pulled the best trick when they hired a small plane to fly over Notre Dame's campus and drop leaflets modeled after Pentagon propaganda sheets. The message was addressed to the Peace-Loving Villagers of Notre Dame and read:

Our friends, why do you struggle against us? Why do you persist in the mistaken belief that you can win freely and openly against us?

Your leaders have lied to you. They have led you to believe you are more powerful than we. They have led you to believe you can win. They have given you false hopes. They have deceived their own people.

We have nothing but affection for Notre Dame.

Signed: A free message from the Michigan State University of America.

Another aerial message was more succinct:

You have heard that the power of our Intercontinental Ballistic Bubba is a myth. The existence of this powerful anti-blocker missile has been questioned. Intercontinental Ballistic Bubba is real. It can destroy you.

With such hijinks afoot, liquor stores and bars in both South Bend and Okemos, the nearest hamlet to East Lansing that allowed drinking (East Lansing was dry), were sending out for reinforcements. A beer distributor in South Bend guessed that beer sales would go up from 20 to 30 percent. One Okemos liquor store stocked fifty extra cases—six hundred bottles—of liquor and hoped it would be enough.

While the student bodies at the two schools blew off steam with their door-to-door pep rallies, their buttons, banners, and pranks, the players waited out what seemed like the longest week of their lives. Both teams were ready to play Monday, and both Parseghian and Daugherty kept practices short and avoided contact drills. The players reacted in opposite ways. At Michigan State the team had one of its best practice weeks ever. At Notre Dame, where Ara personally led calisthenics to the cadence of "Beat who? Beat State!" the team, saddled with the added burden of midterms, was not particularly sharp. The players didn't want to practice. They wanted to play.

The first order of business for both coaches was to decide which aspect of the opponent's game they wanted to stop, and it was no surprise that Duffy and Hank Bullough made it a point of honor to keep Seymour from getting his celebrated mitts on one of Hanratty's passes. They watched films of Hanratty until they were cross-eyed, and when they were done, they decided that the kid quarterback telegraphed all his passes by following the receiver he was going to throw to through the entire pass pattern. A seasoned quarterback will "look off" a defensive back; he will look at a secondary receiver and then shift to his primary receiver. Hanratty, the coaches decided, didn't. They told their defensive backs—Jess Phillips, Jim Summers, George Webster, and Sterling Armstrong—to watch Hanratty's eyes. Wherever he looked, he would throw.

They also noticed that Larry Conjar tended to set up in his stance with his weight shifted forward when the play was going to be a run and with his weight on his heels when he was going to stay back to block for a pass. They developed several calls for the defense to make at the line of scrimmage so the linebackers and backfield could play tight or loose depending on how Conjar set up.

Parseghian was one of the most thorough coaches alive. He not only studied opponents' films, he had two assistants whose job it was to study his own team's films, looking for just the sort of cues that Daugherty and his staff had spotted. Parseghian's staff didn't spot them.

Ara and John Ray were determined to stop Clinton Jones first. Jones had carried the ball 149 times going into the game, 48 times more than quarterback Jimmy Raye, whose carries included set plays and times he had to scramble when trying to pass. Bob Apisa, who was out with a bad knee that had been further damaged against Indiana, had 84 carries, and Dwight Lee at left halfback had 58 carries. Apisa's 5.2 yards per carry led the team, as did his 8 rushing touchdowns and 9 total touchdowns. Jones had gained 771 yards for 5.1 yards a carry and 6 touchdowns, but a Big Ten record 268 of those yards had come two weeks earlier in the blowout against Iowa, in which Jones had touchdown runs of 70 and 79 yards. The three backs had caught 17 passes as well. Regis Cavender, who would replace Apisa, had carried 34 times for 164 yards and a 4.8 average and 6 touchdowns, but he had not caught a pass.

If the Irish could stop Jones, they would force Raye to pass, and although his primary receiver, Gene Washington, was averaging a whopping 25.1 yards a catch and had 7 touchdown catches, he had caught only 22 passes all year. Raye, in fact, had thrown only 103 passes in nine games, just over 11 a game. He was still considered a far more dangerous runner—particularly on the option play when he could keep or pitch to Jones—than a passer.

Parseghian talked up Raye as much as he could to the writers and didn't mention Jones that much, an old coach's trick to draw attention from his real designs. "Our biggest overall problem is Michigan State's speed," Parseghian said. "Individually, we know that a key man is Raye. He can get big chunks of yardage passing, and when everyone is covered, he's dangerous as a runner."

Although forcing Raye to throw would be the Irish strategy, Parseghian knew his assessment of his skills was right on the mark. Raye looked funny throwing the ball. He tended to stand very erect when he threw and seemed to release the ball with his entire upper body and without much of a stride. He looked as if he were throwing darts rather than footballs. But he could get it to Washington, and Washington was fast enough to run under it and athletic enough to bring it down. His passing yardage—968 yards—was considerably less than Hanratty's 1,221 yards on 77 completions in 143 attempts. But his completion rate of 53 percent was virtually identical to Hanratty's 53.8 percent. And he had thrown for 10 touchdowns as opposed to Hanratty's 8.

After stopping Jones, Parseghian and Ray's second defensive priority was to stop Jimmy Raye's ground game. What they didn't know was that Duffy was preparing Raye to run keepers on his options instead of pitching the ball to Jones going outside. Duffy also wanted Raye to pass early and deep to Washington. If Michigan State had to pass, it would be on its terms, not Ara's. Duffy hoped that hitting some big passes early would set up the short stuff underneath Notre Dame's three-deep zone later in the game.

As for what he would do on offense, Parseghian gave nothing away. He was repeatedly asked whether he would run at Bubba Smith, something few other teams had attempted. Ara avoided answering the question by praising Bubba. "Smith has stripped blockers allowing linebackers to get the job done," Ara said. "Whether we run away from Smith would be divulging some of our game plans." Teams expended so much effort avoiding Bubba that he had only thirteen solo tackles and eleven assists going into the game. The unimpressive statistics led one paper to state that Bubba Smith was a myth. In East Lansing the statement, attributed to Regner and Goeddeke, was passed along to Bubba, who spent the week thinking about what he would do to those two gentlemen and anyone else in a white jersey he met on the field. Knowing that wouldn't have made Bob Kuechenberg's nights any more restful. Bubba was known to play middle guard but his usual post was left defensive end, and it would be Kuechenberg's job to block him.

"I kept hearing this 'Kill, Bubba, kill,'" Kuechenberg said. "And being an English major, I knew that wasn't a complete sentence because it lacked an object. Kill whom? Since I was the guy who was going to be blocking him, it must be me."

It also would have been no comfort to Kuechenberg to know that his counterpart on the Spartan offensive line, Jerry West, was having similar nightmares. West, a 218-pound overachiever of small size but enormous strength, would draw Pete Duranko most of the day. He'd get Mitch Pruiett to help him, but that was small consolation as he watched the Notre Dame films. "You don't want to watch films of him," West said of Duranko. "He's beating up people, tearing their limbs off. He was the toughest player I ever played against. I played against several All Americans, and they didn't compare to Pete Duranko. I'd much rather block anyone else. I wish I had Kevin Hardy. I worried about Duranko all week. I was seeing him in my dreams."

In fact, Parseghian thought he could move the ball on Michigan State. The year before he hadn't been able to, but then he had had no quarterback. Now he had the most balanced team he had ever had, a team that could strike from anywhere. He had Nick Eddy who could score from scrimmage or on a kickoff return. He had Hanratty and Seymour who could get it all in one giant bite. He had a defense that had intercepted 21 passes and a punt returner who could break it all the way. And since he could run each of 8 basic passing plays and 8 more running plays from a wealth of formations, he felt he could disguise his intentions well.

But there was a problem with that game plan. Nick Eddy, who had carried the ball only 67 times in eight games but nonetheless gained 498 yards—a daunting 7.4 yards per carry—was among Notre Dame's top ten of all-time leading rushers, but he had injured his shoulder against Pitt and reinjured it against Duke. Then in practice on Wednesday he had hurt it again. Parseghian said he would play, and Eddy believed he would, too. But it was an iffy proposition. If he came out, Rocky Bleier, who had run 50 times for a 4.6-yard average and 5 touchdowns, would assume the burden of being the featured halfback while Bob Gladieux would take over Bleier's duties as blocker, receiver, and sometime runner. Gladieux had carried 26 times for 110 yards and 3 touchdowns and had caught 9 passes for 137 yards and a touchdown. He was a tough back and a winner, but he couldn't break a game open as Eddy could.

Neither could Bleier. He was as tough and steady a performer as Notre Dame had, but he lacked Eddy's speed and shiftiness. He was just the sort of marginal halfback that Ara liked to turn into a defensive back or linebacker, but at 5 feet 11 and 185 pounds, he was too small to be a linebacker and was too slow to play the defensive backfield. What he lacked in size and speed he made up for in determination. After graduating from Notre Dame in 1968, Bleier joined the Pittsburgh Steelers. But before he could start his pro career, he was drafted by the Army and sent to Vietnam, where he had, by his own admission, the good fortune to get part of his foot blown off. It didn't seem like a lucky break at the time. When he got back to the Army hospital he was a cadaverous shadow of his former self. When he said he still wanted to make the Steelers, everyone's head shook sadly. He'd be lucky to walk normally let alone run with a football. But the Steelers let him try, and over the course of two years he tortured himself back into shape and came out of the ordeal a faster runner than he had been before he was wounded.

When Bleier arrived at Notre Dame, he worked and he listened to the coaches and won a starting job because, technically, there wasn't anyone better at executing plays. That extended to blocking, a task at which he excelled because he learned how to do it right. "What kept him in the pros," said Pagna, "was that he could block your can off."

"If you want to see desire personified," said Pete Duranko, "look at Rocky Bleier."

But if you wanted a 70-yard touchdown run with three cutbacks, two head fakes, and a hip juke, you needed Nick Eddy.

Seymour would play, but his ankle wasn't anywhere near healed. (His ankle, in fact, never healed, not then and not twenty-five years later.) But that was something only Seymour, the doctors, and the coaches knew. As far as the rest of the world knew, Seymour's ankle injury had been a sprain and it was healed. Let Duffy Daugherty find out how well the big end could run and cut on his own.

The bookies had made Notre Dame a 3 1/2-point favorite, and the line rose during the week to 5 points. The initial betting line was based on the bookies' perception of the relative strengths of the two teams, and a look at the statistics gave almost every edge to Notre Dame. The Irish had averaged more first downs (20.4 to 17.6), more total yards (405 to 363.7), more points (37.6 to 31.4), and more yards per play (5.8 to 5.4). Defensively, the Irish had better numbers in first downs allowed (11.4 to 13.4), total yards allowed (175.5 to 208.2), points allowed (3.5 to 9.9), interceptions (21 to 10), and yards allowed per play (2.9 to 3.4). The Michigan State advantages were in rushing yardage on offense (240.7 to 226.7), rushing yardage allowed on defense (47 to 75.6), and fumbles recovered (16 to 8). Also, Raye had thrown for 10 touchdowns—5 in the past two games—and 6 interceptions compared to Hanratty's 8 touchdowns and 10 interceptions. It was true that Notre Dame would have to play on the Spartans' turf, but no one had yet invented the automatic 3-point home field advantage that is part of today's betting lines.

Parseghian was asked whether he liked going into the game as the top-rated team. "Sure I do," he said. "Absolutely. I have no qualms about it, but . . . there's not enough difference between number one and number two to say that whoever wins, it could be an upset. The National Championship is part of it, but there are so many other things riding on this game. For one thing, it's a big traditional game. Both teams are going in undefeated. This is State's last home game and their last game of the season. That has to be important to them. Maybe we've got even greater motivation from the defeat last year. Would I call it a kind of revenge motivation?" he asked, grinning. "Yeah, maybe I would."

That was pretty much what Ara told his own troops in private, too. Every one of the Notre Dame players could remember Thornhill insulting Ara on the sidelines during the 1965 debacle at Notre Dame, as clearly as they could remember being held to negative rushing yards and having their noses rubbed in the dirt by the arrogant Spartans. They had not only a National Championship to win, they had their self-respect to recapture.

The Phantom, who worked overtime that week, hit hard on that theme. The Phantom wrote the team:

> One thing burned my ears and stuck with me. Thornhill said, "You don't want it!"
>
> They are not supermen, they swarm you and try to be belligerent enough to force you to back off. Duranko, no two men should ever block you out. . . . Last year, we were not prepared for the assault. . . . This year will be different. We want it. Thornhill, Webster, Smith, Jones, Washington, when you hit them and they fall, you'll begin to know—they are vulnerable.

The Irish were so keyed up that Tom Pagna started to think maybe he, as The Phantom, should do something to loosen them up a bit. He talked to Dan Martin, who was with WNDU, the university's radio and television station, and they got the idea of faking some interviews with various Michigan State players. So Martin played the role of John Alexander, a Detroit broadcaster, and Pagna played the other characters. When they were done, they thought it was pretty funny. Without wall-to-wall electronic coverage of every team and every player in the country, he didn't have to worry about sounding exactly like the Michigan State players as he would today. No one really knew what they sounded like anyway. So Martin and Pagna made up a tape, and in the middle of the week, while the team was eating dinner after practice, Pagna broke in on the dining hall's public address system and told the team they might want to listen to a broadcast he had picked up out of Detroit. He started the tape.

Martin's well-modulated voice came on first: "Good afternoon, ladies and gentlemen. This is John Alexander, and I have with us today, without question, the outstanding defensive end in the country, Bubba Smith of Michigan State."

He proceeded to ask "Bubba" questions, and the answers came back in Pagna's version of Bubba Smith—a broad, southern black accent, not real jive but just broken enough to fit the team's idea of how he might talk. The voice said,

> Well, it gon' be the kind of game I think where breaks gonna make the difference. . . . They say they number one, but all them scores that those fellows had there—and they runs up the score

—and that make us number two, but I think that the game this week gonna prove who the number-one team is.

Pagna and Martin were cracking up, but the team wasn't as amused by the performance as the two conspirators thought they'd be. In fact, it became very quiet in the cafeteria. Instead of seeing through the joke, the players bought into it. They thought they were listening to actual Spartans, and the more they heard, the quieter and more angry they got.

"Charlie Thornhill" came on next, and Pagna gave him a soft, slightly lisped voice, sort of like a 1966 version of Mike Tyson. "Thornhill" 's favorite word was "uh," and he brought up the thrashing of the Irish at Notre Dame in 1965 and said that Michigan State had the best defense in the country.

These were things no player would say. From the beginning of time football players had been taught not to say anything to get the other guys angry, and everything these characters were saying was geared to do just that. But the Irish didn't catch on, and they didn't notice when "Alexander" slipped and said he had just talked to "Bubba Phillips."

Pagna and Martin moved from Thornhill to Bob Apisa. Not knowing what a Samoan Hawaiian might sound like, Pagna gave him a voice with an Hispanic accent and said things like "Meester Alexander" and "I theenk." The players accepted it.

The tape stopped for a while, and then it came back on again, this time with "Clinton Jones," who took on the Michigan State theme that Notre Dame was getting all the publicity while the Spartans had all the talent:

> Well, you know, uh, every time you pick up a paper you read about some of these suckers until they just kind of like a household word. But I don't think they any better than the kids we been playing against. Matter of fact, sometimes I don't think they're as good. You know, they get all the writers behind Notre Dame . . . and I think they just kind of ridin' the crest, so to speak, of a kind of publicity campaign to make some of those boys All American. I think that they got a shock comin' when they play us.

It was a joke, but Pagna had hit it right on the head as far as capturing the Spartan point of view. And it was true, as it had

been since the days of Rockne, that Notre Dame always got the
ink, and a good Notre Dame team would always get the benefit
of the doubt from the writers and voters in the polls.

The tape finished with a long segment purportedly with Henry
Bullough, the defensive coach. And now Pagna went directly
after his own offense, digging at their pride.

"Bullough," to whom Pagna gave a clipped, nasal twang, said
things like, "We think they're overrated" and Nick Eddy "was
an average back, just a very average back." "We're not afraid
of them, any more than we would be of an average back," he
said of the entire Notre Dame backfield. "I'm not saying that
facetiously. I mean that sincerely." As for Hanratty, he said,
"We're really not that concerned about him. As a matter of
fact, I'll go on record and say that he won't hold up under our
rush." His comment about Seymour was: "He's going to find
himself not as wide open as he has in other instances. . . . I would
really say that if he holds up at all, it's going to be a surprise
to me."

The players didn't say anything. They just mumbled and stored
it all away. Parseghian, who was in on the trick, saw that and saw
how quiet everybody was. Later that night he told Pagna to lay
off the jokes because nobody was getting them.

At Michigan State no one was playing head games. They went
through their practices, watched their films, and got higher with
each day. On Thursday, to cut the tension, Duffy had the team
run relay races after practice. Then he sent them back to their
dorms with orders to get to their Kellogg Center rooms on Friday.

With the writers Duffy previewed how he saw the game:

> You can throw psychology out the window because both teams
> have so much going for them that it just doesn't figure. . . . Past
> games won't mean anything. It is a game that will be attacked
> technically and not emotionally. I think the honest feeling of both
> myself and Parseghian is that there is greatness of both teams
> involved. . . . The only apprehension that exists is the possibility
> of mistakes, breaks, or whatever you want to call them. They
> determine games like this.
>
> Notre Dame is, I believe, bigger and stronger physically than
> Michigan State, but we may have more quickness. . . . I'm trying
> to be honestly frank in this appraisal. There is not much chance
> in a coach's lifetime for two teams such as these to play each

other. We'll do anything humanly possible to win. The game actually is getting to me. I mean, its interest and greatness are such that my fear is that I may not fully appreciate it.

It was speeches like that that made Daugherty such a favorite of the writers. He had laid it all out without giving anything away, but he had given them a bit of himself—and a good story.

One thing both coaches agreed on was that the game would be close. As Parseghian opined in South Bend that "the kicking game may prove decisive," Daugherty was saying in East Lansing that "it could all come down to a field goal."

Finally, the week ended and all that remained was the ritual screaming of the student bodies. Notre Dame's pep rally came first, on Thursday night. Normally, Notre Dame didn't have pep rallies before away games because the rallies were a Friday night ritual. But this was special. The team would be leaving on Friday, so the rally had to be Thursday. All the writers attended. For many it was their first brush with a Notre Dame pep rally—"a thing that makes strong men tremble," as one writer put it.

"They tore the roof off Notre Dame's field house," the *Chicago Sun-Times* reported.

"More than 4,500 Notre Dame students and fans arrived an hour early for a 'Game of the Year' pep rally and roared themselves hoarse for almost two hours until coach Ara Parseghian finally addressed them," wrote the more staid *Chicago Tribune*.

The students built their human pyramids up to the big iron tie rods, and then they literally hung from the rafters, where a stuffed dummy representing Bubba Smith was hung. Finally, they threw the dummy into the mob, which tore it limb from limb and shred from shred until there was nothing left of it but a memory.

When Ara finally got up to speak, the place rattled with a noise that didn't seem possible. Every roll of toilet paper on campus that hadn't already been thrown into the trees during the band's march around campus now sailed through the air. One of them flew up toward the balcony, up toward Parseghian. He stuck out his left hand and snagged it cleanly. The crowd roared louder, as Ara motioned them to be quiet. Finally, Parseghian got them settled down enough for him to speak.

"There are only five undefeated teams," he began.

"Four, four, four," the crowd chanted back at him, consigning Michigan State to the ranks of the defeated without trial.

"There's nothing wrong with the Notre Dame intelligence and spirit," Ara observed, and the crowd roared in appreciation of itself. "We respect the Spartans, but we are not going to Lansing to lose," he concluded, and turned it over to the mob again.

While Notre Dame held its pep rally, Duffy was holding his first evening meeting of the week with his team. It was held immediately after dinner and lasted only fifteen minutes. "Nothing special," Duffy reported. "No chalk talk. Just talking over what this game means to them as a team and as individuals." And what was that, someone asked. "The National Championship, if you can believe what you read," he said. "Few young men ever get the opportunity to play for what these two teams are playing for."

Michigan State held its pep rally on Friday night. The rally was bigger but not louder since it was held outdoors with a bonfire. By then the Irish were already in East Lansing along with a contingent of students who went armed with a list of activities and parties they could attend. The list was provided by the Michigan State student government in the interests of goodwill. To give them further help, *The Observer* printed a guide to the East Lansing–area night life:

> There are two types of people at Michigan State, the hippies and the straights. The hippies hang out in hippy bars, do hippy dances, drink hippy drinks. The straights go to the corner bars, drink beer and carouse, talk, and wander around East Lansing.
>
> Upon arrival at East Lansing, the Notre Dame student must make a decision. It's either hippy or straight, because a phony hippy is neither accepted by the legit hippy nor the true straight. . . .
>
> All the hips and the straights will emerge on the campus Friday night and march to Landon Field for a pep rally. If you're a hippy you must be hopped for the rally and if you're straight, you must be crocked.
>
> According to the Michigan State paper nearly every State pep rally's end is signaled by the arrival of the Michigan State police who escort some of the hippies back to their pads and some straights to their rooms.

More than a few terminally straight Notre Damers read that and couldn't figure out what it meant. But they read on and learned that Paul Revere's, on the East Side of town, "is the high place for the holy hips. Artsy stuff like paintings, proverbs, and a jukebox supply the atmosphere where the 'in' can intrigue one another. . . . Other hippies will retreat to one of the many fraternity or sorority halls to discuss Kant, Sartre, and Clinton Jones."

Straights could dance and drink at the Coral Gables Show Bar or Dagwood's, a local bar also frequented by local factory workers. "Troubled hips and straights may get some relief from Bert Mitchell Bail Bonding Co . . . Bill Turk Bonds . . . or William Couch Bonds," the article advised, providing advice that is no longer standard fare in student newspapers. "The Bert and two Bills are open 24 hours a day to salvage the hopes of the unhappy." The article also gave the addresses of two hospitals, just in case.

Michigan State officials were genuinely worried that the Notre Dame fans—even though only five hundred students were coming—meant to wreak destruction on East Lansing. *The Observer* had some fun with that, writing about Michigan State athletic director Biggie Munn's terror. "All he knows is that *they*, the Notre Dame student body, are coming and that the approach of that nefarious cult, second only in reputation to the Huns or the SS, is of more consequence than any game."

If the paper was having fun with Munn, it also showed that it knew what the game really meant for this generation of Notre Dame students:

> It's still a dream. . . . No longer will they hear of the "good old days" and the great players and coaches. They will offer their own. But more important, they and their football team will have proved conclusively something that never really changed, but for a short time appeared to be forgotten in other places: Notre Dame is number one, Notre Dame is the best—no matter what the score. . . . For literally millions of Notre Dame fans across the globe, this is the long-awaited day. This is the return of the Notre Dame football team to greatness.

The article didn't mention that Michigan State might have something to say about that. That job was left to another article written by the paper's sports editor, W. Hudson Giles, under the headline, A COLLISION OF TWO TEAMS—AND TWO WORLDS:

> History is marked with titanic struggles: Rome vs. Carthage, Don Juan vs. the Turks, North vs. South, East vs. West, Kennedy

vs. Johnson. And this Saturday at East Lansing comes the biggest confrontation since the Berlin Wall: Notre Dame vs. Michigan State. . . .

The difference will be in the breeding: The worlds from which they have been sired will mark the champion. And it is here, in a comparison of the worlds, that the competitors are contrasted.

The people who shall represent State have much to be proud of. One of the ten biggest universities in the nation . . . Lots of nice trees and shrubs. Football players from Hawaii. Students from 50 states and 90 foreign nations, 17,000 research projects. A 56-million-dollar cyclotron. According to *Ramparts*, a campus home for the CIA . . . a hedonistic paradise. A tradition as a party school and a football factory. Loyal fans. An excellent football team. And a coach who says, "The Notre Dame football team can do everything with a football but autograph it."

Notre Dame has many of these things. Lots of nice trees and shrubs. Students from many states and nations. An eight-million-dollar library. A nuclear reactor. A tradition as a football factory. An excellent football team.

But through the years the Irish have picked up some things no one—not even almighty State—can hope to equate. One of the greatest collegiate histories and traditions in the world. Knute Rockne, more than a football coach. Tom Dooley, more than a man. Academic excellence and athletic excellence together. 7,000 of the finest men God has put on earth. Fans who have never seen a campus or a college but who clamor for the chance to glory in that name. A coach, articulate, marked in every sense as a man of distinction. A Grotto. A magic *name*.

The difference, Giles concluded, was in the breeding. Notre Dame's pedigree and the superior character of the Notre Dame man would win the day. It was the Protestant Ethic in a Roman collar; that the best things happen to the best people. Certainly, Notre Dame did take great pride in Dr. Tom Dooley, who had given his life helping the people of Southeast Asia at a time when such selflessness didn't earn feature stories on the evening news, just as it took pride in being something more than just the home base for a great football team. And certainly Notre Dame was more selective in its admissions than a state land-grant college. But Giles had not considered the fierce pride of Michigan State's minorities who had been given a chance to play a major role in pursuing a National Championship, a role that no one else had been willing to give them. Yes, Notre Dame had fierce pride. But Michigan State had that, too. Yes, Notre Dame had an appetite for the top that had gone unassuaged for seventeen years. But Michigan State had its own brand of hunger. Finally, as Duffy Daugherty would have been glad to point out, ghosts don't win football games any more than do columnists. No, this one they'd have to play.

The final prelude to Saturday was a meeting of the Notre Dame and Michigan State freshmen teams in the second of two games for each squad. One of the defensive backs on the Michigan State squad was a kid named Steve Garvey who was shortly to give up football for a job playing baseball in the Dodger organization. Played on Friday night, the game attracted sixty-five hundred people to a four-thousand-seat high school field, with hundreds more turned away at the gate. It was a real barnburner, too, with Ara and Duffy watching from the press box and Parseghian admitting to firing and rehiring his freshman coach, Wally Moore, a half-dozen times as Notre Dame blew a 21–0 lead in the third quarter, rallied to tie it at 27–27, and finally won on a last-second field goal, 30–27. Ed Ziegler, a running back, kicked the 32-yard winning field goal after Moore, who didn't have a place kicker, turned to his bench and asked, "Can anyone here kick a field goal?" Ziegler volunteered, Moore sent him in, and the game was won. It was the only field goal Ziegler ever made—or attempted—in his college career.

Both the Notre Dame and Michigan State varsities watched the game, and the Irish went back to their dorm feeling that the game had been an omen. It had been tough. It had swung back and forth, with neither team showing a breaking point. And it had been won by Notre Dame on a field goal. They'd take it the next day, take it gladly.

Some time after the game, Michigan State athletic director Biggie Munn received a call from the last place he expected—or wanted. It was from the East Lansing police station, and the message was that they had Bubba Smith. The story was that Bubba, Jimmy Raye, and some others were cruising down the main drag of town in Bubba's big white Riviera with the gold lettering on the door. A local cop picked that moment to make a statement that any cop could have made at any time. Bubba had collected some parking tickets in his travels around town and had neglected to pay them. He had no reason to feel that he should since he had long since learned he could pretty much do anything he wanted. He just hadn't reckoned on a cop with a sense of the dramatic.

When Bubba saw the flashing lights and pulled over, he couldn't believe what he was hearing. This guy with the badge was going to take him downtown and book him for a few unpaid tickets? "You got to be kidding, man," he told the cop. "We're about to play the biggest game in the school's history, and you're arresting me for traffic tickets?"

"That's right," the cop said.

When they reached the station, Bubba began to believe the man. The police wanted $45 bail, and neither he nor his friends had the money on them. So the call went out to Biggie, who went to the police station, walked up to the cop on duty, and said, "How could you?"

"Yeah," Bubba thought. "You tell him."

It all took about an hour, but finally Bubba was sprung. But if you were cheering for Michigan State and were looking for signs, Friday had provided two, and neither one was good.

12

You have a dream, and one day it's not a dream anymore. It's real and it still seems like a dream.
—Pete Duranko

For Nick Eddy the dream was a nightmare with few clear memories. It began on Wednesday during practice when he reinjured his damaged right shoulder. The doctors had determined when he originally injured it that the damage was muscular and not skeletal, so they told him to take the rest of the week off. Parseghian, meanwhile, said only that he would play. They had a light workout before leaving for the train station and Lansing. After the workout the doctors hunted up an industrial-sized syringe and shot a load of cortisone into the shoulder to reduce the inflammation.

On the train, as the gray countryside punctuated by banners and signs and the people holding them flashed by, Eddy sat and talked with Tom Pagna. Among other things Eddy talked about how important the game was to his future, how it could determine how much money he would get to sign a pro contract. And here he was, a man who had never missed a game in his college career, with a throbbing shoulder, and he didn't know if he'd be able to play at all. Pagna had great affection for Eddy and knew that he would play if he could. "He was too great a ballplayer to quit," Pagna says. "And I felt for him."

Finally, the train pulled into the Lansing station, where another crowd was waiting with their banners on the platform. Even there, in the heart of Spartan country, a few of the fans had come not to jeer but to cheer the Irish. One of Ara's rules was that team members had to dress "appropriately" on road trips; that meant jackets, ties, and dress shoes. Wing tips with heavy leather soles and heels were the preferred footwear among the players. Just before the Michigan State game, Eddy's wife had persuaded him to get a new pair of wing tips, a purchase made possible by his income from ticket sales. Eddy took Jean's advice and wore the brand-new shoes with their slick, leather soles to Lansing.

To get off the train the players walked down a set of slick, steel steps. As Eddy walked down the steps, just ahead of Joe Azzaro, Bob Gladieux, and Tom Pagna and right behind Larry Conjar, Rocky Bleier, and Pete Duranko, he stepped on the edge of a steel riser and his feet flew out from under him. He instinctively threw out his right arm and caught the stair railing with his elbow. He kept from falling, but he also ripped the damaged muscles in his shoulder. Duranko heard Eddy disgorge a muffled scream and turned around. Gladieux heard the same scream and thought, "I might have to play." By the time Eddy got to the platform, lights were flashing in his head, and he was trying to keep from passing out from the pain. After getting himself together he got on the bus that would take them to the hotel. The pain subsided a bit on the trip, and he told himself he might be able to play after all. But deep down he knew he'd need a miracle to do it.

By the time the team settled in its rooms, word had gotten around that Nick had reinjured the shoulder. The less emotional players, such as Kevin Hardy, had known during the week that he probably wouldn't be able to play, and this just sealed it. The more emotional players hoped that he would come through. A few thought it didn't matter how bad the damage was, unless the arm actually fell off he had a duty to play.

Eddy sat up all night with ice bags on the shoulder, and as the pain began to subside his spirits picked up. The next morning when the team got to the locker room at Spartan Stadium, the doctors got out their needles and pumped his shoulder full of novocaine, telling him that since the damage was muscular, he couldn't hurt the joint permanently if he played. The novocaine killed most of the feeling in the shoulder, but even so, the damaged area was so swollen it still hurt. Parseghian told Eddy to go out and warm up and see how it felt.

Eddy did that, and the way it felt was dead. He couldn't move it, couldn't make it pump so he could run, couldn't use the arm to hang on to the football. He knew if he tried to play, the first hit of any intensity would finish him. He also knew that with one arm he wouldn't be able to maintain his balance to cut and wouldn't be able to protect the ball well when he was tackled. He went to Parseghian and told him all of this. "I'll play if you want me to, Coach," he said, "but I can't move my arm."

Parseghian decided right there that Eddy wouldn't play in the biggest game of his career and one of the biggest in the fabled history of Notre Dame. When they returned to the locker room, Parseghian told Gladieux to get ready to take Bleier's spot while Bleier took over for Eddy. It was a loss, but neither the team nor the coaches thought it was fatal. The feeling, said Pagna, was that they were deep in solid running backs. "Rocky was a bread-and-butter back," he said. "You can win with bread-and-butter backs, guys who give you everything they have. It might not be greatness, but if they win the game for you, who cares?"

Word had reached the Michigan State team that Eddy had hurt his shoulder getting off the train, and now they heard that he might not play. Bubba Smith and his defensive mates snorted with derision when they heard that. "He don't want that heat," Bubba told his teammates. "He remembers us from '65." Smith knew that half of what he said was for effect, and this was one of those times. He just wanted to convince the defense that Notre Dame was afraid of them, and all they had to do once the game started was reinforce that fear.

While Eddy was testing his shoulder and the other players were running through their pregame routine, Ara and Duffy wandered to midfield, where they stopped to chat. Ara, bareheaded in the 33-degree weather, wore dark slacks and a navy blue pullover with Notre Dame in ornate letters across the chest. Duffy wore a baggy parka with the hood down, and Spartans in block letters across the back, and a navy blue watch cap pulled down over the tops of his ears. They didn't say much, but it was the thought. Both wanted to win this game as badly as they had ever wanted to win a game, but they could be gentlemen about it.

Duffy spent time during the warmups touching base with a lot of people. One of the players he sauntered up to was Joe Azzaro, Notre Dame's kicker, who was practicing field goals and checking the footing on the field. He hadn't seen Daugherty approach him, and when he did, Azzaro had no idea who the little man was.

"What do you think of the wind?" Duffy asked him of the brisk breeze blowing from east to west and swirling around the field.

Azzaro said it wasn't a problem. They chatted a little more, and it was only after Daugherty walked away that the kicker realized who it had been and that Duffy was probably trying to mess him up—in a friendly sort of way—by getting him to worry about the weather conditions. It didn't work. Azzaro wasn't the sort to worry about those things. Still, it was worth a try.

As the teams were working out, the hordes were descending on the stadium. "Wearing everything from minks to mackinaws, the people swarmed into Spartan Stadium today long before the kickoff. Their eyes were much clearer than the lead-gray sky," wrote Dave Anderson in the *New York Times*. "The Notre Dame–Michigan State game, unlike some other college football games, apparently was not an excuse for an early cocktail party."

Not every fan who got in the gate had a ticket. A few got in through the courtesy of Biggie Munn. Two free admissions, in particular, were a genuine act of mercy. They were for two men from DeKalb, Illinois, who had arrived the night before the game and purchased two tickets for the game from a scalper. When they looked at the tickets, they found that they had purchased two unused tickets left over from the October 8 Michigan State–Michigan game. By then the scalper was long gone. The men told others they met of their bad luck, and they told others, until Win Shuler, a local restaurateur, heard what happened and took the men to see Biggie Munn. On hearing their story Munn let them through the gate. They wouldn't have seats, but at least they'd be in the stadium.

Several got in with less official help. Their method, both ancient and effective, was to slip some green to the ticket takers. Then there was Notre Dame's team security guard, a deputy sheriff from St. Joseph County in Indiana. He used his authority

to pass in a batch of fans from South Bend who had arrived with
no tickets but the promise of entry. He told them to find a place
to sit on the sideline. Of course, there was no place to sit anywhere except for the team bench, so that's where they sat. Others
stood wherever there was room and a view, joining others who
had also found their way to the sidelines, where they stayed for
the duration. Many of them got there at the invitation of Duffy
Daugherty. "Duffy couldn't say no to anybody," said Vince Carillot. "I think half of Pennsylvania was on the sideline. He let
them in and said, 'Find a seat,' and they all ended up on the
field."

Today, you can't stand on a sideline without an official pass.
Even coaches have to wear them in some stadiums. But back then
if you could get on the sidelines, nobody chased you out. Knute
Rockne, in fact, had designed Notre Dame Stadium with almost
no room on the sidelines because he saw that as the only way to
limit the number of people who wound up there. And Michigan
State, which had never seen a crowd so large, was not prepared
to deal with gate-crashers. They, too, would have an effect on
how the game was played.

In the Spartan Stadium press box, which was known as the
Stabley Hilton after the school's public relations man, Fred Stabley, the writers were finding that even though it was one of the
largest and most modern in the game, there was barely enough
room to move. They had used up the town's hotel rooms, used up
every rental car within miles of East Lansing, and now they had
used up the press box. Among the luminaries of the press who
covered that game were Frank Dolson from Philadelphia; Jimmy
Cannon, Arthur Daley, Dave Anderson, Jimmy Breslin, Jess
Abramson, and Paul Zimmerman from New York; Bill Gildea
from Washington; Dan Coughlin from Cleveland; Furman
Bisher from Atlanta; Don Jenkins and John Underwood for
Sports Illustrated; Bill Gleason from Chicago; Tom Harmon from
California; and a rookie sportswriter from Chicago named Brent
Musberger. Although many remember Red Smith, a Notre Dame
graduate and perhaps the best sportswriter ever, as being there,
too, Red covered the game from a gin mill in New York.

To accommodate the 754 journalists—the most ever to cover a
game and more than would cover a Super Bowl for years to come
—Stabley sent his staff into the science labs to commandeer every

stool they could find. He crammed them behind the third and last row in the press box for the overflow. And even that wasn't enough.

In the locker rooms the teams were getting ready for the coming battle. Despite Bubba Smith's bravado, no one had any delusions that it was going to be easy. They thought about their assignments, about the men they would have to block and tackle and run against. To others they were legends. To the players they were muscle and bone and blood, men like themselves who would not quit, who had no breaking point. The seniors knew best what it was about. On both sides they had had immortality by the throat and had watched it wriggle free. This was their chance to make it all right, to avenge UCLA and the Rose Bowl, to erase USC, to be perfect, to answer the call to greatness. They would not lose. Of that both teams were certain.

The sophomores did not grasp the full significance of the game. They didn't have the perspective. Cavender, for one, had watched the varsity win every game except the Rose Bowl the year before and now was part of another team that had also won every game. He would come to realize how naive it was to believe that it was always like that; that every year would bring another huge game and another chapter in the legend. He could see the intensity in his teammates' eyes and felt waves of camaraderie in their every glance, looks that said, "I'll do anything for you, and you for me." It wasn't that he wasn't pumped up. Cavender was the kind of guy who'd have smoke coming out of his nostrils over a game of checkers. On the walk from Kellogg Center to the stadium before the game, as the team passed the Red Cedar River and proceeded across campus whistling the fight song, Cavender visualized himself taking on trees—big trees that had been rooted in the ground for twenty years and more—and just knocking them over, breaking them into splinters. He was always in a mood to play football. He just didn't know how enormous this game was.

Gladieux had a better idea of what was happening, but he had been raised on the legend of Notre Dame and had been reminded all year that this was the season in which the Irish would reclaim their rightful place at the peak of the college football world. Unlike Cavender, he had never started a game. His ambition in spring and summer practice had been just to make the traveling squad and get in some plays during garbage time. And now, after Eddy had determined that he could not play, he was faced with starting the biggest game Notre Dame had played in twenty years. He was as ready as he could be. He had run with the varsity the last half of the week, after Eddy reinjured the shoulder. Just the same, when Parseghian came up to him and said, "You're starting," and he said, "Okay," his stomach felt as if it had been turned inside out. "It's like you've played flag football all your life and for the first time you put on pads and go into combat," he said. "It's a big test of courage."

Nobody on either side remembers what either coach said. Ara doesn't remember himself. But it's safe to say that Parseghian was short, to the point, and intense, while Duffy told a horrible joke to cut the tension.

The officials who waited on the field were as nervous as the players. Jerry Markbreit, who would become a top NFL referee, was a thirty-one-year-old rookie Big Ten back judge that year on a five-man crew headed by referee Howard Wirtz. (Five-man crews were new, and some conferences still went with four, saying that five officials would lead to the calling of too many marginal penalties.) Markbreit wrote about the game in his book, *Born to Referee* (with Alan Steinberg). The crew had been assigned to the game at the beginning of the year, and they had known from the start it would be a big one, but they had no idea how big until they arrived in East Lansing the night before.

"The atmosphere was like that of a Super Bowl game today," he wrote in 1988. "It was late November, but people were driving around like it was summertime, hanging out their windows and honking their horns; the press was twenty-deep. . . . It was the most highly charged pregame atmosphere I'd ever experienced." Before the game Wirtz told the crew how important it was that they get every call right. Then Wirtz said, "Gentlemen, this is the biggest game of the year, maybe the biggest game of the next hundred years. . . . We must work this game so expertly that, later, it will seem as if we weren't even there."

Finally, the players left their locker rooms, gathered in the tunnel leading to the field, and then ran out into a brutish November day that was awash with an energy they had never imagined. "You could see the waves of vibrations from the fans in the air," Rocky Bleier remembers. "You could actually see it in the air."

They ran quickly to the sideline followed by the coaches and joined in a last team huddle. Jim Lynch for Notre Dame and Clinton Jones and George Webster for Michigan State trotted to midfield where Wirtz was waiting for the pregame coin toss. When the coin hit the closely cut, firm turf, Wirtz and the players bent to look at it. Notre Dame had won. Lynch told Wirtz the Irish would receive. Daugherty and Vince Carillot liked that, and Webster, Thornhill, Smith, Phillips, and the rest of the defense loved it. If they had won the toss, they may have put Notre Dame on offense themselves, just to let them taste the fury of the Spartan defense, which felt certain that the first drive would be shorter than anyone at Notre Dame expected. Jones and Webster chose to defend the south goal, which would put the wind at their backs in the second quarter. It was time to play.

Unlike Parseghian, Daugherty's kick coverage squad was not made up primarily of the starting defense. Instead, he used a suicide squad that included a number of nonstarters who could get down the field quickly. They lined up across their own 38-yard line, 2 yards behind the ball, and got down into 3-point stances. Kenney, his right foot as bare as the day he was born, lined up 1 yard behind them on the right hash mark. Then, as the crowd roared in anticipation, he took two steps, swung his foot, and the game was on.

The kick into the wind was short, and Larry Conjar fielded it ahead of the two deep backs, Tom O'Leary and Rocky Bleier. As O'Leary and Bleier sprinted past him to join a wall of five blockers in tight formation, Conjar fell in behind and headed for the middle of the field. Gladieux, on the left of the five-man wedge, took a bead on his man, reserve halfback William Ware, moved to block him, and suddenly realized Ware wasn't there anymore but was sailing overhead, reaching for Conjar and screaming like a banshee. "Baby, these guys are high," Gladieux thought.

Meanwhile, in the middle of the wedge, another reserve halfback, Frank Waters, was running through an attempted block by Brian Stenger as if Stenger weren't there and driving into Conjar at the Michigan State 27, where Ware joined him for the tackle. It was a great play by both defenders, and when the coaches watched the films, they would see that had Stenger been able to

get Waters, the hole would have been there and Conjar might
still be running.

Hanratty trotted onto the field, walked into the huddle, and
called the first play: Conjar over right guard—straight at Charlie
Thornhill. Michigan State stacked seven men on the line of
scrimmage, with four men to the defensive left and three to the
right, including Webster, who lined up over tackle Paul Seiler. At
the snap Goeddeke fired out into Thornhill and blew him backwards while the left guard and tackle, Dick Swatland and Bob
Kuechenberg, closed off the hole to the outside. On the other side
of the line, Regner fired across Jeff Richardson's bow, screening
him from the play, while Seiler put a solid hit on Webster. With
Gladieux flanked out, Bleier ran right to decoy the defense and
Hanratty handed to Conjar, who piled into the hole. The blocking
was nearly perfect, but Webster, who never stayed blocked for
long, fought through Seiler and brought Conjar down at the 31
after a 4-yard gain. When the whistles blew, fourteen of the
twenty-two men on the field were within 3 yards of Conjar. On
second-and-6, Notre Dame came to the line again with Gladieux
flanked and Bleier in a slot right. This time Michigan State
stacked two men over center and only two men over Notre
Dame's left side, Phil Hoag and Webster. As Hanratty called the
signals, Bleier dropped back from just behind the line to his right
halfback position. At the snap Hanratty turned and handed to
Bleier, who took two steps to the right, toward the onrushing
Bubba Smith, then crossed over to the left toward a hole off left
tackle. It was a play put in especially for Smith, who was incredibly fast in a straight line but couldn't cut quickly. It worked. As
Smith went sailing through the air behind him, Bleier turned into
the hole. This time George Chatlos made the big play for the
Spartans, crashing through the blockers from left defensive tackle
to pull Bleier down, but not before Notre Dame had gained another 4 yards.

On third-and-2 from the 35 and with Thornhill blitzing over
the left side of the defense, Hanratty took the snap, stepped to his
right, and as Bubba Smith stormed into the backfield from the
outside, ducked behind Swatland and broke into the clear for 10
yards to the 45, where Webster grabbed him by the ankles and
Jess Phillips put a vicious hit on his kidney. First down, Notre
Dame.

Irish fans were celebrating. This was going to be easy. On first down Michigan State now dropped into a four-man line with Webster looking for a pass. But again Hanratty gave the ball to Conjar over left tackle, where Notre Dame had a double team on Jeff Richardson and Bleier leading the play, blocking end Phil Hoag. But Richardson fought off both Regner and Seiler, and Hoag fought through Bleier, and both men hit Conjar at the line. The fullback took the hit, broke the tackle, and lunged forward, touching ground at the 49 for another 4 yards. On second down Parseghian stuck with what was working and called Conjar's number again into the center of the line. But now Bubba Smith had moved into the gap between Goeddeke and the left guard, Regner, who hit him but could not get his head in front of the big lineman. Bubba grabbed Conjar around the neck and brought him down at State's 49-yard line. Conjar fumbled on the play but fell on the ball himself, setting up third-and-4. Now Smith moved back to left defensive end, and Webster moved back up to the line of scrimmage on the right side of the defense. At the snap Webster and Thornhill started to rush, but when they saw the Notre Dame line drop back to protect for a pass, they both reversed direction to get into pass coverage, leaving only four men rushing Hanratty. The play was a draw to Bleier, and it would have worked but for Jeff Richardson who stormed past the blockers on the right and collared Bleier in the backfield for a 4-yard loss, setting up fourth down at the Notre Dame 47 and the day's first punt.

Bleier had started the year as Notre Dame's punter, but after he bruised his leg against Oklahoma, Gladieux took over. But Gladieux had had a kick blocked against Navy and was not getting the ball as high and deep as Ara would have liked. So in the week leading up to the Michigan State game, Parseghian decided to have big Kevin Hardy punt. Hardy had never punted in college before, but he had a strong leg and was totally unflappable. Hardy now came in to punt, and Gerald Kelly came in at center to snap it to him. Goeddeke, who couldn't snap long, normally would have come out under Parseghian's scheme, but since Jim Seymour was a mediocre blocker, Goeddeke moved to end and Seymour came out.

Kelly snapped the ball low, but Hardy fielded it without a hitch at his ankles, stepped into it, and boomed one down to Michigan

State's 13, where Al Brenner fielded it and started running across the field to his left, trying to get behind the wall of blockers setting up a return. Gladieux foiled the plan, bursting through the blockers much as Ware had flown over him on the opening kickoff, and nailed Brenner on the 11 for a 2 yard loss.

Michigan State was used to taking over after punts in good field position, but now they began their first series on their own 11, with the small contingent of Notre Dame fans in the stands making enough noise for ten thousand. On the first play Notre Dame brought eight men to the line of scrimmage against a State offense that had seven men in tight and a slot back between the left tackle and end. At the snap Raye kept the ball, started down the left side of the line, and was nailed in his tracks by John Horney, who came through untouched, hit Raye in the chest, and drove him down on the 9 for a 2-yard loss. On second down the Spartans again came out in a seven-man balanced line, and now Raye dropped back, faked a handoff, and retreated to his own 1, where he turned around and looked to pass. Instead of a receiver he found Tom Rhoads coming at him unblocked from the front side, and if he had had time to look behind him, he would have seen Alan Page doing the same from the back side. Raye pulled the ball down and started to run just as Rhoads and Page met at the spot he had just occupied. But in bringing the ball down, Raye dropped it. Cavender, who had stayed in to block, saw the loose ball and fell on it at the 4. It was the first huge play of the game, and the sophomore from Detroit had saved his team from a turnover in the shadow of their own goal line.

The Spartans had the ball, but they seemed shell-shocked. They took too much time deciding on a play and got flagged for delay of game, pushing the ball back to their own 2-yard line. On third-and-19, Raye kept again and finally saw the first block of the day that sprung him through the right side for a modest gain of 6 yards. Not that it would have mattered if he had gained more. State was flagged for clipping Kevin Hardy on the play, but Notre Dame declined the penalty to set up a punt.

With Kenney setting up 5 yards deep in his own end zone, Parseghian called for a blocked punt, and now Michigan State got a break. Again Cavender had a hand—or, more accurately, a head—in it. At the snap Rhoads stormed in from the right and Page from the left. Normally, as the blocking back on punts,

Cavender would look first for the man coming from the right, which was the side Kenney kicked from. But Cavender saw that Rhoads delayed at the line, so he made a quick decision and turned toward Page, who was coming full tilt. Cavender didn't so much block him as put his head down, aim for the middle of Page's chest, and hope he lived to tell about it. Page hit him and knocked him backwards into Kenney. The transfer of momentum from Page to Cavender caused just enough of a delay to let Kenney get the kickoff a moment before Cavender crash-landed at Kenney's feet.

The ball carried only to State's 44-yard line, but here they got another break. Schoen had taken his position as safety too deep and decided not to risk trying to run forward and field the low punt on the fly. He let it bounce, and when it did, instead of bouncing to him, it skittered to his left and rolled all the way to the Notre Dame 38—a 36-yard punt that turned into a 54-yarder. Instead of having the ball in Spartan territory, the Irish had to start in their own territory.

It didn't seem that it would matter. Notre Dame had them on the run, and it was only a matter of time before the Irish offense got rolling. And Parseghian had decided that this was the time. After keeping the ball on the ground for the first series, Parseghian turned Hanratty loose. On first down, with Seymour split to the left, Hanratty dropped back, Conjar dropped the onrushing Bubba Smith in his tracks, and "the young soph-ah-more," as the announcers liked to say, fired for Bleier in the right flat, where the Spartans made a great play to bat it away. Undeterred, Hanratty dropped back again, this time with Conjar faking into the line and Bleier sprinting right for a screen. Kuechenberg was supposed to delay Bubba and then sprint out in front of Bleier to lead the blocking. Only he didn't delay Smith at all, and Hanratty, with Bubba bearing down on him like a human avalanche, unloaded it behind Bleier, and it fell incomplete.

No problem, Hanratty figured. On third-and-10 he dropped back again, and now Kuechenberg cut Bubba down at the ankles, and the rest of the line took care of everyone but George Chatlos who was rushing inside of Bubba. Hanratty gave ground and circled to his right as Chatlos missed a swipe at his ankles. From his own 25 and throwing off the wrong foot, Hanratty rifled the ball 37 yards downfield to Gladieux who, with Jess Phillips all over him, pulled it in for a 26-yard gain to Michigan State's 36.

On first down the Irish went to Gladieux over the right side, but he was stacked up after one exceedingly difficult yard. Then, on second-and-9, the Spartans got another break. Parseghian tried to call a halfback draw for the next play, but somehow when the play was sent in by messenger, Hanratty was told it was a quarterback draw. He called the play, went to the line, took the snap, and quickly dropped back 7 yards as if to pass. Here he was supposed to hand off to Bleier, but instead he ran the play he had received from the sidelines and turned upfield, running for daylight around the right side. He was met at the 35 by Thornhill, and as he twisted to his right and tried to get another yard or two, out of the corner of his eye he saw Bubba closing in for the kill. "Uh-oh," Hanratty thought. "Here's a collision I'm not going to win." Thornhill had also seen Smith and was thinking the same thing as Hanratty. "Bubba was coming like a train, so I just ducked. Oh, my goodness, he was *moving*."

Smith hit him high on the right shoulder, driving Hanratty's left shoulder into the turf, where it made what Bubba thought was a squishy sort of sound. Not a good sound, even to the man who did the hitting. Hanratty moaned when he hit, and although it didn't particularly hurt, he knew the left shoulder was history. Thornhill and Smith knew it, too, as did Tom Pagna, who was watching from the sideline.

Pagna tried to get to Parseghian, but the uninvited guests on the sidelines were so thick that they forced the coaches 2 yards out onto the field. Pagna couldn't get around enough people to tell Parseghian that Hanratty was injured. By the time he worked his way to Ara, another play, a pass to Bleier on the left side, had been sent in, and Hanratty was determined to see if he could make it work.

As the team lined up, Pagna told Ara, "You have to get him out of there. He's hurt."

"How do you know?" Ara wanted to know.

"I can see it," Pagna said.

It was too late. Hanratty took the snap, dropped back, and with his left arm flapping at his side like an empty shirt sleeve, tried to throw. He had Bleier open, too, but without his left arm to lead the throw, he couldn't get anything on it and put up a knuckleball that floated toward Bleier. By the time the pass got there, so had Phillips, who knocked it away to set up a fourth down.

Hanratty came off the field and approached Parseghian.

"Why did you run the quarterback draw?" was the first thing Ara asked him.

"You called it," Hanratty replied.

"No," Parseghian said. "I called a halfback draw."

Since that conversation wasn't going any further, Hanratty told his coach about his shoulder. Ara sent him to the doctors, who sent him to the locker room; closer inspection revealed a separated shoulder. Hanratty would watch the rest of the game with his arm in a sling on the sideline. Pagna, meanwhile, had tracked down O'Brien in the mob on the sideline and told him to get ready to take over. O'Brien hadn't expected to get in the game at all. His work was usually done in the second halves of games that had already been won. He had seen plenty of action that way, but he hadn't come to East Lansing expecting a blowout that would give him a chance to play.

The son of a career Navy officer, O'Brien had played his high school ball at St. John's College High in McLean, Virginia. As a high school quarterback he was not known as a great passer, but he was the kind of kid who won ball games any way he could. He wasn't big, only 5 feet 11 and 173 pounds, and although he developed into a good passer, his arm strength was not the equal of Hanratty's rifle-arm, but this was nothing to apologize for.

Since he had not expected to play, he wasn't particularly nervous when Pagna told him to get ready. He knew the plays, and one of the starting halfbacks, Bob Gladieux, had worked with him all year on the second unit and was used to the way he handed off the ball and the speed of his passes. Most important, his teammates, who had taken the loss of Eddy in stride, had total confidence in him. Since they had lost Hanratty, they'd win with O'Brien.

Meanwhile, Hardy had gone in to punt again, along with Kelly, the snapper. Seymour came out and Goeddeke moved to end. Kelly's first snap had been low, and his second was even lower. It hit the ground in front of Hardy, who fielded it on the hop and juggled it briefly. By the time he gained control of the ball, several Spartans had broken through the line and were almost on top of him. Hardy considered the alternatives and realized he had no time to kick the ball and no hope of running it, so he did the only thing he could think of: He heaved it downfield, hoping that maybe the Spartans would intercept it and they'd at least get some yardage out of it.

It was a good thought, but it was doomed from the start because Notre Dame's linemen, unaware of Hardy's troubles, had already released downfield. When Hardy threw the ball, they became illegal receivers, and the officials started throwing red hankies (this was before the switch to yellow flags) all over the field. Regardless of what happened, the play was coming back. Even worse, the closest man to the ball as it came down was Goeddeke, who had no idea that Hardy had thrown it or that the Spartans thought he was a receiver. Jess Phillips saw the ball, saw Goeddeke, and dove at the center's legs, getting him below the right knee with his helmet. Goeddeke went down, rolled over, stood up, and realized immediately that the pain he felt was not going to go away. He hopped off the field as best he could and informed Parseghian and Wampfler that they might want to rustle up a new center.

In 3 plays Notre Dame, which had started the game without its All-American halfback, lost its All-American center and its sensational quarterback. And after the Spartans declined the penalty and took the ball, they had given State valuable field position at their own 33.

While Pagna talked to O'Brien, Jerry Wampfler called for Tim Monty, Goeddeke's backup at center. Monty, at 6 feet and 205 pounds, was considerably smaller than Goeddeke. A sophomore, he went to Notre Dame from St. Albans, West Virginia, and went into his sophomore year with the same ambition as many of his classmates on the team—not so much to start but to make the traveling team. He had done that and had gone in with O'Brien and the second team many times to put the icing on the team's many blowout wins. Like O'Brien, the thought of playing against Michigan State had never occurred to him, and now he was about to be thrown into an incredibly important game. "It was a crazy experience for a sophomore," he remembers. "I don't know that I've ever been able to conceptualize the magnitude of that game. At the time I certainly didn't. I wasn't even aware of the crowd in the stands."

As Monty and O'Brien received their instructions and took some practice snaps on the sideline, the defense went back on the field to try to stop Michigan State for the second time. They did, but this time the Spartans looked a little sharper than in their first disastrous possession. On first down from the State 33, Raye handed to Dwight Lee, who made only a yard before Lynch introduced him to the turf. On second-and-9, Raye took the snap, took three steps back, rolled a couple of steps to his right, and flicked a short pass to Lee, who had come out of the backfield. Lee took the ball 3 yards across the line of scrimmage and made another 8 yards on his own before Horney hauled him down at the 45 for a gain of 11 and State's first, first down.

That got the crowd back into the game, and Raye followed it with a keeper to the right. With Cavender also running right, Notre Dame expected Raye to draw in the defense and then pitch the ball ahead to the leading back—in this case, Cavender. It was a bread-and-butter play for the Spartans, but it was also a play that Daugherty had decided not to run. Instead, Raye turned quickly upfield inside of Tom Rhoads, the defensive end whose job it was to watch for the pitch. Rhoads dove for Raye but could get only one hand on the quarterback's hip, and Raye ran through the arm-tackle and had 8 more yards to Notre Dame's 47 before Pergine brought him down. On second-and-2 Raye tried the same play again, but this time Pergine and Lynch were waiting for him, and he was lucky to get back to the line of scrimmage. On third down Raye went back to pass again. The first time he had thrown, Notre Dame had been in a run defense, and he had had time to get his pass off. This time Pergine came up the middle on a blitz and was on Raye just as he started moving his arm forward to throw another short toss to Lee in the left flat. The ball tumbled out of his hand as Pergine hit him, but it rolled forward and fell to the ground, an incomplete pass that had come within an eyelash of being a fumble.

On fourth down Kenney punted for the second time. The kick traveled 28 yards to the Notre Dame 19, where Tom Schoen ran toward it, signaling for a fair catch. Dwight Lee, running down to cover the punt, didn't see Schoen's signal and ran into him at the 20, a 15-yard penalty that moved the ball to the Notre Dame 35, where Coley O'Brien took over for his first series.

Parseghian called a handoff to Conjar over the left side on O'Brien and Monty's first play. Monty delivered the snap and fired out to put a good block on George Chatlos away from the play. Regner and Seiler opened up a quick hole against Phil Hoag and Jeff Richardson, but Hoag and Richardson both fought off the blocks and closed it down before Conjar got any farther than 2 yards. On second down Ara showed the confidence he had in

O'Brien by calling a pass to Bleier. O'Brien did everything right. He took the snap, dropped back quickly, spotted Bleier at the Michigan State 48 in the middle of the field, and, ignoring Hoag and Bubba Smith who were closing in from each side, fired a low, tight spiral at Bleier. The ball was perfectly thrown, but as Bleier stretched his arms out to catch it, George Chatlos, who had dropped into pass coverage, dove through the air in a desperate try to bat the pass away. He swiped at it and barely hit it, but he altered its path enough so that Bleier couldn't handle it even though he got his hands on it.

O'Brien picked himself off the turf, where Hoag had deposited him after he got rid of the ball, ready to try again. This time Parseghian sent in a screen pass to Bleier. With Chatlos and Thornhill blitzing, O'Brien flicked the ball to his halfback, but now Notre Dame started to look shaky as Bleier turned upfield, collided with Dick Swatland, his own guard, and went down for a loss of 2 yards. It was time to punt again, and for his first 3 plays O'Brien had 1 completion in 2 attempts for negative yardage.

The fans were delighted. Few of them had noticed Goeddeke's absence, but they knew the little quarterback wearing number 3 wasn't Hanratty. He hadn't moved the ball on his first possession, and they figured that was it for Notre Dame's offense. But while the crowd was cheering, Vince Carillot was having anxiety attacks. As the assistant defensive coach to Henry Bullough, Carillot's post during games was in the coaches' box attached to the press box. From there he and an offensive assistant could see the whole field better than anyone on the sidelines and call plays down by a telephone connection. Carillot had spent a lot of time watching films of Hanratty, and he thought he knew the quarterback better than Hanratty's own mother did. "I knew exactly what he was going to do and how he was going to do it," Carillot said. And he taught what he knew to his defensive backs.

But O'Brien was a different matter. "What's a Coley O'Brien?" is how Bubba Smith put it. "We never heard of him. Who is he? What can he do? Is he a runner or a passer?" They didn't know. And because they didn't, they had to play him straighter than they thought they could play Hanratty. Putting Hanratty out of the game was the worst thing they could do. "Everybody in the stands is saying 'Oh, boy!' and I'm saying 'Oh, hell!' " Carillot said. To this day Michigan State says that O'Brien hurt them because he was quicker of foot than Hanratty.

Hanratty listened to all that and laughed. "I don't think I was predictable," he said. "I was the second or third fastest guy on the team. If those guys got me running, I would have had no trouble gaining yardage. What I did best was improvise.

"No question," he said, "if I had played, we would have lit up the board. They wanted to double-team Seymour, but no way could they have done that the way I moved in the pocket. I would have loved not to have gotten hurt in that game."

On the only pass Hanratty completed, the 26-yarder to Gladieux, he had shown what he could do, sprinting away from a rush and throwing quickly and accurately on the run. He had carried the ball twice and gained 12 yards. And knowing what somebody is going to do is not the same as stopping him from doing it. Maybe Hanratty is right, and maybe Carillot is. It's one of the great things about the game. Nobody will ever know. All we know is what happened.

And what happened next brought the crowd to its feet and buried the field in noise. After Hardy's punt the Spartan offense took over on its own 27-yard line. The first two times Michigan State had had the ball, they had started their drives with a run and had had little success because John Ray's troops were stacked for it. So this time Daugherty told Raye to go deep on the first play of the drive. O'Leary was in single coverage on Gene Washington and about 7 yards off the line, giving the big end plenty of running room. At the snap Raye dropped straight back, waited a beat to give Washington a chance to get into the secondary, then stepped up and heaved the ball downfield into the wind. Had he thrown it a foot shorter, Washington might have caught it in full stride and gone all the way. But he had to reach forward for the ball, and in catching it, he couldn't keep his feet under him. Still, when he hit the ground, he was 42 yards farther downfield than he had been when the play started, and the Spartans had a first down at Notre Dame's 31.

Until now Clinton Jones had been used as a decoy, but now Raye handed off to him over the right side. The defense collapsed on the hole, but somehow Jones found a crack where none seemed to have existed and squirted through for 5 yards, with Lynch saving a bigger gain with a shoestring tackle. On the next play Raye went to Jones again, and this time Lynch burst through the center of the line and met him head-on in the backfield. Normally, this would have been a battle that Lynch would win, but Jones bounced out of Lynch's arms, skipped outside, was met by Rhoads, spun out of his arms, and plowed forward for 4 more yards to bring up third-and-1 at the 22.

Daugherty told Raye to take it himself for the first down, but when Raye tried to go over right guard, Rhoads crashed down and buried him inches short of the first down. Today, a coach would send in his kicker and put 3 points on the board, but in 1966 Daugherty told Raye to sneak it again on fourth down. Had he failed, it would have been another big boost for the Irish, but he didn't. Going straight over center, he picked up 2 yards and kept the drive alive.

Daugherty had wanted Raye to run, and he did. On first down from the 20, Raye kept right again, only to be stopped for no gain by Pergine. The Spartans regrouped and stepped to the line again, but before they could run a play, the first quarter came to a close. For the rest of the half Michigan State would have the wind at their backs.

On the first play of the second quarter, Daugherty called on Cavender. On a straight handoff over left tackle, Cavender took the ball and found not a single white shirt anywhere within 5 yards of the line of scrimmage. That's how well the Spartans had the play blocked. By the time the defense caught up with him, he had gained 11 yards and the Spartans had a first-and-goal at the 9. The offensive line was on a roll now. Pruiett and West on the right, Joe Przybycki and Tony Conti to the right, Al Brenner and Gene Washington at the ends, and Larry Smith in the center had gotten into a rhythm in which they could almost read the minds of the Notre Dame defenders. Big drives are like that. Players who had been getting beat or fighting to stalemates suddenly become certain they can handle the guy across from them. The defense, meanwhile, is hoping desperately for a stop, something that will allow the players to get their acts together. Notre Dame didn't get that break, and all Lynch, who called the signals, knew was that "the things we did against everybody else weren't working anymore."

The house that Biggie Munn built was rocking as the Spartans came to the line and the Irish dug in to stop them. Again Raye turned and handed to Cavender over left tackle, and again there was a big hole waiting for him. He got to the 4-yard line before O'Leary stopped him. In Ray's defensive scheme a cornerback having to make a tackle on a running play was a sign of total failure, and the right defensive side of Ray's line had been buried by green shirts. The only man not blocked was Page, who came across the line on a containing route and waved at Cavender as he drove through the hole. It was second and goal at the 4.

Michigan State broke the huddle and came out with the line packed in tightly and Dwight Lee in a slot between the left tackle and end, with Cavender and Jones lined up tight behind Raye. John Ray had called a defense that had the linemen crashing down to the inside, which was where Jones was supposed to run with the ball. The play was designed to go off the left tackle, with Lee blocking from the slot and Cavender kicking Page outside. With Mitch Pruiett pulling from his right guard slot and coming across, the formation gave the Spartans six blockers at the point of attack. It wasn't enough.

When the defensive line crashed in toward the center, it wiped out the blocking—and very nearly wiped out Cavender. The fullback knew he would be called on to block Page on many plays, and he had studied the All-American end on film all week. He noticed that Page's assignment called for him to get across the line of scrimmage and hold his position until the play developed. It was utterly predictable, and Cavender thought he could pull it off because, as he put it, "if you know where he's going, you can be there." However, he admitted, "they did pull a few surprises with their stunts." One of the surprises came right then. Instead of coming across the line, Page came down the line, and Cavender, who was supposed to block Page out, didn't have a chance. He drove into Page's legs with his left shoulder and barely slowed him up. Page didn't make the tackle—he didn't make any tackles that day—but he helped stack up the play for no gain. Meanwhile, Cavender knew something was wrong. He had come into the game with a rib injury that hurt whenever he twisted. The trainers had wrapped that up, and the pain was tolerable. Now when he hit Page, his left arm from the shoulder on down went numb. Then it started hurting. Bad. He got back into the huddle, and Pruiett noticed he was wincing.

"What's wrong?" Pruiett asked.

"I gotta get out of here," Cavender said. "My shoulder's hurt."

"There's no time for that," Pruiett told him.

"I'm really hurting," Cavender said.

"My shoulder's hurting, too," Pruiett said. "There's no time for pain."

This happened in a few seconds, while Raye was getting the play from the sideline. It was third down at the 4, and if the Spartans were going to score, it had better be now. Cavender considered what Pruiett had said and decided he was right. There was no time for pain.

Raye called the play—an off-tackle dive to the right side. Cavender would carry. He lined up directly behind Raye, and when the ball was snapped, he took a step forward and then veered to the right toward the hole, taking the ball from Raye as he went by. The first step was enough to suck Lynch into the middle, where he got tangled up in the pile Pruiett and West created. West sealed off the inside of the hole with a great block on Duranko, and Gene Washington screened Rhoads from the play on the outside. The only man left to fill, O'Leary, was waiting at the goal line, and Clinton Jones, leading Cavender through the hole, took him head-on and simply ran over him. When Cavender got through the line, he saw the goal line, which was highlighted by a stripe of red paint, and dove forward, aiming to hit the ground a foot inside the end zone. That's where he landed, and that's where his teammates pulled him upright and jumped up and down in a circle around him.

Cavender's injury was diagnosed after the game as a stretched ligament. Although it was his left shoulder and he took his stance on his right arm, it hurt every time he got down to start a play. He couldn't use it to block anymore, and so he spent the rest of the day throwing his body across his targets and blocking with his hip. He didn't come out, though. There was no time for that. But after the game, when he took his jersey off, the hard plastic armor on the shoulder flap part of his pads was shattered radially like an automobile windshield that has stopped a head. That's how hard he had hit and been hit by Alan Page.

Michigan State had drawn first blood. After Kenney kicked the extra point, they held a 7–0 lead with 1:40 gone in the second quarter. They knew what it meant, too. Notre Dame's first-string defense hadn't allowed a touchdown since the first game of the year, against Purdue. They had given up one score in that game and hadn't given up another since. Now the question was how they would react to the insult and how O'Brien and the offense would answer.

Kenney kicked off shallow again, and Conjar again took the kick on the 15. This time there was no chance of breaking it. The pursuit closed in on him in a green wave after 11 yards, and Notre Dame's offense took over on their own 26. As the Spartan defense left the sideline to go back to work, Daugherty gave them one piece of advice: "There's your touchdown. Now hold them."

Notre Dame came out as though it would answer immediately. On first down O'Brien dropped back as if to pass, then handed to Bleier on a draw play. Bleier flashed through the right side for 12 yards before Webster hauled him down. Then it was Conjar through the middle for 4 more punishing yards to the 42. On second-and-6 Bleier tried the middle again for 3 more yards, setting up third-and-3 at the 45. Parseghian now sent in Brian Stenger, the sophomore end, in place of Gmitter and called a pass to Stenger. He caught the pass, too, for what would have been a first down on State's 45, but before the snap, Stenger had jumped and didn't have time to get set again before the play started. The flags came out, and the play was wiped out. On third-and-8 O'Brien again went back to pass, had plenty of time, but missed Gladieux cutting into the middle of the field. Hardy punted to the 19, and Michigan State went back to work.

Jones started the drive by trying left tackle, but again the play was stacked up for no gain. Then, on second down from the 19, Raye took the snap and sprinted out to the right. Lynch crashed through the line after him, but Cavender got just enough of him to let Raye turn the corner. Duranko had the next shot at him, but Raye was a step too fast for the big tackle. At the 25, Clinton Jones wiped out O'Leary as Raye faked inside to freeze Horney, and then moved back toward the sideline as Horney dove for him. Horney got a hand on his hip, but it only slowed him down a step; Raye was off to the races down the sideline in front of the Notre Dame bench. Looking back on it, Raye feels he could have taken it all the way if he had cut it back to the middle of the field, but in one of those instinctive decisions you make on a football field, he continued down the sideline, where Smithberger and Schoen eventually hemmed him in and Rhoads finally caught up to him from behind.

It was a gain of 30, and now the home crowd was certain the Irish were going to be pushed all the way back to South Bend. But the play pointed out the best and the worst of the Spartan offense. In the last 2 drives they had picked up 72 yards on 2 plays, the pass to Washington and now this run. That was just about half of the total yardage they would gain for the half on 33 plays. So while 2 plays gained 72 yards, 31 others gained only 86. For this offense, if they didn't get it in big hunks, they weren't going to get it at all.

Right now they were getting it. On first down from their own 49, Dwight Lee got the call and burst through the right side for 14 more yards and a first down at the Notre Dame 37. A run by Cavender gained only 1 yard, and then Michigan State received yet another huge break.

On second-and-9, Raye rolled left to pass, stopped, and threw downfield for Dwight Lee. The pass was short, and Lynch stepped in front of Lee, picked it off at his own 30, and headed the other way. He got to the 35 where he confronted Clinton Jones, who was driving forward, diving at his legs. At that moment Lynch had what seemed like a brilliant idea. With Jones coming in low, he would jump over him and keep running. But just as he planted his left leg to jump, Jones hit him. With the leg still on the ground, Lynch's knee hyperextended, and then he went flying in a somersault. He came down on his head, and if the game were played today, that would be the end of it. The play ends when the ball carrier hits the ground. But back then it didn't end there. When Lynch hit, the ball popped free, and Jones swept it up at the original line of scrimmage.

Lynch was furious with himself for giving up the football. Besides that, his knee hurt. He got up hopping on one leg and for a moment considered going out of the game, but he decided to stay in. "He'd rather play on a bum knee than come out and face me," John Ray explained.

Clinton Jones told everyone after the game that the hit he put on Lynch "was the hardest I've ever hit anybody." He's still telling people that. And Lynch is still bristling every time he hears it. "He didn't hit me hard at all," said Lynch. It was his dumb decision to try to jump over Jones that caused all the trouble, not the force of the hit.

Back in South Bend several thousand students had paid a buck or two a head to watch the game on large-screen closed-circuit television in Notre Dame's Stepan Center, an all-purpose building with a geodesic dome that from the inside looks like an aircraft hangar, but without the glitter. The students were restless as they watched Michigan State have it all their way. And then Lynch intercepted. Everyone leaped to their feet and screamed. In doing so, someone kicked the cable out of the television projector, and the screen went dead. If not for some quick work by a technician, Stepan Center may have ceased to exist that day. The cable was plugged back in as everyone waited in near hysteria to see what had happened, and the picture came back on just in time to see the instant replay and send everyone into a deep depression.

Given a second life, the Spartans went to work again. Lee ran for 1 yard, and then, after a 5-yard penalty for delay of game, Raye passed 17 yards to Washington, who was run out of bounds at the 26. That was as close as they got. Cavender ran for 1 yard, and then Raye went back, found Washington over the middle, and got the ball to him for 13 more yards to the 12. But tight end Al Brenner had moved before the snap, and the play was called back. Raye tried to get it to Washington again, but the pass glanced off his fingertips. After another incompleted pass, on which Raye was chased over half the field by the entire defensive line, Dick Kenney came in to try a 47-yard field goal.

That was a major field goal, a distance most coaches attempted only at the end of a game when they were behind and had no other choices. But Kenney had just missed on one of almost 60 yards the week before, and there was no doubt he could kick it far enough. The only question was whether he could keep it straight in the swirling wind. Although he was celebrated as one of the best kickers in college, he had started the year hitting only 1 of his first 6 attempts. In the past two games he had hit 3 of 4 and came into the game with 4 field goals in 10 attempts. Now he made it 5 in 11, as he made the long kick with 10 yards or more to spare. Rolls of toilet paper arced through the big stadium, and Sparta celebrated.

Down 10–0, Notre Dame had to get something going soon. The longer they went without scoring, the more they'd have to put the ball in the air and the easier it would be for the Spartan defensive line to put the heat on O'Brien. The Irish had lost no confidence. The prevailing sentiment was summed up by Don Gmitter: "So we're down 10–0. We'll get it back," he thought.

After they cleared the field of toilet paper, Michigan State kicked off. Again, Kenney's kick was high but not quite as short as his others. It carried past Conjar this time and was taken by Tom Quinn, a reserve halfback, at the 8. This time the wedge worked, and Quinn, with Bleier leading the way, burst through a huge hole in the middle of the field and set sail for the opposite end zone. He got to the 40, where Chatlos started closing in from Quinn's left while Jim Summers, a starting defensive back who was playing safety on the return unit, came at him from an angle to the right. Bleier could block either man, and he picked Summers, on whom he had a better angle. Perhaps Nick Eddy would have juked inside and run out and around Summers, who was tied up with Bleier, but Quinn faked outside and went in, trying to slip between Summers and Chatlos. He didn't quite make it as Chatlos made the tackle.

But it was a fine return—38 yards to the Notre Dame 46. In a game in which any drive was hard to sustain, field position was paramount. On the first play from the 46, O'Brien faked to Bleier, dropped back 10 yards, and, with excellent protection, fired down the middle to Seymour, who was all alone at the Michigan State 42. He dropped the ball. "Short-armed it," he confessed, meaning he didn't extend his hands to the ball but tried to catch it with his arms tucked in. After the pass dropped harmlessly to the ground, Phillips, who was hitting Notre Dame receivers as if every one of them had just mugged his grandmother, gave Seymour a shoulder to the midsection.

"One thing we told our kids," said Carillot, "was if Seymour catches one, make him pay dearly. We wanted him thinking about them. We wanted him to know he was going to be hit. I don't care who you are, if you know that, you're going to lose some concentration; you're going to be looking around."

The defense took Carillot at his word. Phillips, Thornhill, Webster, Summers, and Armstrong hit Seymour as hard as they could as often as they could. In their minds it was no surprise that Seymour short-armed the pass. They had intimidated him and took him right out of the game. They shut him out without a catch.

In Seymour's mind he just didn't concentrate. It happened at least once every game. He'd simply drop one, and this was the one. Sure, they hit him, "but I was from Michigan and knew most of those guys, so there wasn't any way they were going to intimidate me." The reason he didn't catch any passes, he said, was not that he was scared but that he was double and triple covered most of the day, so darned few were thrown his way; the fact was that he was open frequently but was used often as a decoy to draw the coverage away from other receivers. His teammates laugh at the idea that he was scared of anybody. He had been hit plenty of times before and would be hit just as hard again. It was all part of the job.

Seymour's dropped pass didn't hurt the team, though. On the next play O'Brien dropped back, rolled right to avoid a heavy rush up the middle, and drilled the ball to Gladieux at the Michigan State 43, for a gain of 11 and a first down. Then he rolled left behind good protection and found Bleier slanting out toward the sideline for 9 more yards to the 34. Now it was second down at the 34, and Ara sent in a formation with Seymour split to the sideline on the left and Bleier and Gladieux flanked next to each other on the right. Conjar stayed in the backfield to block. Bullough had called the right defense—a prevent with three down linemen and the other eight defenders split between linebackers and defensive backs. When O'Brien dropped back to pass, one linebacker joined the rush. The play was designed to go to Seymour on a curl over the middle, but O'Brien saw that Drake Garrett, in as a fourth defensive back, followed Bleier, who ran down the field and in, and failed to pick up Gladieux coming off the line. Gladieux was supposed to cut the pattern short, but when no one covered him he ran straight downfield toward the goalposts. Jess Phillips, who was on Seymour's side of the field, saw what had happened and sprinted for the end zone as O'Brien heaved the ball toward Gladieux. Had Phillips lined up 3 yards farther off the line, he would have broken up the pass or even intercepted it. As it was, his desperate leap was an inch or two short, and Gladieux, who had thrown his arms out at the 20 to show O'Brien he was clear, cradled the ball with both arms at his waist, tucked it in at the 1, and stepped into the end zone. He immediately jumped in celebration, and as he jumped and skipped, he looked back upfield but turned around just in time to miss running smack into the goalpost at the back of the end zone. Then Bleier and Seymour converged on him and escorted him to the Notre Dame sideline, where his happy teammates proceeded to hit him harder than the Spartans had.

There were still 4:30 remaining in the half. After Azzaro kicked the point to make it 10–7 in favor of Michigan State, he teed it up and kicked off into the wind to the 12, where it was fielded by Waters and returned 20 yards to the 32. With the pressure back on them to move the ball, Raye and the Spartan offense took the field and ran into a defense that was determined not to allow another score. On first down Raye nearly broke another big one. Rolling to his left, he sprinted around Page, who got caught rushing inside instead of protecting against the sweep. Raye turned the corner and took it upfield to the State 47-yard line for an apparent 15-yard gain. But the officials had caught him stepping out of bounds on the 30, and a big gain turned into a 2-yard loss. The Spartans tried a short pass to Washington in the left flat, but O'Leary smelled it out and knocked it away. On third down Cavender lost a yard, and Kenney punted 31 yards to Schoen, who returned it 5 yards to the Notre Dame 45, where Al Brenner buried a shoulder in his midsection, picked him up, and drove him into the turf.

Notre Dame could gain only 7 yards in 3 plays, and after a delay-of-game penalty pushed them back 5 more, Hardy punted. He dropped the ball inside the 20, and it took a couple of fast hops toward the goal line. Seymour, back on the punt team, made a good play to bat it backwards just before it rolled into the end zone, and Notre Dame downed it on the Spartan 1-yard line.

Time was running out, and Daugherty wanted it to run out quickly. He told Raye to run it himself and to just keep the clock running. He ran 2 plays with Notre Dame calling time-outs in the hope of forcing a punt, which they might be able to either block or return. After a third-down run brought the Spartans 3 yards short of a first down, Notre Dame was out of time-outs, but there seemed to be enough time on the clock to force State to run a fourth-down play. As the Spartans waited in their huddle for the clock to run out, the officials didn't call them for delay of game and let the final seconds tick away.

The teams ran off together through the tunnel at the south end of the stadium while the fans settled down to talk about the first half and either laugh or jeer at the banners that several students unfurled while the bands marched onto the field. One sign that the columnists agreed was funny was held up in the Notre Dame section for the benefit of the television cameras: HI, MOM. WE'RE

MARRIED, it read. Two others earned near-unanimous censure—
at least outside of Michigan: BUBBA FOR POPE and HAIL MARY, FULL
OF GRACE, NOTRE DAME'S IN SECOND PLACE. Both signs, the columnists said, were either disrespectful, blasphemous, or both.

For the moment Notre Dame was in second place, although it
didn't seem as if a 3-point halftime deficit was insurmountable.
If anything, the Irish had reason to feel good. They had absorbed
the loss of Eddy, Hanratty, and Goeddeke, and Seymour had not
caught a pass; yet they hadn't collapsed. Rather they had answered the Spartans' second score with one of their own and had
shown they could move the ball in a hurry. As the grimly determined players reached for soft drinks and orange quarters, the
coaches went into their huddles and agreed that they didn't need
to make major adjustments. Outside of a few big plays, they had
contained the Spartans in general and Clinton Jones in particular. Michigan State had gained 157 yards in the first half, and
Raye and Washington together had accounted for 103 of that
total—59 of it on Washington's 2 receptions. And of Raye's 44
yards rushing, 30 of it had come on 1 play and 14 on Raye's other
11 carries. If they needed to do anything, it was put double coverage on Washington. But a few big gainers didn't mean the
defense was bad. It just meant that Michigan State had done its
job a couple of times and had caught a few breaks. If the defense
could crank it up a notch, they'd be fine.

Against the offense, Michigan State had used George Chatlos
to run a variety of defensive fronts, few of which looked like their
normal six-man line. They had run a number of stunts with linebackers and linemen, and those had at times messed up Notre
Dame's blocking assignments. They would just have to block
better.

Outside of the disabling injuries, everyone else was reasonably
healthy for a game that was, by consensus, the hardest-hitting,
most tightly played they had ever been in. That applied to the
seniors as well as men like Tim Monty, who had never played
with the varsity and had discovered that Charlie Thornhill, for
one, would have felt quite comfortable on John Ray's defense
because "he'd tear your head off every time you got near him."
(And every time Monty did, he saw a little *ND* lettered on Thornhill's helmet, a decoration he had added before the game "because every time I hit Notre Dame, I wanted them to see that ND
stuck on their back.")

Michigan State went into the locker room angry. The defense, handed a 10–0 lead, thought they should have stopped the Irish in their tracks. They had stuffed them in 1965, and they expected to do it again, no matter who the quarterback was. Instead of stopping them, they had let them back in the game. Some of the defenders blamed the offense, which kept giving Notre Dame the ball in good field position and hadn't been able to sustain anything other than the two scoring drives.

Still, they had held the Irish to 5 first downs and 130 total yards, only 52 of those on the ground. More than half of those yards had been gained by Gladieux on his 3 pass receptions for 71 yards. No one had ripped off a long run, and Seymour had been hammered without mercy. The one adjustment the coaches decided to make was to take advantage of the kid who had come in to replace Goeddeke. He was young and he was small. In the first half he had been uncovered by a lineman and had been blocking linebackers—usually Thornhill. It would be interesting to see what he could do if they moved Bubba Smith right over his head. Yes, that's what they would do. They'd make Tim Monty's day the longest of his young life.

Offensively, Daugherty was determined to get Clinton Jones untracked and into the flow of the game. Raye had run well on his option-keepers, but Jones had been their big back, and as with all big backs, he needed to carry the ball to be successful. In the second half he would carry it more than the four times for 9 yards he had had it in the first half. And if he carried more, it would set up another play that Daugherty designed at halftime. It was called an influence-keep, and it called for Raye to fake to Jones off tackle to draw the defense and then step quickly over guard, where, Duffy hoped, there would be a hole.

The teams ran back out onto the field and wedged themselves into the mob that had taken over their seats at halftime. Monty looked at one man standing next to him and realized he was smoking a cigar and drinking whiskey from a bottle—on the Notre Dame bench.

Michigan State chose to receive the second-half kick, and this time Notre Dame took the wind in the fourth quarter. Azzaro kicked to the 10 where Waters caught it, cut to his right, and sped upfield for 20 yards before Pergine wrapped him up. Waters hit the ground, and the crowd gasped as the ball popped free and Rhoads leaped on top of it. Rhoads held the ball in the air, and

Don Gmitter leaped in the air and pointed toward the Spartan end zone, indicating Notre Dame had recovered. But the official on the play pointed at the ground, the signal that the ball had been dead before the fumble.

The Spartans had dodged one bullet, but on the first play of the second half they stepped right in front of another. Keeping with his halftime strategy of getting Jones more involved, Duffy called a handoff to his halfback over the right side. Raye took the snap, stepped to his right, and stuck the ball out to hand it off. But Jones's adrenaline was pumping, and he got to the point of the handoff a split second early and didn't get a firm grip on the ball. Horney leaped on the loose ball, and the defense danced happily off the field, slapping hands with the offense that was already running out to take advantage. As the rest of the offense got in its huddle, Parseghian kept O'Brien on the sideline an extra few seconds, shouting instructions in his ear. When Ara was done, he sent O'Brien out, then spun around, threw a fist in the air, gave a little leap, paced quickly back to midfield, clapped, then turned around and paced slowly back toward the play, his excitement in check and his mind turned back to the coldly logical science of calling plays. It was a typical reaction from Ara, a man who made his decisions with as much logic as anyone mustered, yet had not lost the ability to get excited. He had charmed the sportswriters when he first took over the team by his tendency to get so excited during big plays that he sometimes raced a ballcarrier down the sideline all the way to the end zone. He had toned that down a bit, but he could never stop from showing his emotions at big moments. And this looked like the moment that would turn the game around.

He had told O'Brien to go for the end zone on the first play, a tactic that, if successful, would test the Spartan breaking point as the Spartans had tested theirs. Seymour, split to the left, would run a curl pattern over the middle to draw the defense while Bleier, flanked wide left, would run down the sideline. O'Brien made the call, got protection from the line, and threw. The ball was underthrown just enough for Jess Phillips to run over from his safety position and cut in front of Bleier. Bleier saw him coming, realized he was going to intercept the ball, and changed from receiver to tackler, a decision he has regretted ever since.

"The whole game was a kind of a fog," Bleier says. "I knew

where the plays were going, but everything is meshed together."
He was in his first year as a starter and operating on automatic
pilot, doing the things he had been taught without being con-
scious of what they were. Later, in the pros, he would gain the
football awareness that allowed him to recognize what the other
team was doing and adjust accordingly. That older Rocky Bleier
would have seen Phillips coming, and instead of thinking about
tackling him, would have played pass defender and knocked the
ball out of Phillips's hands. At least they would still have possession. "I let him intercept it," Bleier says.

Had Phillips not come over, it would have been a touchdown.
The pass was there. But Phillips had made a great play and Bleier
hadn't, and now it was a turnover. On the Notre Dame sideline
—which was 2 yards out on the field—Parseghian spun around
again and spat out a gutter profanity.

Duffy had wanted to get Jones more involved, but now, with
the ball resting on the Michigan State 2, he turned to Raye to
give him some breathing room. Raye kept over left guard and
made 3 difficult yards, then tried right tackle, where he made
another yard to the 6. On third-and-6 he went back to the left
side. Giving ground to the goal line, Alan Page came up to hem
him in, but the near guard, Tony Conti, threw a tremendous
block on Page, and Raye turned it upfield. He got hit at the 8 by
two or three defenders, but he squirmed free and dove for 5 more
yards and a critical first down that would save Kenney from having to kick from the end zone.

With a fresh set of downs, Raye faked to Clinton Jones up the
middle, dropped back to pass, and just before Hardy engulfed
him, snapped off a pass 12 yards downfield, where Washington
had gotten free in the short zone. The pass wasn't pretty and
Washington had to go to the ground to catch it, but it was another
first down at the 25 and gave Michigan State a little more breathing room. Three more plays—another sneak, a run by Lee, and
an end run by Jones—produced only 3 more yards. With the ball
on the 28, Kenney came in and went back to his own 15-yard line
to punt. And now Michigan State, which had just gotten out of a
big hole, narrowly missed falling into another one. Center Larry
Smith messed up the snap and sent it sailing high on a trajectory
that seemed certain to take it over Kenney's head. But Kenney
leaped high and, while turning to his right, stuck his right hand

up and just managed to catch the ball and bring it down to his chest. Facing sideways, and with Rhoads bearing in from his right, he took two quick steps and kicked the ball high as Rhoads leaped for it. The ball cleared Rhoads's hands by as little as O'Brien's touchdown pass to Gladieux had cleared Jess Phillips's fingertips. The ball traveled only 30 yards to the Notre Dame 42, where Schoen made a fair catch, but it was far enough.

With Bubba lined up over Monty, the Irish went outside with a handoff to Bleier running around left end. Conjar knocked Hoag off the play, and Bleier cut upfield and made 5 quick yards before being stopped by Armstrong on a driving tackle that lifted Bleier completely off the ground. Next, Conjar ran at Hoag with Bleier leading, and Notre Dame picked up 4 more quick yards to the Michigan State 47. On third down O'Brien faked a handoff, then took it himself off right tackle, diving 2 yards for the first down.

On first down Bleier took it again over Hoag for 3 more yards, and the Irish looked as if they were on the move. The line was making holes. They weren't huge holes and they were closing quickly, but they were holes. With the Spartans thinking run, Parseghian sent in a pass, but now the Spartans recognized the play. At the snap Bubba Smith put a big hit on Monty and simply ran over him. Jeff Richardson, working on Regner, took a hit and then leaped over the big guard. George Chatlos beat his man and came through from the right. O'Brien ran back to set up, turned around, and saw the wall of green. He tried to run out of trouble but didn't get anywhere. The loss was big—12 yards—and faced with a third-and-19, Ara called a draw play to Bleier. Bleier managed to slip through Bubba's arms in the backfield and pick up 4 yards, but the drive was over and Hardy came in to punt.

Hardy hit another high kick that hit around the 20 and bounced down to the 12, where Brenner fielded it and tried to run right. In doing so he made the cardinal mistake of giving ground, and before he could turn it upfield, Gerald Kelly, the center, ran him down at the 5.

Again, the Spartans were pinned deep in their own territory, and again Raye got them out of the hole with a first-down heave to Washington. The play started with a fake to Jones. Raye then retreated 2 yards deep into his own end zone, and with two men holding off Hardy and Duranko bearing down on him from his right, Raye threw it long. Washington, who had drawn single coverage from O'Leary, ran under it. The ball was thrown to Washington's left and again was a little long, or it would have been a touchdown. As it was, Washington made a spectacular diving catch at the 46 for a 41-yard gain. It was his fourth reception, and he had already gained 112 yards.

Duffy, a gambling man by nature who could as often as not be found at a racetrack during the off-season—if he wasn't on a golf course—decided he wanted it all. He sent in another pass, but this time Raye went back, found no one open, and ate it for a 2-yard loss. Jones gained 9 yards to Notre Dame's 47 on a delay up the middle, and then Duffy sent Apisa in to see if he could find any magic in his damaged knee. Raye handed to him, but it was no good. He was stuck for a loss of 1 by Pergine, and Kenney came in to punt.

This time Page just missed blocking the kick, which bounced into the Notre Dame end zone for a touchback.

Starting from the 20, O'Brien went back to the air and immediately hit Bleier for 9 yards on a rollout. Bleier took a major hit from Summers on the play. On second-and-1, O'Brien went to the air again. After faking a handoff, he hit Conjar over the middle for 18 and a first down at the 47, where Garrett struck the fullback hard and drove him back 4 yards. With the quarter winding down and the wind behind them for the last time, Parseghian kept calling passes. And on first down from the 47, an incompleted pass cost Ara yet another player. The play was Flank Right, Roll 78, Harpo Individual. "Harpo" was Gladieux and "individual" meant he was supposed to find a seam in the zone and run to daylight, where O'Brien would presumably hit him. To do that Gladieux had to be able to read the defense, a daunting task for a second-string rookie halfback who answered to the name Harpo. If anyone had asked Gladieux, he would have told them he didn't know what the heck he was supposed to do. Tell him to run a curl or a hook or a post, and he'd do it. Tell him to make up his own pattern, and he was lost. But since no one asked, he did the best he could.

"I ran a very poor route," he admitted. "They had underneath coverage, and I ran across it, completely against the grain."

That meant the coverage was coming toward him, and when he went up to try to catch O'Brien's pass, Jess Phillips piled into him at full ramming speed. Phillips caught Gladieux on the right thigh pad with his helmet, and the moment he hit, Harpo knew he wouldn't be playing any more football that day. The impact shattered the hard plastic thighboard as thoroughly as Page had busted Cavender's shoulder pad. And then, in Gladieux's words, it "dismantled my quadricep into sixteen trillion thousand pieces." He wasn't going to get an "A" in calculus, but he did have a way with words.

With Seymour's help, Gladieux got himself up and off the field, where he reported the damage and explained what had happened. The coaches apologized for calling the play, which didn't make the thigh feel any better. Then they turned him over to the doctors, who diagnosed a serious thigh bruise. With the limb rapidly blowing up to twice its normal size, Gladieux had suspected as much. It didn't fully heal, in fact, until the following fall. That's how hard Jess Phillips could hit.

Pagna looked down the bench and noticed he was running low on halfbacks. He called on Dave Haley, a 5 feet 11, 190-pound junior from Hingham, Massachusetts. Haley remembers that at the time "there was considerable excitement."

Like Monty and O'Brien, Haley hadn't expected to play. But, again like Monty, he worked with O'Brien every day on the second unit and was used to his handoffs and passes. Just the same, Notre Dame was down to its number-two quarterback and center and number-four halfback. The odds of making a comeback weren't getting better.

Fortunately, nobody had told O'Brien he was in trouble, and nobody told Haley he had no business being in there. And nobody told Parseghian and Pagna that they had better be careful about going to Haley. On Haley's first play, O'Brien sent him down the left sideline and drilled a 23-yard completion to him at the Michigan State 30. "You were given a job to do, and you just did it," Haley says. "You didn't have time to think about it. All of a sudden you were in the game, and once you realized you were in it to the end, then it was just a matter of staying focused and getting the job done."

With a first down deep in Michigan State territory, Parseghian now looked for the play that would put the Spartan defense in total disarray. He called a tackle eligible pass for Paul Seiler, the left tackle. It was a play that had worked before. It called for Seiler to take his normal spot next to Regner but for both Seymour and Gmitter to line up on the other side of the line. Sey-mour dropped back to become a flanker, but he split so far to the left that the defense didn't stop to think he wasn't an end any-more; and if he wasn't, somebody else must be.

At the snap Seiler brushed past the defensive end and headed straight downfield. Monty hit Bubba just enough to hold him up, and Regner pulled to his left and took the end. The play was designed to hit quickly, and O'Brien took three steps straight back, turned, and threw. It was a good pass and any other receiver probably would have caught it, but it wasn't right into Seiler's body; instead, he had to reach out for it. Receivers and running backs wear shoulder pads with small plates above the shoulders that allow them to move their arms relatively freely, but a tackle wears big plates that make it difficult to fully extend the arms. Seiler stretched as far as he could, got his hands on the ball, and then watched it fall to the ground at the 15-yard line.

On second-and-10, the Irish got a huge break. The play was a straight handoff to Conjar over left guard. With George Webster dropping off just before the snap in expectation of another pass, a big hole opened, and Conjar had gained 5 yards by the time Webster reversed direction and drove into the fullback headfirst. His helmet hit the ball, which popped free and rolled forward into the hands of Sterling Armstrong. The stadium erupted in gleeful noise, cheerleaders did jumping jacks, and the Spartan defense leaped and shouted in triumph. And then Wirtz, the ref-eree, said, Sorry, guys, but number 95 was offsides. The fumble doesn't count.

That was Bubba. Trying to get a quick jump to get past Monty and Swatland and into the backfield, Bubba had jumped into the neutral zone an instant before the snap. Instead of having the football, the Spartans were lining up on defense again, with the Irish coming up with a second-and-5 at the Spartan 25.

With the Spartans thinking pass, Parseghian went again to Haley, who took the handoff, skipped outside off left end, and made 4 yards before being driven out of bounds. On third-and-1 the Irish went again to Haley, the freshest man on the field, and he burst over the left side for 4 more and a first down on the Spartan 17.

After everything that had happened, there was no doubt in anyone's mind on the Notre Dame side of the field that the Irish were going to get the go-ahead touchdown. Joe Azzaro, the kicker, had as much belief in that certainty as anyone and wasn't even thinking about going in to kick a field goal. He'd tried only two all year and had made them both, so there wasn't anything to worry about. On first down at the 17, O'Brien sent Bleier around right end, and as he bounced outside there was a sliver of room, a sliver that maybe Nick Eddy, had he been healthy, could have accelerated through. There were a dozen plays like it that day, plays where Bleier, Haley, and Gladieux picked up 4 or 5 yards where one could only wonder whether Eddy might have broken it big. Still, it was 5 yards and the Spartans were in retreat.

On second down, Ara abandoned the ends, where Haley and Bleier had been finding room, and turned to Conjar over center. This time there wasn't much there, and Jungle—as Conjar was called—was hauled down on the 10 to set up third-and-3. (This is one of two plays that O'Brien would like to be able to try again, just once, because he's certain it could have won the game.)

It was a pass, and O'Brien took his five-step drop and set up 9 yards deep. With Hoag coming from the left side around Conjar's block, Coley waited, looked for a receiver, and finally pulled the ball in and set out around right end with Hoag in pursuit. He ran past Bubba, who was rushing up the middle. He ducked inside of Chatlos, who made a diving swipe at his ankles. Only one man was left to beat, Jeff Richardson, who was coming at him from the middle. O'Brien, who thought the end zone was his, cut back to the right and tried to ward off Richardson with his left arm, but Richardson managed to get an arm around his waist and pulled him down at the line of scrimmage for no gain. It was the last play of the third quarter and one of the biggest of Richardson's life.

On the first play of the fourth quarter, Parseghian sent Azzaro in to try a field goal from the 18. Azzaro had been following the play down the sideline, staying close to the coaches in case they wanted him. And now Ara not only wanted him but for the first time all year desperately needed Azzaro to pull them even.

While the teams switched ends of the big stadium and the huge crowd caught its breath for the final fifteen minutes that would decide everything that a college football game could decide, Azzaro previewed the kick in his head, a process now known as visualization. On the field he showed O'Brien his spot, just inches ahead of the 18-yard line and on the line of the right hash marks. He didn't use a kicking tee; such devices weren't allowed. When the referee signaled for play to begin, Kelly snapped, O'Brien held, Azzaro took two quick steps straight forward, and swung the squared-off tip of his right shoe into the ball. He kept his head down, he hit it square, he followed through. Just like hitting a golf ball. The ball sailed through the uprights, and with just a few seconds gone in the fourth quarter, it was 10–10.

It had taken Notre Dame just under twenty-eight minutes to catch up since State's first score at the beginning of the second quarter; twenty-eight minutes of pain and mighty effort. They had shown that they would not be broken. "Now," Azzaro thought as he trotted back to kick off, "it's just a matter of time."

The Michigan State offense was thinking the same thing. It was just a matter of time for them to retake the lead for good. They had scored on these suckers before, they had beaten Ohio State in the fourth quarter. They would beat Notre Dame the same way. Azzaro kicked off, and the ball carried to Waters at the 10. He returned it 13 yards, and Raye led the offense out. The wear and tear was showing on both sides. Pruiett's shoulder, repeatedly abused by being thrown at Duranko, Lynch, Rhoads, and the other Irish defenders, was getting progressively worse and would soon give out altogether. Cavender was still hurting but kept going. Lynch's knee hurt. Nearly everyone's head had been ringing at one time or another from the collisions. Rocky Bleier had taken a hit from Webster in the kidney and was running on willpower. After the game, when urinating, he found he was passing blood; he turned himself over to the doctors, who diagnosed a lacerated kidney that ended his season. O'Brien, unaccustomed to such sustained effort, was wearing down, too, and the doctors kept an eye on him to make sure he didn't go into insulin shock. They had all entered the zone where pride and desire take over, the zone that marathoners know when they hit The Wall, the zone that boxers know as the last rounds of a title fight.

Duffy was determined to get the lead back all at once. On the first play from scrimmage Raye dropped back and looked once again down the sideline for Washington. He had great protection, took his time, and threw it hard and deep from his own 15. Like the two other bombs he had connected with, this one was long, but where Washington had been able to catch up with the first two, this one was too far by a yard or two. With Schoen and O'Leary playing him tight, he dove and missed at the Notre Dame 30—a 55-yard throw. No matter. On second down Raye dropped back again. This time Notre Dame had a rush on, and with Rhoads in his face, Raye threw short to Washington for 11 yards. As Washington caught it, O'Leary closed fast and put his helmet right into the ball, but somehow Washington held on and the Spartans had a first down.

Notre Dame called a blitz up the middle, and with Lynch storming over the center, Raye took the snap from Larry Smith and ran the influence play put in at the half. He calmly ducked under Lynch's outstretched right arm, and burst into the secondary, where Schoen finally caught him at the Notre Dame 46 after a gain of 20 yards. That play and the next one epitomized Michigan State's game. If the Spartans caught the Irish in a favorable defense, plays broke for major yardage. If they didn't, they went nowhere. That's what happened next, as Jones got the call off right tackle, and had to fight just to get a yard as Hardy fought off a block and hauled him down. On second-and-10, Daugherty figured the Irish would be looking to blitz again and sent in the same quarterback keeper that had just gained 20 yards. Again Raye caught Lynch blitzing, but Lynch was no dummy. Remembering what Raye had done 2 plays earlier, Lynch lowered his right arm this time, caught the slippery quarterback, and dropped him for a loss of 2 to set up third-and-11 at Notre Dame's 46. Raye again dropped back to pass and looked for Washington coming across the field. He couldn't find him, and with Page closing in from the left and Rhoads circling from the right, Raye started to run. He was back to midfield when Duranko loomed in his path. As Duranko crashed into him, he flipped the ball downfield to the right sideline where Washington and the ball disappeared into the swarm of humanity—a few of them actually players and coaches—on the Michigan State sideline. The officials signaled incomplete, the crowd groaned, and Kenney came in to punt. The Irish defense had had some scary moments, but it had held. And neither they nor the Spartans knew that in getting to the Irish 46, Michigan State had advanced farther than it had at any time since Kenney kicked the second-quarter field goal to go up 10–0.

But now, as Kenney punted to Schoen on his own 7, field position was in the Spartans' favor in the critical final minutes. From that deep in Notre Dame territory Ara wasn't going to pass. He ordered three runs—Conjar for 2, Bleier for 3, and Bleier for 3 more—and sent Hardy in to punt.

Hardy kicked to the Spartan 46, where Brenner caught it and lost another yard to the 45. When the State offense came out, Pruiett was no longer with them. He had been alternating with Dave Techlin, bringing in plays from the sidelines, but as the game went on and his shoulder got worse, he finally found it impossible to get into a proper stance. After the previous series the coaches had asked him what was wrong, and he told them about the injury. They told him to take the rest of the afternoon off.

On first down Apisa came in and carried for his second and final time of the game. He gained 2 yards. Jones then tried the left side, but Hardy broke through a block, leaped, caught Jones by the shoulder pads, and hung on, flapping behind Jones like a 290-pound cape for the 2 yards Jones was able to advance before going down under the weight. On third down Raye went back to pass, found Horney in his face, and threw high off Washington's fingertips on the right sideline. As the ball bounced away, O'Leary crashed into him, just to make sure.

Kenney punted again, this time down to the 13, where Schoen was tackled immediately. O'Brien tried to move the team again. After making 2 yards on a rollout to the right, O'Brien dropped back and looked for Seymour over the middle. The ball was thrown maybe a foot behind the receiver, and as he reached back to grab it, Jim Summers climbed on his back and pulled him down. It looked as if Summers had gotten there a fraction before the ball, but no flags went down for interference and no one argued. On third-and-8, O'Brien sent out three receivers, while the Spartans responded with a prevent defense that had six men dropped back in coverage. Seymour found the hole in the blanket defense, ran to the 30-yard line, and turned around to look for the ball. The ball was right at him, only it sailed six feet over his head. Ara watched the pass from the sideline and couldn't believe it. It was a simple pattern, Seymour was as wide open as he could be and still be on the field, O'Brien had an accurate arm, and there went the ball, sailing so high Wilt Chamberlain couldn't have caught it. When O'Brien came out and Hardy went in to punt, Ara asked his quarterback what the heck was going on out there—only in somewhat stronger language. O'Brien said the pass got away from him.

Parseghian knew that O'Brien's diabetes could wear him down and take away his coordination if he didn't keep his blood sugar up. But O'Brien had a doctor on the sideline monitoring his condition, and if O'Brien said he was fine, Ara took his word for it.

Back on the field Michigan State had tried to block Hardy's punt and had come up short. So the offense took over on its own 48 and went back to work, still convinced that there was no way they weren't going to get to the end zone. Raye started the possession by handing off to Lee, who got 3 tough yards to the 49. On second down Raye tried to hit Lee with a pass, but the halfback was jarred loose from the ball. On third down Raye dropped back and again tried to get the ball to Lee. With three gold helmets in his face, Raye threw into triple coverage, and Schoen picked off the ball and brought it to within a yard of midfield.

Emotions seesawed back to Notre Dame. On first down O'Brien handed to Bleier, who squirted off right tackle through a hole that wasn't there and picked up 5 yards before Thornhill dragged him down. Despite the badly overthrown ball to Seymour on the previous series, Parseghian sent another pass in to O'Brien. With Thornhill blitzing unchecked up the middle, O'Brien barely had time to dump the ball incomplete in the middle of the field, 5 yards in front of Bleier. On third down O'Brien tried a screen pass to Bleier in the right flat. With Chatlos crashing in from right end, O'Brien jumped and threw the ball short, and Bleier couldn't scoop it up. It was fourth down and the Irish had to punt again.

On the sideline Parseghian was worried that O'Brien had reached the limits of his endurance. Pagna felt the same and started looking for Bob Belden, the third-team quarterback who would spend three years playing behind Terry Hanratty and still be drafted by the Cowboys. But when Pagna looked, he couldn't find Belden in the mob of interlopers on the sidelines.

It wouldn't have mattered. When Parseghian asked O'Brien if he wanted to come out, O'Brien said, "No way. This is my game, and I'm going to finish it."

That was good enough for Ara, and he sent O'Brien off to the doctors to be stuffed with candy bars and orange juice for the final effort.

"I was tired because it was a tough game," O'Brien, who knows his sugar situation well, insists to this day. "The diabetes had nothing to do with it."

Others, including Dr. Nicholas Johns, who wasn't O'Brien's physician but was on the sidelines with the team, thought that it was the diabetes that was causing O'Brien to miss the passes. At one point in the game he had been 7-for-13 passing. He wound up missing his last 6 passes against defenses stacked against the pass and finished 7-for-19.

After Hardy kicked it 45 yards into the end zone, Raye came out and immediately went back to the air, and here he made the second play he'd like to have back. Notre Dame had gone to double coverage on Washington, and when Raye went to the line of scrimmage and looked at the defense, Tom Schoen, the single safety, had rotated away from the middle of the field and toward the right side of the offense, where Washington had lined up. Seeing that, Raye decided to look for Al Brenner, who was split out to the left. But while Raye was taking the snap and dropping back, Schoen, who had been disguising his intentions, moved back to the center of the field. Raye didn't look for him because he wasn't supposed to be on the left side, and by the time he did see Schoen, it was too late. The ball was on its way toward Brenner, who was running stride for stride with Smithberger. The ball never got there. Schoen, crossing from the middle, stepped in front of Brenner, leaped high, caught the ball at the top of his jump on the Michigan State 49, and took off for the goal line. He got all the way to the 25 before anyone showed up in front of him. The Spartans met him at the 20, and Schoen tried to break through the last two men. One of them was Jerry West, who grabbed for Schoen as he went by and got hold of a handful of jersey. He pulled Schoen off balance and out of bounds at the Michigan State 18.

The Spartans had been playing a prevent defense with six defensive backs, but now, their backs to the wall, they stacked five men on the line and three more behind them. On the sidelines the rest of the team felt sure they had lost it. "We're in trouble now," Pruiett thought. "All they have to do is kick a field goal." On the other side of the field, Azzaro wasn't thinking that at all.

He had seen enough of his team to know that from that close, they wouldn't need him. They'd take it in themselves.

O'Brien handed to Conjar over the right side. The blocking broke down, but Jungle bulled for 2 brutish yards entirely on his own. It was second-and-8 at the 16.

Notre Dame had been running most of its ground game with a lead blocking back ahead of the ballcarrier. But now, with Michigan State stacking up the run, Pagna and Parseghian decided to show them a new wrinkle. They sent in a play called a buck trap left that went away from the lead back and sent Haley over left tackle. To kick end Phil Hoag out, the play called for a special blocking stunt called a J block between Gmitter and Seiler, the offensive end and tackle. Normally, if a man was on Seiler's head and another was on Gmitter's outside shoulder, Seiler and Gmitter double-teamed the tackle and a back kicked out the end to create the hole. The J block called for Gmitter to block the man over Seiler in and for Seiler to step behind Gmitter and block the end out. The scheme gave both men a good blocking angle. Meanwhile, Regner would be pulling from right guard to either seal off any leakage on the left side or, if no one was coming through, to lead Haley through the hole. The hole Regner left when he pulled was to be stopped up by Conjar, who was to take a fake from O'Brien while Haley ran from right halfback to his left, taking the handoff deep in the backfield and turning upfield.

The blocking scheme was not used frequently. When O'Brien called it in the huddle, Gmitter recognized what he and Seiler had to do. He told Seiler it was a J block, but he got the impression from Seiler's reaction that the tackle wasn't sold on the idea. They broke from the huddle, and Gmitter told him again what they had to do. He knew Seiler heard him, but as they got down in their stance against a six-man Spartan front, Gmitter had a bad feeling about the play.

In the backfield Conjar was lined up behind O'Brien, and Haley was to his right. At the snap O'Brien faked to Conjar, going over right guard to freeze the pursuit on that side of the line. O'Brien then continued back to hand the ball to Haley, who was crossing from right to left behind Conjar.

On the line Gmitter's fears were realized. Seiler, who was a tremendous blocker, went with his gut feeling and fired out on the tackle with all his heart and soul. Gmitter did the same, and together they drove the man halfway to the end zone. But Hoag was now storming across the line utterly unblocked.

Haley never had a chance. Hoag was on him as soon as he got the handoff, and with more pressure coming from the backside, Haley was a dead duck. Hoag dropped him on the 24 for an 8-yard loss. On the State sideline, hope, which had been nearly extinguished, was suddenly renewed, while on the other side Azzaro knew that it would come down to his right foot after all.

Parseghian makes no apologies about the call. The blocking scheme was in the playbook, and the players were supposed to know it. It had been a well-designed play that could easily have popped Haley through the charging Spartans for a good gain. But somebody had missed an assignment, and they lost 8 yards. Ara wasn't happy about that, but those things happen. They'd been happening in various ways all afternoon. That's football. And he still had a down left.

On third-and-16 he had to try a pass. The Spartans brought five men on the rush this time, and the line picked them up, with Conjar, who blocked his behind off all day, wiping out Charles Bailey, who was rushing from the right side—the side O'Brien was rolling toward. O'Brien set up on the 35, spotted Bleier who had run to the first-down marker and was wide open at the 8, stepped up, and fired. As he threw, Chatlos, who had been knocked down at the line and had scrambled to his feet again and had gotten to within a few yards of O'Brien, leaped as high as he could and threw up his arms. As the ball passed over him, Chatlos got a tiny piece of it, just enough to take some of the steam off it. As Bleier watched helplessly, the ball hit the ground 7 yards in front of him and skipped away. (This is the other play O'Brien wants back.)

It was fourth-and-16 at the 24, and on the sideline Azzaro knew it was his moment. He went to Parseghian who told him to get out there. As he started to run onto the field, John Ray, the maniac of the defense, grabbed Azzaro and gave him a last bit of fatherly advice. Azzaro doesn't remember it precisely because he wasn't really listening. Besides, Ray had given him the same advice before and the sense of it was always the same: "Goddamn it, you son of a bitch, you'd better not miss." In quiet moments Ray would admit he didn't understand kickers. All they had to do was kick the bleeping ball through the bleeping uprights. How hard can that be? In truth, with the straight-on kicking style used at the time, it could be remarkably hard. Kenney himself, one of the best, had hit only four of ten that year. In the NFL anything over 50 percent was good, and 60 percent was nearly unheard of. It wasn't the kickers but the technique. Few coaches really taught players how to kick. It was an acquired art. Also, kicks hit from straight on could start out straight and take the craziest moves in midair for no apparent reason. It had to do with aerodynamics.

Azzaro wasn't thinking about any of that. Instead, he went over his mental checklist, showed O'Brien where to spot the ball, and got ready to kick. The spot couldn't have been better—dead square in the middle of the field. Piece of cake.

He took his position two steps behind O'Brien. Kelly made a perfect snap, O'Brien made a perfect placement, Azzaro took his two steps, keeping his head down, hit the ball dead solid perfect, and followed through. When he had completed the motion he looked up and saw the ball sailing straight and true. Charlie Thornhill, who had rushed from end, looked up, saw the same thing, and thought, "We lost." More than eighty thousand people in East Lansing and more than thirty million more around the world held their breath.

"I did everything right. It was a good, solid hit," Azzaro said, "and at the last instant the wind kicked up or something, and it started tailing right a little bit."

Underneath the right upright, back judge Markbreit looked straight up and watched the ball pass over it perhaps a foot and a half wide. He gave the signal indicating an unsuccessful attempt, and the stadium exploded in noise. Maybe God was a Spartan fan after all. The clock read 4:39 to play.

Azzaro says he wouldn't do anything differently if he had it to do over. He did everything right, and it just didn't work. Again, that's football.

The game wasn't over. Michigan State took over on the 20 with plenty of time for one more drive and plenty of time for Notre Dame to get the ball back. The one thing they didn't have was the cooperation of the Notre Dame defense. Maybe they had missed the field goal, but now the Irish dug in, determined that they would stop it right here and get the ball back for one more chance.

On first down Raye handed to Jones on a delay, and Duranko

stopped him before he could move for a 6-yard loss. On second-and-16, Raye dropped back and Duranko again blew past West and crashed into Raye an instant after the quarterback threw the ball out of bounds to stop the clock and save another loss. Now, on third-and-16 with Notre Dame looking for a pass, Daugherty called a running play—a draw to Cavender. With only three linemen and one linebacker to block, Cavender burst through the line and charged upfield for 15 yards, 2 feet, and about 6 inches. The first down was at the 30, and the ball was half a foot short.

Daugherty told Raye to get the six inches himself, and the quarterback took it over left guard, where he was met by all of South Bend. He needed six inches and he got eighteen. First down, Michigan State.

From the start of the drive Raye had wanted to go deep to Washington. The whole team wanted him to go deep to Washington, but after Schoen's second interception that had put the Spartans in such a precarious position just minutes before, Daugherty decided to run the ball instead of risking another interception. And he wanted Jones to run it.

Many Spartans didn't understand the call. Jones hadn't gained any significant yardage all day, and that didn't seem likely to change. If they were going to run, let Raye do it; he had been their steadiest runner with 75 yards on 21 attempts. But Jones it was, and on first down Raye sent him around left end, where he was met in the backfield and dropped by Lynch and Horney for a 2-yard loss. On second-and-12, Duffy called a pass, but not the deep one Raye wanted. Instead, he threw underneath to Brenner, who caught it and was tackled immediately by Schoen at the 36 —4 yards short of a first down.

On third down Raye dropped back again. Again Duranko nearly dropped him, and again Raye passed not to Washington but to Brenner. The pass was behind Brenner and fell to the turf. It was fourth-and-4, and the clock was down to the last two minutes of the game.

If Daugherty punted, Notre Dame could finish out the game on offense by getting a first down or two and the Spartans wouldn't get another chance at the goal line. But if he didn't punt, the odds weren't good on making a first down on fourth-and-4. A turnover in his own territory might hand Notre Dame the game. Duffy weighed all that and decided to punt. His thinking was that he could get lucky and get a fumble on the punt return. Or, failing that, Parseghian would have to put the ball in the air from deep in his own territory, and Duffy's defense might get a shot at picking one off. Then, with the wind at his back, Kenney could try a field goal, which would be dangerous anywhere from midfield on in.

Duffy considered the possibilities and sent Kenney in to punt. Ara sent his men in after Kenney, but the Spartan line did its job and, despite a low snap, Kenney got the ball away. It was another high kick, and Duffy almost got his wish immediately. Schoen moved under it at the 30, signaled for a fair catch, and dropped it with six Spartans almost on top of him. Footballs bounce funny ways, everyone knows that, and this one bounced the funniest way of all, which is to say it didn't bounce a bit. Schoen was able to drop to the ground, reach out his left arm, and sweep the ball to safety just before the green wave landed on top of him.

All across the country the Notre Dame faithful spent a couple of seconds trying to recover from their collective heart attack. But the Irish had the ball with 1:24 on the clock and time-outs left. There was still time.

While the fans were pleading with their televisions during Michigan State's last drive, Ara was weighing his options. For all his fire on the sidelines, Parseghian didn't operate on impulse, as Daugherty sometimes did. He had played football under Woody Hayes and Paul Brown and had risen to the coaching pinnacle not through accident but through careful planning. By all accounts it was nearly impossible to find another football coach as organized and with as fine an eye for detail as Ara Parseghian. It was the reason for his success. He didn't do things because he thought they might work but because he was convinced they would work. If the risk of failure greatly outweighed the chance of success, he didn't do it.

He was not a gambler in the sense that Daugherty was. Daugherty loved to play the horses, Parseghian didn't. He didn't believe in long shots. He was willing to put a few dollars on a game of golf or handball, but he could control his performance and thus his fate. When he played, whether it was for $100 or a milkshake, he played to win; and if he was losing, he demanded to play some more. If the poor soul who was playing him went along with that, sooner or later he lost. He lost because Parseghian had gotten him to play his game. Football was no different. The way to win was to get the other guy to do what you wanted him to. The way to lose was to be the other guy.

Daugherty wanted Ara to be the other guy. Rather than try to make a first down on fourth-and-4 and keep his drive going, rather than let Raye throw deep to Washington and risk another interception, Daugherty elected to kick to Parseghian and let him beat himself. He knew what a fierce competitor Ara was and figured that Parseghian, wanting to win the game, would have O'Brien put it in the air. When he did, Duffy would be waiting with seven and even eight defensive backs and linebackers, each with instructions to go for the ball. With the Irish starting on their own 30, the Spartans wouldn't have far to go after a turnover to get within Kenney's field goal range.

Daugherty had figured Parseghian's will to win correctly, but he didn't factor in Ara's overall goal, stated back in August in his letter to his players. It was to win the National Championship. Nothing else. And one thing Ara knew as he prepared to call his last sequence of plays: Lose this game, and he could forget about a National Championship.

Ara explained his thinking immediately after the game and hasn't changed a word of it in more than a quarter century. He had brought in a team that started without Nick Eddy. On the second series, it had lost its starting quarterback and center. Later, it lost another halfback. Still it had rallied from a 10–0 deficit against some of the greatest defensive players in the country and had forged a 10–10 deadlock. He had had a chance to win it, but the field goal had trickled wide at the last moment. It was, he said, "one of the greatest comebacks in Notre Dame history."

His choices were obvious only to him. To everyone else he had only one choice: Put the ball up and hope the guy who catches it is wearing a white jersey. But he knew he didn't have to win to reach his goal; he just couldn't lose. At the same time, Daugherty did have to win. That was because this was Duffy's last game. He had no bowl to go to, no chance for redemption, no overtime. Notre Dame did have overtime—its final game the following week against nationally ranked Southern Cal. Tie this one and beat Southern Cal, and the National Championship might still be attainable. Lose this one on a stupid play in the closing minute, and there was no chance of winning the championship. As others would point out then and forever, Duffy had gambled by putting the ball up deep in his own territory. Sure, and he had just about lost the game because of it. And after the last interception, Duffy became rather conservative, too, figuring it was Ara's turn to make a mistake.

Finally, no matter how O'Brien said he felt, Ara could not be sure he still could throw the ball with accuracy. Maybe he could and maybe he couldn't, but did Ara really want to find out?

Ara decided he didn't. He wasn't going to try to tie the game, but he was going to make darned sure he didn't lose it. Though you'll have a hard time convincing everyone, there's a difference.

So Ara sent O'Brien in, and on first down, with the Spartans rushing five men hard, Ara sent O'Brien around right end on a power sweep that picked up 4 yards. On second down O'Brien dropped back as if to pass, the Spartans dropped back to cover, and then he handed it to Bleier on a draw—the same play Daugherty had run the previous series when he was backed up, third-and-16. The hole was there, too, but Hoag made a terrific play to shake free of Gmitter's block and tripped Bleier up after a gain of 3 yards. If Hoag hadn't made the play, Bleier would have bounced outside for a big gain, and Parseghian might have put the ball in the air. It was, even Carillot admits, a good call against the defense.

On third-and-3, Notre Dame packed it in tight, and O'Brien handed to Conjar for 2 yards. Now it was fourth-and-1 on their own 39 with under a minute to go. Duffy had kicked on fourth-and-4 and was looking for Parseghian to do the same, but again Ara refused to go along with the plan. It was a gamble to go for the first down, but it was a gamble Ara could control. The alternative was to punt, and the chances of a bad snap, a blocked kick, or a big return were better than the chances that his huge offensive line would fail to get a yard in front of O'Brien on a quarterback sneak.

Ara figured it right. The line fired out into the Spartan defense, our eleven against yours, and pushed the whole pile forward 2 yards for the first down at the 41.

Ara had figured that if he got to the 45, he could risk one pass to get close enough for a last-second field goal try. Complete the pass, and he still had time-outs. But he wasn't going to stop the clock until he thought it would help.

After O'Brien sneaked for the first down, the Spartans saw what was going on and called a time-out. Less than half a minute remained. In the huddle Bubba Smith and Charlie Thornhill were screaming at their teammates, saying that Notre Dame was trying to run out the clock. When the Irish came to the line, Smith and Thornhill called them sissies, cowards, and every other insulting thing they could think of—which in Bubba's case covered a lot. "You don't want it," he said, repeating a line from 1965. "C'mon. Throw the ball. Try to win," they yelled. They said that the Notre Dame linemen were crying and were saying that they wanted to go for it but had no choice. They had to run what the coach called.

Bubba Smith admits that he didn't really believe the things he was saying, although Thornhill did at the time. The Spartans had played too long and too hard against men every bit as tough as they were to think they were sissies. By the end of the game the players on both sides of the line were like heavyweight boxers who give everything they have to the common goal of knocking the other guy silly, and when the final bell sounds, fall into an embrace. There was that kind of respect on the field. Showing it was for after the game. Right then Bubba and his teammates were interested only in doing and saying whatever they could to try to get the Irish to do something stupid that would give Michigan State the ball.

Bubba, Jerry West, Jimmy Raye, and others on the team were just as unhappy with their own coach's play-calling at the end. "Duffy went conservative," said West. Daugherty didn't throw deep to Washington, but of his last 8 plays, 4 were passes. One of them lost 6 yards on a sack. Two were incomplete to receivers who were tightly covered. One was complete for 8 yards in a situation where 12 yards were needed. Finally, with fourth down at his own 36 and 1:30 left, Duffy punted, knowing that if his defense gave up one first down, he'd never get the ball back.

O'Brien admits to wanting to go for it, but he also was committed to whatever Parseghian called. Bleier, too, wondered why Ara wasn't trying to throw the ball. But almost everyone else accepted whatever Ara called. If he called a draw, they were blocking for it with everything they had, convinced that if they did their jobs, it would work. In fact, the Bleier draw almost did break for big yardage. Against that prevent defense, any running play had a chance of being a big gain. They heard Bubba, Thornhill, and Phillips, who joined in the taunting, but they say nobody was crying. They were too busy trying to win the game.

On first down from the 41, Ara finally called a pass. With the clock down to ten seconds and the crowd booing, O'Brien dropped back on a sprint out. But Bubba, still playing over Monty, timed the snap perfectly, blew past the center, and dragged O'Brien down 7 yards behind the line of scrimmage before Coley had a chance to get out of the way. As Bubba hit the ground, he signaled frantically for another time-out.

He got it, but the game was over. O'Brien ran a sneak for 5 yards, and that was that.

The players hauled themselves off the tattered grass and looked around as if to say, "Is that all there is?" Jeff Richardson, who had played magnificently, like everyone else on the Spartan defense, ran screaming toward an official. It couldn't be over. There must be another play to be run. There must be another minute that had been hiding on the clock. Bubba pulled him away.

Charles Bailey shook hands with Bob Kuechenberg. Half of the Notre Dame offense stopped to shake hands with George Webster. Kevin Hardy came off the sideline and patted Webster on the back. "George Webster," said Jim Lynch, "should have won the Heisman trophy that year."

The players distinctly remember that the stadium, which had been so incredibly noisy, went dead silent at the final gun. No one left. Like the players, the fans just stood around, thinking that it couldn't be over, it couldn't be a tie. Somebody had to win. The photographers were rushing onto the field, snapping pictures, but the players were unaware of them. Ara and Duffy found each other, patted each other on the back, and went their separate ways. Neither one of them looked happy. Neither one was.

The fans on the sidelines milled around, too. One of them, carrying a snootful of liquor, walked past the players spewing invective. "They went for a tie," he hollered. "They didn't want to win."

Slowly, the teams walked to the tunnel and filed out, while the Michigan State band marched on the field to play songs no one cared to hear. The fans stayed but didn't listen. Forty minutes later a radio reporter told his audience that the fans had just started to file out.

As the players walked out of the stadium, the game officials and sideline officials walked off with them. The official in charge of the down marker carried his equipment high over his head, where it stuck out among the mass of Notre Dame and Michigan State players. In a black numeral on a white metal plate, the marker said "1."

13

The only person it has really driven crazy is Ara.
                                        —Charles "Bubba" Smith

Ara Parseghian never thought "Let's get a tie" as he managed the last minutes of the game. He didn't hum the fight song to himself and substitute the words that appeared in *Sports Illustrated*—and provoked a magazine-burning on the Notre Dame campus: "Tie, tie for old Notre Dame." First, he wanted to win. Second, he wanted not to lose. There was no third. "I knew there was going to be a winner and a loser, and I thought we were going to win," he said. "I never thought about a tie. The last thing Duffy Daugherty or I wanted was a tie."

What he thought about as he left the field was what he was going to tell his players. He had heard the drunk who had run onto the field and shouted that they were going for the tie, and that angered him. His players had spilled their guts on that field, just as the Michigan State players had. It may not have been the prettiest game in history, but it was, said Lynch, the hardest-hitting college football game he had ever been in. It was also the biggest he ever would be in. "The Super Bowl was not as big as the Michigan State–Notre Dame game," he said after having played in both. "It was as electrifying a game as you had," said George Young, who was coaching high school ball in Baltimore in 1966 and went on to become the general manager of the New York Giants.

"If we had won that game, we would have gone down in history as the greatest football team ever," said Charlie Thornhill. "There's not a month that passes that somebody doesn't mention it."

Thornhill may exaggerate, but he may also be right. Certainly, few defenses have ever put together four athletes like Jess Phillips, George Webster, Bubba Smith, and Charlie Thornhill, and then filled in with the likes of Phil Hoag and Jeff Richardson, and still have a George Chatlos in reserve. Notre Dame sent more men to the pros, but Michigan State's best were better than Notre Dame's best. That's not an insult to Notre Dame. It's impossible to insult the abilities of players like Jim Lynch, Pete Duranko, Alan Page, and Kevin Hardy. No one would believe you. But people who played against Webster swear there was no better defensive player in college football. Notre Dame had a collection of offensive linemen who would go on to play more than a half century of professional ball. Every interior lineman on the team had a pro career. And not one of them could hold a block on Webster. These were players who simply blew away everyone else they faced, who were the engine of an offense that averaged 400 yards a game when that was an enormous figure. They got just over half that against the Spartans—219 yards: 91 on the ground and 128 in the air. Some of that can be attributed to the loss of Hanratty, Eddy, and Goeddeke, and then Gladieux as well. Hanratty and Eddy were both men who could find a way to get a whole lot of yards at once. But Hanratty, Goeddeke, and Gladieux left the game because Michigan State hit them so hard things went pop in their bodies. Throw in Bleier's lacerated kidney, and you have a good day's hitting. Phillips, particularly, hit that day with frightening force, and not one of the hits was a cheap shot because the Spartans, like the Irish, played clean. Only 5 yards in penalties were assessed against Notre Dame, and 32 against the Spartans. The officials didn't call a single holding penalty, personal foul, or pass interference penalty. That says a lot about the play of the game. It was hard and it was clean, as football is supposed to be and so seldom is.

Against that defense, with so many starters knocked out, Notre Dame's comeback was remarkable. Michigan State not only had great athletes, but Hank Bullough and Vince Carillot also did a magnificent job of presenting multiple defensive fronts and calling the right defense at the right time. They wanted to take away Seymour and they did. They forced Notre Dame to do things the Irish would rather not have done.

Michigan State's offensive performance was no less impressive. Notre Dame took away Clinton Jones utterly. The man who had gained more than 250 yards in a single game was held to 13 net yards on 10 carries. Cavender had a few big runs and finished with 36 yards on 7 carries. But Raye was magnificent, gaining 75 net yards on 21 attempts. Eleven of those attempts resulted in losses, but many of the losses came on pass plays and not runs. Raye completed only 7 passes in 20 attempts, but he gained 142 yards on them—20 yards a catch. Nobody passed well that day anyway. O'Brien was 7 for 19, and Hanratty was 1 for 4.

Michigan State had more first downs, 13 to 10, and more total yards, 284 to 219. On the other hand, each team punted 8 times, so the possessions were even in the end.

Twenty years earlier, Notre Dame had played to a 0–0 tie with Army. In that game neither team really tried to win by going for the big play. Both teams played it tight, and as a result, neither team could score. But the Spartans threw the ball 20 times, and Notre Dame threw it 23 times (24, counting the pass by Hardy on the aborted punt). The effort was there, if not the results.

Some writers saw it that way, as a magnificent effort in which Notre Dame came back against frightening odds and managed to escape with a tie.

William Gildea of the *Washington Post* wrote: "As it is at the end of all wars, there was really no winner. This was war today, with the colossi of collegiate football, Notre Dame and Michigan State, marshalling their forces, then kicking the bejabers out of one another, only to have victory escape both."

Dana Mozley of the New York *Daily News* wrote: "Notre Dame, with the tenacity of a has-been trying to hold on to her millionaire love, probably retained its No. 1 rating, and with it all but locked up the national football championship."

David Smothers of UPI said simply, "Once again the big game proved nothing."

It was left to a few, led by Dan Jenkins of *Sports Illustrated* and

Jim Murray of the *Los Angeles Times*, to set the agenda for the ages. They saw the game as a case of Ara purposely playing for a tie. Murray, a magnificent writer, was viciously sarcastic, as only he could be. He set up his column as one end of a dialogue, with the speaker being an Irish Catholic Notre Dame fan. The headline said it all: 'TIS A PITY WHEN IRISH 'TIE ONE FOR THE GIPPER.' Murray wrote: "The Four Horsemen, indeed! The Four Rabbits! The Four Mice! 'Outlined against a blue-gray October sky, the Four Mice went into hiding again today.' . . . May George Gipp never hear of it!"

Jenkins began his lead story in the nation's sports magazine, "Old Notre Dame will tie over all. Sing it out, guys. . . . No one really expected a verdict in that last desperate moment," he wrote. "But they wanted someone to try."

That's the legacy of the game, and Ara saw it coming as soon as he talked to the first wave of newspaper reporters; maybe even as soon as he heard the drunken goof on the field taunting him about tieing the game. The first thing he did when he got off the field and had his few minutes with his team in the closed locker room was explain to his own players what had happened. They had come off the field thinking that their dreams of a National Championship were finished. They thought they had lost, and when they got behind closed doors, they sat at their lockers and wept.

Ara asked for their attention and explained that they hadn't lost, and that was the main thing. He told them how magnificently they had played to come back and tie the Spartans with five key players hurt. He told them how college football did not have overtime in a game but how they had overtime in their season. Michigan State was through, their record carved in stone at 9-0-1. But Notre Dame had USC yet to play. Beat them and they could still save the season, they could still win their championship.

The players listened and the players believed because Ara Parseghian had never misled them. They still felt empty, but no longer as empty as the Spartans, who were raging in their own locker room at the cruel trick fate had played on them. When the writers came in, Bubba led the charge by telling everyone how Notre Dame had played for a tie and how it was Parseghian's fault.

The writers ran over to the Notre Dame locker room and asked

Ara, "What about it?" They've been asking the question ever since. Ara's answer never changes. The following is as good a rendition as any:

> Tying is bad, but there's something worse. That's losing. I can understand why Michigan State gambled late in the game deep in its own territory. I can understand why Bubba Smith called time-out when we had the ball. It was all over for Michigan State right then. They don't play overtime games in football, but in a sense Notre Dame had an overtime chance. We were the last team on Michigan State's schedule, but we still had Southern Cal the following week. Now look at it my way. If we get a tie, we don't lose. Then the next week, we get a chance to get back Number One alone by beating Southern Cal. Like I said, it depends on how you look at it. If we gamble and lose to Michigan State, the next week we're fighting for Number Two and maybe Number Ten in the rankings.

Two days after the game, when asked about trying a desperation heave, he said:

> That's a stupid gamble. Everybody's making a federal case out of the last minute of the game when we closed with six straight running plays in our own territory. Our whole game plan, which certainly was hit hard by key injuries, was not to open up until we had good field position. At the end, if we had moved to their 45 or so, we might have gone to the air, but we weren't going to gamble against percentages and lose on an interception and possible field goal. We didn't achieve the success we have enjoyed this season by making stupid mistakes.

It went on for a long time that way. Ara saw it as a great comeback. Some of the writers didn't. "They wanted an outcome," Parseghian said.

That's the allure of sports. It's why many sports writers choose their profession. If you had the Berlin beat on the international desk, you had to wait almost thirty years to find out who won the game with the Berlin Wall. You can cover Congress for your entire life and never get a firm resolution to anything. That's how life is. You have a few big wins, a few big setbacks. You have lots of minor wins and setbacks. But most days you're lucky to come out even; you're lucky to tie. So people turn to sports, where games happen in discrete packages of time, and at the end of that time, somebody wins and somebody else loses. Then you know who's better. If two teams tie, it throws everything out of whack.

The writers wanted a resolution, and if they didn't get one, somebody would pay. In 1946, Leahy and Blaik could play to a tie and not have it haunt them forever. In 1966, Parseghian couldn't.

The more the writers questioned his strategy, the more frustrated Ara became. What, he said, could he have done in the last minute that he hadn't done in the first fifty-nine? He had tried everything. There was nothing left to do but get out and win the title the next week. Most coaches understand that. The goal is not to win any one game but the big prize at the end of the season. If a pro coach tied a game on purpose and got into the postseason because of it and went on to win the Super Bowl, he'd be a genius. "That's what you're playing for," said George Young of the Giants. "It's not how you win things. It's whether or not you do."

Ara and Duffy, the analyst against the gambler, had played a chess game on a field 100 yards long. They traded pieces and tried different gambits. At the end Duffy made the move that he thought would win. Ara foiled the move and won a stalemate. In chess that's a legitimate tactic. In football it is as well. If it weren't, the rules wouldn't provide for ties. As in basketball, the rules would allow only for wins and losses.

Ara also felt for his players. He had been with the seniors through 1964 when they had come within ninety seconds of a national title and then lost. That had been a devastating defeat, and it had been the incentive to do better now, in the last year for that senior class. They had done so much for him. They had given everything they had. "I didn't want to throw away all that effort," he said.

"I made the judgments for all the games I coached, and I wasn't going to let some writer in the press box make a decision about what I should have done at the end of the game. Who knows better my team and the capabilities of the team?" Ara argued, his eyes flashing. "One of the writers said, 'Well, why didn't you throw the bomb out of bounds to make it look good?' What! I'm not trying to impress anybody. Doing that would be truly phony to me."

When the writers finally left the locker room, Ara knew how it would come out. He had played for a tie, and that made him unmanly. To get away from everyone, he went into the shower. On the way in he picked up an apple from a pile of fruit that was there for the team to eat after the game. "I was so goddamned frustrated," he said. "I picked up that apple and threw it left-handed, just smashed it. I threw it as hard as any Dwight Gooden fastball. I mean, *whomp*. That thing just splattered."

He was alone for the first time that day, and as the bits of apple dribbled down the wall, Ara finally let himself go. Pagna came in and found him there. "It was the only time I really saw him come apart," Pagna said years later. As he recounted the story, tears welled up in his own eyes at the memory. "Privately, he went into the shower room and just sobbed. He knew we gave everything we had, and what else can you ask of the kids? But we didn't pull it off."

After he had composed himself, Ara got on the bus with the team and they drove to the rail siding at the Lansing station where their car was waiting for them. Attached to the team's coach was a private coach that was owned by a wealthy Notre Dame fan who liked to travel to the games in his railcar. Joe Doyle, the *South Bend Tribune* writer and Ara's friend, took the coach back to the private car, and Doyle, the fan, and Ara had a drink and then a big steak dinner. The dinner, the drinks, and the conversation with friends loosened him up a bit, Doyle thought. Finally, Ara excused himself to be with his team.

He may have seemed a bit brighter, but he wasn't. He has no recollection of the car or the meal. He has no recollection of the trip back to South Bend, for that matter. When he did get back and the buses took the players back to campus, he went home. His wife asked him to go with her to a small social gathering at the house of a friend who lived two blocks away. He went, and while he was there with a few friends, the phone rang. His host told Ara it was for him. Somebody—he was from the South, Ara thinks—had tracked him down with a little help from the baby-sitter at his house. Ara took the phone, and the guy started reaming him out for his strategy at the end of the game. "I said, 'I don't give a damn what you think,' and I slammed down the receiver. That's what kind of mood I was in," Ara said. "Normally, I would be diplomatic." Several years later Ara finally got an unlisted phone number. He didn't really want to, but he'd taken too many calls from too many drunks.

"I've always prided myself on saying, 'Okay, fine. You want to talk? You make any kind of common sense, I'll talk to you.' I wasn't afraid of that," he said.

He's still not afraid, and he'll still talk to you. But over the years, since he retired from coaching because he was afraid the job would kill him, the question that comes up most is, "Why did you go for the tie?" It's become an obsession for him, his Moby Dick that he keeps sticking harpoons into but can't kill. And having always relied on the power of reason, he's never been able to say, "Screw it. I did what I did and that's that. End of discussion." He seems to feel that if he can only get people to see the game the way he did, if they could only look at the big picture instead of the little picture, they'd understand.

In fact, most of the people who count do understand. Rocky Bleier, one of the few among the Irish who openly questioned Ara's strategy, said,

> It makes sense now. If I were coaching today, I'd probably do the same thing. It's just at the time, the mentality of the player was to throw the ball, throw the ball, throw the ball. But we were running the ball, and you don't even get the satisfaction of saying, "Hell, we tried." If you lose, it takes away from the success of the whole season. I would tie it for the guys, because if you lose it, nobody remembers you. If you lose, you can say all you want, "We could have won. We went for it." But that's bull. Who cares? To win the championship, which was our goal, you have to win every game, or, in this case, not lose that game. That's the point. We didn't lose the game.

On the other side of the field, Bubba Smith, who was most vocal in criticizing Parseghian, has come to appreciate the fact that nobody won the game.

> I told George Webster that the best thing that ever happened was that the game ended in a tie. The only person it has really driven crazy is Ara, and the older he has gotten the more it has preyed on him because the game comes up every year. But he did exactly what he should have done. I knew during the game that Ara's strategy was right. I was calling them names because

that's all we had left to do—play head games. I told our guys in the huddle, "If this game ends in a tie, Notre Dame is going to win. All the sportswriters are Catholic." I said, "Do you think we're going to win the National Championship even if they run the clock out? We got too many niggers on this team to win the National Championship. We have to find a way." I was saying that to try to motivate the guys, but it's true. I don't think any other school would have won the championship if they had done that. But he did the right thing. They couldn't have thrown the ball against the defenses we were running. I'm just being honest.

"It was so frustrating," said Clinton Jones. "But over the years I've come to see it was a great testimony to both clubs. We played our hearts out. It was a classic game, a real classic. Knute Rockne would have been proud."

In his strategy, Jones said, "Ara had a broader perspective. He knew there was another game for him and not for us."

Vince Carillot insists that Duffy would never have gone for the tie. Indeed, Duffy pressed most of his coaching life for a change in collegiate rules to allow overtime to settle tied games. "There's no way Duffy would have done what Ara did," Carillot said.

But Duffy did do what Ara did. He kicked the ball away with a fourth-and-4 from his own 36 and little or no hope of getting it back except by a turnover. Duffy explained at the time that the situation dictated a punt and then trying to get it back. If that was so, then the situation also dictated to Ara not to give it back.

"What Ara did turned out to be right," Carillot admitted. "I'd have gone for the win, but I guess I'm not bright enough to think that far ahead. If Ara thought the way he says he did, then he did the right thing."

Duffy himself, before he died, never criticized Ara for his strategy. He and Ara were friends. He told Ara that he had done the right thing.

Regis Cavender was another angry Spartan after the game, but he came to understand, too. It all came together in his mind in June 1991 when he went to a dinner in Chicago commemorating the twenty-fifth anniversary of the tie. Some of the players from each team were there along with some coaches. Ara couldn't be there but sent a letter of three or four paragraphs that was read aloud at the dinner. Half of the letter was devoted to explaining his decision again. As Cavender listened to it, he thought,

Why is he explaining? He doesn't have to justify it. There's no pointing fingers or saying this is right or wrong. It was a decision he made, one of thousands that had to be made that day. He was a fantastic coach, and one thing Notre Dame people don't have to do is justify that game. I don't see Michigan people criticizing Ara these days. We came off that decision a long time ago. The preponderance of evidence is that they played for a tie. It's a decision, right, wrong, or indifferent. I'm not saying it was bad. But from that point on, many coaches go for a win now.

They have to. They don't want to have to put up with what Ara's been through.

"That's a shame," said Cavender. "I have a tremendous amount of respect for him and for that team."

But again, the problem was that the writers needed a winner. They had to vote for one in the polls, and how could they vote if the game was tied? Duffy got it right when he said Notre Dame and Michigan State should be co–National Champions. The awarders of the MacArthur Bowl, one of the National Championship awards, did just that. They split the award between the two teams. Notre Dame kept the trophy for six months, and Michigan State kept it for the next six.

The day after the game of the century, Ara Parseghian was back in his office getting ready for the game that would decide the season. He was worried. He had no idea how his team would respond after Saturday's mighty effort and the disappointment that followed. And USC was no pushover, with future pros Tim Rossovich, Adrian Young, and Ron Yary on its roster. In addition, USC had something to prove after its Saturday loss to cross-city rival UCLA.

That loss had spawned a storm on the West Coast. Both teams had gone into the game with one loss. At stake, both teams thought, was a berth in the Rose Bowl, with the winner playing Purdue on New Year's Day and the loser going to the beach. But the Rose Bowl selection wasn't automatic. The team to represent the PAC-8 was chosen by the conference, and it didn't have to be the team with the best record. Like the Big Ten's rule that prevented Michigan State from going to the Rose Bowl for a second straight year, the events of 1966 would help change the PAC-8's selection process. UCLA beat the Trojans, 14–7, and the Bruins went home thinking they had won the Rose Bowl trip since they had one loss to USC's two and had beaten USC. They were also ranked ahead of USC in both polls—sixth place as opposed to tenth. Then the committee met and chose USC. At UCLA angry students rioted. At USC the football team felt it had to beat Notre Dame to justify the choice of the conference.

The Irish were horribly beat up. Parseghian had no idea if Eddy could return, and he knew Bleier, Hanratty, Gladieux, and Goeddeke were definitely out. He didn't even know if Coley O'Brien could recover from his grueling day against Michigan State. With only Conjar definitely healthy in the backfield, Parseghian decided to convert defensive back Dan Harshman into a halfback for the USC game. He needed bodies.

At Sunday's team meeting he told his men again how they could rescue their season by beating the Trojans. He didn't say they had to blow them out. Any victory would be good enough. He reminded them, and the seniors specifically, how USC had dashed their championship hopes two years earlier after Notre Dame had led at the half, 17–0. USC had scored in the last ninety seconds to win, 20–17. Until Saturday and Michigan State, neither Ara nor his players had ever been as miserable.

"We have one game left," Regner remembers Parseghian saying. "You can prove what you are."

On Monday, Ara held a brief workout and handed out the weekly awards for Saturday's top performers. In addition to Regner's game ball, he cited Larry Conjar, who had been as good a blocker as there was on either side of the ball, and Coley O'Brien in the backfield. He also cited Jim Lynch, Kevin Hardy, and Tom Schoen on defense.

The two polls came out on Monday, with Notre Dame leading the AP version and Michigan State first in the UPI coaches' poll. The first of the many All-American teams, chosen by the American Football Coaches Association, was also announced. Notre Dame placed four players on the first team: Tom Regner, Nick Eddy, Pete Duranko, and Jim Lynch. Michigan State had three on the first team: Bubba Smith, George Webster, and Gene Washington. Others on the squad included Heisman trophy–winning quarterback Steve Spurrier of Florida and Purdue quarterback Bob Griese, Ron Yary at tackle, guard Cecil Dowdy, and end Ray Perkins of Alabama, halfback Floyd Little of Syracuse, and halfback Mel Farr of UCLA. Honorable mentions went to

Notre Damers Jim Seymour, Paul Seiler, George Goeddeke, Larry Conjar, Alan Page, and Tom Schoen, and to Spartans Jerry West, Jimmy Raye, Clinton Jones, Bob Apisa, and Charlie Thornhill. That was eighteen of the forty-four offensive and defensive starters from the two schools. In the weeks to come, Eddy, Lynch, Page, and Regner would be named consensus All Americans, and Duranko, Hardy, Seymour, Seiler, Goeddeke, Schoen, Conjar, Horney, Pergine, and Hanratty were all named to one or more teams. Michigan State saw Jones, Raye, Apisa, West, Washington, Thornhill, Smith, Przybycki, Hoag, Gallinagh, and Kenney named to All-American squads, one of which also listed a Colorado defensive back named Hale Irwin, who would give up football for golf. In all, twenty-five of the forty-four starters for the Spartans and Irish received All-American mention.

The USC game would be played over the Thanksgiving break, a traditional date for the two schools. In 1964, Parseghian had taken his team out to Arizona in the middle of the week to get accustomed to the heat. Having done that and lost, this year Parseghian decided not to go out until Friday morning. So on Thursday and Friday the players had the campus virtually to themselves, as most students went home on Wednesday for the holiday. On Thursday the team had its own Thanksgiving meal, prepared by the dining hall cooks. They put tablecloths out to give it a holiday air, and they cooked turkey and dressing and all the accessory dishes. The players were even allowed to bring their girlfriends to the dinner. But it was still in the dining hall, and it was still dining hall food. "It was," said Seymour, "boring."

On Friday they left for Los Angeles. Probably the most nervous player on the flight was O'Brien. He hadn't had time to be nervous against Michigan State. He had not expected to play, and then suddenly he was in the game. But now he knew from the beginning of the week that he was the man. Parseghian's fears about his recovering from Saturday had proved to be unfounded. He felt fit and strong. "I feel much more pressure than I did when I went into the game Saturday," he told writers. "I knew from the start of the week that I'm the number-one quarterback, and I know I have to play a good game. I have time to think, and I'm getting plenty excited about the prospects." To make it better, his father, the career Navy officer, was captain of an aircraft carrier, and he would be in Los Angeles for the game.

When the Irish landed in Los Angeles and got off the plane, they were surprised to be welcomed by the leaders of the UCLA student government and a big contingent of UCLA fans. The student leaders told the team that if they would be so kind as to beat those no good so-and-so's from USC who had stolen UCLA's Rose Bowl bid, the town would be theirs for the rest of the weekend. And they wouldn't have to worry about being asked for their IDs before they could get a beer.

Nick Eddy was almost as anxious as O'Brien to play. His shoulder felt considerably better after a week of rest. And California was his home base. Many of his friends had gone to USC, and some were playing football there. It would be his last college game, his last chance to play in front of his friends. So he let the doctors stick their huge needles in his shoulder again to deaden it enough so he could give it a try, but not so much that he couldn't move his arm. He did play and played well. Soon after he signed a pro contract with the Lions for $525,000—considerably more than the $400,000 Namath was said to have gotten a year before.

When Notre Dame came out into the Rose Bowl, they were greeted by a throng of 88,520 fans, the biggest crowd to see a college football game anywhere that year. A surprisingly large number of them were cheering for the Irish, either because they were freeway alumni or because they were UCLA fans there to see USC get beat. On the back of their bench someone had hung a banner that said: TO HELL WITH UPI. WE'RE NO. 1. But as they warmed up, Lynch felt totally flat and exhausted. After Michigan State, he was running on empty. Duranko was still sore and stiff, and thought it would be a long afternoon.

It wasn't long at all, at least not for Notre Dame. For USC it lasted longer than the Roman Empire.

It started well enough. After Notre Dame won the coin toss and elected to receive, Rossovich kicked off into the end zone, and Eddy did the Trojans the favor of downing it there. Notre Dame's offense trotted out, and on the first play O'Brien handed to Conjar running over left guard, and the USC line stopped him after 3 yards. USC had targeted Conjar. A year earlier in South Bend, Conjar had scored 4 touchdowns against them, and they were determined that it wasn't going to happen again. When they tackled him on that first play, they told him as much. "You're not going to do it again, Conjar," they said. Six minutes later, after a merciless drive made up entirely of short, crashing plays, Conjar scored from the 2, and for the only time in his career he couldn't resist saying something to the enemy. As he turned to trot off the field, he passed the USC defenders and said, "Thank you, gentlemen."

The teams traded punts, and then Schoen picked off a pass at the USC 40 and ran it into the end zone. Azzaro, who would have a busy day, kicked his second extra point, and it was 14–0.

The interception return ended the first quarter. In the second quarter Azzaro added a field goal to run it to 17–0, the same as the halftime score in 1964. The very thought of a repeat of 1964 made everyone so nervous they vowed to score again before the half. After USC turned the ball over on downs, O'Brien obliged, getting the score on a 13-yard pass to Seymour. It was 24–0 and only fifty-seven seconds remained in the half. But the Irish weren't done. For some reason Coach John McKay punted the ball back to them with only seconds left in the half when he could have let the clock run out. The punt was short, and with time for only 1 play, Parseghian told Seymour to see if he could get clear in the end zone. He didn't exactly get clear, but O'Brien threw it anyway. Seymour went up in a covey of defenders and brought it down for a 31–0 halftime lead.

When Notre Dame went into the locker room at the half, someone had written on the top of the blackboard, "No. 1." Underneath was a brief reminder: "We relaxed in '64."

Ara needn't have worried. As beat-up as they were, the Irish were finding this game easy. "When we went out there, they could have put a pro team against us," said Regner. "I didn't care who they put out, we would have beaten them." By halftime Regner's day was already over. He had taken a hit and ripped the ligaments in his knee. When he returned to South Bend the following week, he had surgery on it and went into a cast for six weeks. When they took the cast off, the rehab people put him on a machine to see how much strength he had lost. They were astounded to see that the injured leg was just as strong as the uninjured one. Regner can't explain it and neither can the doctors, but he went straight to pro ball and never missed a beat.

The second half was more of the same, and by the time the game ended, the scoreboard read Notre Dame 51, USC 0. The

Trojans who had given up 63 points in nine previous games nearly equaled that total in the tenth game. It was the worst loss in the history of USC.

The final score only drew further criticism for Ara. He ran up the score to influence the voters, people said. Nonsense, Parseghian replied, and even McKay didn't argue with him. The simple fact was that USC kept turning the ball over and taking fourth-down chances and getting passes picked off, and the Irish kept finding the end zone.

When the gun finally sounded, the Irish knew they had climbed their mountain. With their jerry-built offense, they had gained 461 yards. O'Brien had passed for 255 of them on 21 completions in 31 attempts. Three were for touchdowns. Seymour had come back to catch 11 passes for 150 yards and 2 touchdowns, his best performance since the first game of the season against Purdue.

They carried Ara off the field and into the locker room, where they chucked him in the shower. Bill Cosby, enjoying the fame generated by his Emmy-winning role in the television series "I Spy," came down to congratulate the team. Lynch pulled out his false teeth and waved them at the comedian. Cosby offered Parseghian a job coaching at Temple, Cosby's alma mater.

During the season Parseghian kept a distance between himself and his players. It ran against his nature, but he knew he couldn't be pals with men he had to discipline and lead. But now he didn't care what they did to him. "They could have done any god-damned thing they wanted," he said. "I was proud they were able to do something that I wasn't sure they were going to be able to do in that last game."

His players gave him the game ball, and as he talked to reporters, he held the ball. "I'll cherish this for a long, long time," he said softly. "This is the best team by far that I've ever coached. Not only that, it is the best balanced college football team I've ever seen in my life."

As good as it was, the 51–0 final was beyond anything he would have dared to dream. "I never envisioned that 51–0 score. I just thought if we could win this thing, I'd be very happy. I felt we had to win it, and if we had won it by, say, one point on a fluke, then I don't think we would have been named National Champions. But we demonstrated we were a helluva solid team that comes back."

It was his one-hundredth coaching victory.

After the game the team went out for a night of fun. One large group went to the home of Don Gmitter's friend Doug Simon, whose father was a powerful and wealthy Hollywood attorney. They had a huge house with a pipe organ and scads of servants. Jimmy Durante came to the party and sat at the piano singing songs and comparing noses with Terry Hanratty, who had come out with Bob Gladieux to be with the team, and Frank Criniti. Gmitter finally found his way to the wine cellar stocked with the best stuff around. Gmitter, who hadn't had a beer since spring practice began, drank a few bottles and took some with him when he left to check out the town and see if the UCLA guys had been serious about carte blanche.

They went to a place called the Oar House, a hangout for the UCLA rowing team. Gmitter walked in and asked for an empty beer mug, pulled out one of the bottles of wine he had in his coat pocket, and drank some more.

Hanratty, Gladieux, and Ron Dushney, a reserve halfback who was the third member of what was known variously as the Rat Pack and the Unholy Three, decided to catch a show in a strip joint. But Gladieux was on crutches because of his thigh injury and hadn't been getting around very well. Dush and the Rat—Hanratty—decided Harpo was slowing them down, so they put him in a cab, gave the driver some money, and told the driver to take Harpo back to the hotel while they went to the strip joint. An hour later when they were walking into the hotel, they heard a noise in the bushes. They looked over and saw a crutch sticking out and waving around in the air. They followed the crutch into the bush and found Harpo. He had staggered out of the cab, fallen into the shrub, and hadn't been able to get out.

The next day, Saturday, they had a tour of Universal Studios and Disneyland. Then a bunch of them went to Tijuana, where they did whatever it is that young men did there.

Ara enjoyed himself, too, but he never got the satisfaction out of the season he might have. The Michigan State thing kept coming up,

and I found myself defending myself, and after a while it got frustrating. I remember being at a banquet in Houston and a writer had put in the paper that I was chicken. I was making a speech, and I said, "I was in the Navy for three years, and I came up the hard way through the Depression. If you think I'm chicken, come up and try me."

Normally, I wouldn't do that, but I know the kind of person I am. I'll compete. I'm going to give my best effort. I'm not going to give up easy. That's not in my nature. But if you're in this business long enough, they're going to find something in your career that they're going to get after your ass about.

The belligerence has worn off. Ara won't offer to punch you in the nose anymore. "I feel comfortable with the situation," he said. "If I didn't, that would be pretty tough to live with."

The team returned to school on Monday. Because a snowstorm had socked in South Bend, the plane had to divert to Chicago, where the team mounted buses to the campus. In 1964, on their way back from their heartbreaking loss, they had driven into town in the middle of the night and had been touched to find that the residents of South Bend along the route had all turned on their porch lights to welcome them home.

This time, a pep rally was waiting for them in the old field house. In the middle of the rally word had come to the school and was announced to the crowd that the final polls had come in. Both UPI and AP had voted Notre Dame number one and Michigan State number two. Alabama, the only undefeated and untied team in the nation, finished third. The announcement brought a huge roar from the crowd and the usual chants. Soon word would come from East Lansing that Duffy Daugherty had sent his congratulations. "They are as fine as any team ever selected National Champions," Duffy said. "But I also salute the Spartans who are, in my mind, equally as good as the Notre Dame team." To prove it, he would see to it that the Spartans got their diamond rings. He also said he would say no more about the game because "I would hate to see this great game deteriorate into a name-calling, controversial thing."

Spoken like a champion.

Epilogue

*Now the media makes whoever's playing this week a
star so you'll want to watch the game.*
—Bubba Smith

Notre Dame–Michigan State was part of a continuum that
started in a vacant lot in 1869 in New Brunswick, New Jersey,
when the boys from Princeton went up to play the boys from
Rutgers. When Rutgers won, Princeton had to return the following year to try to square things. The first rivalry was born. Rival-
ries created fan interest, and as more and more colleges took up
this new game of football, observers naturally argued about
which team was the best. By 1883 the Helms Athletic Foundation
started the obsession with number one by declaring Yale to be
the best team in the country. No fewer than eight organizations
were awarding championships by 1936 when the Associated
Press chipped in with a national poll of sportswriters and broadcasters. The AP poll soon became the most coveted of all the
championships, but over the years at least fifteen organizations
have awarded championships.

Some of those championship races created more national interest than others, and the biggest of them mark pivotal points in
the continuum. Notre Dame–Michigan State was one of those

pivotal points because it demonstrated the power of television and showed how far beyond the stadium a game could reach. It ushered in the modern TV-football era just as surely as the Notre Dame–Army game in 1913 had shown the power of the forward pass.

The seeds of the change that bloomed in 1966 had been sown in 1964 when the last rules against platoon football were dropped by the NCAA. With the introduction of full substitution, many of the big football schools started awarding more scholarships to athletes. Rosters exploded, and the talent available to marginal programs shrank. The rich got richer, and by the time the NCAA got around to limiting scholarships, the damage had been done. College football was clearly divided into the haves and the have-nots. In 1966 the Ivy League was still part of major college football, at least in name. In time the old divisions of major colleges and small colleges would be scrapped to reflect the new reality. There would be the big schools—Division I. The Ivy League would retain a claim to the big-time by being shunted off into something called Division IA. The small colleges were divided into Divisions II and III. Division I would shake down again after the biggest schools formed the College Football Association. The rest of Division I just became cannon fodder for the big boys.

Not all the changes were for the better. A lot of them—maybe most of them—were for the worse. College football lost whatever innocence it still had; it had let the money changers into the temple. Television would call the shots in the future, and college teams would be run more like professional franchises than like amateur sports programs. Rankings became more important than competition. Television audiences became more important than the people who paid their money to see the game live. College football was big business.

Everyone wanted a piece of the frenzy that Notre Dame–Michigan State had inspired; everybody wanted to be number one. To do that, they would have to follow the rules that the voters—the sportswriters and broadcasters—were making up as they went along. The University of Alabama went undefeated and untied in 1966 but could do no better than third in the polls. The pollsters decided the Crimson Tide hadn't proved itself because it hadn't played an intersectional schedule. That year Bear Bryant started talking about the need for the Crimson Tide to play three national games every year along with seven conference games. To win those games, Bryant knew he'd need to have some of the black players who were being recruited away in ever-increasing numbers by midwestern and western schools. The University of Minnesota had shown that a championship could be won with a black quarterback. Now Duffy Daugherty showed that you could start a black quarterback with blacks at virtually every key position and not only win but dominate. Just as important, he showed that if the team won games, it didn't matter what color the players were, the fans would flock to the ticket windows.

All in all, 1966 was an important year for black college athletes. First, Texas Western became the first major college to put five blacks on a basketball floor, on their way to beating all-white Kentucky to win the National Championship. Then Michigan State went undefeated with a majority of blacks on its football team. The old prejudices that said blacks weren't leaders or didn't have the alleged necessities pretty much died right there.

In fact, the old wisdom—which wasn't wisdom at all—changed almost overnight. Where once people said you couldn't win with blacks, now they realized you couldn't win without them. It took a long time for the college sports establishment to come to that realization. Baseball had noticed it a long time ago, and after the Dodgers brought up first Jackie Robinson and then Roy Campanella, Don Newcombe, Jim Gilliam, Maury Wills, Willie Davis, and Tommy Davis, among others, everyone realized that there was a huge pool of talent out there that could help win games.

It's doubtful that Duffy Daugherty was consciously trying to drag the rest of college football into the modern world. More likely he was just trying to win a championship, and he realized that color wasn't important. Talent was. He probably would have preferred that his rivals continued to wallow in their ignorance and bigotry. That way he could have kept the best talent for himself. But consciously or not, he helped change recruiting.

Even though there were new opportunities for black athletes, there was little change on the mostly white campuses. As long as the players were stars, they were enormously popular. Bubba Smith, Clinton Jones, and Gene Washington were as popular as a student could be at Michigan State, just as Alan Page was at Notre Dame. But other black students, blacks who were not athletes, didn't necessarily find their lives made any easier. They were still a tiny minority in a white world. And any ideas they may have had that their athletic brethren were breaking new ground were dashed when they looked around and saw that all the black All Americans in the country didn't translate into any black coaches, administrators, or professors. It didn't even mean more black students. At many campuses blacks were liberally represented on the football field and on the basketball court, but no more than a handful of minority students were on the campus as a whole.

The men who played in 1966 were just happy to have a chance to attend a big, traditionally white school. They were grateful for the chance to play for the best teams; grateful, even, for the chance to get a good education. But with time some of them came to see that they were there only because of their ability to run and jump and tackle and catch. They were being used. Alan Page came to that conclusion, and although he says today his Notre Dame experience was positive, he has separated himself from the school and his football past. He is on the board of trustees at the University of Minnesota and laments the fact that minority enrollment at that school is minuscule. He has come to the conclusion that athletes should be paid for their efforts.

The members of the NCAA quail at such suggestions. They make big money from the labors of their athletes. They want to keep it. Besides, they argue, the athletes are getting scholarships; they are getting the opportunity for an education. It has become clear over the years, however, that as far as many athletic departments are concerned, education is secondary. Even traditionally black colleges fight proposals to stiffen academic requirements for athletes. If standards are raised too high, they say, many blacks will be denied an education. But the standards would deny no one an education; they would just prevent them from playing sports. And the schools that protest are only saying that if they aren't allowed to play football, we don't want them as students.

Every school did recruit more blacks after Daugherty's success. A couple of years later, at a coaches' conference, Bryant told Daugherty that Duffy wouldn't be able to keep recruiting southern blacks much longer. The Bear had just about convinced the Crimson Tide alumni that they needed to keep the talent at home. The intersectional games he had scheduled hammered home that point. The clinching argument was provided in 1970 when USC, led by Sam "Bam" Cunningham, a southern black, trashed 'Bama and turned the tide of athletic racism. Within two years Bryant had his first black player and the Big Ten, which had mined the South for a decade, began to lose those players and with them its status as the premier conference in the nation.

To be number one, boosters were willing to do anything, and university presidents went along with their desires. The following years saw the construction of special dorms for athletes at many schools. The petty abuses that had always existed—altering transcripts, spreading money around, getting cars for the star players—reached new levels as well; recruiters started going after kids who would never have been able to get into most schools before the frenzy began. Before Michigan State fielded its great team, coaches tended to recruit close to home. After the 1965–66 squad moved on, other coaches at other schools with championship aspirations started following Duffy Daugherty's footprints to the far corners of the country in pursuit of talent.

The huge rewards of success made trainers, coaches, and players more willing to turn to the medicine cabinet to gain an edge, and more players started going to the weight room. The first weight lifters were undersized players like Jerry West and Mitch Pruiett, who lifted weights to get up to the 215–220-pound range so they could play the line. When they got that big, natural 220-pounders had to lift to get bigger, too, so they could keep their jobs. When they got up to 240, the 240-pounders had to bulk up, and so it went. The discovery that a class of drugs called steroids could add enormous bulk in a short time accelerated the process, which continued until men the size of Bubba Smith and Kevin Hardy were no longer the exception on the line, they were the rule.

At the same time, coaches demanded more and more that athletes stick to one sport. Jim Brown had been a phenomenon in the fifties at Syracuse by being an All American in football, basketball, and lacrosse, but few followed in his footsteps. By 1966, Kevin Hardy, who lettered in three sports in one year, was an extreme rarity, but a substantial number of players still played at least two sports—football in the fall and track or baseball in the spring. Now even that is rare. In the race for number one, football has become a full-time job with players spending as much time working at it in the off-season as they do during the season.

It all followed the new importance of what would become college football's cash cow—television. Notre Dame–Michigan State was the first mega-game of the modern television era; the first monster game seen in color, with instant slow-motion replay. ABC had even flown in a special zoom lens from England for the game, a lens that allowed viewers to see not only Dick Kenney's bare kicking foot but whether he had dirt under his toenails. It was the first time a lens of such power had been used to cover a sporting event.

Television brought every aspect of the game into the nation's living rooms in detail never seen before. Some of the feature stories even mentioned the signs in the stands that were shown on television. It wasn't the first time signs were shown on the tube, but it helped teach the fans how to get on television. Soon enough, they would be trained to spot the cameras. They would stand and wave when it swept over them, and to help attract the glass eye, they would make more signs and would be sure to include the network's call letters to improve their chances of being chosen for their five seconds of fame. In 1968 one student at Notre Dame took his shirt off in the stands during a snow-storm. He did it on a dare, with the prize being possession of the all-important wineskin. It seemed like fun at the time, but when someone told him the next day he had been on television, he was shocked. Doing it was one thing, being shown on television was embarrassing. What if his mother saw? He vowed never to do it again. But others who saw similar stunts thought, "Hey, if I take my shirt off and paint myself blue, I can get on television, too. I can even wave to my Mom."

The players, too, would discover the all-seeing eye. In Notre Dame's first game that year, against Purdue, Hanratty and Sey-mour had to be coaxed by an ABC employee to turn away from the game and smile into the sideline camera. Waving an index finger and mouthing "Hi, Mom" was out of the question. You watch a tape of any game from that year, and you'll see the same attitude. In the Notre Dame—Michigan State game, not one player from either side can be seen gloating over a fallen oppo-nent. The contest was filled with monster defensive hits, with great efforts, with tackles for losses, tackles for no gains, passes broken up along with the receivers who were trying to catch them. And after every great play, the athletes picked themselves up and got back into the huddle. That was it. No pointing. No gloating.

No woofing. No sack dances. Not even a little leap of triumph. Just business.

But a new generation would soon be watching Joe Namath take the New York Jets to the Super Bowl while wearing white football shoes and sporting hair that hung out of the back of his helmet. Cool. Then Billy "White Shoes" Johnson would join the Houston Oilers in 1974 and introduce the sport to the end zone boogie. After Johnson, Mark Gastineau did the same thing for defensive linemen with his sack dance. And every time someone did something unusual on the field, the cameras picked it up and the replay machines showed it again and again on the sports shows. It got to the point where the first thing players did when they made a play was jump up and down and dance and gesture for the cameras. Then they'd look for a teammate to celebrate with.

Television did all that, and the Game of the Century gave television its stage. The enormous ratings the game attracted— thirty-three million viewers for a game that was shown on tape delay in the South and Northwest—attracted the most attention of all. It was the largest audience ever to see a college football game. The 22.5 Nielson rating for the game was also the greatest ever and remains the second highest in history for a regular season game, surpassed only by the 22.9 rating for the 1968 Notre Dame–Southern Cal game in O. J. Simpson's senior year. No one knows what the rating would have been if the two sections of the country hadn't had to wait to see the game until after it was broadcast on the radio.

Dr. Paul Brechler, commissioner of the Western Athletic Conference, said coverage of the game "just killed college football as a Saturday afternoon spectator sport." A member of the NCAA television committee, Brechler revealed that the vote to allow the game to be broadcast nationally on a delayed basis had been narrow. He said at the time:

> Fans who demanded and got the championship game may be shortsighted. We are not so concerned about offering the game as competition to the major [local] game of the day because the real football fan will still go see his school play. . . . What we are concerned about is the effect telecasting the big game has on the schools that play before only one thousand or three thousand

fans. These small schools cannot afford to lose any fans or they may be forced to drop football, and I'm afraid that the committee's majority action may cause untold damage to hundreds of small schools.

Now that we have bowed to pressure, I'm wondering what happens in the future. This decision could have far-reaching effects, and I'm afraid a lot of fans who demanded to see this game may be sorry.

He was right about the effects. In 1966 the NCAA limited ABC to eighteen minutes of commercials per game. They asked the network to run them during regular time-outs, between halves, before and after the game, and, if they couldn't wedge them all in, they begrudgingly allowed them to call "a TV time-out," a phrase so new it was enclosed in quotes in newspaper stories. But when the massive ratings poured in and the NCAA members learned what that meant in ad revenue—and what it could mean if the networks could sell even more ad minutes—the days of a two-and-a-half hour game were gone forever.

Brechler was not so correct about fans regretting their demands to see the big game.

Notre Dame–Michigan State was the Super Bowl before the Super Bowl became what it is today. Had the game been played on a day with no competing games available, as the Super Bowl is, there's no telling what the viewership would have been. As it was, attendance at most high school and college games across the nation was significantly lower because of the availability of the game on television. Notre Dame–Michigan State had drawn that viewership on merit, just as it had drawn more than seven hundred reporters. And the publicity focused on the two teams and the players helped those players to get jobs in the pros. Rocky Bleier admits that if he had gone to Boston College instead of Notre Dame, he never would have gotten to the pros at all, not even as a last-round draft choice, which is how he made it. But going to Notre Dame meant being on television and getting attention. That attention helped attract the professional scouts who drafted every offensive starter on Notre Dame's team with the exception of tight end Don Gmitter. And Gmitter wasn't drafted because he didn't enter the draft. On the defensive side, every member of the front eight was drafted except John Horney, who opted for medical school instead of the draft. They were good football players. Most of them had careers in the pros. George Kunz, who started the season at tackle but missed most of the year with an injury, played eleven pro seasons, and Bob Kuechenberg played fifteen. Notre Dame's top six offensive linemen combined for more than fifty years in the pros. The defensive front eight, led by Alan Page's fifteen-year Hall of Fame career and Jim Lynch's eleven years, also played more than a half century of pro ball. In all, twenty-two members of Notre Dame's team played in the pros, including third-team quarterback Bob Belden. Another eleven from Michigan State had pro careers.

Had those athletes played elsewhere, they might not have gotten the chance. Certainly they would not have gone as high in the draft as they did. As it was, the two teams produced eight first-round draft choices in the spring of 1967.

If the players were interested in what television could do for their careers, the colleges and the networks were interested in what the sport could do for their pocketbooks. Television ratings meant money, and ABC was rolling in it that year. In the years that followed, other schools would look at that money and look at the NCAA's restrictive television policies and decide they wanted a bigger piece of the pie. Oklahoma and Georgia eventually challenged the NCAA TV monopoly in court, and won in 1984. The College Football Association followed—an alliance of the biggest schools that cut its own TV deal. The Big Ten and the PAC-10 cut separate deals, and now college football is on all the networks and across the cable spectrum as well. The segmentation of the audience meant that no one would ever get the ratings Notre Dame had generated against Michigan State in 1966 and against USC in 1968. Ultimately it also meant that Notre Dame, the king of the ratings, would one day have its own network.

In all the TV deals over the decades, Notre Dame played the team game. The original NCAA rules against multiple national exposure were adopted in the early days of television to prevent Notre Dame from being the national game of the week. Notre Dame went along with those rules. The Irish then went along with the CFA after the Georgia and Oklahoma court challenge, and didn't criticize the Big Ten and the PAC-10 for cutting an exclusive multi-million-dollar deal to televise the Rose Bowl. But in 1990, when the CFA cut a new national deal that relegated Notre Dame to regional broadcast status, the Irish went off on their own and signed a separate deal with NBC to televise all their home games. The drawing power of Notre Dame that was demonstrated in 1966 finally ended in Notre Dame's having what the NCAA had sought to prevent in the beginning—its own network.

Television was not the only medium that changed because of the game. Newspapers, too, became slaves to the hype. They had covered the game with every resource at their disposal because the game demanded it. When the television ratings came in, they assumed they had helped to create that interest. So they covered the next big game just as thoroughly. It didn't matter if that game wasn't as naturally compelling. No future regular season game could be. In the first place, Notre Dame–Michigan State had been a freak of scheduling. Never before had the number-one-and-two-ranked teams met so late in the regular season, and never again would such a game—if it were to happen—decide the National Championship. Within three years Notre Dame would be in the bowl picture, and the polls would no longer take their final vote before the bowl games were played.

It didn't matter. Travel had become easier and cheaper. The era of train travel was officially dead. Electronic data transmission would make coverage easier than ever. The era of media overkill had dawned, and the mode of attack used for what was called the Game of the Century became the pattern. It was, in fact, the first media Super Bowl week, a phenomenon that debuted in January 1967. That first Super Bowl was a pale imitation of Notre Dame–Michigan State and would remain that way for several years to come. It just wasn't as big a game. With time, that didn't matter either. Good or bad, the big game had to be drowned in ink.

Neither the writers nor the broadcasters thought of any of this as they filed their eager prose. They were just trying to dig out a story anywhere they could, and they didn't care whom they deified to do it: Let the halos fall where they may. How could anyone know the players would become so inflated with their own images and so much money would wash over the sport that the players would eventually demand a share of the profits?

One game was not the sole cause of all these changes. Just as someone would have discovered the forward pass without Rockne and Dorais, the combination of television and football would have grown into the monster it is without The Biggest Game of Them All. The point is that the game defined a turning point and pointed out the possibilities which lay down the road. It accelerated the process. Part of that had to do with the times. Much more than football was changing. The entire nation was changing its focus from traditional values to the solipsistic society that would follow. The year 1966 was at the middle of the change from the crew-cut post–World War era to the long-haired Flower Generation, which would soon enough become the Me Generation. Rocky Bleier remembers walking across campus in the spring of 1968, his senior year, and seeing a group of students demonstrating against the Vietnam War. "Why are they doing that?" he thought. Soon enough, as he was recuperating in a VA hospital, he would know. Bleier had a brother, four years younger than he, who participated in such demonstrations. For Rocky's brother the world was a different place with far fewer certainties than it was for Rocky. The brothers are close in age but a generation apart in outlook. The elder accepted authority, the younger questioned it.

A big part of the new generation was the quest for social justice, for fundamental fairness. That, too, was mirrored in college football in rule changes that governed how national champions were chosen and who went to bowl games. Michigan State might have won the national title that year if it could have gone to a bowl game—and if the final polls were taken after the bowl games. But Big Ten rules prohibited the Spartans from going to the Rose Bowl because they had been there the year before. The Rose Bowl was considered a treat to be spread out among the conference members, not an end in itself. The PAC-8's rule was different but equally inequitable. That conference voted on a representative, a policy that prevented UCLA from representing the conference after the 1966 season. Because of the uproar that arose when both UCLA and Michigan State were shut out of the bowl, both conferences changed their rules. From then on, the conference champion would go.

Once bowls became an important part of the race for the National Championship, Notre Dame, which for decades had claimed that bowl games would detract from the academic mission of the university, changed its mind, too. Predictions that the school's no-bowl rule would be dropped appeared immediately after the end of the 1966 season. By 1969 the academic year had been restructured to end at the Christmas break instead of after the New Year, and the Notre Dame administration decided that there were no longer any academic reasons not to go to a bowl. The scramble was then on among the bowl committees to land the Irish and their big TV audience for their postseason classics. From a fan's viewpoint, Notre Dame's entry into the postseason meant new opportunities to decide who was number one. From the school's viewpoint it meant millions of dollars more, not only for the expanding athletic program but also for scholarships and academics, for Notre Dame remained—and remains—one of a minority of schools whose athletic department budget is part of the university's overall budget, not separate from it.

But people don't still talk about Notre Dame–Michigan State for any of those reasons. They still talk about it because it ended in a tie—an immortal tie. They talk about it and argue about who was better. They browbeat Ara Parseghian for playing for a tie instead of a win. It's been terrific grist for debate. Unlike other matchups of undefeated teams since, which created their own splash and then were relegated to the back of the memory because someone did win and someone did lose, Notre Dame–Michigan State lives forever because there was no resolution.

In the fall of 1991, Ara Parseghian sat in his downtown South Bend office, surrounded by the relics of a great career, defending himself again for his strategy. I listened to him that day, and finally I said, "Ara, you did the right thing. If someone had won or lost, it would have been a great game, but we wouldn't be sitting here talking about it twenty-five years later."

We may never talk about a game for as long again. After the criticism Ara took, few other coaches are as willing to follow the dictates of sensible strategy at the end of a big game. It's better to lose a game and the National Championship, as Nebraska's Tom Osborne did in the Orange Bowl against Miami, by taking a big gamble to win, than it is to lose by refusing to lose.

Ara was just trying to win a trophy. He wasn't trying to create a debate for the ages. That's just the way it turned out. You can criticize him for that, but what's the point? He did what he did for a lot of good reasons, and it came out a tie. And that seems right. It was truly a game no one deserved to lose, and no one did. They were Notre Dame and Michigan State, the two best teams that ever met by the quirk of a schedule at the end of a season to play for it all. That's how they should be remembered —not as a winner and a loser but as two great champions that fought to a draw. The polls said Notre Dame won. History says they both did.

Notre Dame 10, Michigan State 10
November 19, 1966

Notre Dame...	0	7	0	3—	10
Michigan State	0	10	0	0—	10

MSU—Cavender 4 run (Kenney kick); MSU—FG Kenney 47; ND—Gladieux 34 pass from O'Brien (Azzaro kick); ND—FG Azzaro 28.

TEAM STATISTICS

	MSU	ND
First Downs	13	10
Total Net Yards	284	219
Net Yards Rushing	142	91
Net Yards Passing	142	128
Passes (Comp/Att/Int)	7-20-1	8-24-3
Punts-Average	8-38.0	8-42.0
Fumbles-Lost	2-1	3-1
Penalties-Yards	5-32	1-5

INDIVIDUAL STATISTICS
Rushing
MSU—Raye 21-75; Cavender 7-36; Lee 6-17; Jones 10-13; Apisa 2-1.
ND—Bleier 13-53; Conjar 11-32; Hanratty 2-12; Gladieux 1-1; O'Brien 9-(3); Haley 2-(4).
Passing
MSU—Raye 7-20, 142.
ND—O'Brien 7-19, 102, 1 TD; Hanratty 1-4, 26; Hardy 0-1, 0.
Receiving
MSU—Washington 5-123; Lee 1-11; Brenner 1-8.
ND—Gladieux 3-71; Bleier 3-16; Haley 1-23; Conjar 1-18.
Tackles
MSU—Thornhill, 16; Richardson, 13; Webster, 10; Chatlos, 6; Smith, 6; Phillips, 5; Summers, 4; Hoag, 4; Armstrong, 3; Garrett, 2; Gallinagh, 2; Bailey, 2; Waters, 2; C. Jones, 2; Brawley, 1; Brenner, 1; Washington, 1; Lee, 1.
ND—Lynch, 13; Pergine, 12; Horney, 11; O'Leary, 9; Hardy, 7; Rhoads, 4; Schoen, 4; Smithberger, 4; Duranko, 3; Martin, 2; Gladieux, 1; Regner, 1.

INDEX